40,001 best Baby names

40,001 best Baby names

Diane Stafford

Vermilion
LONDON

First published in the United States in 2003 by Sourcebooks, Inc.
First published in the United Kindom in 2004 by
Vermilion, an imprint of Ebury Press
Random House UK Ltd.
Random House,
20 Vauxhall Bridge Road,
London SW1V 2SA
www.randomhouse,co,uk

The Random House Group Limited Reg. No 954009

Addresses for companies within The Random House Group Limited
can be found at: www.randomhouse.co.uk/offices.htm

The Random House Group Limited supports The Forest Stewardship Council (FSC),
the leading international forest certification organisation.
All our titles that are printed on Greenpeace approved FSC certified paper carry the FSC logo.
Our paper procurement policy can be found at www.rbooks.co.uk/environment

A CIP catalogue record for this book is available from the British Library

ISBN 9780091900007

Printed and bound in Great Britain by
CPI Mackays, Chatham ME5 8TD

For precious Ben, with all my love

Acknowledgements

Sincere thanks to: Ed Knappman of New England Publishing Associates, for giving me the opportunity to write this book—and to Elizabeth Frost Knappman, literary agent and friend, who has made my dreams come true.

Hillel Black of Sourcebooks, for his patience, support, direction, and kindness. Amy Baxter of Sourcebooks for her hard work on *40,001 Best Baby Names*.

Dana Chandler, Slavek Rotkiewicz, Camilla Pierce, Gabriela Baeza Ventura, and Jennifer Shoquist San Luis, for their help with this book.

And special thanks to my wonderful family and friends, whose names will always be tops on my list of favorites:

Jennifer, Benjamin, Robert, Clinton, Belle, Allen, Christina, Austin, Xanthe, Richard, Camilla, Britt, Gina, Curtis, Lindsay, Cameron, Josh, Jake, David, Amber, Dan, Fletcher, Russ, Martin, Dinah, Chris, Donna, Annie, Angela, Jami, Lucy, Tessie, Bob, Lily, Carolyn, Beth, Dot, Laurens, Cynthia, Laura, Jeffrey, Dana, Clarence, Eddi, Jay, Jim, Martha, Carrie, Natasha, Kathleen, Rachel, Renee, Wendy, Kristina, Jennifer, Liz, Elizabeth, Christy, Shannon, John, Shari, JoAnn, Alice, Gary, C.D., Bernice, Karla, Karen, Doug, Michael, Tom, Joanne, Mark, Fred, Spiker, Scott, Dominique, Russell, Evin, Dennis, Patrick, Cari.

Table of Contents

Introduction

Your name. Those two words should make you smile.

Nothing is more personal. Whether one-of-a-kind (Shawnikwaronda) or most-popular-of-the-century (Jennifer), your name gives you an identity that sets you apart from the twenty other kids in nursery school and labels you the first day of a new job. If your name is memorable or a perfect fit, people say it more often. But if yours is hard to pronounce or difficult to remember, chances are good that you will go through life rarely hearing your 'Daphinola' at all.

Indeed, a name can affect the ebb and flow of your entire existence. That's exactly why parents-to-be often give the baby-naming process numerous hours of list-perusing, head-scratching, and poll-taking.

For a kid who feels 'stuck' with an albatross name, life can be long and bumpy. While people with better names seem to glide through social encounters effortlessly, the name-challenged types are more likely to stumble and bungle their way through the jungle.

If you have any doubt, note the baby-naming efforts of a person who grew up as Nyleen or Hortense, Huelett or Drakeston, and you'll probably find that this individual will have offspring named John or Ann. Just having a sibling with a tough moniker will nudge us in the direction of plain when it comes to naming a tiny, innocent baby.

What's the significance of all of this for you, the parent-in-waiting? You are dead right in thinking that finding the 'right' name constitutes a major responsibility. This occasion is momentous enough to merit lots of discussion and lots of thumbing through the baby-naming book until you finally hit on it—The Right Name.

Whether or not you want to admit it, you really and truly want your child to like his name. No wonder you feel awed by the job! Most parents fret and falter, marvel and malinger, worry and wonder—sometimes for the entire nine months of pregnancy.

And that's because authors and songwriters immortalize names. People in love grow misty-eyed just thinking of them. Names are glorified and mocked, loved and loathed.

You're looking for a name that resonates, one that's memorable and perfect—but not *frighteningly* memorable or overly perfect. You're out to locate a name that is absolutely sure, 100 percent guaranteed, to have a positive effect on your little tyke's life. For that reason alone, you're willing to give the baby-naming gig quite a few hours of over-analysis.

We all want great names. We all struggle with the thousands of contenders.

Couldn't that little embryo give us a hint as to what name he would prefer? Is it better to be one of ten Davids in your class at school, or is it more of a challenge to try to pull off a quirky Ringo?

Maybe you're already submitting name-nominees to the acid tests: Is it too cute? Overly hip? Brutally boring? And, what's wrong with just going with your gut? This is your baby, after all. So why not tag that little biscuit with the way-cool name you've had squirrelled away since your Barbie-and-Ken days!

Have fun with the name game. Approach it with wackiness, high spirits, and good insider information. Stay on message, and don't let yourself get sidetracked by relative-schmoozing or movie-star-mimicking. Carefully assess the pros and cons of your finalists, and you're bound to come up with a winner.

And while you're at it, do weigh the fact that a name can shape personality, career, and self-esteem. And just as clearly, a person's name can be a lifelong drawback, as in the guy whose parents reversed the letters of their surname, and came up with an unpronounceable humdinger that made kids laugh at the boy all the way through school. So what happens to this kind of nuisance-name? When the man turns twenty-one, he banishes by deed poll that kookiness forever. What used to be 'Enord' becomes the benign letter 'E'.

Also, consider any nasty connotations. Erica took on a whole new and scary feel after thirty years of being kicked around by the malevolent Erica Kane on the U.S. soap *All My Children*. And, by a different, somewhat slatternly yardstick, who could in good conscience name an innocent baby girl Monica in the post-Bill Clinton era?

At the same time, names can be an asset, a source of pride and distinction. Who would bet on anything other than a promising future for a Theodore or a Saul, a Grace or a Claire?

Some parents get so confused that they throw up their hands and pick a generic name. That way, the child can make what he wants of it. (Think how many times you've met Anne, Patricia, Carol, Michael, Richard, David, and Mark.)

Everyone knows what his own name did for him growing up (and what it didn't do). Maybe your parents envisioned a man becoming Prime Minister and chose Jim, Tony, Harold, or Alec. Or, perhaps, your mother had warm, fuzzy feelings about a good old boy she knew growing up, so you were christened Billy Bob, certainly well suited for country-western singing (or for tattooing Angelina Jolie). Or your aunt loved the 'artist formerly known as Prince' and made sure your birth certificate registered the eccentric 'Purple Rain'.

Boggled by mega-input, many parents toss around names for the entire nine months. And adding to the confusion is the steady stream of names offered by well-meaning grandparents, aunts, uncles, cousins, co-workers, employees, repairmen, and friends.

Baby-naming can even become so daunting that perplexed parents-to-be waffle daily. And then after they have identified a few winners, a couple faces the key issue that often comes into play—finding a name they can agree on. Usually, the result is a rush to judgement on delivery day, when Mum and Dad are finally forced to choose a name in the maternity ward.

Basic attitudes toward baby-naming can range from frivolous and cavalier to serious and tradition-laden. One Houston mother with the surname Palms named her African-American son White so that each time he introduced himself, 'I'm White Palms,' he was greeted with a grin or a look of disbelief. The same goes for a Texan named King Solomon, whose name is so memorable that this author was introduced to him at age fifteen, and decades later can still remember the shock of meeting a very confident kid who actually managed to pull off that spectacular name. (Some children can make a traffic-stopping name a big asset. But, some can't.) A friend of mine named Jeffrey wore her boy-name like a badge of honour, growing up to be both funny and popular. But, another girl whose parents chose a masculine name (Christopher) struggled with the name lifelong, forced to live with kids' ridicule.

That brings up a major trend going strong currently in the U.S., the meshing of names to come up with something brand new. The U.S. Social Security Administration shows growing numbers of 'creations' such as Tamikas and Rayshons, but don't mistake the proliferation for anything resembling approval by the kids so named. Most children don't appreciate their parents' inventiveness because teachers either mispronounce or avoid made-up names (as they have through the ages), and classmates make a hobby of terrorizing kids with odd names.

Some folks consider the practice of giving an old name a new spelling—Genefur for

Jennifer, for example—a very cool way to go, while others scoff at this as downright laughable. By the same token, plenty of parents contend that giving new spellings to old names lends a fresh and splashy feel.

In some ethnic groups, a baby's name reflects the mother's pregnancy impressions. One book titled *Narco* tells of a Spanish mother who had a complicated process for naming seven sons. Each long name was a three-pronged affair consisting of a number for the birth order, a word that represented the mother's main obsession during the nine months, and the name of a famous writer. Cuatro Conrad Confabulation was the fourth son—Cuatro, meaning fourth son; Conrad, for the writer Joseph Conrad; and Confabulation, indicating that she spent her pregnancy gossiping with other pregnant women. Cinco Cervantes Cirrus, by the same token, was the fifth child, named for the writer Miguel Cervantes, and Cirrus, a cloud name that represents the mother's daydreaming pregnancy.

On the other end of the spectrum from those parents who dream up bizarre, fanciful names are the families who view baby-naming as a holy act, right up there with baptism. Some societies believe that names hold spiritual and prophetic significance, and that a child's name is sure to have an enormous impact on his future. The people of Ghana, for instance, think that a name is a mark of religious identification that carries honour and respect. A good name is highly treasured in Ghanaian society, and each baby is honoured with a naming ceremony.

Obviously, no science has ever been devised to pinpoint the whys and hows of choosing a name. But, in this book, we give you 40,001 names, tips on the selection process, and, most importantly, clues as to how our names affect us. Be sure to read Part Two, which features anecdotes from people who reflect on their names and how they were shaped (or weren't) by their names.

part one

Tips for Naming Your Baby

What do most people do? Some of the baby-naming approaches frequently used include the following:

- Mesh two names together to form a new one.
- Pick a name you've always loved.
- Find a name that bodes well for a promising career.
- Go with a name that connotes a trait—honesty, friendliness, *savoir faire*.
- Use the mother's maiden name for the first name.
- Honour a beloved relative by using his name.
- Stick with something time-honoured and safe.
- Make up a name, a practice that some people consider *tres gauche*, and others rate high on the creativity scale.

And while you are dabbling in the name game, be sure to remember these naming taboos:

- Avoid a name that's carrying baggage equivalent to Amtrak, as in Cher, Michael Jackson, Richard Simmons, Billy Joel, or Sting.
- Don't let family members talk you into a 'junior' unless you don't mind your child being called 'Little John' or 'Junior' lifelong. Listen to all the suggestions relatives fling your way, but you make the call.
- Don't be too bothered by existing connotations that you associate with a name ('I knew a Margaret in school, and she was the meanest person in our class,' 'I sat next to a Stone in college, and he had a million moles,' or 'I dated a Morgan, and she was the most boring girl I've ever known'). The reason you shouldn't let old associations trip you up is that once you name your child Tasha or Truman, there isn't another person in the world with that name who matters. *Trust me on this.*

Ten Great Tips for Successful Baby-Naming

A 'set of rules' can ratchet up your confidence. If you don't really need a framework, just read the following tips as a fun diversion.

Here are ten steps for naming your baby:

1. Consider the sound—does it work with your last name?
When the full name is said aloud, you want something that has a nice ring, not a tongue-twister or a rhyme. You may find that a long last name jibes best with a short first name; by the same token, put a long first name with a short last name, and you may have a winner.

The union of a first name ending in a vowel paired with a last name that starts with a vowel is not the greatest choice. For example: Ava Amazon. It's just hard to say. Puns aren't good omens for a happy life, either. Look at the infamous Ima Hogg, name of a Houston philanthropist. If the poor woman wasn't burdened enough, she also had to deal with life-long rumors of a sister named Ura.

2. Know exactly what happens when you give your baby a crowd-pleaser name.
Give your kid a common name, and she'll probably end up Sarah B. in a classroom with six Sarahs. She may be comfortable with the anonymity that a plain-Jane name lends her—considering it far better than being the class Brunhilda, who gets ridiculed daily. Or, she may ask you every other day of her childhood why you weren't more original in naming her: 'Why did you give me the same name fifty million other kids have? Why couldn't you have come up with something better? Why didn't you take more time?'

3. Think seriously about the repercussions of choosing a name that's over-the-top in uniqueness.
You are definitely sticking your neck out by giving your child the name Rusty if your last name is Nail. Sure, he may muster up enough swagger to pull it off, but what if he doesn't? Lots of people with unusual or hard-to-spell last names will purposely opt for a simple first name for their child, just to ease the load of having two names to spell over and over. Some research suggests that kids with odd names get more taunting from peers and are less well socialized. You can be sure that primary school kids will make fun of a boy named Stone, but later, as an adult, he may enjoy having an unusual name.

Just make sure you don't choose a 'fun' name simply because you like the idea of having people praise your creativity—instead, ask yourself how your child will feel about being a Bark or a Lake.

4. Ponder the wisdom of carrying on that family name.
Aunt Priscilla did fine with her name, but how will your tiny tot feel in a classroom full of Ambers and Britneys? Extremely old-fashioned names sometimes make their way back into circulation and do just fine, but sometimes they don't. (Will we really ever see the name Durwood soar again?)

5. Consider the confusion that is spawned by a namesake.
A kid named after a parent won't like being 'Junior' or 'Little Al'. Ask anyone who has been in that position about the amount of confusion it generates in regard to credit cards and other personal I.D. information. You'll spend half your life unravelling the mix-ups. Psychiatrists (many of them juniors themselves) will tell you that giving a child his very own name is a much better jumpstart than making him a spin-off or a mini-me.

At the same time, Trey or a III are still popular in the U.S. because the name represents tradition and history.

6. Make your family/background name an understudy (the middle name).
Let's say you want your baby's name to reflect his heritage or religion, but you strongly prefer more mainstream names. You can fill both bills by using the ancestry name as a middle name.

7. Ponder whether the name's meaning matters to you.
For some people, knowing a name's meaning is extremely important, often much more so than its Greek or German origin. And your child could turn out to be the type who loves investigating such things. So what happens when that offspring of yours finds out that her name Delilah means 'whimpering harlot guttersnipe'? She may wish you had taken a longer look at the name's baggage.

8. Look at shortened versions of a name and check out initials.
Don't think your child's schoolmates will fail to notice that his initials spell out S.C.U.M. And, you can be sure that Harrison will become 'Harry' or, occasionally, 'Hairy'. View the teasing as being as much a given as school backpacks, and think twice about whether you want to give your child's peer group something they can really grab onto. Tread lightly. Naming always starts with good intentions, but you can do your kid a favour by considering each name-candidate's bullying potential.

9. After you've narrowed your list, try out each name and see how it feels.
Say, "Barnabus Higgins, get yourself over here!" Or, "Harrison Higgins, have you done your homework?" Or, "Hannibal Higgins, would you like some fava beans?"

10. Once you and your mate have decided on a name, don't broadcast it.
You may want to keep your name choice a secret, otherwise relatives and friends are likely to share all of their issues with the name and a long string of other, 'better' options. Another possibility is that people will start calling the unborn baby that name, which will be unfortunate if you happen to find one you like better.

Bottom line: take the Name Game seriously, but don't be afraid to go with the one that just *feels right*. That precious infant who will change your life dramatically is sure to be the best thing that has ever happened to you—give him or her a name that you will love singing and saying every single day, a million times over.

Baby Ben (Jen), I'm so glad you're mine.

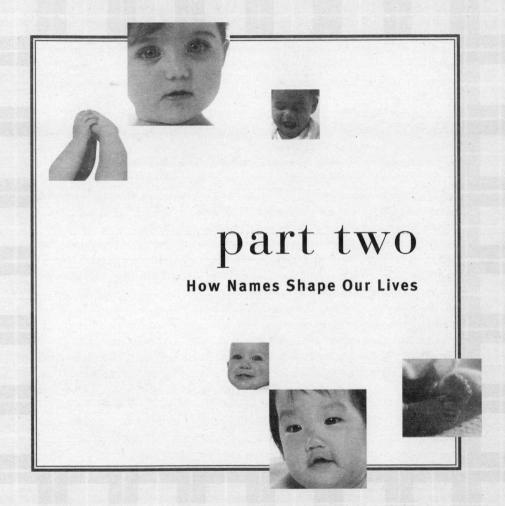

part two

How Names Shape Our Lives

Here, twenty-one people share their thoughts on their names:

Camilla Shirley Pierce, homemaker and mother: 'Although I was named after a beloved great aunt, I always felt that carrying around such an unusual name was not great. When I was a child, no one could pronounce it or spell it. It was a source of embarrassment and aggravation. Now, at the age of sixty-two, when people read my name they still mispronounce it, and I always feel like saying, "How hard can it be? I could pronounce it at age three!"'

David Nordin, proposal writer: 'I always liked my name because it had more character than other names. David has Biblical history, and it's more elegant and regal than your average name. On the flip side, my odd middle name caused me years of embarrassment. Teachers would call out that name during roll call, and people would laugh and make fun of me...As soon as I was grown, I had it legally changed. Parents should never name their kids anything that could make them objects of ridicule.'

Clarence Raymond Chandler: 'I was named after my dad's favourite brother, who was a great guy I admired. I was raised in south Texas (Benavides), where my friends were called Roberto, Jose, Ricardo, Jesus, and Francisco, so being a George, Bill, Jerry, Charles, or Roger never really came up on my "wish list". I was content! Today, technology has caused the minor inconvenience of not being able to find enough room on forms to print out my long name, much less my signature.' Chandler adds: 'I had it easy compared to my dad, who was born in an era when children were named after famous people; he got incessant ribbing, not to mention playground fights, when he was growing up, because his challenge was answering to Napoleon Bonaparte Chandler, which is right up there with the ranks of Johnny Cash's "How do you do, my name is Sue." In school, it was common knowledge that you only picked on him once, or you had a real dogfight on your hands. To avoid "you gotta be kidding" comments, he adopted the name "Nap"' Chandler. He was a great dad, patriot, WWII veteran, ethical businessman, champion for the little guy, and a loving and tough SOB—he was my hero!'

Jennifer Wright, a psychiatrist: 'I've always liked my name. Some of my best friends have been named Jennifer also, and I think it suits our personalities. The benefit of having a "common" name is that I never have difficulty finding personalized items. Plus, I like the nicknames "Jen" and "Jenny".'

Kristina Kaczmarek Holt, a graphic artist: 'I have always liked my name because it was unique. I had never come across a Kristina with a "K" until I was a teenager, and then it was usually a Kristy or Kristine. I liked the sound of my first and last name together (the two Ks)—that seemed to work. My name was a heck of a thing to learn to spell in kindergarten, but it was all mine. They used to tape your name to those thick green pencils you learned to write with, and I was always sharpening my pencil down into my name. It wasn't until I recently had a child of my own (Noah) that my dad told me where he got my name. I assumed he picked it because it was a Polish name, and his family was half-Polish. But instead, he named me after a woman who was especially nice to him when he was young, who must have made a strong impression because the name stuck with him until I was born.'

Homemaker Dana Huggins Chandler: 'I like to be just a little different from everyone else around me, so I always loved my name. There are now many people named Dana, but most don't have the same pronunciation. My name rhymes with Anna and Lana. I always tell people I was named after my dad—Dan—which isn't true, but it does help people remember how to pronounce my name.'

TV anchor Dominique Sachse: 'Considering you can't pick your name at birth, I'm quite pleased with the one my parents chose for me. I think it has a level of sophistication, and it's unique and European, which I am. I've never considered changing it, shortening it, or going by a nickname. It's a name I feel I've had to live up to.'

Cari LaGrange, Internet business owner: 'I liked my name growing up, but like most kids, I went through a phase when I wished I could change it, the way girls with straight hair want curly hair and vice versa. Thankfully, my name and its spelling were unique in the town where I grew up, so there was no other girl by my name to compare my identity to.'

Jane Vitrano, homemaker: 'My mother named my sister Linda and me Jane because she hated her own name, Lula Mae, and said she would never want her daughters to have anything but plain names—and no middle names.'

Donna Pate, technical writer: 'I was neutral about my name. It was okay but not too exciting or interesting. At least it didn't lend itself to juvenile humour. There was the chance of being labelled "Prima Donna", but that was beyond the vocabulary of most kids. I liked my name better after I learned what it meant, but that wasn't until I was an adult.'

Natasha Graf, acquisitions editor: 'My name is pretty special because I was named after a very important woman in my father's life. When I was young and wanted to be like every other girl, I didn't always like my name because it was unusual at the time, being Russian and all. However, when my father shared with me who I was named after, I came to love it because I feel like I am connected to her somehow. She was a professor at my father's college, and she spoke seven languages—a brilliant woman who had emigrated from Russia. She was his mentor—the first really intellectual person he met during college, and they stayed friends after he went to medical school. It was not an affair—more a meeting of the minds. They wrote to each other. He saved every letter she wrote, and he let me read them. It was so interesting to see my father as a young person through these letters. She died before I was born, before my father was married. I wish I could have met her; I wonder what she would have thought of me. As you can tell, I wouldn't want my name to be anything else.'

JoAnn Roberson, fifth-year teacher: 'I didn't like my name because it reminded me of a boy's name—Joe. My dad said they were going to name me Jacquelyn, but an uncle said that was too long a name for a little baby, and I would never learn to spell it. I always wished that was my name.'

Trey Speegle, art director: 'I've always appreciated my name, although when I was very young and wanted to fit in, I wished I had a more normal name, like Chris, or a cool name like Skip. My great-grandmother named me; I was born on her birthday, April 13, and I was her thirteenth great-grandson. Her son (my grandfather) was John Hugh Speegle Sr., and my father is John Hugh Speegle Jr., so she named me Trey John—"the third" John.'

Angela Theresa Clark, co-owner of Court Record Research, Inc.: 'My mother called me Angela Theresa after two of her favourite Carmelite nuns. I was known as Theresa until year six, when I tired of telling teachers that I didn't go by Angela and just surrendered to being called that. I thought it was stupid to be named something so close to the word "angel". Angels are imaginary, soft, and I saw them as easy prey. I was also afraid people might think I was angelic. I thought I had to be tough in my family, with five brothers and two big (mean) older sisters (ha!). I was tomboyish, and Theresa just fit better. Some family members still call me Theresa, although it doesn't fit me anymore because now I'm softer and much more vulnerable. I love my name.'

Spiker Davis, dentist: 'I really liked my name because people always remembered it, and there's no one to get confused with. Also, with a last name like Davis, you need something to separate you from the crowd.'

Cristy Ann Hayes, journalist and mother of two: 'My name became a primary focus when I was young and searching for a sense of self, like other pre-teens. I was disappointed when people would ask what Cristy was short for, and I had to reply "nothing". I would wish my mum had taken more time to give me a name as substantial as Christina or Christian. My name also worked well as a taunt for my brother, who insisted I was the only one of the three siblings whose name didn't start with W, so I was not part of the family. Will and Wendy could be rascals that way. My mom thought it was clever to give my name an unconventional spelling, so I have, my entire life, had to take special care in spelling my name, and often people will add an *h*. My driver's licence is incorrect because of this, and many of my in-laws still spell it wrong. But after years of frustration regarding the spelling, I now appreciate the measuring tool it has become for me, showing how attuned someone is to me. I hold in high regard those who actually take the time to recognize the unique spelling and write it correctly. I believe it says something about one's character and approach to life when you take care to get a name right!'

Frank Vitrano, retired petroleum engineer: 'I was born in Waco, Texas, of a Sicilian father, and I was named after my grandfather, Frank Anthony, which is the Italian custom for the first-born son. You get your grandfather's name.'

Jennifer Colwell, commercial property management: 'Since I'm in my fifties, there were not very many Jennifers when I was growing up, and I always loved my name. I thought it was pretty and considered it an asset.'

Christopher (Chris) Fleming, female computer consultant: 'Growing up, I hated my name, Christopher Anne. I was called Christopher Columbus, was sent a draft notice, and was labelled "effeminate" on an aptitude test in secondary school. I finally told my mother how much I had hated my name, and she was surprised. In my opinion, parents should choose a name that indicates the child's sex (not one that's androgynous), and that's easy to spell. I don't think it's good to give a baby a name that's bizarre or made up from several words.'

Wendy Schnakenberg Corson, EMT: 'I have always hated my name. There were never any other Wendys, and if there were, they certainly weren't popular. My parents said they also liked the name Robin, which is a name I love; I told them how mad I was that they chose such a terrible name for me. Also, my middle name, Anne, is just boring. I was never teased about my name, so I suppose that is a positive. But, of course, kids had my last name—Schnakenberg—to tease me with!'

Carey Layne Davis, male landscape architect: 'I have always liked my name and never wanted to be called anything else. It was somewhat unique, and I was never teased.'

part three

Changing Your Name

Typically, U.S. hospital officials require parents to name their child before leaving the hospital. Other places, such as the U.K., give you six weeks in which to register your baby (and its name) at the local Town or City Hall.

In the U.S., if you want to change your name, you can hire a lawyer to give you all of the specifics and forms, or you can go to LawGuru.com on the Internet. The latter route gives you, for a fee, the legal forms your state requires.

In the U.K. you can change your name by deed poll, or, as it is legally known, by a Deed of Change of Name. This is a legal document that binds the person who signs it to: abandoning the use of his or her former name; using the new name only at all times and requiring all people to address him or her by the new name. In order for it to be recognized by all U.K. government departments, companies and organizations, it must be prepared by a competent authority such as the U.K. Deed Poll Service (Freephone helpline 0800 783 3048 or *www.ukdps.co.uk*) or a solicitor.

part four

75 Fun Lists

Boy names that give you a leg up in life

Barrett
Benjamin
Blake
Burke
Daniel
David
Ethan
Graham
Gus
Julian
Kyle
Lance
Logan
Mason
Matt
Max
Michael
Nathaniel
Patrick
Ralph
Samuel
Tyler
Will

Girl names that give you a leg up in life

Anna
Ashley
Bella
Caroline
Celeste
Claire
Danielle
Dominique
Elizabeth
Emma
Grace
Isabella
Jennifer
Julia
Kim
Margaret
Marion
Merit
Michelle
Natalie
Nicole
Rose/Rosa
Sadie
Sidney
Sophie

Patriotic names

America
Amerigo
Andrew
Asia
Blue
Brittany
Cherokee
Cheyenne
Columbus
David
Eagle
Elizabeth
Flag
Free
George
Liberty
Librada
Lincoln
Loyalty
Nation
Pacifika
Patrick
Patriot
Peace
Queenie
Red
Sailor
Salute
Spirit
Starr
Utopia
Victory

Burdensome boy names

Ambrose
Ankoma
Archibald
Bartholomew
Boaz
Bouvier
Cord
Dakarai
Durwood
Gershom
Godfrey
Hercules
Humphrey
Ignatius
Kalunga
Lafayette
Lazarus
Marmaduke
Mortimer
Percy
Reginald
Thelonius
Vladimar
Wolfgang
Zacharias

Burdensome girl names

Alfre
Antigone
Bathsheba
Chastity
Clotilde
Columbine
Cornelia
Cricket
Edna
Elspeth
Flannery
Henrietta
Indiana
Keturah
Majidah
Millicent
Minerva
Muriel
Priscilla
Prudence
Purity
Thomasina
Ursula
Zona
Zuwena

Boy names for children of lesbians and gays

Alex
Anson
Avery
Bevan
Brett
Caleb
Carson
Casey
Clay
Derek
Ethan
Forrest
Jake
Kyle
Logan
Marco
Matt
Noel
Owen
Ray
Silas
Spencer
Yale
Zack
Zeke

Girl names for children of lesbians and gays

- Amber
- Annabelle
- April
- Bianca
- Brianna
- Candace
- Celeste
- Chloe
- Daisy
- Darcy
- Feo
- Gloria
- Hilary
- Ingrid
- Jessica
- Kirsten
- Lara
- Lola
- Maura
- Mia
- Molly
- Noele
- Pia
- Ramona
- Sharon

Famous gangster names

- Angelo 'Docile Don' Bruno
- Aniello Dellecroce
- Antonio 'Tony Bananas' Caponigro
- Dominick 'Little Dom' Curra
- Frank 'Frankie Fap' Fappiano
- James J. 'Whitey' Bulger
- John 'Jackie Nose' D'Amico
- John Gotti
- Joseph 'Skinny Joey' Merlino
- Louis 'Big Louie' Vallario
- Lucky Luciano
- Michael 'Mikey Scars' DiLeonardo
- Nicky 'The Little Guy' Corozzo
- Paul Castellano
- Paulie Cimino
- Peter 'The Crumb' Caprio
- Ralph Natale
- Salvatore 'Sammy the Bull' Gravano
- Sonny Visconti
- Stephen 'The Rifleman' Flemmi
- Vincent 'The Chin' Gigante
- Vincent Palermo

Over-the-top boy names to avoid

- Achilles
- Adonis
- Amadeus
- Aristotle
- Attila
- Bark
- Beauregard
- Brando
- Caesar
- Eagle
- Goliath
- Hamlet
- Jock
- Lancelot
- Laramie
- Lobo
- Lord
- Lothario
- Rambo
- Rip
- Rocco
- Rod
- Stormy
- Sylvester
- Titan

Over-the-top girl names to avoid

- Aphrodite
- Asp
- Bijou
- Birdie
- Blaze
- Bless
- Blossom
- Blush
- Butter
- Chantilly
- Chastity
- Cher
- Cleopatra
- Desire
- Fantasia
- Fashion
- Fawn
- Fluffy
- Honesty
- Jezebel
- Loyalty
- Ophelia
- Psyche
- Purity
- Tempest

Androgynous names

- Andy/Andi
- Bailey
- Cameron
- Carol, Carroll
- Chris
- Corey
- Dakota
- Dale, Dell
- Darcy
- Darryl
- Dylan
- Gail/Gale
- Jamie
- Jean, Gene
- Jordan
- Kat
- Kelly
- Kerry/Carrie
- Lane
- Lee
- Leslie
- Morgan
- Pat
- Shawn, Sean
- Terry

Names that make you smile

Angel
Bambi
Bitsie
Boots
Buffalo
Buffy
Bunny
Champagne
Cheer
Cherry-Sue
Cookie
Corky
Dusty
Fluffy
Galaxy
Harmony
Honey
Peach
Poppy
Ritz
Snooks
Sundancer
Sunny
Tweetie

Soap opera names for boys

Alfie
Blake
Carson
Cyrano
Darren
Dario
Dean
Del
Den
Dexter
Duke
Grant
Jack
Kirk
Max
Oscar
Phil
Romeo
Ryan
Sebastian
Scott
Spencer
Taj
Todd
Tyrone

Soap opera names for girls

Amanda
Amber
Bethany
Bianca
Carmen
Chardonnay
Charity
Charmaine
Crystal
Gail
Janine
Kelly
Madonna
Monica
Nina
Samantha
Sasha
Sharon
Simone
Skye
Stephanie
Summer
Tracy
Zoe

Made-up names for boys

Bryton
Damarcus
Dantrell
Daquan
Dashawn
Derlin
Devonte
Donyell
Jabari
Jaquawn
Jashon
Javaris
Juwon
Keshon
Kyan
Leeron
Markell
Quintavius
Raekwon
Roshaun
Shaquille
Shawnell
Tevin
Tre
Tyree

Made-up names for girls

Alexakai
Amberkalay
Bryelle
Dalondra
Danelle
Darlonna
Darshell
Dashawn
Dashika
Dasmine
Davelyn
Dawntelle
Jaleesa
Jameka
Kaneesha
Keoshawn
Latasha
Noemi
Quanisha
Shalonda
Shanique
Shawanna
Tamika
Tamyrah
Teagan

Alternative spellings for boy names you can't pronounce

Adolfus (Adolphus)
Amadayus (Amadeus)
Booveeay (Bouvier)
Breeahno (Briano)
Byorn (Bjorn)
Dalanee (Delaney)
Dameetree (Dmitri)
Dolf (Dolph)
Eve (Yves)
Flavean (Flavian)
Gweedo (Guido)
Jordahno (Giordano)
Keyohtee (Quixote)
Klev (Cleve)
Loocho (Lucho)
Lukah (Luca)
Makale (Mikhail)
Malla-Ki (Malachi)
Odisius (Odysseus)
Playtoh (Plato)
Preemoh (Primo)
Shawn (Sean)
Sonteeahgo (Santiago)
Ulissus (Ulysses)

Alternative spellings for girl names you can't pronounce

Afrodytee (Aphrodite)
Alaygrah (Allegra)
Alaytheea (Aleithea)
Anewk (Anouk)
Dafnee (Daphne)
Dayna (Dana)
Duhnell (Danelle)
Egzanth (Xanthe)
Elkie (Elke)
Felisha (Felicia)
Hiah (Heija)
Kamela (Camilla)
Katelyn (Kaitlin)
Margo (Margot)
Mazie (Maisie)
Maxeeme (Maxime)
Moneek (Monique)
Q-malee (Cumale)
Sade (Sharday)
Salowmee (Salome)
Shanade (Sinead)
Sheelyah (Shelia)
Shivan (Siobhan)
Skyler (Schulyer)
Tateeahna (Tatianna)

Biblical and saintly names for boys

Abel
Adam
Benjamin
Daniel
David
Elijah
Ezekial
Isaac
Isaiah
Jacob
Jesus
Job
John
Jonah
Joseph
Joshua
Judas
Lazarus
Luke
Mark
Matthew
Moses
Noah
Paul
Peter
Samuel
Solomon

Biblical and saintly names for girls

Anna
Bathsheba
Deborah
Delilah
Dinah
Esther
Eve
Joanna
Judith
Julia
Leah
Magdalene
Martha
Mary
Miriam
Naamah
Naomi
Phoebe
Rachel
Rebekah
Ruth
Salome
Sarah
Tamar
Zipporah

Names for future architects (boys)

Aaron
Alan
Alexander
Art
Ed
Jack
Jay
Lawrence
Liam
Paul
Rafael
Robert
Ron
Royce
Sage
Sam
Sebastian
Seth
Shaw
Smith
Sterling
Taylor
Theo
Victor
Walt

Names for future architects (girls)

Adrianna
Alana
Annie
Beata
Candace
Deandra
Diana
Ernestine
Fawn
Fortune
Grace
Hannah
Janna
Joann
Justine
Katy
Kelly
Landa
Marianne
Olga
Penelope
Queen
Stella
Susannah
Treece

Good names for racing drivers

Al (Unser)
Alex (Tagiliani)
Bruno (Junqueira)
Damon (Hill)
Danny (Sullivan)
Dario (Resta)
David (Coulthard)
Eddie (Irvine)
Fernando (Alonso)
Helio (Castroneves)
Jacques (Villeneuve)
Johnny (Rutherford)
Juan (Montoya)
Jules (Goux)
Leo (Kinnunen)
Mario (Andretti, Dominguez)
Mark (Webber)
Mauri (Rose)
Michael (Schumacher)
Olivier (Panis)
Ralf (Schumacher)
Rick (Mears)
Rubens (Barrichello)
Sam (Hanks)

Boy celebrity names

Antonio
Ashton
Ben
Brad
Burt
Caspar
Damon
Denzel
Fabrice
Fernando
Gareth
Goran
Harrison
Hudson
Kiefer
Kurt
Liam
Marc
Matthew
Mel
Patrick
Quentin
Roman
Russell
Ryan
Tom

Girl celebrity names

Catherine
Charlize
Courtney
Daryl
Demi
Drew
Fiona
Gisele
Halle
Isabella
Jennifer
Jessica
Julia
Kate
Lara
Liberty
Liv
Natasha
Nicole
Oprah
Penelope
Portia
Reese
Renee
Rosanna
Sheena
Simone
Sophie
Trisha
Uma

Names celebrities give their baby boys

Aaron (Robert De Niro and Toukie Smith)
Bailey (Anthony Edwards and Jeannine Lobell)
Blanket (Michael Jackson)
Boston (Kurt Russell and Season Hubley)
Chance (Larry King and Shawn Southwick)
Chester (Tom Hanks and Rita Wilson)
Connor (Tom Cruise and Nicole Kidman)
Elijah Blue (Cher and Gregg Allman)
Giacomo (Sting and Trudie Styler)
Gib (Connie Selleca and Gil Gerard)
Griffin (Brendan Fraser and Afton Smith)
Hughie (Marg Helgenberger and Alan Rosenberg)
Jett (John Travolta and Kelly Preston)

Joaquin (Kelly Ripa and
Mark Consuelos)

Miles (Eddie and Nicole
Murphy)

Pedro (Frances
McDormand and Joel
Coen)

Prince Michael (Michael
Jackson)

Rafferty (Jude Law and
Sadie Frost)

Roman Caruso (Dee Dee
and Dan Cortese)

Satchel (Woody Allen
and Mia Farrow)

Theo (Kate Capshaw and
Steven Spielberg)

Zachary (Robin Williams
and Valerie Velardi)

Names celebrities give their baby girls

Bria (Eddie and Nicole
Murphy)

Briella Nicole (Desiree
and Blair Underwood)

Carys Zeta (Catherine
Zeta Jones and
Michael Douglas)

Cassidy (Kathy Lee and
Frank Gifford)

Ella Bleu (John Travolta
and Kelly Preston)

Eulala (Marcia Gay
Harden and Thaddeus
Scheel)

Fifi Trixibelle (Paula
Yates and Bob
Geldof)

Giovanna (Vanna White
and George Santo
Pietro)

Gracie (Faith Hill and Tim
McGraw)

Greta (Phoebe Cates and
Kevin Kline)

Ireland (Kim Basinger
and Alec Baldwin)

Kenya (Natassja Kinski
and Quincy Jones)

Maggie (Faith Hill and
Tim McGraw)

Mary Willa (Meryl Streep
and Donald Gummer)

Paris (Michael Jackson)

Peaches (Paula Yates
and Bob Geldof)

Rumer Glenn (Demi
Moore and Bruce
Willis)

Sailor (Christie Brinkley
and Peter Cook)

Scarlett (Mick Jagger
and Jerry Hall)

Scout LaRue (Demi
Moore and Bruce
Willis)

Shayne (Eddie and
Nicole Murphy)

Starlite Melody (Marisa
Berenson)

Tigerlily (Paula Yates
and Michael
Hutchence)

Zola (Eddie and Nicole
Murphy)

Cool names for athletes

Althea (Gibson)
Arnold (Palmer)
Babe (Ruth, Dedrikson)
Ben (Hogan)
Bill (Russell)
Billie Jean (King)
Bo (Jackson)
Boris (Becker)
Carl (Lewis)
Cy (Young)
David (Beckham)
Evander (Holyfield)
Fatima (Whitbread)
Frank (Bruno)
Frankie (Dettori)
Gabriel (Batistuta)
Greg (Louganis)
Hank (Aaron)
Jack (Nicklaus)
Jackie (Robinson, Joyner-
   Kersee)
Jerry (Rice)
Jesse (Owens)
Jim (Brown, Thorpe)
Joe (DiMaggio, Louis,
   Montana, Namath)
Jonny (Wilkinson)
Julius (Erving)

Kareem (Abdul-Jabbar)
Lance (Armstrong)
Larry (Bird)
Lou (Gehrig)
Magic (Johnson)
Mark (Spitz)
Martin (Johnson)
Martina (Navratilova)
Michael (Jordan, Owen)
Muhammad (Ali)
Paula (Radcliffe)
Rio (Ferdinand)
Sandy (Koufax)
Serena (Williams)
Steve (Redgrave)
Sugar Ray (Robinson)
Tiger (Woods)
Tyler (Hamilton)
Venus (Williams)
Walter (Payton)
Wayne (Gretzky)
Willie (Mays)
Wilma (Rudolph)
Wilt (Chamberlain)

Old-fashioned boy names that are cute again

Atticus
Barney
Casper
Charlie
Chester
Clem
Curtis
Dexter
Duane
Duke
Elmer
Gill
Harvey
Homer
Luke
Mitchell
Monty
Mort
Myron
Ned
Norm
Oscar
Stanley
Wilbur
Wyatt

Old-fashioned girl names that are cute again

- Abby
- Alma
- Annette
- Arden
- Arlene
- Ava
- Belle
- Betsy
- Beulah
- Corinna
- Ethel
- Flo
- Hazel
- Inez
- Irene
- Isabel
- Kay
- Kyra
- Laverne
- Loretta
- Lorraine
- Lydia
- Mabel
- Polly
- Trudy

Names for future doctors (boys)

- Bryant
- Charles
- Dimitri
- Frazier
- George
- Herbert
- James
- John
- Judd
- Lister
- Mark
- Martin
- Mason
- Murray
- Newell
- Nick
- Niles
- Peter
- Philip
- Ralph
- Randall
- Reagan
- Rell
- Russell
- Sabin

Names for future doctors (girls)

- Ann
- Athena
- Brenda
- Bryce
- Catrice
- Claire
- Dana
- Donna
- Elaine
- Elizabeth
- Freda
- Greta
- Jane
- Jennifer
- Linda
- Lydia
- Lynn
- Marianne
- Mary
- Maureen
- Miriam
- Sarah
- Suzanne
- Tina
- Victoria

Names for future artists (boys)

Ballard
Blaze
Ceron
Eduardo
Francesco
Francoise
Frederic
Gansta
Graham
Hector
Jean-Claude
Jean-Pierre
Jose
Laurent
Lionel
Maximilian
Michael
Octavio
Oscar
Paulo
Pash
Pedro
Ronnie
Sancho
Sebastian
Stephan

Names for future artists (girls)

Alexis
Ashantia
Azure
Caramia
Chantal
DeeDee
Emelle
Eve
Janice
Jenna
Kavita
Lace
Lanee
Lavonne
Margina
Mary-Catherine
Michaele
Mona
Regine
Sisteene
Skyler
Tallulah
Zora

Names for future lawyers (boys)

Atticus
Bryan
Caleb
Carlson
Dick
Gary
Jack
Jacob
John
Josh
Lawrence
Noble
Preston
Price
Quinn
Reese
Roark
Robert
Rush
Rusty
Ryder
Samuel
Sander
Sandford
Tom

Names for future lawyers (girls)

Ann
Brianna
Campbell
Carlisle
Charlotte
Dana
Emily
Haley
Joanna
Kate
Kendra
Lane
Madison
Marlel
Mason
Meg
Parker
Rachel
Sally
Sarah
Serena
Sloan
Taylor
Tekla
Terese

Good names for mechanics

Brewster
Carl
Chubby
Ernie
Fred
Gary
Hal
Hank
Harry
Jake
Joey
Leon
Max
Merle
Moey
Ralph
Red
Rusty
Sonny
Spanky
Terry
Toby
Zeke

Names from mythology and astrology

Ajax
Alala
Argus
Aries
Bacchus
Bran
Cadmus
Cressida
Evander
Galatea
Gawain
Gemlnl
Kalliope
Lake
Lancelot
Merlin
Nestor
Ocean
Penelope
Phoenix
Tane
Terra
Thor
Venus
Zeus

Scary/creepy boy names

- Bigram
- Brick
- Bruno
- Butcher
- Delete
- Dweezil
- Elmo
- Graven
- Gruver
- Horatio
- Izzy
- Modred
- Nada
- Napoleon
- Narcissus
- Nellie
- Neptune
- Nero
- Percival
- Pontius
- Seymour
- Sindbad
- Sisyphus
- Socrates
- Zero

Scary/creepy girl names

- Adelaide
- Agnes
- Arlette
- Beatrix
- Crispy
- Denz
- Earlene
- Edna
- Hortense
- Lakeesha
- Nunu
- Nyleen
- Peta
- Phyllida
- Quinceanos
- Randelle
- Scylla
- Sharama
- Swoosie
- Tashanee
- Uzbek
- Winnie
- Wyetta
- Zeb
- Zulemita

World's strangest names

- Adjanys
- Bego
- Blue
- Bucko
- Bukola
- Car
- Dix
- Dweezil
- Edju
- Idarah
- Kermit
- Kiwa
- Lovella
- Moon Unit
- Nimrod
- Oak
- Obey
- Pity
- Rudow
- Swell
- Tiago
- Tilla
- Zap
- Zip
- Zone

Unforgettable names

Allegra
Aura
Bai
Cocoa
Hyacinth
Jumbe
King
Lake
Leelee
Lindberg
Madonna
Momo
Montague
Pink
Prince
Rivers
Santeene
Schmoopie
Spirit
Sting
Symphony
Talent
Tame
Trocky
Wyclef

Boy names teachers can't pronounce

Artemus
Declan
Dionysus
Flody
Gyth
Hamif
Hermes
Hieronymos
Honorato
Iago
Ignatius
Ioannis
Isidro
Jetal
Jovan
Larrmyne
Mihow
Mischa
Moey
Raoul
Revin
Seth
Sladkey
Slavek
Takeya

Girl names teachers can't pronounce

Aisha
Aleithea
Camilla
Carenleigh
Chesskwana
Deighan
Falesyia
Gisbelle
Gresia
Madchen
Maromisa
Mayghaen
Meyka
Naeemah
Nissie
Nunibelle
Rhonwen
Ruthemma
Sade
Shaleina
Sharrona
Shawneequa
Tanyav
Tierah
Twyla

Names for Mister Perfect

Alex
Anthony
Ben
Blake
Brent
Christian
Christopher
Clint
Fletcher
Giancarlo
Harrison
Hunter
James
Joaquin
Justin
Kirk
Kyle
Monty
Reese
Riley
Robert
Rory
Ryan
Wells
Zack

Names for Miss Perfect

Alexandra
Allison
Bailey
Brittney
Celeste
Christiane
Courtney
Danielle
Elizabeth
Hollyn
Jennifer
Jill
Leah
Lexi
Marissa
Meredith
Merit
Mia
Miranda
Natalie
Nia
Riley
Shara
Sloan

Names that will help make your baby boy popular

Britt
Cam
Cody
Dylan
Ethan
Evan
Fletch
Gino
Gus
Heath
Hunter
Ian
Jake
Jason
Jeremy
Jerod
Joshua
Julian
Justin
Kyle
London
Max
Morgan
Nick
Tyler

Names that will help make your baby girl popular

- Ava
- Britney
- Clancy
- Coby
- Coco
- Emma
- Gina
- Lauren
- Lexi
- Lily
- Lindsay
- Lola
- London
- Lyla
- Mackenzie
- Madison
- Morgan
- Nicole
- Piper
- Reese
- Samantha
- Skye
- Sophie
- Tara
- Taylor

Comfy names that boys like having

- Allen
- Ben
- Brent
- Casey
- Chad
- Daniel
- Dave
- Ethan
- Gavin
- Jack
- Jake
- Jason
- Jesse
- Josh
- Justin
- Logan
- Matt
- Max
- Mike
- Nicholas
- Rob
- Sam
- Tyler

Comfy names that girls like having

- Allison
- Amber
- Annie
- Ashley
- Becca
- Callie
- Carrie
- Danielle
- Diane
- Emily
- Hailey
- Heather
- Isabel
- Jessica
- Jordan
- Justine
- Kim
- Lauren
- Liz
- Maggie
- Nicole
- Rachel
- Samantha
- Selena

Names for boys that sound regal

Alexander
Alfred
Andrew
Arthur
Charles
David
Edgar
Edmund
Edward
Egbert
Frederick
George
Harold
Henry
James
John
Julius
Louis
Malcolm
Philip
Rex
Richard
Robert
Rory
Rudolph
William

Names for girls that sound regal

Anne
Beatrice
Caroline
Charlotte
Christina
Cleopatra
Diana
Eleanor
Elizabeth
Eugenie
Helena
Isabella
Jane
Jennifer
Josephine
Julia
Katherine
Louisa
Margaret
Mary
Maud
Regina
Victoria

Season/weather names

Autumn
Cloudy
Dusky
Easter
Fog
Frosty
Holly
Misty
Noel
Rain
Rainbow
Season
Sky
Snow
Soleil
Spring
Storm
Summer
Sunny
Sunshine
Typhoon
Windy
Winter

Exotic names for your baby boy

Desiderio
Destin
Diego
Enrique
Enzo
Esme
Francesco
Franco
Frederic
Gabriel
Gaston
Genaro
Giancarlo
Hamlet
Hansel
Hawke
Heinz
Helio
Hermes
Honorato
Jacques
Janus
Javier
Jean-Paul
Johann

Exotic names for your baby girl

Cherokee
Cheyenne
Chiara
Kia
Kimone
Lakesha
Lani
Laurent
Pax
Pepita
Phaedra
Philomena
Phyllida
Quanda
Rania
Rasheeda
Rhiannon
Saffron
Santana
Sasha
Sequoia
Sheba
Shoshana
Simone
Solange

Names of the rich and famous

Abigail (Johnson)
Amy (Brinkley)
Andre (Agassi)
Andrew (Lloyd Webber)
Barbara (Taylor Bradford)
Bobby (Kotick)
Brad (Pitt)
Colleen (Barrett)
Dan (Snyder)
David (Beckham)
Elton (John)
Elizabeth (HM The Queen)
Jamie (Oliver)
Jennifer (Lopez)
Joe (Liemandt)
John Paul (Getty)
Judy (McGrath, Lewent)
Julia (Roberts)
Karen (Katen)
Lois (Juliber)
Madonna
Michael (Dell, Jordan, Robertson)
Oprah (Winfrey)
Pat (Woertz, Russo)
Richard (Branson)

Robbie (Williams)
Scott (Blum)
Sean (Combs) — P. Diddy
Shaquille (O'Neal)
Sherry (Lancing)
Sting
Tiger (Woods)
Tom (Cruise)
Vinny (Jones)
Will (Smith)

Nerd/dork/wallflower names

Barney
Bruce
Cheryl
Chester
Dabney
Dudley
Durwood
Edgar
Edward
Elwood
Emory
Engelbert
Estes
Ethelbert
Eugene
Eustace
Ewan
Fagan
Fairfax
Gomer
Pembroke
Percy
Priscilla
Ted
Warren

Names that make boys feel weird

Bloo
Butler
Car
Delete
Elmo
Elmore
Ervin
Excell
Fabio
Fable
Fergus
Fife
Forester
Geronimo
Gomer
Maverick
Oswald
Paris
Prince
Rebel
Stone
Stormy
Welcome
Ziggy

Names that make girls feel weird

- Breezy
- Charm
- Chastity
- Cherish
- Delite
- Fashion
- Glory
- Harmony
- Lake
- Leaf
- Liberty
- Michelin
- Misty
- Oceana
- Panther
- Peace
- Pity
- Precious
- Promise
- Purity
- Rain
- Sweetpea
- Tree
- True
- Vixen

Names for eccentrics

- Antigone
- Balfour
- Bark
- Beetle
- Bird
- Chantilly
- Cloudy
- Echo
- Ecstasy
- Flirt
- Free
- Fudge
- Galatea
- Gawain
- Goliath
- Lady
- LaRue
- Lazarus
- Obedience
- Orson
- Oz
- Rambo
- Stoli
- Webb
- Zeus

Names for boys who are handsome

- Allen
- Austin
- Benjamin
- Cal
- Cameron
- Chad
- Cooper
- Dax
- Dylan
- Ethan
- Fletcher
- Gus
- Hudson
- Ian
- Jan-Erik
- Jude
- Julian
- Kyle
- Logan
- Owen
- Riley
- Ryan
- Sebastian
- Shiloh
- Will

Names for girls who are beautiful

Addison
Anabelle
Annie
Ashley
Ava
Belle
Catrice
Dominique
Eden
Gina
Jade
Jennifer
Jessica
Jinx
Jolie
Jordan
Liz
Marisol
Miranda
Natasha
Petra
Rachel
Renee
Sheyn
Trista

Jewish/Hebrew names for boys

Aaron
Abe
Barry
Benjamin
Daniel
David
Eli
Esau
Ethan
Gabriel
Harrison
Ira
Isaac
Jake
Jay
Joshua
Levi
Marvin
Milton
Nathan
Sam
Saul
Sheldon
Solomon
Stanley

Jewish/Hebrew names for girls

Anne
Claire
Esther
Golda
Hannah
Ilana
Jenny
Johanna
Judith
Leah
Lena
Lillian
Linda
Mary
Miriam
Naomi
Rachel
Rebekah
Ruth
Sadie
Sarah
Shara
Sophie
Sylvia
Tovah

Arabic/Islamic names for boys	Arabic/Islamic names for girls	Scandinavian names for boys
Abdul-Jabbar	Aisha	Aksel
Ahmad, Ahmed	Almira	Anders
Ali	Asma	Anton
Amir	Bathsira	Bjorn
Dawud	Cala	Christian
Fariol	Dhelal	Claus
Ghassan	Fatima	Dirk
Habib	Habibah	Erik
Hakim, Hakeem	Hadil	Gustav
Hamid	Hajar, Hagir	Hendrik
Hasan	Hayfa	Ingmar
Ibrahim	Ihab	Isak
Jabir, Jabbar	Jamila	Johannes
Jamal	Kalila	Karl
Kamal, Kamil	Karima	Knut
Kareem	Laila	Krister
Khalid	Leila	Lars
Mahmud	Malak	Matts
Muhammad, Mohammad	Nada	Mikael
	Nima	Niels
Nuri	Rashidah	Niklas
Rafi	Rida	Oskar
Rashid	Sabah	Per
Salim	Salima	Rudolf
Sharif		Stellan
Yasir		

Scandinavian names for girls

Astrid
Birgit
Bonnevie
Dufvenius
Elsa
Erika
Fia
Frida
Gudrun
Gunilla
Inge
Ingrid
Janna
Johanna
Kristina
Liv
Lotta
Mini
Sabina
Sanna
Sigrid
Sofia
Sonya
Ursula
Wilhelmina

Italian names for boys

Aldo
Alessandro
Angelo
Arturo
Carlo
Carmine
Ciro
Cosmo
Dante
Emilio
Enrico
Franco
Gianni
Gino
Giorgio
Guido
Leonardo
Lorenzo
Luciano
Marco
Mario
Salvatore
Tomasso
Vincenzo
Vito

Italian names for girls

Annamaria
Bella
Cara
Caramia
Carissa
Carlotta
Chiara
Elda
Elena
Eliana
Elisa
Elletra
Faustina
Fidelia
Gina
Isabella
Maria
Melania
Paulina
Pia
Rosa
Rosamaria
Sophia

French names for boys	French names for girls	German names for boys
Alain	Aimee	Claus, Klaus
Charles	Amelie	Erik
Claude	Anais	Folker
Francois	Angelique	Freiderich
Frederic	Antoinette	Garrick
Gaston	Arianne	Gerhard
Gerard	Chantal	Gunther
Germain	Claire	Gustaf
Gregoire	Colette	Heinrich
Guy	Daniele	Helmut
Henri	Desiree	Hendrik
Isidore	Dominique	Karl
Jacques	Eliane	Konrad
Jean	Elisabeth	Kurt
Jean-Claude	Emmanuelle	Leopold
Jean-Michel	Esmee	Max
Jean-Paul	Gabrielle	Norbert
Laurent	Genevieve	Oswald
Louis	Giselle	Otto
Luc	Maria	Ralph
Marcel	Michele	Roger
Maxime	Monique	Rudy
Phillipe	Simone	Stefan
Robert	Yvette	Wilhelm
Yves	Yvonne	Wolfgang

German names for girls

Ada
Anke
Anneliese
Annemarie
Beata
Clotilda
Constanze
Cordula
Ebba
Elisabeth
Elsa
Emma
Felicie
Gudrun
Heidi
Hilda
Juliana
Karoline
Katharina
Kristina
Margarite
Maria
Martina
Rosa
Ursula

Polish names for boys

Aleksander
Andrzej
Aniol
Anzelm
Bogdan
Boleslaw
Czeslaw
Dobromir
Helmut
Jacek
Jozef
Karol
Kazimierz
Krzysztof
Marek
Pawel
Ryszard
Slawomir
Waclaw
Walenty
Witold
Wladymir
Wladyslaw
Wojtek
Zbigniew

Polish names for girls

Anna
Barbara
Cecilia
Celestyna
Gabriela
Gizela
Grazyna
Hanna
Honorata
Iwona
Jadwiga
Kamilia
Karolina
Krysta
Krystyna
Lucja
Maria
Marusya
Matylda
Mirka
Monika
Otylia
Roksana
Waleria
Wiktoria

Russian names for boys	Russian names for girls	Irish names for boys
Adya	Anastasiya	Aidan
Alek	Anninka	Art
Aleksei	Dariya	Bran
Denis	Dasha	Brendan
Dmitri	Duscha	Brian
Grigori	Elena	Colin
Igor	Evelina	Curran
Ivan	Inessa	Devin
Karl	Irene/Irina	Farris
Maksimilian	Ivanna	Fergus
Mikhail	Kira	Finn
Misha	Lara	Ian
Nikita	Lia	James
Nikolai	Masha	Jamie
Oleg	Nadya	John
Pavel	Natalia	Kevin
Sasha	Natasha	Kieran, Keiran
Sergei	Oksana	Killian
Sidor	Olga	Liam
Stanislav	Polina	Lochlain
Valentin	Sasha	Owen
Valeri	Sofya	Patrick
Vlad	Sonya	Rowan
Vladimir	Svetlana	Sean
Vladja	Tatiana	Shay

Irish names for girls

Aileen
Amanda
Annie
Brenda
Briana
Catherine
Cathleen
Ciara
Deirdre
Dorren
Eavan
Eliza
Emma
Ethnea
Karen
Kate
Kathy
Maggie
Molly
Nancy
Nessa
Polly
Riona
Sally
Sinead

Scottish names for boys

Ainsley
Alan
Angus
Bean
Bennett
Cally
Cameron
Charles
Clement
Conall
Donald
Fergus
Gregor
Harry
Iagan
Ian
James
Jock
Jon
Kenneth
Peader
Roddy
Scott
Stewart
Walter

Scottish names for girls

Alexandra
Alison
Annella
Christy
Dina
Fiona
Heather
Jeanie
Jenny
Lexine
Lexy
Lindsay
Lucy
Maidie
Maisie
Margaret
Nan
Netta
Nora
Peigi
Robina
Rona
Rowena
Sandy
Tory

English names for boys

Adam
Arthur
Ben
Charles
Clive
Colin
Daniel
Edward
George
Henry
Jack
James
Joseph
Joshua
Luke
Matthew
Max
Michael
Nicholas
Nigel
Oliver
Peter
Philip
Roger
Roland
Sam
Thomas
Toby
William

English names for girls

Agnes
Alexandra
Amanda
Angela
Anne
Charlotte
Chloe
Elizabeth
Ella
Emily
Emma
Esther
Georgina
Grace
Hannah
Hayley
Jennifer
Jessica
Jill
Katherine
Lucy
Margaret
Megan
Olivia
Philippa
Rebecca
Sophie
Wendy

Welsh names for boys

Adeone
Bevan
Bowen
Brice
Bryson
Bryton
Carey
Clyde
Dylan
Davis
Dewey
Drew
Drystan
Evon
Ewand
Griffith
Gwynn
Howell
Llewelyn
Lloyd
Meredith
Newlin
Nye
Owen
Parry
Price
Renfro
Rhys
Romney
Sayre
Vaughn

Welsh names for girls

Aeronwenn
Ariana
Aylwin
Betha
Betriss
Bronwyn
Brynna
Carey
Carys
Crisiant
Delwyn
Dylan
Eleri
Enid
Gladys
Glenda
Glynnis
Griffin
Guinevere
Gwen
Gwendolyn
Gwyneth
Isolde
Jennifer
Meredith
Morgan
Nerys
Olwen
Owena
Price
Rhianna
Rhonwen
Sian
Wynne

African names for boys

Addae
Adio
Ayo
Bakari
Bomani
Dalila
Dumisani
Hamidi
Harun
Hasani
Hondo
Jaja
Kamal
Kamau
Muhhamad
Rudo
Runako
Saeed
Salehe
Salim
Sekani
Themba
Umi
Zikomo
Zuberi

African names for girls

Aamori
Abayomi
Adia
Aisha
Asabi
Bayo
Eshe
Fatima
Femi
Habiba
Hasina
Jumoke
Kibibi
Kissa
Lateefa
Maudisa
Nailah
Nomble
Omorose
Oni
Rufaro
Salama
Taliba
Tisa
Zahra

Spanish names for boys

Adonis
Alejandro
Alfonso
Angel
Benito
Carlos
Damaso
Diego
Emilio
Enrique
Esteban
Fiero
Francisco
Hector
Isidoro
Javier
Jorge
Jose
Juan
Julio
Miguel
Mundo
Raoul
Roberto
Tomas

Spanish names for girls

Angela
Beila
Beilarosa
Bonita
Caliopa
Carlotta
Carmen
Clementina
Consuelo
Delicia
Delfina
Destina
Elena
Flora
Graciela
Guadalupe
Honoria
Juanita
Maria
Mariposa
Odelita
Paloma
Primalia
Soledad

Greek names for boys

- Alexandros
- Andreas
- Ari
- Basil
- Cletus
- Demetri
- Demetrios
- Demos
- Flavian
- Hilarion
- Jason
- Lucas
- Markos
- Nikos
- Paul
- Sander
- Seth
- Socrates
- Stephanos
- Theo
- Theodoros
- Theophilos
- Tito
- Verniamin
- Zeno

Greek names for girls

- Aggie
- Andrianna
- Ariane
- Athena
- Calista
- Calla
- Chloe
- Damalla
- Delos
- Diona
- Filia
- Gillian
- Helena
- Iona
- Isadora
- Kali
- Kalidas
- Kori
- Kynthia
- Leandra
- Nia
- Phyllis
- Pia
- Theodora
- Zoe

Southeast Asian names for boys

- An (Chinese)
- Chang (Chinese)
- Dong (Chinese)
- Hiro (Japanese)
- Huang (Chinese)
- Ibu (Japanese)
- Ji (Chinese)
- Jin (Chinese)
- Jing (Chinese)
- Ju-Long (Chinese)
- Kang (Korean)
- Li (Chinese)
- Liang (Chinese)
- Pin (Vietnamese)
- Quon (Chinese)
- Shen (Chinese)
- Sheng (Chinese)
- Shuu (Japanese)
- So (Vietnamese)
- Tan (Japanese)
- Tung (Chinese, Vietnamese)
- Yen (Chinese)
- Yu (Chinese)
- Yuan (Chinese)
- Zhong (Chinese)

South-east Asian names for girls

Bao (Chinese)
Bay (Vietnamese)
Cai (Chinese)
Connie-Kim (Vietnamese)
De (Chinese)
Fang (Chinese)
Ha (Vietnamese)
Lei (Chinese)
Li (Chinese)
Lian (Chinese)
Ling (Chinese)
Mai (Japanese)
Min (Chinese)
Ming (Chinese)
Niu (Chinese)
Nu (Vietnamese)
Pang (Chinese)
Tam (Japanese)
Thim (Thai)
Veata (Cambodian)
Yu (Chinese)
Zan (Chinese)
Zhi (Chinese)
Zhong (Chinese)
Zi (Chinese)

Indian/Pakistani names for boys

Arun
Babu
Bish
Dalai
Deepak
Gobind
Iranga
Jabal
Krishna
Madan
Madhav
Manu
Mihir
Mohan
Mohana
Motee
Mukul
Perun
Ponnuswamy
Raj
Rakesh
Ram
Rangarajan
Ravi
Shiva
Taj
Varma
Yash

Indian/Pakistani names for girls

Anala
Anand
Anjali
Asharaf
Asra
Ayanna
Chakra
Chana
Chandra
Dama
Deva
Gita
Hansa
Inca
Jaya
Kaleigh
Kashmir
Kavita
Kismet
Lalita
Maya
Nirvana
Opal
Prema
Raka
Rania
Rasheeda
Rubina

Saffron
Sajah
Salma
Sanila
Shamsa
Sheela
Tamirisa
Usha
Veda
Vina
Yadira

Boy names that get shortened

Alexander
Augustus
Barnabus
Bradford
Christopher
Cornelius
Donovan
Emmanuel
Enrique
Franklin
Frederic
Gregory
Jonathon
Nathaniel
Nicholas
Randolph
Roberto
Roderick
Roosevelt
Salvador
Samuel
Solomon
Timothy
Wilfredo
Woodrow

Girl names that get shortened

Alexandra
Anastasia
Angelina
Cassandra
Charmaine
Constance
Deborah
Elizabeth
Evangeline
Gabrielle
Guadalupe
Gwendolyn
Jacqueline
Jennifer
Josephine
Kimberly
Lucretia
Magdalena
Nanette
Penelope
Rebecca
Rosalinda
Roxanna
Susannah

Boy names that spawn nasty nicknames

Adolf
Aldred
Alec, Alek
Alfonso
Apple
Ash
Asher
Ashley
Ashton
Babe
Boris
Bucky
Butler
Byrd
Clement
Dominic
Farley
Farnham
Farr
Ferdinand
Harry
Haywood
Jericho
Titus

Girl names that spawn nasty nicknames

Christopher
Cocoa
Dusky-Dream
Earlene
Feather
Fortune
Gay
Harriet
Haute
Hedy
Hermione
Hodge
Hortense
Lesbia
Monica
Rainey
Romona
Ruta
Scarlett
Sesame
Sigrun
Sweetpea
Taffy
Teddi
Winifred

Hippie-sounding names

Apple
Breezy
Cloud
Dune
Free
Gypsy
Happy
Maverick
Oceana
Peace
Peaches
Rain
Rainbow
River
Sea
Serenity
Sierra
Spring
Star
Summer
Sunny
Tree
True
Willow
Winner

Names for smart boys

Adam
Allen
Barry
Benjamin
Brent
Byron
Chet
Clarence
Curtis
David
Eric
Gray
Guy
Hillel
Jack
Kent
Laurens
Martin
Maximilian
Peter
Philip
Richard
Rob
Russell
Scott
Trevor
William

Names for smart girls

Allene
Beth
Carolyn
Carrie
Colby
Dana
Dominique
Donna
Elizabeth
Jamie
Jennifer
Karen
Kathleen
Kristina
Leticia
Maude
Micheline
Natasha
Page
Shannon
Shari
Shaune
Suzanne
Tessie
Zoann

Names for playful personalities

Babe
Bebe
Bliss
Bunny
Buzzie
Chica
Dusky
Fluffy
Happy
Jandy
Jinx
Lily
Merrilee
Miranda
Pal
Pixie
Poppy
Precious
Queenie
Rabbit
Schmoopie
Skip
Sunny
Trixie
Viveca

Place names (boys)	Place names (girls)	Boy names derived from literature
Aberdeen	Asia	Ahab
Aleppo	Bali	Ali Baba
Alps	Bonn	Boswell
America	Cairo	Cervantes
Beaumont	Capri	Chaucer
Bexley	Chelsea	Cummings
Bradford	China	Cyrano
Brent	Dallas	Dickens
Brooklyn	Devon	Don Quixote
Carson	Easter	Dryden
Cuba	Egypt	Emerson
Cyprus	France	Foster
Douglas	Georgia	Grimm
Gwent	India	Hunter
Hollywood	Indiana	Keats
Hull	Ireland	Lowell
Kent	Jordan	Milton
Lincoln	Kansas	Norman
Logan	Kentucky	Pope
Orlando	Kenya	Rhett
Sydney	Lansing	Sherman
Texas	Odessa	Spenser
	Persia	Swift
	Savannah	Wordsworth
	Venice	Yeats

Girl names derived from literature

Alice
Austen
Bronte
Browning
Cale
Charlotte
Colette
Daisy
Godiva
Grisham
Harper
Jane
Kipling
Lara
McMurtry
Meg
Melanie
Millay
Patricia
Sadie
Scarlett
Scout
Simone
Stella
Whitman
Whittier

Bad-to-the-bone, death-row names for boys

Adolph (Hernandez)
Clydell (Coleman)
David (Hammer, Long)
Fred (West)
Harold (Shipman)
Ian (Brady, Huntley)
Jeffrey (Dahmer, Lund-
    gren)
Jessie (Patrick)
John (Baltazar, Martinez)
Leonard (Rojas)
Mack (Hill)
Peter (Sutcliffe)
Reginald (Kray, Reeves)
Richard (Ramirez, Speck,
    Kutzner, Dinkins)
Ronald (Kray)
Rodolfo (Hernandez)
Stanley (Baker)
Ted (Bundy)
Timothy (McVeigh)
Windell (Broussard)

Bad-to-the-bone, death-row names for girls

Aileen Carol (Wuonmos)
Ana (Cardona)
Andrea (Jackson)
Antoinette (Frank)
Betty (Beets)
Blanche (Moore)
Caroline (Young)
Christa Gail (Pike)
Darlie Lynn (Routier)
Debra (Milke)
Delores (Rivers)
Faye (Copeland)
Frances (Newton)
Gail Kirsey (Owens)
Jaqueline (Williams)
Karla Faye (Tucker)
Kerry (Dalton)
Latasha (Pulliam)
Maria (del Rosio Alfaro)
Marilyn (Plantz)
Mary Ellen (Samuels)
Maureen (McDermott)
Myra (Hindley)
Nadine (Smith)
Pamela (Perillo)
Vernice (Ballenger)

Country-western singer names (boys)

Alan (Jackson)
Billy Ray (Cyrus)
Brad (Paisley)
Buck (Owens)
Cash (Moline)
Chance (Martin)
Charley (Pride)
Chet (Atkins)
Clay (Walker)
Clint (Black)
Conway (Twitty)
Dwight (Yoakum)
Garth (Brooks)
George (Strait)
Hank (Williams)
Kenny (Rogers)
Lyle (Lovett)
Merle (Haggard)
Tex (Ritter)
Tim (McGraw)
Toby (Keith)
Travis (Tritt)
Vince (Gill)
Waylon (Jennings)
Willie (Nelson)

Country-western singer names (girls)

Allison (Krauss)
Anne (Murray)
Barbara (Mandrell)
Brenda (Lee)
Carlene (Carter)
Cristy (Lane)
Dolly (Parton)
Emily (Robison)
Faith (Hill)
Jo Dee (Messina)
Kitty (Wells)
LeAnn (Rimes)
Lee Ann (Womack)
Loretta (Lynn)
Martie (Maguire)
Martina (McBride)
Maybelle (Carter)
Natalie (Maines)
Pam (Tillis)
Patsy (Cline)
Reba (McIntire)
Shania (Twain)
Tamara (Walker)
Trisha (Yearwood)
Wynonna (Judd)

Wimpy names

Babe
Barney
Bobo
Brownie
Brucie
Byrd
Chubby
Clydell
Corky
Denny
Dewey
Dudley
Dusty
Dwight
Feo
Fergie
Fuddy
Perry
Skeeter
Skippy
Spanky
Terry
Timmy
Tippy
Wendell

Girlie-girl names

Bebe
Bubbles
Buffy
Bunny
Cherry
Cinderella
Cinnamon
Cookie
Darlie
Debbie-Jean
Deedee
Dolly
Fluffy
Melrose
Poppy
Posy
Precious
Primrose
Princess
Prissy
Sissy
Sugar
Sweetpea
Tippie
Trixiebelle

Boy names that are so over

Al
Bob
Dennis
Donald
Douglas
Ernie
Frank
Garland
Gary
Glanville
Harold
Harvey
Jaden
Jason
Jerry
Juwon
Ken
Leon
Marvin
Morey
Oscar
Ottis
Randy
Rick
Todd

Girl names that are so over

Bertie
Betty
Carla
Delores
Edith
Faye
Frances
Gail
Hilary
Judy
Loretta
Louise
Marilyn
Maureen
Minnie
Myrna
Nancy
Nina
Priscilla
Stacy
Tiffany
Tracy
Veronica
Wanda
Winona

Overpowering boy names

Abbott
Axelrod
Baldridge
Balthazar
Domenico
Don Quixote
Dontrell
Esmond
Gabbana
Galbraith
Huntley
Hyde
Kensington
Lothario
Montague
Napoleon
Ottway
Pluto
Quintavius
Reginald
Rochester
Ronford
Roosevelt
Thor
Wyclef

Overpowering girl names

Antoinette
Aunjanue
Bjork
Calista
Colemand
Deja-Marie
Gwyneth
Illeana
Ione
Jowannah
Kallioppe
Karalenae
Madonna
Mariangela
Oprah
Perabo
Penelope
Philomena
Russo
Sahara
Siphronia
Stockard
Teah
Thora
Winifred

Macho names

Bucko
Butch
Buzz
Cal
Cash
Duke
Esteban
Evander
Hud
Hugo
Jock
Judd
Mack
Ram
Rebel
Reem
Rip
Rocco
Sam
Santiago
Spike
Stone
Trocky
Waylon
Zoom

Sweetie-pie names	Powerful boy names	Powerful girl names
Alicia	Andrew	Anna
Angie	Angus	Blake
Annabelle	Anthony	Campbell
Bay	Charles	Candace
Brook	Cole	Elizabeth
Darcy	Colin	Evan
Dolce	Easton	Grace
Dove	Ford	Greta
Faith	Grant	Harper
Goldie	Harrison	Honor
Honey	Heath	Hope
Jenny	Jacob	Jessica
Julianna	James	Julia
Kate	Jon	Lauren
Laurel	Justice	Madison
Lisa	Lamar	Margaret
Marina	Louis	Olivia
Robin	Michael	Pace
Rosa	Nash	Parker
Roseanne	Nolan	Pilar
Sarah-Jessica	Quentin	Quinn
Tammy	Reagan	Reeve
Wylie	Solomon	Rhea
Yolie	Thomas	Sarah
	William	Wylie

Most popular names of the 1990s (boys)

1. Michael
2. Christopher
3. Matthew
4. Joshua
5. Jacob
6. Andrew
7. Daniel
8. Nicholas
9. Tyler
10. Joseph
11. David
12. Brandon
13. James
14. John
15. Ryan
16. Zachary
17. Justin
18. Anthony
19. William
20. Robert
21. Jonathan
22. Kyle
23. Austin
24. Alexander
25. Kevin
26. Cody
27. Thomas
28. Jordan
29. Eric
30. Benjamin
31. Aaron
32. Jose
33. Christian
34. Steven
35. Samuel
36. Brian
37. Dylan
38. Timothy
39. Adam
40. Nathan
41. Richard
42. Sean
43. Charles
44. Patrick
45. Jason
46. Luis
47. Jeremy
48. Stephen
49. Mark
50. Jesse

Most popular names of the 1990s (girls)

1. Ashley
2. Jessica
3. Emily
4. Sarah
5. Samantha
6. Brittany
7. Amanda
8. Elizabeth
9. Taylor
10. Megan
11. Stephanie
12. Kayla
13. Lauren
14. Jennifer
15. Rachel
16. Hannah
17. Nicole
18. Amber
19. Alexis
20. Courtney
21. Victoria
22. Danielle
23. Alyssa
24. Rebecca
25. Jasmine
26. Katherine
27. Melissa
28. Alexandra
29. Brianna
30. Chelsea
31. Michelle
32. Morgan
33. Kelsey
34. Tiffany
35. Kimberly
36. Christina
37. Madison
38. Heather
39. Shelby
40. Anna
41. Mary
42. Maria
43. Allison
44. Sara
45. Laura
46. Andrea
47. Olivia
48. Erin
49. Haley
50. Abigail

Most popular names of the 1980s (boys)

1. Michael
2. Christopher
3. Matthew
4. Joshua
5. David
6. Daniel
7. James
8. Robert
9. John
10. Joseph
11. Jason
12. Justln
13. Andrew
14. Ryan
15. William
16. Brian
17. Jonathan
18. Brandon
19. Nicholas
20. Anthony
21. Eric
22. Adam
23. Kevin
24. Steven
25. Thomas
26. Timothy
27. Richard
28. Jeremy
29. Kyle
30. Jeffrey
31. Benjamin
32. Aaron
33. Mark
34. Charles
35. Jacob
36. Stephen
37. Jose
38. Patrick
39. Scott
40. Paul
41. Nathan
42. Sean
43. Zachary
44. Travis
45. Dustin
46. Gregory
47. Kenneth
48. Alexander
49. Jesse
50. Tyler

Most popular names of the 1980s (girls)

1. Jessica
2. Jennifer
3. Amanda
4. Ashley
5. Sarah
6. Stephanie
7. Melissa
8. Nicole
9. Elizabeth
10. Heather
11. Tiffany
12. Michelle
13. Amber
14. Megan
15. Rachel
16. Amy
17. Lauren
18. Kimberly
19. Christina
20. Brittany
21. Crystal
22. Rebecca
23. Laura
24. Emily
25. Danielle
26. Samantha
27. Angela
28. Erin
29. Kelly
30. Sara
31. Lisa
32. Katherine
33. Andrea
34. Mary
35. Jamie
36. Erica
37. Courtney
38. Kristen
39. Shannon
40. April
41. Maria
42. Kristin
43. Katie
44. Lindsey
45. Alicia
46. Vanessa
47. Lindsay
48. Christine
49. Allison
50. Kathryn

Most popular names of the 1970s (boys)

1. Michael
2. Christopher
3. Jason
4. David
5. James
6. John
7. Robert
8. Brian
9. William
10. Matthew
11. Daniel
12. Joseph
13. Kevin
14. Eric
15. Jeffrey
16. Richard
17. Scott
18. Mark
19. Steven
20. Timothy
21. Thomas
22. Anthony
23. Charles
24. Jeremy
25. Joshua
26. Ryan
27. Paul
28. Andrew
29. Gregory
30. Chad
31. Kenneth
32. Stephen
33. Jonathan
34. Shawn
35. Jose
36. Aaron
37. Patrick
38. Adam
39. Justin
40. Edward
41. Sean
42. Benjamin
43. Todd
44. Donald
45. Ronald
46. Keith
47. Bryan
48. Gary
49. George
50. Nathan

Most popular names of the 1970s (girls)

1. Jennifer
2. Amy
3. Melissa
4. Michelle
5. Kimberly
6. Lisa
7. Angela
8. Heather
9. Stephanie
10. Jessica
11. Elizabeth
12. Nicole
13. Rebecca
14. Kelly
15. Mary
16. Christina
17. Amanda
18. Sarah
19. Laura
20. Julie
21. Shannon
22. Christine
23. Tammy
24. Karen
25. Tracy
26. Maria
27. Dawn
28. Susan
29. Andrea
30. Tina
31. Cynthia
32. Patricia
33. Rachel
34. April
35. Lori
36. Crystal
37. Wendy
38. Stacy
39. Sandra
40. Jamie
41. Erin
42. Carrie
43. Tara
44. Tiffany
45. Monica
46. Danielle
47. Stacey
48. Teresa
49. Pamela
50. Sara

Most popular names of the 1960s (boys)

1. Michael
2. David
3. John
4. James
5. Robert
6. Mark
7. William
8. Richard
9. Thomas
10. Jeffrey
11. Steven
12. Joseph
13. Timothy
14. Kevin
15. Scott
16. Brian
17. Charles
18. Daniel
19. Paul
20. Christopher
21. Kenneth
22. Anthony
23. Gregory
24. Ronald
25. Donald
26. Gary
27. Eric
28. Stephen
29. Edward
30. Douglas
31. Todd
32. Patrick
33. George
34. Keith
35. Larry
36. Matthew
37. Terry
38. Andrew
39. Randy
40. Dennis
41. Jerry
42. Peter
43. Jose
44. Frank
45. Craig
46. Raymond
47. Jeffrey
48. Bruce
49. Mike
50. Tony

Most popular names of the 1960s (girls)

1. Lisa
2. Mary
3. Karen
4. Susan
5. Kimberly
6. Patricia
7. Linda
8. Donna
9. Michelle
10. Cynthia
11. Sandra
12. Deborah
13. Pamela
14. Tammy
15. Laura
16. Lori
17. Elizabeth
18. Julie
19. Jennifer
20. Brenda
21. Angela
22. Barbara
23. Debra
24. Sharon
25. Teresa
26. Nancy
27. Christine
28. Cheryl
29. Denise
30. Tina
31. Kelly
32. Maria
33. Kathleen
34. Melissa
35. Amy
36. Robin
37. Dawn
38. Carol
39. Diane
40. Rebecca
41. Tracy
42. Kathy
43. Theresa
44. Kim
45. Stephanie
46. Rhonda
47. Wendy
48. Cindy
49. Janet
50. Michele

Most popular names of the 1950s (boys)

1. Michael
2. James
3. Robert
4. John
5. David
6. William
7. Richard
8. Thomas
9. Mark
10. Charles
11. Steven
12. Gary
13. Joseph
14. Donald
15. Ronald
16. Kenneth
17. Paul
18. Larry
19. Daniel
20. Stephen
21. Dennis
22. Timothy
23. Edward
24. Jeffrey
25. George
26. Gregory
27. Kevin
28. Douglas
29. Terry
30. Anthony
31. Jerry
32. Bruce
33. Randy
34. Frank
35. Brian
36. Scott
37. Raymond
38. Roger
39. Peter
40. Patrick
41. Lawrence
42. Keith
43. Wayne
44. Danny
45. Alan
46. Gerald
47. Jose
48. Carl
49. Christopher
50. Ricky

Most popular names of the 1950s (girls)

1. Mary
2. Linda
3. Patricia
4. Susan
5. Deborah
6. Barbara
7. Debra
8. Karen
9. Nancy
10. Donna
11. Cynthia
12. Sandra
13. Pamela
14. Sharon
15. Kathleen
16. Carol
17. Diane
18. Brenda
19. Cheryl
20. Elizabeth
21. Janet
22. Kathy
23. Margaret
24. Janice
25. Carolyn
26. Denise
27. Judy
28. Teresa
29. Rebecca
30. Christine
31. Joyce
32. Shirley
33. Judith
34. Catherine
35. Betty
36. Maria
37. Beverly
38. Lisa
39. Laura
40. Gloria
41. Theresa
42. Connie
43. Gail
44. Julie
45. Ann
46. Martha
47. Joan
48. Paula
49. Robin
50. Bonnie

Most popular British names (boys)

1. Jack
2. Joshua
3. Thomas
4. James
5. Daniel
6. Oliver
7. Benjamin
8. Samuel
9. William
10. Joseph
11. Harry
12. Matthew
13. Lewis
14. Luke
15. Ethan
16. George
17. Adam
18. Alfie
19. Callum
20. Alexander

Most popular British names (girls)

1. Emily
2. Ellie
3. Chloe
4. Jessica
5. Sophie
6. Megan
7. Lucy
8. Olivia
9. Charlotte
10. Hannah
11. Katie
12. Ella
13. Grace
14. Mia
15. Amy
16. Holly
17. Lauren
18. Emma
19. Molly
20. Abigail

Most popular American names (boys)

1. Jacob
2. Michael
3. Joshua
4. Matthew
5. Ethan
6. Joseph
7. Andrew
8. Christopher
9. Daniel
10. Nicholas

Most popular American names (girls)

1. Emily
2. Madison
3. Hannah
4. Emma
5. Alexis
6. Ashley
7. Abigail
8. Sarah
9. Samantha
10. Olivia

Most popular Australian names (boys)

1. Joshua
2. Jack
3. Thomas
4. Ethan
5. Liam
6. Jacob
7. Matthew
8. Mitchell
9. Lachlan
10. Daniel

Most popular Australian names (girls)

1. Chloe
2. Jessica
3. Emma
4. Grace
5. Sarah
6. Shakira
7. Emily
8. Amy
9. Hannah
10. Hayley

Most popular French names (boys)

1. Thomas
2. Lucas
3. Theo
4. Hugo
5. Maxime
6. Antoine
7. Quentin
8. Clement
9. Alexandre
10. Nicolas

Most popular French names (girls)

1. Lea
2. Manon
3. Chloe
4. Camille
5. Emma
6. Oceane
7. Sarah
8. Marie
9. Laura
10. Julie

part five

Boys

Aaron
(Hebrew) revered; sharer
*Aarone, Ahren, Ahron,
Arin, Aron, Arron*

Abacus
(Word as name) device
for doing calcalutions;
clever
Abacas, Abakus, Abba

Abbas
(Arabic) harsh
Ab, Abba

Abbey, Abby
(Hebrew) spiritual
Abbie, Abie

Abbott
(Hebrew) father; leader
Abbitt, Abott, Abotte

Abdiel
(Arabic) serving Allah

Abdul
(Arabic) servant of Allah
Ab, Abdel, Abul

Abdul-Jabbar
(Arabic) comforting

Abdullah
(Arabic) Allah's servant
*Abdallah, Abdulah,
Abdulla*

Abe
(Hebrew) short for
Abraham; father of many
Abey, Abie

Abel
(Hebrew) vital
*Abe, Abele, Abell, Abey,
Abie, Able*

Abelard
(German) firm
*Abbey, Abby, Abe, Abel,
Abelerd*

Abelino
(Spanish) from Biblical
Abel, son of Adam and
Eve; naive
Abel, Able

Aberdeen
(Place name) serene
Aber, Dean, Deen

Abilene
(Place name) town in
Texas; good-old-boy
Abalene, Abileen

Abir
(Hebrew) strong
Abeer

Abner
(Hebrew) cheerful leader
Abnir, Abnor

Abraham
(Hebrew) fathering
multitudes
*Abe, Abrahim, Abrahm,
Abram, Bram*

Abram
(Hebrew) short for
Abraham
Abe, Bram

Abraxas
(Spanish) bright
Aba

Abs
(Hebrew) short for
Absalom; muscular
Abe

Absalom
(Hebrew) peaceful;
handsome
Abe, Abs

Abundio
(Spanish) living in
abundance
Abun, Abund

Ace
(Latin) one; unity
Acey

Achilles
(Greek) hero of *The Iliad*
Achille, Ackill, Akilles

Acker
(American)
Aker

Acton
(English) sturdy; oaks
Acten, Actin, Actohn,
Actone

Adair
(Scottish) negotiator
Adaire, Adare, Ade

Adalberto
(Spanish) bright;
dignified
Adal, Berto

Adam
(Hebrew) first man;
original
Ad, Adahm, Adamo,
Addam, Addams, Addie,
Addy, Adem

Adamson
(Hebrew) Adam's son
Adamsen, Adamsson

Adan
(Irish) bold spirit
Aden, Adin, Adyn, Aidan,
Aiden

Addae
(African) the sun

Addis
(English) short for
Addison; masculine
Addace, Addice, Addy,
Adis

Addison
(English) Adam's son
Ad, Adison, Adisson

Addy
(German) awesome;
outgoing
Addi, Addie, Adi

Adel
(German) royal
Adal, Addey, Addie,
Addy

Adelard
(German) brave
Addy, Adelarde

Adeone
(Welsh) royal
Addy, Adeon

Adio
(African) devout

Adlai
(Hebrew) ornamented
Ad, Addy, Adlay, Adley,
Adlie

Adler
(German) eagle-eyed
Adlar

Adnee
(English) loner
Adni, Adny

Ado
(American) respected
Ad, Addy

Adolf
(German) sly wolf
Adolfe, Adolph

Adolfus
(German) form of
Adolphus

Adonis
(Greek) gorgeous
(Aphrodite's love in
mythology)
Addonis, Adones,
Adonys, Andonice

Adrian
(Latin) wealthy; dark-
skinned
Ade, Addie, Adreeyan,
Adriann, Adrien, Adrion,
Adryan, Aydrien,
Aydrienne

Adriano
(Italian) wealthy
Adriannho, Adrianno

Adriel
(Hebrew) God's follower
Adrial, Adryel

Adrien
(French) form of Adrian
Ade, Adriene, Adrienn

Adya
(Russian) man from
Adria

Adyn
(Irish) manly
Adann, Ade, Aden,
Aidan, Ayden

Aeneas
(Greek) worthy of praise
Aineas, Aineias, Eneas,
Eneis

Afton
(English) dignified
Affton, Aftawn, Aften

Agamemnon
(Greek) slow but sure
Agamem

Agustin
(Latin) dignified
Aguste, Auggie,
Augustin

Ahab
(Hebrew) father's
brother; sea captain in
Moby Dick

Ahmad, Ahmed
(Arabic) praised man
Achmed, Amad, Amed

Aidan
(Irish) fiery spirit
Adan, Adin, Aiden,
Aydan

Aiken
(English) hardy;
oakhewn
Aikin, Ayken, Aykin

Ainsley
(Scottish) in a meadow
Ansley, Ainslee, Ainsli,
Aynsley, Aynslie

Ajax
(Greek) daring
Ajacks

Ajay
(American) spontaneous
A.J., Aj, Ajah

Akeem
(Arab) form of Hakeem;
skilled; introspective
Ackeem, Ackim, Akieme,
Akim, Hakeem, Hakim

Aki
(Scandinavian)

Akilles
(Greek) form of Achilles;
heroic

Aksel
(Scandinavian) calm

Al
(Irish) short for
Alexander and Alan;
attractive

Aladdin
(Arabic) believer
Al, Aladdein, Aladen

Alain
(French) form of Alan
and Allen
Allain, Alun

Alair
(Gaelic) happy
Alaire

Alan
(Irish) handsome boy
Al, Aland, Alen, Allan,
Allen, Alley, Allie, Allin,
Allyn, Alon, Alun

Alando
(Spanish) form of Alan;
attractive
Al, Alaindo, Alan , Aland,
Alano, Allen, Allie, Alun,
Alundo, Alyn

Alasdair
(Scottish) form of
Alistair; highbrow
Al, Alasdaire, Alasdare,
Alisdair

Alastair
(Scottish) strong leader
Alastere, Alastaire,
Allastair, Alystair

Alaster
(American) form of
Alastair; staunch
advocate
Alaste, Alester, Allaster

Alban
(Latin) white man (from
Alba's white hill)
Abion, Albee, Alben,
Albi, Albie, Albin, Alby

Albanse
(Invented) from the place name Albany, New York; white
Alban, Albance, Albanee, Albany, Albie, Alby

Albany
(Place name) restless
Albanee, Albanie

Albert
(German) distinguished
Al, Alberto, Albie, Alby, Ally

Alberto
(Italian) distinguished
Al, Albert, Bertle

Albie
(German) short for Albert; smart
Albee, Albi, Alby

Albion
(Greek) old-fashioned
Albionne, Albyon

Alcordia
(American) in accord with others
Alcord, Alkie, Alky

Alden
(English) wise
Al, Aldan, Aldon

Aldo
(Italian) older one; jovial
Aldoh

Aldorse
(American) form of Aldo; old
Al, Aldo, Aldorce, Aldors

Aldred
(English) advisor; judgmental
Al, Aldrid, Aldy, Alldred

Aldren
(English) old friend
Al, Aldran, Aldie, Aldrun, Aldy, Aldryn

Aldrich
(English) wise advisor
Aldie, Aldrick, Aldrish, Alldrich

Alec
(Greek) high-minded
Al, Aleck, Alic

Alejandro
(Spanish) defender; bold and brave
Alejandra

Alek
(Russian) short for Aleksei; brilliant
Aleks

Aleksander
(Greek and Polish) defender
Alek, Sander

Aleksei
(Russian) defender; brilliant
Alek, Alik, Alexi

Aleppo
(Place name) easygoing
Alepo

Alessandro
(Italian) helpful; defender
Allessandro

Alex
(Greek) short for Alexander; leader
Alecs, Alix, Allex

Alexander
(Greek) great leader; helpful
Al, Alec, Alex, Alexandor, Alexsander

Alexandre
(French) form of Alexander; helpful

Alexandros
(Greek) form of Alexander; helpful
Alesandros, Alexandras

Alexis
(Greek) short for Alexander
Alexace, Alexes, Alexi, Alexy, Lex

Alfeus
(Hebrew) follower
Alpheus

Alfie
(English) short for Alfred; friendly
Alf, Alfi, Alfy

Alfonso
(Spanish) bright;
prepared
*Alf, Alfie, Alfons,
Alfonsin, Alfonso,
Alfonz, Alphonsus, Fons,
Fonzie, Fonzy*

Alfred
(English) counselor
*Al, Alf, Alfie, Alfrede,
Alfryd*

Alfredo
(Italian and Spanish)
advisor
*Alf, Alfie, Alfreedo,
Alfrido*

Alfredrick
(American) combo of
Alfred and Fredrick;
pretentious
*Al, Alf, Alfred, Freddy,
Fredrik*

Alger
(German) hardworking
Algar

Algernon
(English) man with facial
hair
Al, Alger, Algie, Algy

Algia
(German) prepared; kind
Alge, Algie

Ali
(Arabic) greatest
Alee, Aly

Ali-Baba
(Literature) *A Thousand
and One Nights*

Alisander
(Greek) form of
Alexander
Alissander, Alsandare

Allan
(Irish) form of Alan
Allane

Allard
(English) brave man
Alard

Allegheny
(Place name) mountains
of the Appalachian
system; grand
*Al, Alleg, Alleganie,
Alleghenie*

Allen
(Irish) handsome
*Al, Alen, Allie, Allin,
Allyn, Alon*

Almar
(German) form of
Almarine; strong
Al, Almarr, Almer

Almere
(American) director
Almer

Alonzo
(Spanish) enthusiastic
*Alonso, Alonze, Elonzo,
Lon*

Aloysius
(German) famed
Aloisius

Alphonse
(German) distinguished
*Alf, Alfonse, Alphonso,
Fonsi, Fonsie, Fonz,
Fonzie*

Alps
(Place name) climber
Alp

Alquince
(American) old and fifth
*Al, Alquense, Alquin,
Alquins, Alquinse,
Alqwence*

Alrick
(German) leader
Alrec, Alric

Alroy
(American) combo of Al
and Roy; sedate
Al, Alroi

Alston
(English) serious;
nobleman
Allston, Alsten, Alstin

Altarius
(African-American) from
Greek Altair; shining star
*Altare, Altair, Altareus,
Alterius, Alltair, Al*

Alter
(Hebrew) old; will live to
be old

Alto
(Place name) town in
Texas; alto voice;
easygoing
Al

Alton
(English) excellent; kind
*Allton, Altawn, Alten,
Altyn*

Altus
(Latin) form of Alta; high
Al, Alta

Alva
(Hebrew) intelligent;
beloved friend
Alvah

Alvarado
(Spanish) peacemaker
*Alvaradoh, Alvaro, Alvie,
Alvy*

Alvaro
(Spanish) just
*Alvaroh, Alvarro, Alvey,
Alvie, Alvy*

Alvern
(English) old friend
Al, Alverne, Alvurn

Alvin
(Latin) light-haired;
loved
Alv, Alven, Alvie

Alvincent
(American) combo of
Alvin and Vincent; giving
friend
*Alvin, Alvince, Vin,
Vince, Vincent, Vinse*

Alvis
(American) form of Elvis;
old friend
Al, Alviss, Alvy

Amadayus
(Invented) form of
Amadeus
Amadayes

Amadeo
(Italian) blessed by God;
artistic

Amadeus
(Latin) god-loving
Amad, Amadayus

Amado
(Spanish) loved
*Amadee, Amadeo,
Amadi, Amadis, Amadus,
Amando*

Amadour
(French) loved
Amador, Amadore

Amal
(Hebrew) hardworking;
optimistic
Amahl, Amhall

Amar
(Arabic) making a home
Ammar

Amarillo
(Place name) in Spanish,
it means yellow;
renegade
Amarille, Amarilo

Amato
(Italian) loving
Amahto, Amatoh

Ambrose
(German) everlasting
*Amba, Ambie, Ambroce,
Amby*

America
(Place name) patriotic

Americo
(Spanish) patriotic
*Ame, America, Americus,
Ameriko*

Amerigo
(Italian) ruler (name of
Italian explorer)
Amer, Americo, Ameriko

Ames
(French) friendly
Aims

Amiel
(Hebrew) my people's
God
Ameal, Amheel, Ammiel

Amin
(Arabic) honorable;
dependable
Aman, Ameen

Amir
(Arabic) royal; ruler
Ameer, Amire

Amiti
(Japanese) endless friend

Amor
(Latin) love
Amerie, Amoree, Amori,
Amorie

Amory
(German) home ruler
Amor

Amos
(Hebrew) strong
Amus

Ampy
(American) fast
Amp, Ampee, Ampey,
Amps

Amyas
(Latin) lovable
Aimeus, Ameus, Amias,
Amyes

An
(Chinese) peaceful; safe

Anan
(Irish) outdoorsy
An, Annan

Anastasius
(Greek) reborn
Anastase, Anastasio,
Anasticius

Anatole
(French) exotic
Anatol, Anatoly, Anitolle

Ancel
(French) creative
Ance, Ancell, Anse,
Ansel, Ansell

Andel
(Scandinavian) honored

Ander
(English) form of
Andrew; masculine

Anders
(Swedish) masculine
Ander, Andirs, Andries,
Andy

Andras
(French) form of Andrew;
masculine
Andrae, Andres, Andrus,
Ondrae, Ondras

André
(French) masculine
Andre, Andree

Andreas
(Greek) masculine
Andrieas, Adryus, Andy

Andres
(Spanish) macho
Andrez, Andy

Andretti
(Italian) speedy
Andrette, Andy

Andrew
(Greek) manly and brave
Aindrew, Anders, Andi,
Andie, Andreas, Andres,
Andru, Andrue, Andy

Andros
(Polish) masculine
Andrus

Andru
(Greek) form of Andrew;
masculine
Andrue

Andrzej
(Polish) manly

Andy
(Greek) short for
Andrew; masculine
Andee, Andie

Anferny
(American) variation of
Anthony
Andee, Anfernee,
Anferney, Anferni,
Anfernie, Anfurny

Angel
(Greek) angelic
messenger
Ange, Angele

Angelberto
(Spanish) shining angel
Angel, Angelbert, Bert,
Berto

Angelo
(Italian) angelic
Ange, Angeloh, Anjelo

Angle
(Invented) word as
name; spin-doctor
Ange, Angul

Anglin
(Greek) angelic
Anglen, Anglinn, Anglun

Angus
(Scottish) standout;
important
Ange, Angos

Anibal
(Spanish) brave noble

Aniello
(Italian) risk-taker

Aniol
(Polish) angel
Ahnjol, Ahnyolle

Ankoma
(African) last-born child

Annatto
(Botanical) tree; tough
Annatta

Anolus
(Greek) masculine
Ano, Anol

Anrue
(American) masculine
Anrae, Anroo

Ansel
(French) creative
Ancell, Anse, Ansell

Anselm
(German) protective
Anse, Ansehlm, Ansellm

Anselmo
(Spanish) protected by
God
*Ancel, Ancelmo, Anse,
Ansel, Anselm, Anzelmo,
Selmo*

Anson
(German) divine male
Anse, Ansonn, Ansun

Anthony
(Latin) outstanding
*Anth, Anthoney,
Anthonie, Anton, Tony*

Antoine
(French) worthy of
praise
*Antone, Antwan,
Antwon, Antwone*

Anton
(Latin) outstanding
Antan, Antawn

Antonce
(African-American) form
of Anthony; valued
Antawnce

Antonio
(Spanish) superb
*Antone, Antonioh,
Antonyo, Antonyia, Tony*

Antony
(Latin) good
*Antawny, Antonah,
Antone, Antoney,
Antonie, Tone, Tony*

Antrinell
(African-American)
valued
Antrie, Antrinel, Antry

Antroy
(African-American) form
of Anthony; prized
Antroe, Antroye

Antwan
(American) form of
Antoine; achiever

Antwone
(American) variant of
Antoine; achiever
Antwonn

Anwar
(Arabic) shining
Anwhour

Anzelm
(Polish) protective
Ahnzselm

Apolinar
(Spanish) manly and
wise
Apollo

Apollo
(Greek) masculine (a
god in mythology)
*Apolloh, Apolo,
Apoloniah, Applonian*

Apostle
(Greek) follower;
disciple
Apos

Apostolos
(Greek) disciple
Apos

Apple
(American) favorite;
wholesome
Apel

Aquila
(Spanish) eagle-eyed
Aquile, Aquilla

Aquileo
(Spanish) warrior
Akweleo, Aquilo

Aramis
(French) clever
Arames, Aramyse,
Arhames

Arbet
(Last name as first
name) high
Arb, Arby

Arceneaux
(French) friendly;
heavenly
Arce, Arcen, Arceno

Arch
(English) short for Archie
and Archibald; athletic
Arche

Archer
(English) athletic;
bowman
Arch, Archie

Archibald
(German) bold leader
Arch, Archibold, Archie

Archie
(English) short for
Archibald; bold
Arch, Archi, Archy

Ardee
(American) ardent
Ard, Ardie, Ardy

Ardell
(Latin) go-getter
Ardel

Arden, Ardon
(Latin) ball-of-fire
Ard, Arda, Ardie, Ardin,
Ardon, Arrden

Ardmohr
(Latin) more ardent than
others
Ard, Ardmoor, Ardmore

Arenda
(Spanish)

Aristeo
(Spanish) best
Aris, Aristio, Aristo, Ary

Argan
(American) leader
Argee, Argen, Argey,
Argi, Argie, Argun

Argento
(Spanish) silver
Arge, Argey, Argi, Argy

Argus
(Greek) careful; bright
Arjus

Ari
(Greek) best
Ahree, Arie, Arih, Arri

Aric
(English) leader
Arec

Ariel
(Hebrew) God's spirited
lion
Ari, Arie, Ariele, Arielle,
Arriel

Aries
(Greek) god of war
(mythology)
Arees

Arion
(Greek) enchanted man
Ari, Arrian, Arie, Ariohn

Aristides
(Greek) son of the
outstanding
Ari, Aris

Aristotle
(Greek) best man
Ari, Aris, Aristie,
Aristottle

Arkyn
(Scandinavian) royal
offspring
Ark, Arken, Arkin

Arle
(Irish) sworn
Arlee, Arley, Arly

Arledge
(English) lives by a lake
Arleedj, Arles, Arlidge

Arleigh
(Irish) sworn
Arly

Arlen
(Irish) dedicated
Arl, Arlan, Arle, Arlin

Arlis
(Hebrew) dedicated; in charge
Arlas, Arles, Arless, Arly

Arlo
(German) strong
Arloh

Arlonn
(Irish) sworn; cheerful
Arlan, Arlann, Arlen, Arlon

Arlys
(Hebrew) pledged
Arlis

Arm
(English) arm
Arma, Arman, Arme

Armand
(German) strong soldier
Armando, Arme, Ormand

Armando
(Spanish) entertainer
Armand, Arme, Armondo

Armani
(Italian) army; disciplined talent
Amani, Arman, Armanie, Armon, Armoni

Armen
(Spanish) from the name Armenta
Arme, Arment, Armenta

Armitage
(Last name as first name) safe haven
Armi, Armita, Army

Armon
(Hebrew) strong as a fortress
Arman, Arme, Armen, Armin

Armstrong
(English) strong-armed
Arme, Army

Arnaud
(French) strong
Arnaldo, Arnauld

Arnborn
(Scandinavian) eagle-bear; animal instincts
Arn, Arne, Arnborne, Arnbourne

Arndt
(German) strong
Arne, Arnee, Arney, Arni, Arnie

Arne
(German) short for Arnold; ruler
Arn

Arnie
(German) short for Arnold; ruler
Arne, Arney, Arni, Arny

Arnithan
(African-American) form of Arnie and Jonathan; eagle-eyed
Arnee, Arnie, Nithan

Arno
(German) far-sighted
Arn, Arne, Arnoh

Arnold
(German) ruler; strong
Arnald, Arne, Arnie, Arny

Arnome
(Invented) powerful
Arnom

Arnst
(Scandinavian) eagle-eyed (arn means eagle)
Arn

Arnulfo
(Spanish) strong
Arne, Arnie, Arny

Aron
(Hebrew) generous
Aaron, Arron, Erinn

Arsenio
(Greek) macho; virile
Arne, Arsinio, Arsonio

Art
(English) bear-like;
wealthy
Arte, Artie

Artemus
(Greek) gifted
*Art, Artemis, Artie,
Artimus*

Arthisus
(Origin unknown) stuffy
Arth, Arthi, Arthy

Arthur
(English) distinguished
*Art, Arther, Arthor, Artie,
Artur, Arty, Aurthur*

Artie
(English) short for
Arthur; wealthy
Art, Artee, Arty

Arturo
(Italian) talented
Art, Arture, Arturro

Arun
(Hindi) the color of the
sky before dawn

Arvin
(German) friendly
Arv, Arven, Arvy

Arwen
(German) friend
*Arwee, Arwene, Arwhen,
Arwy*

Ary
(Hebrew) lionine; fierce
Ari, Arye

Asa
(Hebrew) healer
Ase, Aza

Ash
(Botanical) tree; bold
Ashe

Ashbel
(Hebrew) fiery god

Ashby
(Scandinavian) brash
*Ashbee, Ashbey, Ashie,
Ashy*

Asher
(Hebrew) joyful
Ash, Ashur

Ashford
(English) spunky
Ash, Ashferd

Ashley
(English) smooth
Ash, Ashie, Ashlee, Ashly

Ashton
(English) handsome
Ashteen, Ashtin

Atam
(American) form of
Adam; tough
Atame, Atom, Atym

Atanacio
(Spanish) everlasting
Atan, Atanasio

Atkins
(Last name as first
name) linked; known
Atkin

Atlas
(Greek) courier of
greatness
Atlass

Atticus
(Greek) ethical
Aticus, Attikus

Attila
(Gothic) powerful
Atila, Atlya, Att

Atwell
(English) place name;
the well; full of gusto

Atwood
(English) place name;
the woods; outdoorsy

Auberon
(German) like a bear;
highborn
Aube

Aubert
(German) leader
Auber, Aubey

Aubin
(French) ruler; elfin
Auben

Aubrey
(English) ruler
*Aube, Aubree, Aubry,
Bree*

Auburn
(Latin) brown with red
cast; tenacious
Aubern, Aubie, Auburne

Auden
(English) old friend
Aude, Audie

Audencio
(Spanish)
Auden

Audie
(German) strong man
Aude, Audee

Augie
(Latin) short for Augustus
Aug, Auggie , Augy

August
(Latin) determined
Auge, Augie

Augustine
(Latin) serious and revered
Aug, Augie, August, Augustene, Augustin

Augusto, Augustin
(Spanish) respected; serious
Agusto, Augey, Auggie, Austeo

Augustus
(Latin) highly esteemed
Aug, Auge, Augie, August

Aulie
(English) form of Audley
Awlie

Aurelius
(Latin) golden son
Aurel, Aurie, Aury

Austin
(Latin); capital of Texas; ingenious; Southwestern
Aust, Austen, Auston, Austyn

Auther
(American) form of Arthur; brave and smart
Authar, Authur

Averill
(French) April-born child
Ave, Averil, Avryl, Avrylle

Avery
(English) softspoken
Avary, Ave, Averie, Avry

Avion
(French) flyer
Aveonn, Avyon, Avyun

Axel
(German) peaceful; contemporary
Aksel, Ax, Axe, Axil

Ayo
(African) happy

Ayson
(Origin unknown) lucky
Aison

Azael
(Spanish) God-loved
Azzael

Babe
(American) athlete

Babu
(Hindi) fierce

Bacchus
(Greek) reveler; jaded
Baakus, Bakkus, Bakus

Bach
(Last name as first name) talented
Bok

Bacon
(English) literary; outspoken
Baco, Bake, Bakon

Badger
(Last name as first name) difficult
Badge, Badgeant, Bage, Bagent

Bailey
(French) attentive
Baile, Baily, Baley, Baylie

Bainbridge
(Irish) bridge; negotiator
Bain, Banebridge, Beebee

Baines
(Last name as first name) pale
Baine, Baynes

Bainlon
(American) form of Bailey; pale
Bailey, Baily

Baird
(Irish) singer/poet; creative
Bard, Bayrde

Bakari
(African) promising

Baker
(English) baker
Baiker, Baykar

Baldemar
(Spanish) form of Balthasar; brave and wise
Baldy

Baldric
(German) leader
Baldrick, Baledric, Bauldric

Baldridge
(English) persuasive

Baldwin
(German) steadfast friend
Baldwinn, Baldwynn, Bally

Baley
(American) form of Bailey
Baleye

Balfour
(Scottish) landowner
Balf, Balfore

Balfre
(Spanish) brave

Ballance
(American) courageous
Balance, Ballans

Ballard
(German) brave
Ballerd

Balthasar
(Greek) God save the king
Bath, Bathazar

Balwin
(Last name as first name) friendly and brave
Ball, Winn

Bancroft
(English) bean field; gardener
Banc, Bankie, Bankroft

Bandy
(Origin unknown) gregarious
Bandee, Bandi

Banks
(Last name as first name) focused
Bank

Banning
(Irish) fair-haired
Bannie, Banny, Bannyng

Barclay
(Scottish) audacious man; birch tree meadow
Bar, Barclaye, Bark, Barklay, Barky

Bard
(Irish) singer
Bar, Barr

Barden
(English) peaceful; valley-dweller
Bardon

Bargo
(Last name as first name) outspoken
Barg

Bark
(English) short for Barker; outgoing
Birk

Barker
(English) handles bark; lumberjack
Bark, Barkker

Barlow
(English) hardy
Barloe, Barlowe

Barman
(Last name as first name) bright; blessed
Barr

Barn
(American) word as name; works in barns
Barnee, Barney, Barny

Barnabas
(Hebrew) seer; comforter
Barn, Barnaby, Barnebus, Barney, Barnie, Barny

Barnaby
(Hebrew) companionable
Barn, Barnabee, Barnabie, Barnie, Barny

Barner
(English) mercurial
Barn, Barnerr, Barney, Barny

Barnes
(English) powerful; bear

Barnett
(English) leader of men
Barn, Barnet, Barney

Barney
(English) short for Barnett
Barn, Barni, Barnie, Barny

Barnum
(German) safe; barn
Barnham, Barnhem, Barnie

Baron
(English) noble leader
Bare, Baren, Barren, Baryne

Barrett
(German) strong and bearlike
Bar, Baret, Barett, Barette, Barry

Barrington
(English) dignified
Bare, Baring, Berrington

Barry
(Irish) candid
Barre, Barrie, Bary

Bart
(Hebrew) persistent
Bartee, Bartle, Barty

Bartley
(Last name as first name) rural man
Bart, Bartle, Bartlee, Bartli, Bartly

Barth
(Hebrew) protective
Bart, Barthe, Barts

Bartholomew
(Hebrew) friendly; earthy
Bart, Barthlolmewe, Bartie

Barto
(Spanish) form of Bartholomew; upward
Bartelo, Bartol, Bartoli, Bartolo, Bartolomeo

Barton
(English) persistent man; Bart's town
Bart, Barty

Bartram
(English) intelligent
Bart, Barty

Baruch
(Hebrew) most blessed
Barry

Basford
(American) charming; low-profile
Bas, Basferd, Basfor

Bash
(American) party-loving
Bashi, Bashey, Bashy

Basil
(Greek) regal
Basel, Basey, Basile, Bazil

Bass
(Last name as first name) fish; charmer
Bassee, Bassey, Bassi, Bassy

Bassett
(English) small man
Baset, Basett, Basey, Basse

Benny
(Hebrew) short for
Benjamin
Benge, Benjy, Benni,
Bennie

Benoit
(French) growing and
flourishing
Ben, Benoyt

Bensey
(American) easygoing;
fine
Bence, Bens, Bensee

Benson
(Hebrew) son of Ben;
brave heart
Bensahn, Bensen

Bent
(English) short for
Benton
Bynt

Bentley
(English) clever
Bent, Bentlee, Leye

Benton
(English) formidable
Bentan, Bentawn,
Bentone

Benvenuto
(Italian) welcomed child
Ben

Benz
(German) from carmaker
Mercedes-Benz; upscale
Bens

Ber
(Hebrew) bear

Berfit
(Origin unknown)
farming; outdoorsman
Berf

Berg
(German) tall; mountain
Bergh, Berj, Burg, Burgh

Berger
(French) watchful;
shepherd
Bergher, Bergie

Bergin
(Swedish) loquacious;
lives on the hill
Bergan, Berge, Bergen,
Berger, Bergin, Birgin

Berkeley
(English) place name;
idolized
Berk, Berkeley, Berki,
Berkie, Berklee, Berkley,
Berklie, Berkly, Berky

Berko
(Hebrew) bear
Ber

Berks
(American) adored
Berk, Berke, Berkelee,
Berkey, Berkli, Berksie,
Berkslee, Berky, Birklee,
Birksey, Burks, Burksey

Berman
(German) steady
Bermahn, Bermen,
Bermin

Bernabe
(German) bold
Bernabee, Bernabey,
Bernaby, Bernby,
Bernebe, Berns, Bernus,
Burnby

Bernal
(German) bear-like
Bern

Bernard
(German) brave and
dependable
Bern, Bernarde, Bernee,
Bernerd, Bernie, Berny,
Burnard

Bernardo
(Spanish) brave; bear
Berna, Bernardo,
Barnardoh, Berny

Bernave
(American) form of
Bernard; smart
Bernav, Bernee,
Berneve, Berni

Bernd
(German) bear-like
Bern, Berne, Bernee,
Berney, Berny

Berne
(German) courageous
Bern, Berni, Bernie,
Bernne, Berny

Bernie
(German) brave boy
Bern, Berni, Berny,
Birnie, Burney

Bert
(English) shining
example
Berti, Bertie, Berty, Birt,
Burt

Berthold
(German) bold ruler
Bert, Berthol, Berthuld,
Berty

Berthrand
(German) form of
Bertram; strong; raven
Bert, Berthran, Bertie,
Bertrand, Berty

Bertin
(English) form of Burton;
dramatic
Berton, Burtun

Bertoldo
(Spanish) ruler
Bert

Berton
(American) form of
Burton; brave; dramatic
Bert, Bertan, Berty

Bertram
(German) outstanding
Bert, Bertie, Bertrem,
Bertrom, Berty

Bertrand
(German) bright
Bert, Bertie,Bertran,
Bertrund, Birtryn

Berty
(English) form of Bert;
shining
Bert, Bertie, Burty

Bervick
(American) upwardly
mobile; brave
Bervey

Berwyn
(English) loyal friend
Berrie, Berwin, Berwynd,
Berwynne

Besley
(Last name as first
name) calm
Bes, Bez

Best
(American) word as
name; quintessential
man
Beste

Bettis
(American) vocal
Bettes, Bettus, Betus

Beuford
(Last name as first
name) form of Buford;
country boy
Beuf, Bu, Bueford

Bevan
(Welsh) beguiling
Bev, Bevahn, Beven,
Bevin

Bever
(English) form of Bevis;
sophisticated

Bevil
(English) form of Bevis;
dignified

Bevis
(French) strong-willed
Bev, Bevas, Beves,
Bevvis, Bevys, Bevyss

Bexal
(American) studious
Bex, Bexlee, Bexly, Bexy

Bexley
(Place name)
distinguished

Biaggio
(Italian) stutters; unsure
Biage, Biagio

Biffy
(American) popular
Bibbee, Biff

Bigram
(Origin unknown)
handsome
Bigraham, Bygram

Bill
(German) short for William; strong; resolute
Billi, Billie, Billy

Billings
(Place name) sophisticated

Billy
(German) short for William; strong
Bilie, Bill, Billee, Billi, Billie, Bily

Billybob
(American) combo of Billy and Bob
B.B., Billibob, Billiebob, BillyBob, Billy Bob

Billy-Dale
(American) from William and Dale; countrified
Billidell, Billydale

Billyjoe
(American) combo of Billy and Joe
Billiejoe, Billijo, Billjo, BillyJoe

Billymack
(American) combo of Billy and Mack
Billiemac, Billimac, Billy, BillyMack, Mackie

Billyray
(American) combo of Billy and Ray
Billirae, Billy Ray

Bing
(German) outgoing
Beng

Bingo
(American) spunky
Bengo, Bingoh

Binkie
(English) energetic
Bink, Binki, Binky

Birch
(English) white and shining; birch
Berch, Bir, Burch

Bird
(American) soaring
Byrd

Biren
(American) form of Byron
Biran

Birkett
(English) living in birches; calming
Birk, Birket, Birkie, Birkitt, Burkett, Burkette, Burkitt

Birley
(English) outdoorsy; meadow
Berl, Birl, Birlee, Birly

Birney
(English) single-minded; island
Birne, Birni, Birny, Burney

Bish
(Hindi) universal

Bishop
(Greek) supervisor; serving the bishop
Bish, Bishie, Bishoppe

Bix
(American) hip
Bicks, Bixe

Bjorn
(Swedish) athletic
Bjarn, Bjarne, Bjonie, Bjorne, Bjorny

Black
(Scottish) dark
Blacke, Blackee, Blackie

Blade
(Spanish) prepared; knife
Bladie, Blayd

Blaine
(Irish) svelte
Blain, Blane, Blayne

Blair
(Irish) open
Blaire, Blare, Blayree

Blaise, Blaze
(French) audacious
Blasé, Blayse

Blake
(English) dark and handsome
Blaike, Blakey, Blakie

Blakeley
(English) outdoorsy; meadow
Blake, Blakelee, Blakely, Blakie

Blame
(American) sad
Blaim, Blaime

Blanchard
(Last name as first name) white
Blan

Blanco
(Spanish) light
Blancoh, Blonco, Blonko

Blank
(American) word as name; blank slate; open
Blanc

Blanket
(Invented) baby attached to a security blanket
Blank, Blankee, Blankett, Blankey, Blankie, Blanky

Blanton
(English) mild-mannered
Blanten, Blantun

Blasio
(Spanish) stutterer
Blaseo, Blasios, Blaze

Blaze
(English and American) daring
Blaase, Blaise, Blazey, Blazie

Bliss
(English) happy
Blice, Blyss

Blithe
(English) merry
Bly, Blye, Blythe

Blitzer
(German) adventurous
Blitz, Blitze

Blocker
(Last name as first name) block
Bloc, Block, Blok

Bloo
(American) zany

Blue
(Color name) hip
Bleu, Blu

Blye
(American) joyful
Blie

Bo
(Scandinavian) lively
Beau

Boat
(American) word as name; sealoving
Bo

Boaz
(Hebrew) strong; swift
Bo, Boase, Boaze, Boz

Bob
(English) short for Robert; bright; outstanding
Bobbi, Bobbie, Bobby

Bobby
(English) short for Robert; bright; outstanding
Bob, Bobbie, Bobi

Bobbydee
(American) combo of Bobby and Dee; country boy
Bobbidee, Bobby D, Bobby Dee, Bobby-Dee

Bobbymack
(American) combo of Bobby and Mack; jovial
Bobbimac, Bobbymac, Bobby-Mack

Bobby-Wayne
(American) combo of
Bobby and Wayne;
small-town boy
Bob, Bobbiwayne,
Bobbi-Wayne, Bobby,
Bobby Wayne,
Bobbywayne, Wain,
Wayne

Boden
(French) communicator
Bodin, Bodun, Bowden

Bodhi
(Buddhist) Bodhi-
Dharma was founder of
Ch'an Buddhism in
China
Bodhee

Bogart
(German) bold, strong
man
Bo, Bobo, Bogardte,
Boge, Bogert, Bogey,
Bogie

Bogdan
(Polish) God's gift

Bogdari
(Polish) gift from God
Bogdi

Boggle
(American) confusing
Bogg

Bojesse
(American) comical
Boje, Bojee, Bojeesie,
Bojess

Bola
(American) careful; bold
Bolah, Boli

Bolden
(American) bold man
Boldun

Boleslaw
(Polish) in glory
Boleslav

Bolin
(Last name as first
name) bold
Bolen

Bolivar
(Spanish) aggressive
Bolley, Bollivar, Bolly

Bolley
(American) strong
Bolly

Bomani
(African) fighter
Boman

Bon
(French) good
Bonne

Bonar
(French) gentle
Bonarr, Bonnar, Bonner

Bonaventura
(Spanish) good fortune
Bona, Bonavento,
Buenaventura,
Buenaventure, Ventura

Bonaventure
(Latin) humble
Bonaventura,
Bonnaventura,
Buenaventure

Bond
(English) farmer;
renegade
Bondee, Bondie, Bondy

Bongo
(American) type of
drum; musical
Bong, Bongy

Boni
(Latin) fortunate
Bonne

Bonifacio
(Spanish) benefactor
Bona, Boni, Boniface

Bono
(Spanish) good
Bonno

Booker
(English) lover of books
Book, Booki, Bookie,
Booky

Boone
(French) blessed; good
Boon, Boonie, Boony

Booth
(German) protective
*Boot, Boothe, Boothie,
Bootsie*

Boots
(American) cowboy
Bootsey, Bootsie, Bootz

Booveeay
(Invented) form of
Bouvier
Boo

Bordan
(English) secretive; of
the boar
*Borde, Bordee, Borden,
Bordi, Bordie, Bordy*

Border
(American) word as
name; fair-minded;
aggressive
Bord

Borg
(Scandinavian) fortified;
castle
Borge, Borgh

Boris
(Russian) combative
Boras, Bore, Bores

Bos
(English) woodsman
Boz

Boscoe
(English) woodsman

Bosley
(English) thriving; grove
*Bos, Boslee, Boslie,
Bosly*

Bost
(Place name) from
Boston, Massachusetts;
audacious
Bostt

Boston
(Place name) distinctive
Boss, Bost

Boswell
(English) well near
woods; dignified
*Bos, Bosswell, Boz,
Bozwell*

Botolf
(English) wolf;
standoffish
Botof

Bourbon
(Place name) jazzy
*Borbon, Bourbonn,
Bourbonne*

Bourne
(French) planner;
boundary
*Bourn, Bourney,
Bournie, Byrn, Byrne,
Byrnie*

Bouvier
(French) elegant; sturdy;
ox
*Bouveah, Bouveay,
Bouviay*

Bowen
(Welsh) shy
Bowie, Bowin

Bowie
(Irish) brash; western
Booie, Bowen

Boyce
(French) defender
Boice, Boy, Boyce

Boyd
(Scottish) fair-haired
Boide, Boydie

Bovo
(Last name as first
name) macho
Bovoh

Bowing
(Last name as first
name) blond and young
Beau, Bo, Bow, Bowen

Bowman
(Last name as first
name) young; archer
Bow

Bowry
(Irish) form of Bowie;
able; young
Bowy

Boy
(American) boy child of the family
Boydine
(French) from the woods
Boyse
Boyer
(French) woodsman
Brack
(English) from the plant bracken; fine
Bracke
Bracken
(English) plant name; debonair
Brack, Brackan, Brackin, Brackun
Brad
(English) short for Bradley; expansive
Braddie, Braddy
Bradan
(English) open-minded
Braden, Bradin, Brady, Bradyn, Braedyn, Braid
Bradford
(English) mediator
Brad, Brady
Bradley
(English) prosperous; expansive
Brad, Bradie, Bradlee, Bradlie, Bradly

Bradshaw
(English) broad-minded
Brad, Brad-Shaw, Bradshie
Brady
(Irish) high-spirited
Brade, Bradee, Bradey
Brain
(Invented) word as name; brilliant
Brane
Bram
(Hebrew) short for Abraham; great father
Brahm, Bramm
Bran
(Irish) raven; blessed
Brann
Branch
(Latin) growing
Bran, Branche
Branco
(Last name as first name)
Brank, Branko
Brand
(English) fiery
Brandd, Brande, Brandy, Brann
Brando
(American) talented
Brand

Brandon
(English) hill; high-spirited
Bradonn, Bran, Brandan, Brandin, Branny
Brandt
(English) dignified
Bran, Brandtt, Brant
Brandy
(English) firebrand; bold; brandy drink
Brand, Brandee, Brandey, Brandi, Brandie
Brannon
(Irish) bright-minded
Bran, Brann, Brannen, Branon
Branson
(English) persistent
Bran, Brans, Bransan, Bransen
Brant
(English) hothead
Brandt
Brashier
(French) brash
Brashear, Brasheer
Bratcher
(Last name as first name) aggressive
Bratch
Bravillo
(Spanish) brave
Braville

Bravo
(Italian) topnotch
Bravoh, Bravvo

Braxton
(English) worldly
Brack, Brackston, Brax, Braxsten, Braxt

Bray
(English) vocal
Brae

Brayan
(Origin unknown)
Brayen

Braydon
(English) effective
Braedan, Braedon, Brayden, Braydun

Breck
(Irish) fair and freckled
Breckie, Breckle, Brek

Breeahno
(Invented) form of Briano

Breeon
(American) strong

Breeson
(American) strong
Breece, Breese, Bresen

Breeze, Breezy
(American) happy
Breese, Breez

Brendan
(Irish) armed
Brend, Brenden, Brendie, Brendin, Brendon

Brennan
(English) pensive
Bren, Brenn, Brennen, Brennon, Brenny

Brenson
(Last name as first name) disturbed; masculine
Brens, Brenz

Brent
(English) prepared; on the mountain
Bren, Brint

Brenton
(English) forward-thinking
Brent, Brenten, Brintin

Brett
(Scottish) man from Britain; innovative
Bret, Breton, Brette, Bretton, Britt

Brettson
(American) manly man; Briton
Brett

Brewster
(English) creative; brewer
Brew, Brewer

Breyen
(Irish) strong; aggressive
Brey, Breyan

Brian
(Irish) strong man of honor
Bri, Briann, Brien, Brienn, Bry, Bryan

Brice
(Welsh) go-getter
Bryce

Brick
(English) alert; bridge
Bricke, Brik

Brickle
(American) surprising
Brick, Brickel, Brickell, Bricken, Brickton, Brickun, Brik

Brigdo
(American) leader
Brigg, Briggy

Brigham
(English) mediator
Brigg, Briggie, Briggs, Brighum

Briley
(English) calm
Bri, Brilee, Brilie, Brily

Briscoe
(Last name as first name) forceful
Brisco, Brisko, Briskoe

Britt
(English) humorous;
from Britain
Brit, Britts

Britton
(English) loyal; from
Britain

Brock
(English) forceful
*Broc, Brocke, Brockie,
Brocky, Brok*

Brockly
(English) place name;
aggressive
*Brocklee, Brockli,
Broklee, Broklie, Brokly*

Brockton
(English) badger; stuffy
Brock

Brod
(English) short for
Broderick
Broddie, Broddy

Broderick
(English) broad-minded;
brother
*Brod, Broddee, Broddie,
Broddy, Broderik,
Brodric, Brodrick*

Brodie
(Irish) builder
Brode, Brodee, Brody

Brogan
(Irish) sturdy shoe;
dependable
Brogann

Bromley
(English) meadow of the
shrubs; unpredictable
*Brom, Bromlee, Bromlie,
Bromly*

Bronc
(Spanish) wild; horse
Bronco, Bronk, Bronko

Bronco
(Spanish) wild; spirited
*Broncoh, Bronko,
Bronnco*

Brondo
(Last name as first
name) macho
Bron, Brond

Bronson
(English) Brown's son
*Bron, Brondson, Bronni,
Bronnie, Bronny,
Bronsan, Bronsen*

Bronto
(American) short for
brontosaurus;
thunderous
*Bront, Brontee, Brontey,
Bronti, Bronty*

Bronze
(Metal) alloy of tin and
copper; brown
Bronz

Brook
(English) easygoing
*Brooke, Brookee,
Brookie*

Brooklyn
(Place name) area of
New York

Brooks
(English) easygoing
Brookes, Brooky

Brow
(American) word as
name; highbrow; snob
Browy

Brown
(English) tan
*Browne, Brownie,
Browny*

Brownie
(American) brown-haired
Brown

Bruce
(French) complicated
(from a thicket of
brushwood)
Bru, Brucie, Brucy, Brue

Brumley
(French) smart;
scattered
Brum

Bruno
(German) brown-skinned
Brune, Brunne, Brunoh

Bruiser
(American) tough guy
Bruezer, Bruser, Bruzer

Bryan
(Irish) ethical; strong
Brye, Bryen

Bryant
(Irish) honest; strong
Bryan, Bryent

Bryce
(Welsh) spunky
Brice, Bry, Brye

Brydon
(American)
magnanimous
Bridon, Brydan, Bryden, Brydun

Bryson
(Welsh) Bryce's son; smart
Briceson, Bry, Bryse

Bryton
(Welsh) hill town

Bubba
(German) a regular guy
Bub, Buba, Bubb, Bubbah

Buck
(English) studly; buck deer
Buckey, Buckie, Bucko, Bucky

Buckley
(English) outdoorsy; a meadow for deer
Buckey, Buckie, Bucklee, Bucklie, Bucks, Bucky

Bucko
(American) macho
Bukko

Bucky
(American) warm-hearted
Buck, Buckey, Buckie

Bud
(English) courier
Budd, Buddie, Buddy, Budi, Budster

Buddy
(American) courier
Bud, Buddi, Buddie, Budi

Buell
(German) upward; hill
Bue

Buffalo
(American) tough-minded
Buff, Buffer, Buffy

Buford
(English) diligent
Bueford, Bufe, Buforde

Bulgara
(Slavic) hardworking
Bulgar, Bulgarah, Bulgaruh

Bulldog
(American) rough-and-tough
Bull, Dawg, Dog

Bullock
(Last name as first name) practical

Bumpus
(Last name as first name) humorous
Bump, Bumpey, Bumpy

Bunard
(English) good
Bunerd, Bunn

Bunyan
(English) good and burly
Bunyan, Bunyen

Buran
(American) complex
Burann, Burun

Burditt
(Last name as first name) shy
Burdett, Burdette, Burdey

Burge
(English) form of Burgess; middle-class
Burges, Burgis, Burr

Burgess
(English) businessman
Berge, Burge, Burges, Burgiss

Burke
(German) fortified
*Berk, Berke, Burk,
Burkie*

Burley
(English) nature-lover;
wooded meadow
*Burl, Burlea, Burlee,
Burli, Burly, Burr*

Burnis
(English) by the brook
*Burn, Burnes, Burney,
Burr*

Burr
(English) prickly;
brusque
Burry

Burrick
(English) townsman
Bur, Burr, Burry

Burney
(English) loner; island
*Burn, Burne, Burnie,
Burny*

Burris
(English) sophisticated;
living in the town
*Berris, Buris, Burr,
Burres*

Burt
(English) shining man
*Bert, Bertee, Burtie,
Burty*

Burton
(English) protective;
town that is well
fortified
Burt, Burty, Brutie

Busby
(Scottish) artist; village
*Busbee, Busbi, Buzbie,
Buzz, Buzzie*

Busher
(Last name as first
name) bold
Bush

Buster
(American) fun
Bustah

Butcher
(English) worker
Butch, Butchy

Butler
(English) directing the
house; handsome
*Butler, Butlir, Butlyr,
Buttler*

Buzz
(Scottish) popular
*Buzy, Buzzi, Buzzie,
Buzzy*

Byorn
(American) form of Bjorn

Byram
(English) stealthy; yard
that houses cattle
Bye, Byrem, Byrie, Byrim

Byrd
(English) birdlike
Bird

Byrne
(English) loner
*Birn, Birne, Byrn, Byrni,
Byrnie, Byrny*

Byrnett
(Last name as first
name) stable
*Burn, Burnett, Burney,
Burns, Byrne, Byrney*

Byron
(English) reclusive; small
cottage
*Biron, Biryn, Bye, Byren,
Byrom, Byrone, Byryn*

C

Cab
(American) word as name
Cabby, Kab

Cabrera
(Spanish) able
Cabrere

Cack
(American) laughing
Cackey, Cackie, Cacky, Cassy, Caz, Kass, Kassy, Khaki

Cactus
(Botanical) plant as name; prickly
Cack, Kactus

Cade
(English) stylish; bold; round
Cadye, Kade

Caden
(English) spirited
Cadan, Cade, Cadun, Caiden, Kaden, Kayden

Cadmus
(Greek) one who excels; prince
Cad, Cadmuss, Kadmus

Cady
(American) forthright
Cadee, Cadey, Cadie

Caesar
(Latin) focused leader
Caeser, Caez, Caezer, Cesaro, Cezar, Seezer

Cage
(American) dramatic
Cadge

Cailen
(American) gentle
Kail, Kailen, Kale

Cain
(Hebrew) aggressive
Caine, Cane, Kain, Kane

Cal
(Latin) short for Calvin; kind
Callie, Kal

Calbert
(American) cowboy
Cal, Calbart, Calberte, Calburt, Callie, Colbert

Calder
(English) stream; flowing
Cald, Kalder

Calderon
(Spanish) stream; flowing
Cald, Kald, Kalder, Kalderon

Caldwell
(English) refreshing; cold well

Cale
(Hebrew) slim; good heart
Kale

Caleb
(Hebrew) faithful; brave
Calab, Cale, Caley, Calie, Calub, Kaleb

Calek
(American) fighter; loyal
Calec, Kalec, Kalek

Calf
(American) cowboy
Kalf

Calhoun
(Irish) limited; from the narrow woods
Cal, Calhoon, Calhoune, Callie

Calixto
(Spanish) handsome
Calex, Calexto, Cali, Calisto, Calix, Callie, Cally, Kalixto

Callahan
(Irish) spiritual
Cal, Calahan, Calihan, Callie

Callie
(American) short for Calvin; kind
Cal, Calley, Calli, Cally

Callo
(American) attractive
Cal, Cally, Kallo

Cally
(Scottish) peacemaker

Calman
(Last name as first name) caring
Cal

Calum
(Irish, Scottish) peaceful
Cal, Callum, Calym, Calyme

Calvary
(American) word as name; herding all
Cal, Kal, Kalvary

Calvert
(English) respected; herding
Cal, Calber, Calbert, Calver, Kal, Kalvert

Calvin
(Latin) bold
Cal, Calvie, Kal

Cam
(Scottish) short for Cameron; loving
Camm, Cammey, Cammie, Cammy, Kam

Cambell
(American) form of Campbell; reliable (irregular mouth)
Cam, Cambel, Cammy, Kambell

Camberg
(Last name as first name) valley man
Cam

Camden
(Scottish) conflicted
Cam, Camdan, Camdon

Cameron
(Scottish) mischievous; crooked nose
Cam, Camaron, Camerohn, Cami, Cammy, Camren, Camron

Camilo
(Latin) helpful; (Italian) free
Cam, Camillo

Campbell
(Scottish) bountiful; crooked mouth
Cambell, Cammie, Camp, Campie, Campy

Camron
(Scottish) short for Cameron
Camren

Canaan
(Biblical) spiritual leanings
Cane, Kanaan, Kanan

Canal
(Word as name) waterway
Kanal

Candelario
(Spanish) bright and glowing
Cadelario

Cander, Candor
(American) candid
Can, Candy, Kan, Kander, Kandy

Candido
(Spanish) pure; candid
Can, Candi, Candide, Candy

Candle
(American) bright; hip name
Candell

Cannon
(French) courageous
Canney, Canni, Cannie, Canny, Canon, Canyn, Kannon, Kanon

Canute
(Scandinavian) great
Knut, Knute

Cappy
(French) breezy; lucky
Cappey, Cappi

Carad
(American) wily
Karad

Card
(English) short for
Carden; crafty
Kard

Cardan, Carden
(English) crafty; carder
Card, Cardon

Cardwell
(English) craftsman
Kardwell

Carey
(Welsh) masculine; by
the castle
Care, Cari, Cary, Karey

Cari
(English) masculine
Care, Carie, Cary

Carl
(Swedish) kingly
Karl

Carlfred
(American) combo of
Carl and Fred; dignified
Carl-Fred, Carlfree

Carlin
(Irish) winning
*Carlan, Carle, Carlen,
Carlie, Carly*

Carlisle
(English) strengthens
Carl, Carly, Carlyle

Carlo
(Italian) sensual; manly
Carl, Carloh

Carlon
(Irish) form of Carl;
winning
Karlon, Carlonn

Carlos
(Spanish) manly;
sensual
Carl, Carlo

Carlson
(English) son of manly
man
Carls, Carlsan, Carlsen

Carlton
(English) leader; town
of Carl
*Carltan, Carlten,
Carltown, Carltynne*

Carmel
(Hebrew) growing;
garden
Carmell, Karmel

Carmello
(Italian) flourishing
*Carm, Carmel, Carmelo,
Karmello*

Carmichael
(Scottish) bold;
Michael's follower
Car, Kar, Karmichael

Carmine
(Italian, Latin) dear song
*Carmane, Carmin,
Carmyne, Karmen,
Karmine*

Carmody
(French) manly; adult
Carmodee

Carnell
(Irish) victor
*Car, Carny, Kar, Karnell,
Karney*

Carney
(Irish) winner
Carn, Carnee, Carnie

Carr
(Scandinavian)
outdoorsy
Car, Kar

Carroll
(German) masculine;
winner
*Carall, Care, Carell,
Caroll, Carrol, Carrolle,
Carry, Caryl*

Carson
(English) confident
*Carr, Cars, Carsan,
Carsen*

Cart
(American) word as
name; practical
Cartee, Cartey, Kart

Carter
(English) insightful
Cart, Cartah, Cartie

Cartrell
(English) practical
*Car, Cartrelle, Cartrey,
Cartrie, Cartrill, Kar,
Kartrel, Kartrell*

Cartwright
(English) creative
*Cart, Cartright, Kart,
Kartwright*

Caruso
(Italian) musically
inclined
Karuso

Carvell
(English) innovative
*Carvel, Carvelle, Carver,
Karvel*

Carver
(English) carver
*Carve, Carvey, Karver,
Karvey*

Cary
(English) place name;
pretty brook; charming
Carey

Casdeen
(American) assertive;
ingenious
Kassdeen

Case
(Irish) highly esteemed
Casey

Casey
(Irish) courageous
*Case, Casey, Casi, Casie,
Kacie, Kacy, Kase, Kaysie*

Cash
(Latin) conceited
Casha, Cashe, Cazh

Cashmere
(American) smooth;
softspoken
*Cash, Cashmeer,
Cashmyre, Kashmere*

Cashone
(American) cash-loving
Casho

Casimir
(Polish) peace-loving
Casmer, Casmir

Casimiro
(Spanish) famous;
aggressor
Casmiro, Kasimiro

Casper
(German) secretive
*Caspar, Casper, Caspey,
Caspi, Caspie, Cass*

Cass
(Irish) short for Cassidy;
funny
Kass

Cassidy
(Irish) humorous
*Casidy, Cass, Cassadie,
Cassidee, Cassidie,
Kasidy, Kass, Kassidy*

Cassie
(Irish) short for Cassidy;
clever
Casi, Cass, Cassy

Cassius
(Latin) protective
Cass, Casseus, Casshus

Cast
(Greek) form of Castor;
fiery star
Casta, Caste, Kast

Casto
(Mythology) from Castor,
a Gemini twin
Cass, Kasto

Castor
(Greek) eager protector
Cass, Caster, Castie

Castulo
(Spanish) aggressor
Castu, Kastulo

Cato
(Latin) zany and bright
Catoe, Kato

Catarino
(Spanish) unflawed;
perfect
Catrino

Cavan
(Irish) attractive man
Cavahn, Caven, Cavin

Cavance
(Irish) handsome
*Caeven, Cavanse,
Kaeven, Kavance*

Cayce
(American) form of
Casey; brave
Cace, Case, Kayce

Caynce
(Invented) form of
Cayce; daring
Caincy, Cainse, Kaynse

Cazare
(Last name as first
name) daring
Cazares

Cecil
(Latin) unseeing;
hardheaded; blind
Cece, Cecel

Cedar
(Botanical) tree name;
sturdy
Ced, Sed, Sedar

Cedric
(English) leader
Ced, Ceda, Cedrick

Celso
(Italian) heavenly
*Celesteno, Celestino,
Celesto, Celestyno,
Celsus, Selso*

Celumiel
(Spanish) of the heavens
Celu

Centola
(Spanish) tenth child
Cento

Century
(Invented) remarkable
Cen, Cent

Cerone
(French) serene; creative
Serone

Cervantes
(Literature, Spanish)
original
Cervantez

Cesar
(Spanish) leader
Cesare, Cezar, Zarr

Chad
(English) firebrand
Chadd, Chaddy

Chadwick
(English) warrior
Chad, Chadwyck

Chaggy
(American) cocky
Chagg, Shagg, Shaggy

Chaim
(Hebrew) life
*Chai, Chayim, Haim, Hy,
Hyman, Hymie, Khaim,
Manny*

Chalmer
(Scottish) the lord's son
Chall, Chally, Chalmers

Chalmers
(French) chambers;
surrounded
Chalm

Chamblin
(American) easygoing
Cham

Chance
(English) good fortune;
happy
*Chancey, Chanci, Chancy,
Chanse, Chanz,
Chauncey*

Chancellor
(English) bookkeeper
Chance, Chancey

Chandell
(African-American)
innovator
*Chandelle, Chandey,
Chandie, Shandel,
Shandell*

Chandler
(English) ingenious;
(French) maker of candles
Chand, Chandey

Chaney
(French) strong
Chane, Chanie, Chayne, Chaynee

Chang
(Chinese) free; flowing

Channing
(English) brilliant
Chann, Channy

Chante
(French) singer
Chant, Chanta, Chantay, Chantie

Chapa
(Last name as first name) merchant; spirited
Chap, Chappy

Chaparro
(Spanish) from chaparral (southern landscape); cowboy
Chap, Chaps

Chapman
(English) businessman
Chap, Chappy

Charles
(German) manly; well-loved
Charl, Charli, Charlie, Charly, Chas, Chaz, Chazz

Charles-Wesley
(German) combo of Charles and Wesley; strong and sensitive
Charles Wes, Charles Wesley

Charlie
(German) manly
Charl, Charley, Charli, Charly

Charlton
(English) leader
Charles, Charley, Charlie, Charlt

Charome
(American) masculine
Char, Charoam, Charom, Charrone, Charry

Charro
(Spanish) wild-spirited cowboy
Charo, Charroh

Chase
(French) hunter
Chace, Chass

Chat
(American) happy
Chatt

Chaucer
(Literature, English) distinguished
Chauce, Chauser

Chauncey
(English) fair-minded
Chance, Chancey, Chanse, Chaunce

Chayne
(Scottish) swagger
Chane, Channe, Chay

Chaz
(German) short for Charles; manly
Chas, Chazz, Chazzie, Chazzy

Ché
(Spanish) short for José; aggressive
Chay, Shae, Shay

Chee
(American) high-energy
Che

Cheramy
(American) form of Jeremy; excitable
Cheramee, Charamie, Chermy

Chesley
(American) patient
Ches, Cheslee, Chez, Chezlee

Chester
(English) comfy-cozy
Ches, Chessie, Chessy

Chet
(English) creative
Chett

Chevalier
(French) gallant
Chev, Chevy
Chevalle
(French) dignified
Chev, Chevi, Chevy
Cheven
(Invented) playful
Chevy
Chevery
(French) from Chevy;
elegant
Chev, Shevery
Cheves
(American) from liquor
name Chivas; jaded
Chevez, Shevas
Chevy
(French) clever
*Chev, Chevi, Chevie,
Chevv*
Chick
(English) short for
Charles; friendly
Chic, Chickie, Chicky
Chico
(Spanish) boy
Chicoh, Chiko
Chili
(American) appetite for
hot food
Chilton
(English) serene; farm
*Chill, Chillton, Chilly,
Chilt*

Chip
(English) chip off the old
block; like father, like
son
Chipp, Chipper
Chris
(Greek) short for
Christopher; close to
Christ
Cris, Chrissy, Chrys
Chisholm
(Place name) Chisholm
Trail; pioneer spirit
Chis, Chishom,Chiz
Christer
(Norwegian) religious
Krister
Christian
(Latin) follower of Christ
*Chris, Christen,
Christiane, Christyan,
Cristian, Kris, Krist,
Kristian*
Christophe
(French) beloved of
Christ
Cristoph, Kristophe
Christopher
(Greek) the bearer of
Christ
*Chris, Christofer, Crista,
Cristos, Kristopher*

Christos
(Greek) form of
Christopher
Chris, Kristos
Chito
(American) fast-food
eater; hungry
Cheetoh, Chitoh
Choicey
(American) word name;
picky
Choicie, Choisie
Chonito
(Spanish) friend
Chonit, Chono
Chopo
(American) cowhand
Chop, Choppy
Choto
(Spanish) kid
Shoto
Chotto
(Last name as first
name)
Chubby
(American) oversized
*Chubbee, Chubbey,
Chubbi, Chubbie*
Chuck
(German) rash
*Chuckee, Chuckey,
Chuckie, Chucky*

Chucky
(German) impulsive
Chuckey, Chucki,
Chuckie

Chunky
(American) word name;
large
Chunk, Chunkey, Chunki

Churchill
(English) bright
Church

Chutar, Chuter
(Spanish) aiming for
goals

Cicero
(Latin) strong speaker
Cice

Cicil, Cecil
(English) shy
Cice

Cid
(Spanish) leader; lord
Ciddie, Ciddy, Cyd, Sid

Cimarron
(Place name) cowboy
Cimaronn

Cinco
(Spanish) fifth child
Cinko, Sinko

Ciro
(Italian) lordly
Ciroh, Cirro, Cyro

Cirrus
(Latin) thoughtful; cloud
formation
Cerrus, Cirrey, Cirri,
Cirrie, Cirry, Cirus,
Serrus, Serus

Cisco
(American) clever
Sisco, Sysco

Citronella
(American) oil from
fragrant grass; pungent
Cit, Citro, Cytronella,
Sitronella

Civille
(American) form of place
name Seville

Clance
(Irish) form of Clancy;
redhead; aggressive
Clancy, Clanse, Klance,
Klancy

Clair
(English) renowned
Claire, Clare

Clancy
(Irish) lively; feisty
redhead
Clance, Clancey, Clancie

Claran
(Latin) bright
Clarance, Claransi,
Claranse, Clare, Claren,
Clarence, Clary, Klarense

Clarence
(Latin) intelligent
Clarance, Clare, Clarens,
Clarense, Clarons,
Claronz, Clarrence,
Klarence, Klarens

Clarinett
(Invented) plays the
clarinet
Clare, Clarinet, Clary,
Klare, Klari

Clark
(French) personable;
scholar
Clarke

Claude
(Latin); slow-moving;
lame
Claud, Claudey, Claudie,
Claudy, Klaud, Klaude

Claus, Klaus
(Greek) victorious
Klaas

Claven
(English) endorsed
Klaven

Clawdell
(American) form of
Claudell
Clawd

Claxton
(English) townie
Clax, Klax

Clay
(English) firm; short for Claybrook and Clayton; reliable
Claye, Klae, Klay

Claybey
(American) southern; earthly
Claybie, Klaybee

Clayborne
(English) earthly
Clabi, Claybie, Klay

Claybrook
(English) sparkling smile
Claibrook, Clay, Claybrooke, Clayie

Clayton
(English) stodgy
Clay, Claytan, Clayten

Cleary
(Irish) smart
Clear, Clearey, Clearie

Cleavon
(English) daring
Cheavaughn, Cleavaughn, Cleave, Cleevaughan, Cleevon

Clem
(Latin) casual
Cleme, Clemmey, Clemmie, Clemmy, Clim

Clement
(Scottish) gentle
Clem, Clemmyl

Clemente
(Spanish) pleasant
Clemen, Clementay

Clements
(Latin) forgiving man
Clem, Clement, Clemmants, Clemment

Clemer
(Latin) mild
Clemmie, Clemmy, Klemer, Klemmie, Klemmye

Clemmie
(Latin) mild
Clem, Klem, Klemmee, Klemmy

Clenzy
(Spanish) forgiving; cleansed
Clense, Clensy, Klenzy

Cleopatrick
(African-American) combo of Cleopatra and Patrick
Cleo, Cleopat, Kleo, Kleopatrick, Pat, Patrick

Cleophas
(Greek) seeing glory; known
Cle, Cleofus, Cleoph, Klee, Kleofus, Kleophus

Cleon
(Greek) famed man
Clee, Cleone, Kleon

Cletus
(Greek) creative; selected
Clede, Cledus, Cletis

Cleve
(English) precarious; cliff
Clive

Cleveland
(English) daring
Cleavelan, Cleve, Clevon, Clevy, Cliveland

Cliff
(English) short for Clifford; dashing
Clif, Cliffey, Cliffie, Cliffy

Clifford
(English) dashing
Cleford, Cliff, Cliffy, Clyford

Clifton
(English) risk-taker
Cliff, Clifftan, Clifften, Cliffy

Clint
(English) short for Clinton; bright
Clent, Clynt, Klint

Clinton
(English) curious; bright; cliff in town
Clenton, Clint, Clinten, Clynton, Klinten, Klinton

boys

115

Clive
(English) daring; living near a cliff
Cleve, Clyve

Clooney
(American) dramatic
Cloone, Cloonie, Cloony, Clune, Cluney, Clunie, Cluny

Clotaire
(French) famous
Clotie, Klotair, Klotie

Clovis
(German) famed warrior
Clove, Cloves, Clovus, Klove, Kloves, Klovis

Cloyd
(American) form of Floyd; cloying
Cloy, Cloye, Kloy, Kloyd

Clyde
(Welsh) adventurer
Clide, Clydey, Clydie, Clydy, Clye, Klyde, Klye

Clydell
(American) countrified
Clidell, Clydel

Clydenestra
(Spanish) form of Clyde
Clyde

Coal
(American) word as a name
Coale, Koal

Cobb
(English) cozy
Cob, Cobbe

Coben
(Last name as first name) creative
Cob, Cobb, Cobe, Cobee, Cobey, Cobi, Coby, Kob, Kobee, Koben, Kobi, Koby

Coby
(American) friendly
Cob, Cobe, Cobey, Cobie

Coca
(American) excitable
Coka, Cokey, Cokie, Koca, Koka

Cochise
(Native American) warrior
Cocheece, Cochize

Coco
(French) brash
Coko, Koko

Cody
(English) comforting
Coday, Code, Codee, Codey, Codi, Codie

Cog
(American) short for Cogdell; necessary
Kog

Cogdell
(Last name as first name) needed
Cogdale

Cohn
(American) winner
Kohn

Cokie
(American) bright
Cokey, Coki, Cokie, Cokki, Kokie

Colbert
(English) cool and calm
Colbey, Colbi, Colbie, Colburt, Colby, Cole

Colborn
(English) intimidating; cold brook
Colbey, Colborne, Colburn, Colby, Cole

Colby
(English) bright; secretive; dark farm
Colbey, Colbi, Colbie, Cole, Colie

Colden
(English) haunting
Coldan, Coldun, Cole

Cole
(Greek) lively; winner
Coal, Coley, Colie, Kohl, Kole

Coleman
(English) lively; peacemaker
Cole, Colemann, Kohlman

Colgate
(English) passway
Colgait, Colgaite, Kolgate

Colin
(Irish) young and quiet; peaceful; the people's victor
Colan, Cole, Colen, Collin, Collyn

Colley
(English) dark-haired
Col, Colli, Collie

Collier
(English) hard-working; miner
Colier, Collie, Colly, Colyer

Collin
(Scottish) shy
Collen, Collie, Collon, Colly

Collins
(Irish) shy; holly
Collens, Collie, Collons, Colly, Kolly

Colson
(English) precocious; son of Nicholas
Cole, Colsan, Colsen

Colt
(English) frisky; horse trainer
Colty, Kolt, Koltt

Colten, Colton
(English) dark town; mysterious
Cole, Collton, Colt, Coltan, Coltawn, Kol

Colter
(English) keeping the colts
Colt, Coltor, Colty

Colum
(Latin) peaceful; dove
Colm, Kolm, Kolum

Columbus
(Latin) peaceful (discovered America)
Colom, Colombo, Columbe

Comanche
(Native American) tribe; wild-spirited; industrious
Comanch, Komanche

Como
(Place name) handsome
Comoh

Comus
(Greek) humorous
Comes, Comas, Commus, Komus

Conall
(Scottish) highly regarded
Conal

Conan
(Irish) worthy of praise
Conen, Connie, Conny, Conon

Conant
(Irish) topnotch
Conent, Connant

Concord
(English) agreeable
Con, Concor, Conny, Koncord, Konny

Cong
(Chinese) bright

Conlan
(Irish) winner
Con, Conland, Conlen, Connie, Conny

Conk, Konk
(Invented) from conch (mollusk of the ocean); jazzy
Conch, Conkee, Conkee, Conkey, Conky, Kanch, Konkey, Konkey

Connell
(Irish) strong
*Con, Conal, Connall,
Connel, Connelle,
Connie, Conny*

Connery
(Scottish) daring
*Con, Conery, Connarie,
Connary, Connie, Conny*

Connie
(Irish) short for Connor,
Connery, Conrad
*Con, Conn, Connee,
Conney, Conni, Conny*

Connor
(Scottish) brilliant
*Con, Conn, Conner,
Conor, Kon, Konnor*

Conrad
(German) optimist
*Con, Connie, Conny,
Conrade, Konrad*

Conrado
(Spanish) bright advisor
*Conrad, Conrod,
Conrodo*

Conridge
(Last name as first
name) advisor
*Con, Conni, Connie,
Conny, Ridge*

Conroy
(Irish) wise writer
*Conrie, Conroye, Conry,
Roy, Roye*

Constantine
(Latin) consistent
*Con, Conn, Consta,
Constance, Constant,
Constantyne*

Conway
(Irish) vigilant
*Con, Connie, Kon,
Konway*

Cooke
(Latin) cook
Cook, Cookie, Cooky

Coolidge
(Last name as first
name) wary
Cooledge

Cooper
(English) handsome;
maker of barrels
*Coup, Couper, Koop,
Kooper, Kouper*

Cope
(English) able
Cape

Corbet
(Latin) dark
*Corb, Corbett, Corbit,
Corbitt, Korb, Korbet*

Corbin
(Latin) dark and
brooding
Corban, Corben, Corby

Corbitt
(Last name as first
name) brooding
*Corbet, Corbett, Corbie,
Corbit, Corby*

Corby
(Latin) dark
*Corbey, Korbee, Korby,
Korry*

Corcoran
(Irish) ruddy-skinned
Corkie, Corky

Cord
(Origin unknown) soap
opera macho man
Corde, Kord

Cordel
(French) practical
*Cordel, Cordell, Cordelle,
Cordie, Cordill, Cordy*

Cordero
(Spanish) gentle
*Cordara, Cordaro,
Cordarro, Kordarro,
Kordero*

Corey
(Irish) laughing
*Core, Corie, Corry, Cory,
Korey, Korrie, Kory*

Corin
(Latin) combative
*Coren, Dorrin, Koren,
Korrin*

Cork
(Place name) city in Ireland
Corkee, Corkey, Corki, Corky, Kork

Corky
(American) casual
Corkee, Corkey, Korky

Corn
(Latin) form of Cornelius; horn; yellow-haired
Korn

Cornelius
(Greek) a temptation
Coarn, Conny, Corn, Corni, Cornie, Corny, Kornelius, Neel, Neely, Neil, Neiley

Cornell
(French) fair
Corne, Cornelle, Corny, Kornell

Corrigan
(Irish) aggressive
Coregan, Corie, Correghan, Corrie, Corry, Koregan, Korrigan

Cort
(German) eloquent
Corte, Court, Kort

Cortez
(Spanish) victorious; explorer
Cortes

Corvin
(English) friend
Corwin, Corwynn, Korry, Korvin

Corwin
(English) heart's delight
Corrie, Corry, Corwan, Corwann, Corwyn, Corwynne

Cory
(Latin) humorous
Coarie, Core, Corey, Corrie, Kohry, Kori

Cosgrove
(Irish) winner
Cosgrave, Cossy, Kosgrove, Kossy

Cosma
(Greek) universal
Cos, Kosma

Cosmas
(Greek) universal
Cos, Kosmas, Koz

Cosmo
(Greek) in harmony with life
Cos, Cosimon, Cosmos, Kosmo

Cosner
(English) organized; handsome
Cosnar, Kosner

Costas
(Greek) constant
Costa, Costah

Cotton
(Botanical name) casual
Cottan

Coty
(French) comforter
Cotey, Coti, Cotie, Koty

Coug
(American) short for cougar; fierce
Cougar, Koug, Kougar

Coulter
(English) dealing in colts; horseman
Colter, Coult, Kolter, Koulter

Counsel
(Latin) advisor
Consel, Council, Kounse, Kounsell

Courtnay
(English) sophisticated
Cort, Corteney, Court, Courtney, Courtny

Covell
(English) warm
Covele, Covelle

Covet
(American) word as name; desires
Covett, Covette, Kovet

Covington
(English) distinctive
Covey, Coving, Kovey, Kovington

Cowan
(Irish) cozy
Cowen, Cowie, Cowy
Cowboy
(American) western
Cowell
(English) brash; frank
Kowell
Cowey
(Irish) reclusive
Cowee, Cowie, Kowey
Coye
(English) outdoorsman
Coy, Coyey, Coyie
Coylie
(American) coy
Coyl, Koyl, Koylie
Coystal
(American) coy
Coy, Koy, Koystal
Crad
(American) practical
Cradd, Krad, Kradd
Crago
(Last name as first
name) macho
Crag, Craggy, Krago
Craig
(Irish) brave climber
*Crai, Craigie, Cray, Craye,
Crayg, Creg, Cregge,
Kraig*

Crandal
(English) open
*Cran, Crandall, Crandell,
Crane*
Crawford
(English) flowing
*Crafe, Craford, Craw,
Fordy*
Crayton
(English) substantial
Craeton, Cray, Creighton
Creed
(American) believer
*Crede, Creede, Creyd,
Kreed*
Creighton
(English) sophisticated
Criton
Crey, Creigh
(English) short for
Creighton; slight
Craedie, Cray, Creydie
Creshaun
(African-American)
inspired
Creshawn, Kreshaun
Cresp
(Latin) man with curls
*Crisp, Crispen, Crispun,
Crispy, Cryspin, Kresp,
Krisp, Krispin, Krispyn*
Crew
(American) word as
name; sailor
Krew

Crispin
(Latin) man with curls
*Chrispy, Crespen, Crispo,
Crispy, Krispin, Krispo*
Crispo
(Latin) curly-haired
Crisp, Krispo
Cristo
(Place name, Spanish)
from Count of Monte
Cristo
Kristo
Cristian
(Greek) form of Christian
Kristian
Criten
(American) shortened
version of Critendon;
critical
Critan, Kriten
Critendon
(Last name as first
name) critical
*Crit, Criten, Krit,
Kritendon*
Crofton
(Irish) comforter
Croft, Croften
Cromwell
(Irish) giving
*Chromwell, Crom,
Crommie*

Crosby
(Irish) easygoing
Crosbee, Crosbie, Cross,
Krosbie, Krosby

Croston
(English) by the cross
Cro, Croton, Kroston

Cruze
(Spanish) cross
Cruise, Cruse, Kruise,
Kruze

Cuba
(Place name) distinctive;
spicy
Cubah, Cueba, Kueba,
Kuba

Cucuta
(Place name) city in
North Colombia; sharp
Cucu

Cuernavaca
(Place name) city in
Mexico; cowhorn
Vaca

Cuke
(American) zany
Kook, Kooky, Kuke

Culkin
(American) child actor
Culki, Kulkin

Cull
(American) selective
Cullee, Cullie, Cully,
Kulley

Cullen
(Irish) attractive
Culen, Cull, Cullan,
Cullen, Cullie, Cully,
Kullen, Kully

Culley
(Irish) secretive
Cull, Cullie, Cully, Kull,
Kully

Culver
(English) peaceful
Colver, Cull, Culley, Culli,
Cully

Culverado
(American) peaceful
Cull, Cullan, Culver,
Culvey, Kull

Cummings
(Literature) poetic
Cumming, Kummings

Cuney
(Last name as first
name) serious
Cune, Kune, Kuney

Cunning
(Irish) from surname
Cunningham;
wholesome
Cuning

Cunningham
(Irish) milk-pail town;
practical
Cuningham

Curb
(American) word as a
name; dynamic
Kurb

Curbey
(American) form of
Kirby; high-energy
Curby

Curley
(American) cowboy
Curly, Kurly

Curran
(Irish) smiling hero
Curan, Curr, Curren,
Currey, Currie, Curt

Currie
(English) messenger;
courteous
Kurrie

Curt
(French) short for Curtis;
kind
Kurt

Curtis
(French) gracious; kind-
hearted
Curdi, Curdis, Curt,
Curtey, Curtice, Curtie,
Curtiss, Curty, Kurt

Custer
(Last name as first
name) watchful;
stubborn
Cust, Kust, Kuster

Cutler
(English) wily
Cutlar, Cutlur, Cuttie, Cutty

Cutsy
(English) from Cutler; knife-man
Cutlar, Cutler, Cuttie, Cutty, Kutsee, Kutsi, Kutsy

Cuttino
(African-American) athletic
Kuttino

Cuyler
(American) form of Schuyler; protective
Kuyler

Cy
(Greek) shining example
Cye, Si

Cyll
(American) bright
Syll, Cyl

Cyprien
(French) religious
Cyp, Cyprian

Cyprus
(Place name) outgoing

Cyrano
(Greek) shy heart
Cyranoh, Cyre, Cyrie, Cyrno, Cyry

Cyril
(Greek) regal
Ciril, Cyral, Cyrell, Cyrille

Cyrus
(Persian) sunny
Cye, Syrus

Cyrx
(American) conniving
Cyrxie

Czeslaw
(Polish) honorable
Slav, Slavek

Dabney
(Place name) careful; funny
Dab, Dabnee, Dabnie, Dabny

Dacias
(Latin) place name; brash
Dace, Daceas, Dacey, Dacy, Dayce, Daycie

Dada
(African) curly-haired

Dade
(Place name) county in Florida; renegade
Daide, Dayde

Dag
(Scandinavian) sunny
Dagg, Dagny

Daggan
(Scandinavian) day

Dagny
(Scandinavian) day
Dag

Dagoberto
(Spanish) day
Dagobert

Dagwood
(English) comic
Dag, Dawood, Woody

Dairus
(Invented) daring
Daras, Dares, Darus

Dakarai
(African) happy
Dakarrai, Dakk

Dakota
(Native American) friendly
Dack, Dak, Dakodah, Dakotah, Kota

Dakote
(Place name) from Dakota (states North and South Dakota)
Dako

Dalai
(Indian) peaceful
Dalee

Dalanee
(Invented) form of Delaney
Dalaney, Dalani

Dale
(English) natural
Dail, Day, Dayl, Dayle

Dalen
(English) up-and-coming
Dalan, Dalin, Dallen, Dallin, Dalyn

Daley
(Irish) organized
Dailey, Daily, Dale

Dalgus
(American) loving the outdoors

Dalhart
(Place name) city in Texas
Dal

Dallas
(Place name) good old boy; city in Texas
Dall, Dallice, Dallus

Dallin
(English) valley-born; fine
Dal, Dallen

Dalsten
(English) smart
Dal, Dalston

Dalt
(English) abundant
Dall, Daltt, Daltey

Dalton
(English) farmer
Dall, Daltan, Dalten

Dalvis
(Invented) form of Elvis; sassy
Dal, Dalves, Dalvus, Dalvy

Damacio
(Spanish) calm; tamed
Damas, Damasio, Damaso, Damazio

Damarcus
(African-American) confident
D'Marcus, Damarkes, Damarkus, Demarcus

Damary
(Greek) tame
Damaree, Damarie

Damascus
(Place name) capital of Syria; dramatic
Damas, Damask

Damaso
(Spanish) taming
Damas

Damean
(American) form of Damian; tamed
Dama, Daman, Damas, Damea

Dameetre
(Invented) form of Dmitri; audacious
Dimitri

Damian
(Greek) fate; (Latin)
demon
Dame, Damean,
Dameon, Damey,
Damien, Damion,
Damyean, Damyon,
Damyun

Damon
(Greek) dramatic;
spirited
Damonn, Damyn,

Dan
(Hebrew) short for
Daniel; spiritual
Dahn, Dannie, Danny

Dana
(Scandinavian) light-
haired
Danah, Dane, Dayna

Dandre, DeAndre
(American) light
Dan, Dandrae, Dandray,
DeAndrae, DeAndray,
Diondrae

Dane
(English) man from
Denmark; light
Daine, Daney, Danie,
Danyn, Dayne, Dhane

Daneck
(American) well-liked
Danek, Danick, Danik,
Danike, Dannick

Danely
(Scandinavian) Danish
Dainely, Daynelee

Dang
(Vietnamese) worthy

Dangelo
(Italian) angelic
Danjelo

Danger
(American) word as a
name; dangerous
Dang, Dange, Dangery

Daniel
(Hebrew) judged by
God; spiritual
Dan, Dann, Danney,
Danni, Dannie, Danniel,
Danny, Danyel, Danyell,
Danyyell

Daniele
(Hebrew) form of Daniel
Danyel, Danyell

Danne
(Biblical) from Daniel;
faithful
Dann

Danner
(Last name as first
name) rescued by God
Dan, Dann, Danny

Danno
(Hebrew) kind
Dannoh, Dano

Danny
(Hebrew) short for
Daniel; spiritual
Dan, Dann, Dannee,
Danney, Danni, Dannie

Danon
(French) remembered
Danen, Danhann,
Dannon, Danton

Dante
(Latin) enduring
Dan, Danne, Dantey,
Dauntay, Dayntay,
Dontay

Dantre
(African-American)
faithful
Dantray, Dantrae,
Dontre, Dantrey, Dantri,
Dantry, Don, Dont,
Dontrey, Dontri

Dantrell
(African-American)
spunky
Dantrele, Dantrill,
Dantrille

Danube
(Place name) flowing;
river
Dannube, Danuube

Daquan
(African-American)
rambunctious
Dakwan, Dequan

Darbrie
(Irish) free man; light-
hearted
*Dar, Darb, Darbree,
Darbry*

Darby
(Irish) free spirit
*Dar, Darb, Darbee,
Darbie, Darre*

Darce
(Irish) dark
*Darcy, Dars, Darsy,
D'Arcy*

Darcel
(French) dark
*Dar, Darce, Darcelle,
Darcey, Darcy, Darsy*

Darcy
(French) slow-moving
*Darce, Darse, Darsey,
Darsy*

Dare
(Irish) short for Darroh;
dark
Dair, Daire, Darey

Darian
(American) inventive
*Dari, Darien, Darion,
Darrian, Darrion,
Derreynn*

Darin
(Irish) great
*Daren, Darren, Darrie,
Daryn*

Dario
(Spanish) rich
Darioh, Darrey

Darion
(Irish) great potential
*Dare, Darien, Darrion,
Daryun*

Darius, Darrius
(Greek) affluent
Dare, Dareas, Dareus

Dark
(Slavic) short for Darko;
macho
Dar, Darc

Darko
(Slavic) macho
Dark

Darlen
(American) darling
Darlan, Darlun

Darnell
(English) secretive
*Dar, Darn, Darnel,
Darnie, Darny*

Darold
(American) clever
*Dare, Darrold, Darroll,
Derold*

Daron
(Irish) great
Darren, Dayron

Darrell
(French) loved man
*Darel, Darol, Darrel,
Darrey, Daryl, Derrel,
Derrell*

Darren
(Irish) great man
*Daren, Darin, Darryn,
Derron, Derry*

Darrett
(American) form of
Garrett; efficient
Dare, Darry

Darroh, Darrow
(English) armed; bright
*Dare, Daro, Darrie,
Darro, Darrohye, Darrow*

Darrti
(American) fast; deer
Dart, Darrt

Darryl
(French) darling man
*Darrie, Daryl, Derrie,
Deryl, Deryll*

Dart
(Place name) decisive
Darte, Dartt

Darton
(English) swift; deer

Darwin
(English) dearest friend
*Dar, Darwen, Darwinne,
Darwon*

Daryn
(American) form of
Darren
Darynn, Deryn

Dash
(American) speedy;
dashing
Dashy

Dashawn
(African-American)
unusual
*D'Sean, D'Shawn,
Dashaun, Deshaun,
Deshawn*

Dashell
(African-American)
dashing
Dashiell

Dasher
(American) dashing; fast
Dash

Davao
(Place name) city in the
Philippines; exotic
Davo

Dave
(Hebrew) short for
David; loved
Davey, Davi, Davie, Davy

Daven
(American) form of Dave;
dashing
Davan

Davey
(Hebrew) short for
David; loved
*Dave, Davee, Davi,
Davie, Davy*

Davian
(Hebrew) dear one
Daveon, Davyon

David
(Hebrew) beloved
*Davad, Dave, Daved,
Davee, Daven, Davey,
Davi, Davide, Davie,
Davy, Davydd*

David-Drue
(American) combo of
David and Drue; sweet
and loved
*David-Drew, David-Dru,
David Drue*

Davidpaul
(American) beloved
David-Paul

Davidson
(English) son of David
Davidsen, Davison

Davin
(Scandinavian) smart
Dave, Daven, Dayven

Davins
(American) from David;
smart
Davens

Davis
(Welsh) David's son;
heart's child
Dave, Daves, Davies

Davon
(American) sweet
*Davaughan, Davaughn,
Dave, Davone, Devon*

Davonnae
(African-American) from
David; loved
Davawnae, Davonae

Davonte
(African-American)
energetic
*D'Vontay, Davontay,
Devonta*

Daw
(English) quiet
Dawe, Dawes

Dawber
(Last name as first
name) funny
*Daw, Dawb, Dawbee,
Dawbey, Dawby, Daws*

Dawk
(American) spirited
Dawkins

Daws
(English) dedicated
Daw, Dawsen, Dawz

Dawson
(English) David's son; loved
Dawsan, Dawse, Dawsen, Dawsey, Dawsin

Dax
(French) unique; water-loving
Dacks, Daxie

Day
(English) calm
Daye

Dayton
(English) the town of David; planner
Daeton, Day, Daye, Daytawn, Deytawn, Deyton

Deacon
(Greek) giving
Decon, Deecon, Dekawn, Deke, Dekie, Dekon

Deagan
(Last name as first name) capable
Degan

Deal
(Last name as first name) wheeler-dealer
Deale

Dean
(English) calming
Deane, Deanie, Deany, Deen, Dene, Dino

Deangelo
(Italian) sweet; personable
D'Angelo, Dang, Dange, DeAngelo, Deanjelo, Deeanjelo, DiAngelo, Di-Angelo

Deans
(English) sylvan; valley
Dean, Deaney, Deanie

Deanthony
(African-American) rambunctious
Deanthe, Deanthoney, Deanthonie, Deeanthie, Dianth

Deanza
(Spanish) smooth
Denza

Dearing
(Last name as first name) endearing
Dear

Dearon
(American) dear one
Dear

Deason
(Invented) cocky
Deace, Deas, Dease, Deasen, Deasun

Debonair
(French) with a beautiful air; elegant and cultured
Debonaire, Debonnair, Debonnaire

Debythis
(African-American) strange
Debiathes

Decatur
(American) place name; special
Dec, Decatar, Decater, Deck

Deccan
(Place name) region in India; scholar
Dec, Dek

Deck
(Irish) short for Declan; strong; devout
Decky

Declan
(Irish) strong; prayerful
Dec, Deck, Dek, Deklan, Deklon

Deddrick
(American) form of Deidrich; substantial
Dead, Dedrik

Dedeaux
(French) sweet
Dede, Dee

Dedric
(German) leader
Dedrick, Deidrich

Dee
(American) short for names that start with D
D, De

Deek
(American) short for
Deacon; leader
Deke

Deepak
(Sanskrit) light of
knowledge
Depak, Depakk, Dipak

Deeter
(American) friendly
Deter

DeFoy
(French) child of Foy
Defoy, Defoye

Degraf
(French) child of Graf
DeGraf

Deidrich
(German) leader
*Dedric, Dedrick, Deed,
Deide, Deidrick, Diedrich*

Deinorus
(African-American)
vigorous
Denorius, Denorus

Deion
(Greek) form of
Dion/Deone (god of
wine); fun-loving;
charismatic
Dee

Dejuan
(African-American)
talkative
*Dejuane, Dewaan,
Dewan, Dewaughan,
Dewon, Dwon, Dwonn,
Dwonne*

Deke
(Hebrew) from Dekel;
brilliant; sturdy tree
Deek, Dekel

Del
(English) valley; laid-
back and helpful
Dail, Dell, Delle

Delaney
(Irish) challenging
*Del, Delainie, Delanie,
Delany, Dell*

Delano
(Irish) dark
Del, Delaynoh, Dell

Delbert
(English) sunny
*Bert, Berty, Del, Delburt,
Dell*

Delete
(Origin unknown)
ordinary
Delette

Delfino
(Spanish) dolphin;
sealoving
Define, Fino

Delgado
(Spanish) slim

Delius
(Greek) from Delos
Deli, Delia, Delos

Delmar
(Last name as first
name) friendly
Delm

Delmer
(American) country
Del, Delmar, Delmir

Delmis
(Spanish) friend
Del, Delms

Delmore
(French) seagoing
*Del, Delmer, Delmoor,
Delmoore*

Delmy
(American) from French
Delmore; seagoing
Delmi

Delroy
(French) royal; special
*Del, Dell, Dellroy, Delroi,
Roi, Roy*

Delsi
(American) easygoing
*Delci, Delcie, Dels,
Delsee, Delsey, Delsy*

Delt
(American) fraternity boy
Delta

Delton
(English) friend
Delt, Deltan, Delten

Delvan
(English) form of Delwin; friend
Del, Dell, Delven, Delvun

Delvin
(English) good friend
Del, Dell, Delly, Delven, Delvyn

Delwin
(English) good friend
Del, Dell, Dellwin, Delwyn

Delwinse
(English) friend
Del, Delwen, Delwince, Delwins, Delwy

Demarco
(Italian) daring
D'Marco, Deemarko, Demarkoe, Demie, Demmy, Dimarco

Demarcus
(American) zany; royal
DeMarcus, Demarkes, DeMarkus, Demarkus, Demarquiss, DeMarquiss

Demario
(Italian) bold
D'Mareo, D'Mario, Demarioh, Demarrio, Demie, Demmy, Dimario

Demarques
(African-American) son of Marques; noble
Demark, Demarkes, Demarquis, Demmy

Demete
(American) from Greek Demetrius; a saint
Deme, Demetay

Demetrice
(Greek) form of Demetrius; fertile

Demetrick
(African-American) earthy
Demetrik, Demi, Demitrick

Demetrios
(Greek) earth-loving
Demeetrius, Demetreus, Demetri, Demetrious, Demetris, Demi, Demie

Demetrius
(Greek) form of Demeter, goddess of fertility
Dem, Demetri, Demmy, Demos

Demitri
(Greek) fertile; earthy
Demetrie, Demetry, Demi, Demie, Demitry, Dmitri

Demond
(African-American) worldly
Demonde

Demos
(Greek) of the people
Demas, Demmos

Demosthenes
(Greek) orator; eloquent
Demos

Demps
(Irish) form of Dempsey; sturdy
Demps, Dempse, Dempz

Dempsey
(Irish) respected; judge
Dem, Demi, Demps, Dempsie, Dempsy

Denard
(Last name as first name) envied
Den, Denar, Denarde, Denny

Denby
(Scandinavian) place name; adventurous
Danby, Denbee, Denbie, Denney, Dennie, Denny

Deni
(English) form of Dionysius, god of revelry and wine; festive
Denni

Denis
(Greek) reveler
Den, Denese, Dennis

Denk
(American) sporty
Denky, Dink

Denman
(English) dark; valley-
dweller
*Den, Deni, Denmin,
Denney, Denni, Dennie,
Dennman, Denny,
Dinman*

Dennis
(Greek) reveler
*Denes, Deni, Denis,
Deniss, Denni, Dennies,
Denniz, Denny, Deno,
Dino*

Dennisen
(English) Dennis's son;
partier
Dennison, Dennizon

Denny
(Greek) short for Dennis;
fun-loving
*Den, Denee, Deni,
Denney, Denni*

Denton
(English) place name;
valley settlement; happy
*Dent, Dentan, Denten,
Dentie, Dentin*

Denver
(Place name) capital of
Colorado; climber
Den, Denny

Denzel
(English) sensual
*Den, Denny, Densie,
Denz, Denze, Denzell,
Denzelle, Denzil,
Denzille, Denzylle,
Dinzie*

Deondray
(African-American)
romantic
*Deandre, Deeon,
Deondrae, Deondrey,
Deone*

Deone, Dion
(Greek) short for
Dionysius, god of wine;
fun-loving; charismatic
Deion, Deonah, Deonne

Deonté
(French) outgoing
*De'On, Deontae,
Deontay, Deontie,
Diontay, Diontayye*

Deordre
(African-American)
outgoing
Deordray

Deotis
(African-American)
combo of De and Otis;
scholar
Deo, Deoh, Deotus

Depp
(American) movie-star
surname; theatrical
Dep

Derald
(American) combo of
Harold and Derrell;
content
*Deral, Dere, Derry,
Deruld*

Derek
(German) ruler; bold
heart
*Darrick, Derak, Dere,
Deric, Deriqk, Derk,
Derrek, Derrick, Derryck,
Dirk, Dyrk*

Derlin
(English) from Derland,
deer land; sly
*Derl, Derlan, Derland,
Derlen, Derlyn, Durland,
Durlin*

Dermod
(Irish) from Dermot;
guileless; thoughtful
Dermud

Dermond
(Irish) unassuming
*Dermon, Dermun,
Dermund, Derr*

Dermot
(Irish) unabashed; giving
*Der, Dermod, Derree,
Derrey, Derri*

Dermott
(Irish) guileless;
freedom-loving
*Derie, Derm, Dermot,
Derrie*

Deron
(African-American)
variation on Darren;
smart
*Dare, Daron, DaRon,
Darone, Darron, Dayron,
Dere*

Derrell
(French) another form of
Darrell; loved
Dere, Derrel, Derrill

Derri
(American) breezy
Derree, Derry

Derrick
(German) bold heart
Derak, Derick

Derry
(Irish) red-haired
*Dare, Darry, Derrey,
Derri, Derrie*

Derward, Durward
(Last name as first
name) clunky
*Der, Derr, Derwy, Dur,
Durr, Ward*

Derwin
(English) bookish
*Derwynn, Durwen,
Durwin*

Deseo
(Spanish) desire
Des, Desi, Dezi

Deshawn
(African-American)
brassy
*D'Sean, D'Shawn,
Dashaun, Dashawn,
Deshaun, Deshaune;
Deshawnn, Deshon*

Deshea
(American) confident
*Desh, DeShay, Deshay,
Deshie*

Deshon
(African-American) bold;
open
Desh, Deshan, Deshann

Desiderio
(Italian, Spanish)
desirable
Des, Desi, Desie

Desire
(American) word as
name; desirable
Des, Desi, Desidero

Desmee
(Irish) form of Desmond;
from Munster
*Desi, Dessy, Dezme,
Dezmee, Desmey,
Dezmie, Dezmo, Dezzy*

Desmond
(Irish) from Munster;
profound
*Des, Desi, Desmon,
Desmund, Dezmond,
Dizmond*

Desmun
(Irish) form of Desmond;
profound
Des, Dez

Desperado
(Spanish) renegade
*Des, Desesperado,
Dessy, Dezzy*

Destin
(Place name) city in
Florida; destiny; fate
*Desten, Destie, Deston,
Destrie*

Detroy
(African-American)
outgoing
Detroe

Detton
(Last name as first
name) decisive
Deet, Dett

Deuce

(American) two in cards; second child

Doos, Duz

DeUndre

(African-American) child of Undre

Deundrae, DeUndray, Deundry

Devann

(American) divine child

DeVanne, Deven

Devaughan

(American) bravado

Devan, Devaughn, Devonne

Devender

(American) poetic

Devander, Deven, Devendar

Deverell

(American) special

Dev, Devee, Deverel, Deverelle, Devie, Devy

Devin

(Irish) poetic; writer

Dev, Devan, Deven, Devon, Devvy, Devyn

Devine

(Latin) divine

Dev, Devinne

Devinson

(Irish) poetic

Dev, Devan, Devee, Deven, Davin, Devy

Devland

(Irish) courageous

Dev, Devland, Devlen, Devlin, Devy

Devlin

(Irish) courageous

Dev, Devlan, Devland, Devlen, Devy

Devon

(Irish) writer

Deavon, Dev, Devin, Devohne, Devond, Devonn, Devy

Devonte

(African-American) variation on Devon; outgoing

Devontae, Devontay

Dewayne

(American) spirited

Dewain, Dewaine, Duwain, Dwain

Dewey

(Welsh) valued

Dew, Dewie, Dewy, Duey

Dewitt

(English) fair-haired

Dewie, DeWitt, Wittie, Witty

DeWittay

(African-American) witty

Dewitt, De Witt, Witt, Witty

Dewon

(African-American) clever

Dejuan, Dewan

Dex

(Latin) from Dexter; right-handed; hearty

Dexe

Dexee

(American) short for Dexter; lucky

Dex, Dexey, Dexi, Dexie

Dexter

(Latin) skillful; right-handed

Decster, Dex, Dext, Dextah, Dextar, Dextor

Diablo

(Spanish) devil

Diamon

(American) luminous

Dimon, Dimun, Diamund

Diamond

(English) bright; gem

Dimah, Dime, Dimond, Dimont

Diaz

(Spanish) rowdy

Dias, Diazz

Dice

(English) risk-taking

Dicey, Dies, Dize, Dyce, Dyse

Dick
(German) short for
Richard; ruler who
dominates
*Dickey, Dicki, Dickie,
Dicky, Dik*

Dickens
(Literature) articulate

Diedrich
(German) form of
Dedrick; ruler
*Dedric, Dedrick, Deed,
Died, Dietrich*

Diego
(Spanish) untamed; wild
*Deago, Deagoh, Dee,
Diago*

Diesel
(American) movie-star
name
*Dees, Deez, Desel,
Dezsel, Diezel*

Dieter
(German) prepared
Detah, Deter

Digby
(Irish) man of simplicity

Dijon
(Place name) France;
mustard
Dejawn

Dill
(Irish) loyal
Dillard, Dilly

Dillion
(Irish) from Dillon; loyal

Dillon
(Irish) loyal
*Dill, Dillan, Dillen, Dilly,
Dilon, Dylan, Dylanne*

Dimas
(Spanish) frank

Dimitri, Dmitri
(Russian) fertile;
flourishing
*Demetry, Demi, Demitri,
Demitry*

Dino
(Italian) short for Dean
*Dean, Deanie, Deano,
Deinoh, Dinoh*

Dinos
(Greek) short for
Constantine; proud
*Dean, Dino, Dinohs,
Dynos*

Dinose
(American) form of Dino;
joyful
*Denoze, Dino, Dinoce,
Dinoz, Dinoze*

Dins
(American) climber
Dinse, Dinz

Dinsmore
(Irish) guarded
Dinnie, Dinny, Dins

Diogenes
(Greek) honest man
Dee, Dioge, Dioh

Dion
(Greek) short for
Dionysius, god of wine;
reveler
Deon, Dio, Dionn

Dionisio
(Spanish) from
Dionysius, god of wine
and revelry; reveler
*Dionis, Dioniso,
Dionysio*

Dionysus
(Greek) joyous
celebrant; god of wine
*Dee, Deonysios, Dion,
Dionysius*

Dirk
(Scandinavian) leader
Derk, Dirke, Dirky, Durk,

Diron
(American) form of
Darren; great
Diran, Dirun, Dyronn

Dit
(Hungarian) short for
Ditrik

Dix
(American) energetic
Dex

Dixie
(American) southerner
Dix, Dixee, Dixey, Dixi

Dixon
(English) Dick's son; happy
Dickson, Dix, Dixie, Dixo

Doan
(English) hills; quiet
Doane, Doe

Dobes
(American) unassuming
Dobe, Doe

Dobie
(American) reliable; southern
Dobe, Dobee, Dobey, Dobi

Dobromir
(Polish) good
Dobe, Dobry, Doby

Dobry
(Polish) good
Dobe, Dobree, Dobrey

Doc, Dock
(American) short for doctor; physician
Dok

Dodd
(English) swaggering; has a small-town sheriff feel
Dod

Dodge
(English) swaggering

Dody
(Greek) God's gift
Doe

Dog
(American) animal as name; good buddy
Daug, Dawg, Dogg, Doggie, Doggy

Doherty
(Irish) rash
Doh, Doughertey

Dolan
(Irish) dark
Dolen

Dolf
(German) short for Rudolph; wolf
Dolfe, Dolfie, Dolfy, Dolph, Dophe

Dolgen
(American) tenacious
Dole, Dolg, Dolgan, Dolgin

Dolon, Dolton
(Irish) brunette
Dole, Dolen

Dom
(Latin) short for Dominic, saint; of the Lord
Dome, Dommie, Dommy

Domenico
(Italian) confident
Dom, Domeniko

Domingo
(Spanish) Sunday-born boy
Demingo, Dom, Domin, Dominko

Dominic
(Latin) child of the Lord; saint
Dom, Domenic, Dominick

Dominique
(French) spiritual
Dom, Dominick, Dominike, Domminique

Domino
(Latin) winner
Domeno, Dominoh, Domuno

Don
(Scottish) short for Donald; powerful
Dahn, Doni, Donn, Donney, Donni, Donnie, Donny

Donaciano
(Spanish) dark
Dona, Donace, Donae, Donase

Donahue
(Irish) fighter
Don, Donohue

Donald
(Scottish) world leader; powerful
Don, Donal, Doneld, Donild, Donn, Donney, Donni, Donnie, Donny

Donatello
(Italian) giving
Don, Donatelo, Donetello, Donny, Tello

Donatien
(French) generous
Don, Donatyen, Donn, Donnatyen

Dong
(Chinese) from the east

Donnell
(Irish) courageous
Dahn, Don, Donel, Donell, Donhelle, Donnie, Donny

Donnelly
(Irish) righteous
Donalee, Donally, Donelli, Donely, Donn, Donnellie, Donnie

Donnis
(American) from Donald; dark; regal
Don, Donnes, Donnus

Donny
(Irish) fond leader
Donney, Donni, Donnie

Donovan
(Irish) combative
Don, Donavan, Donavaughn, Donavyn, Donivin, Donny, Donovon

Don Quixote
(Literature) an original

Dont
(American) dark; giving
Don, Dontay

Dontae
(African-American) capricious
Dontay, Donté

Dontave
(African-American) wild spirit
Dontav, Donteve

Donton
(American) confident
Don, Donnee, Dont, Dontie

Dontrell
(African-American) jaded
Dontray, Dontree, Dontrel, Dontrelle, Dontrey, Dontrie, Dontrill

Donyale
(African-American) regal; dark
Donyel, Donyelle

Donyell
(African-American) loyal
Donny, Danyel, Donyal

Donzell
(African-American) form of Denzel
Dons, Donsell, Donz, Donzelle

Doocey
(American) clever
Dooce, Doocee, Doocie, Doos

Dooley
(Irish) shy hero
Doolee, Dooli, Dooly

Dorian
(Greek) the sea's child; mysterious; youthful forever
Dora, Dore, Dorean, Dorey, Dorie, Dorien, Dory

Dorman
(Last name as first name) practical
Dor, Dorm

Dorral
(Last name as first name) vain
Dorale, Dorry

Dorset
(Place name) county in England
Dorsett, Dorzet

Dotan
(African) hardworking
Dotann

Dov
(Hebrew) bear

Doug
(Scottish) short for
Douglas; strong
*Dougie, Dougy, Dug,
Dugy*

Douglas
(Scottish) powerful;
dark river
*Doug, Douggie, Dougie,
Douglace, Douglass,
Douglis*

Dovie
(American) peaceable
*Dove, Dovee, Dovey,
Dovi, Dovy*

Dowd
(American) serious
Doud, Dowdy, Dowed

Doyal
(American) form of
Doyle; dark and unusual
Doile, Doyl, Doyle

Doyle
(Irish) deep; dark
*Doil, Doy, Doyal, Doye,
Doyl*

Doylton
(Last name as first
name) pretentious
Doyl, Doyle

Dracy
(American) form of
Stacy; secretive
*Dra, Drace, Dracee,
Dracey, Draci, Drase,
Drasee, Drasi*

Dradell
(American) serious
Drade, Dray

Drake
(English) dragon-like;
fire-breathing
Drago, Drakie, Drako

Draper
(English) precise; maker
of drapes
Draiper, Drape

Dravey
(American) groovy
Dravee, Dravie, Dravy

Drew
(Welsh) wise; well-liked
Dru

Drexel
(American) thoughtful
Drex

Dries
(Dutch)
Dre

Driscoll
(Irish) pensive
Drisk, Driskell

Dru
(English) wise; popular
Drew, Drue

Drummond
(Scottish) practical
*Drum, Drumon,
Drumond*

Drury
(French) loving man
*Drew, Drewry, Drure,
Drurey, Drurie*

Dryden
(English) writer; calm
Driden, Drydan, Drydin

Drystan
(Welsh) form of Tristan;
mourning
Drestan, Dristan, Drystyn

Duane
(Irish) dark man
*Dewain, Dewayne,
Duain, Duwain,
Duwaine, Duwayne,
Dwain, Dwaine, Dwayne*

Dub
(Irish) short for Dublin;
friendly
Dubby

Dublin
(Place name) city in
Ireland; trendy

Duc
(Vietnamese) honest

Dude
(American) cool guy
Dudley
(English) compromiser; rich; stuffy
Dud, Dudd, Dudlee, Dudlie, Dudly
Dueart
(American) kind
Art, Duart, Due, Duey
Duff
(Scottish) dark
Duf, Duffey, Duffie, Duffy
Duffy
(Scottish) dark
Duff
Dugan
(Irish) dark man
Doogan, Dougan, Duggie, Duggy, Dugin
Duke
(Latin) leader of the pack
Dook, Dukey, Dukie
Dumisani
(African) leader
Dumont
(French) monumental
Dummont, Dumon, Dumonde, Dumonte, Dumontt
Dunbar
(Irish) castle-dweller
Dunbarr

Dunbaron
(American) dark
Baron, Dunbar
Duncan
(Scottish) spirited fighter
Dunc, Dunk, Dunkan, Dunne
Dunia
(American) dark
Dunya
Dunk
(Scottish) form of Duncan; dark; combative
Dunc, Dunk
Dunlavy
(English) sylvan
Dunlave
Dunley
(English) meadow-loving; sylvan
Dunlea, Dunlee, Dunleigh, Dunli, Dunly, Dunnlea
Dunmore
(Scottish) guarded
Dun, Dunmohr, Dunmoore
Dunn
(Irish) neutral
Dun, Dunne

Dunphy
(American) dark; serious
Dun, Dunphe, Dunphee, Dunphey
Dunstan
(English) well-girded
Dun, Duns, Dunse, Dunsten, Dunstin, Dunston
Dunstand
(English) form of Dunstan; protected
Dunsce, Dunse, Dunst, Dunsten, Dunstun
Duran
(Last name as first name) lasting; musical
Durand, Durante, Durran
Durand
(Latin) from Durant; lasting; dependable
Duran, Durayn
Durant
(Latin) lasting; alluring
Duran, Durand, Durante, Durr, Durrie, Durry
Durban
(Place name) city in South Africa
Durb, Durben
Durham
(Last name as first name) supportive
Duram

Duro
(Place name) Palo Duro
Canyon; enduring
Dure

Durrell
(English) protective
*Durel, Durell, Durr,
Durrel, Durry*

Durwin
(English) dear friend
Durwen, Durwinn

Durwood, Durward
(English) vigilant; home-
loving
*Derrwood, Derwood,
Durr, Durrwood,
Durwould*

Duster
(American) form of
Dusty; deliberate
*Dust, Dustee, Dustey,
Dusti, Dusty*

Dustin
(German) bold and brave
*Dust, Dustan, Dusten,
Dustie, Dusty, Dustyn*

Dusty
(German) short for
Dustin; brave
*Dust, Dustee, Dustey,
Dusti, Dustie*

Dusty-Joe
(American) cowboy
*Dustee, Dusti, Dusty,
Dustyjoe, Joe*

Dutch
(Dutch) from Holland;
optimistic
Dutchie, Dutchy

Duval
(French) valley; peaceful
*Dovahl, Duv, Duvall,
Duvalle*

Dwain
(American) form of
Dwayne; country; dark
Dwaine

Dwan
(African-American) fresh
*D'wan, D'Wan, Dewan,
Dwawn, Dwon*

Dwanae
(African-American) dark;
small
Dwannay

Dwayne
(American) country
Duane, Duwane, Dwaine

Dweezel
(American) creative
Dweez

Dwight
(English) intelligent;
white
Dwi, Dwite

Dwyer
(Irish) wise
Dwire, Dwyyer

Dyer
(English) creative
Di, Dier, Dyar, Dye

Dylan
(Welsh) sea god;
creative
*Dill, Dillan, Dillon,
Dilloyn, Dilon, Dyl,
Dylahn, Dylen, Dylin*

Dynell
(African-American)
seaman; gambler
Dinell, Dyne

Dyron
(African-American)
mercurial; sea-loving
Diron, Dyronn, Dyronne

Dyson
(English) sea-loving
*Dieson, Dison, Dysan,
Dysen, Dysun, Dyzon*

Dyvet
(English) worker; dyes
Dye

Eagle
(Native American) sharp-eyed
Eagal, Egle

Eamon
(Irish) form of Edmund; thriving; protective
Amon, Emon

Earl
(English) promising; noble
Earle, Earley, Earlie, Early, Eril, Erl

Early
(English) punctual
Earl, Earlee, Earley

Earnest
(English) genuine
Earn, Earnie, Ern, Ernie

Earon
(American) form of Aaron
Earonn

Earvin
(English) sea-loving
Dervin, Ervin

Easey
(American) easygoing
Easy, Ezey

Easton
(English) outdoorsy; east town
Easten

Eaton
(English) wealthy
Etawn, Eton

Ebby
(Hebrew) short for Ebenezer; rock; reliable
Ebbey, Ebbi

Ebenezer
(Hebrew) base of life; rock
Eb, Ebbie, Ebby, Eben, Ebeneezer, Ebeneser

Eberhardt
(German) brave
Eb, Eber, Eberhard

Eckhardt
(German) iron-willed
Eck, Eckhard, Eckhart, Ekhard

Ed
(English) short for Edward
Edd, Eddie, Eddy, Edy

Edan
(Scottish) fiery
Edon

Edcell
(English) focused; wealthy
Ed, Edcelle, Eds, Edsel

Eddie
(English) short for Edward
Eddee, Eddey, Eddy

Eden
(Hebrew) delight
Eadon, Edin, Edon, Edye, Edyn

Edenson
(Hebrew) delight
Edence, Edens, Edensen

Edgar
(English) success
Ed, Eddie, Edghur, Edgur

Edgardo
(English) successful
Edgar, Edgard, Edgardoh

Edge
(American) cutting edge; trendsetter
Eddge, Edgy

Edilberto
(Spanish) noble
Edilbert

Edison
(English) Edward's son; smart
Ed, Eddie, Edisen, Edyson

Edmond
(English) protective
Ed, Edmon, Edmund

Edmund
(English) protective
Ed, Eddie, Edmond

Edrick
(English) rich leader;
(American) laughing
Ed, Edri, Edrik, Edry

Edsel
(English) rich
Ed, Eddie, Edsil, Edsyl

Eduardo
(Spanish) flirtatious
Ed, Eddie, Edwardo

Edward
(English) prospering;
defender
Ed, Eddey, Eddi, Eddie,
Eddy, Edwar, Edwerd

Edwin
(English) prosperous
friend
Ed, Edwinn, Edwynn

Efrain
(Hebrew) fertile
Efren

Efrim
(Hebrew) short for
Ephraim
Ef, Efrem, Efrum

Efton
(American) form of
Ephraim; (Hebrew)
fruitful
Ef, Eft, Eften, Eftun

Egan
(Irish) spirited
Eggie, Egin, Egon

Egbert
(English) bright sword
Egber, Egburt, Eggie,
Eggy

Egborn
(English) ready; born of
Edgar
Eg, Egbornem, Egburn,
Eggie

Eghert
(German) smart
Eghertt, Eghurt

Egmon
(German) protective
Egmond, Egmont,
Egmun, Egmund,
Egmunt

Egeus
(American) word as
name; protective
Aegis, Egis

Egypt
(Place name)

Elam
(Hebrew) from Eliam;
God-centered;
distinctive

Elan
(French) finesse
Elann, Elon

Elbis
(American) exalted
Elb, Elbace, Elbase,
Elbus

Elbridge
(American) presidential
Elb, Elby

Elder
(English) older sibling
El, Eldor

Eldon
(English) place name;
charitable
El, Elden, Eldin

Eldorado
(Place name) city in
Arkansas (El Dorado)
El, Eld, Eldor

Eldread
(English) wise advisor
El, Eldred, Eldrid

Eldridge
(English) supportive
Eldredge

Elgin
(English) elegant
Elgen

Elegy
(Spanish) memorable
Elegee, Elegie, Elgy

Elendor
(Invented) special
Elen, Elend

Eli
(Hebrew) faithful man; high priest
El, Elie, Eloy, Ely

Elian
(Spanish) spirited
Eliann, Elyan

Elias
(Greek) spiritual
El, Eli, Eliace, Elyas

Eliezer
(Origin unknown) of God

Elijah
(Hebrew) religious; Old Testament prophet
El, Elie, Elija

Elijah-Blue
(American) combo of Elijah and Blue; devout
Elijah-Bleu, Elijah-Blu

Eliseo
(Spanish) daring
Elizeo

Ellard
(German) brave man
Ell, Ellarde, Ellee, Ellerd

Ellery
(English) dominant
El, Ell, Ellary, Ellerie, Ellie

Elliott
(English) God-loving
Elie, Elio, Ell, Elliot

Ellis
(English) form of Elias; devout
Ellice, Ells

Ellis-Marcelle
(American) combo of Ellis and Marcelle; achiever
Ellis, Ellismarcelle, Marcelle

Ellison
(English) circumspect
Ell, Ellason, Ellisen, Ells, Ellyson

Elman
(American) protective
El, Elle, Elmen, Elmon

Elmer
(English) famed
Ell, Elm, Elmar, Elmir, Elmo, Elmoh

Elmo
(Greek) gregarious
Ellmo, Elmoh

Elmot
(American) lovable
Elm

Elmore
(English) radiant
Elm, Elmie, Elmoor, Elmor

Elsworth
(Last name as first name) pretentious
Ells, Ellsworth

Elof
(Swedish) the one heir
Loff

Eloi
(French) chosen one
Eloie, Eloy

Elonzo
(Spanish) sturdy; happy
El, Elon, Elonso

Elroy
(French) giving
Elroi, Elroye

Elsden
(English) spiritual
Els, Elsdon

Elson
(English) from Elston; affluent
Elsen

Elston
(English) sophisticated
Els, Elstan, Elsten

Elton
(English) settlement; famous
Ell, Ellton, Elt, Eltan, Elten

Elvin
(English) friend of elves
El, Elv, Elven

Elvind
(American) form of Elvin/Alvin; friend of elves
Elv

Elvis
(Scandinavian) wise; musical
El, Elvyse, The King

Elwen
(English) friend of elves
Elwee Elwy, Elwyn, Elwynn, Elwynt

Elwond
(Last name as first name) steady
Ellwand, Elwon, Eldwund

Elwood
(English) old wood; everlasting
Ell, Elwoode, Elwould, Woodie, Woody, Woodye

Ely
(Hebrew) lifted up
Eli

Emanuel
(Hebrew) with God
Em, Eman, Emanuele

Emberto
(Italian) pushy
Berty, Embert, Emberte

Emerson
(German) Emery's son; able
Emers, Emersen

Emery
(German) hardworking leader
Em, Emeri, Emerie, Emmerie, Emory, Emrie

Emil
(Latin) ingratiating
Em, Emel, Emele

Emilio
(Italian) competitive; (Spanish) excelling
Emil, Emile, Emilioh, Emlo

Emjay
(American) reliable
Em-J, Em-Jay, M.J., MJ

Emmanuel
(Hebrew) with God
Em, Eman, Emmanuele

Emmett
(Hebrew) truthful; sincere
Emit, Emmet, Emmitt

Emory
(German) industrious leader
Emmory, Emori, Emorie

Emuel
(Hebrew) form of Emmanuel (God with us); believer
Emanuel, Imuel

Eneas
(Hebrew) much-praised
Ennes, Ennis

Engelbert
(German) angel-bright
Bert, Bertie, Berty, Engelber, Inglebert

Enlai
(Chinese) thankful

Enoch
(Hebrew) dedicated instructor
En, Enoc, Enok

Enos
(Hebrew) mortal
Enoes

Enrick
(Spanish) cunning
Enric, Enrik

Enrico
(Italian) ruler
Enrike, Enriko

Enrique
(Spanish) charismatic ruler
Enrika, Enrikae, Enriqué, Quiqui

Enzo
(Italian) fun-loving

Ephraim
(Hebrew) fertile
Eff, Efraim, Efram, Efrem

Erasmus
(Greek) beloved
Eras, Erasmas, Erasmis

Erazmo
(Spanish) loved
Erasmo, Eraz, Ras, Raz

Erhardt
(German) strong-willed
Erhar, Erhard, Erhart,
Erheart

Eric, Erik
(Scandinavian) powerful
leader
Ehrick, Erek, Erick, Eryke

Erin
(Irish) peace-loving
Aaron, Aron, Erin, Eryn

Erlan
(English) aristocratic
Earlan, Earland, Erland,
Erlen, Erlin

Ernest
(English) sincere
Earnest, Ern, Ernie, Erno,
Ernst, Erny, Ernye

Ernesto
(Spanish) sincere
Ernie, Nesto, Nestoh

Ernie
(English) short for Ernest
Ernee, Erney, Erny

Erol
(American) noble
Eral, Eril, Errol

Eros
(Greek) sensual
Ero

Erose
(Greek) from the word
eros; sensual; resolute
Eroce

Erskine
(Scottish) high-minded
Ers, Ersk, Erskin

Ervin
(English) sea-loving
Earvin, Erv, Ervan, Erven,
Ervind, Ervyn

Ervine
(English) sea-lover
Ervene, Ervin

Esau
(Hebrew) rough-hewn
Es, Esa, Esauw, Esaw

Esaul
(American) combo of
Esau and Saul; hairy
Esau, Esaw, Esawle, Saul

Esmé
(French) beloved
Es, Esmae, Esmay

Esmond
(French) handsome
Esmand, Esmon,
Esmund

Esmun
(American) kind
Es, Esman, Esmon

Esperanza
(Spanish) from
esperance;
(English) hopeful
Esper, Esperance,
Esperence

Essex
(Place name) dignified
Ess, Ez

Esteban
(Spanish) royal; friendly
Estabon, Estebann,
Estevan

Estes
(Place name) eastern;
open
Estas, Este, Estis

Estridge
(Last name as first
name) fortified
Es, Estri, Estry

Etereo
(Spanish) heavenly;
spiritual
Etero

Ethan
(Hebrew) firm will
Eth, Ethen, Ethin, Ethon

Etheal
(English) of good birth
Ethal

Ethelbert
(German) principled
Ethelburt, Ethylbert

Euclid
(Greek) brilliant
Euclide, Uclid

Eugene
(Greek) blue-blood
Eugean, Eugenie, Ugene

Eural
(American) form of Ural
Mountains; upward
Eure, Ural, Ury

Eurby
(Last name as first
name)
Erby, Eurb

Eurskie
(Invented) dorky
Ersky

Eusebio
(Spanish) devoted to
God
*Eucebio, Eusabio,
Eusevio, Sebio, Usibo*

Eustace
(Latin) calming
Eustice, Eustis, Ustace

Eustacio
(Spanish) calm;
visionary
*Eustacio, Eustase,
Eustasio, Eustazio,
Eustes, Eustis*

Evan
(Irish) warrior
*Ev, Evann, Evanne, Even,
Evin*

Evander
(Greek) manly;
champion
Evand, Evandar, Evandir

Evanus
(American) form of Evan;
heroic
*Evan, Evin, Evinas,
Evinus*

Evaristo
(Spanish) form of Evan;
heroic
Evariso, Evaro

Eve
(Invented) form of Yves
Eeve

Evelyn
(American) writer
Ev, Evlinn, Evlyn

Everard
(German) tough
Ev, Evrard

Everett
(English) strong
*Ev, Everet, Everitt, Evret,
Evrit*

Everhart
(Scandinavian) vibrant
Evhart, Evert

Everly
(American) singing
*Everlee, Everley, Everlie,
Evers*

Evetier
(French) good

Evett
(American) bright
*Ev, Evatt, Eve, Evidt,
Evitt*

Evon
(Welsh) form of Evan;
warrior
*Even, Evin, Evonne,
Evonn, Evyn*

Ewan
(Scottish) youthful spirit
Ewahn, Ewon

Ewand
(Welsh) form of Evan;
warrior
Ewen, Ewon

Ewanell
(American) form of
Ewan; hip
Ewanel, Ewenall

Ewart, Ewert
(English) shepherd;
caring
Ewar, Eward

Ewing
(English) law-abiding
Ewin, Ewyng

Excell
(American) competitive
Excel, Exsel, Exsell

Exia
(Spanish) demanding
Ex, Exy

Eza
(Hebrew) from Ezra;
helpful
Esri

Ezekiel
(Hebrew) God's strength
*Eze, Ezek, Ezekhal,
Ezekial, Ezikiel, Ezkeil*

Ezequiel
(Spanish) devout

Ezra
(Hebrew) helpful; strong
Esra, Ezrah

Ezzie
(Hebrew) from the name
Ezra; helpful
Ez

Faber
(German) grower
Fabar, Fabir, Fabyre

Faberto
(Latin) form of Fabian;
grower; deals in beans
*Fabe, Fabey, Fabian,
Fabien, Fabre*

Fabian
(Latin) grower; singer
*Fab, Fabean, Fabeone,
Fabie*

Fabio
(Italian) seductive;
handsome
Fab, Fabioh

Fable
(American) storyteller
Fabal, Fabe, Fabel, Fabil

Fabrizio
(Italian) fabulous

Fabryce
(Latin) crafty
*Fab, Fabby, Fabreese,
Fabrese, Fabrice*

Fabulous
(American) vain
Fab, Fabby, Fabu

Faddis
(American) loner; deals
in beans
Faddes, Fadice, Fadis

Faddy
(American) faddish
Fad, Faddey, Faddi

Fadil
(Arabic) giving

Fagan
(Irish) fiery
*Fagane, Fagen, Fagin,
Fegan*

Fahd
(Arabic) fierce; panther;
brave
Fahad

Fahim
(Arabic) intelligent

Fairbanks
(English) place name;
forceful
Fairbanx, Farebanks

Fairfax
(English) full of warmth
*Fairfacks, Farefax, Fax,
Faxy*

Faisal
(Arabic) authoritative
*Faisel, Faizal, Fasel,
Fayzelle*

Faladrick
(Origin unknown)
Faldrick, Faldrik

Falcon
(American) bird as name; dark; watchful
Falk, Falkon

Falk
(Hebrew) falcon
Falke

Fam
(American) family-oriented
Fammy

Famous
(American) word as name; ambitious
Fame

Fannin
(English) happy
Fane

Far
(English) traveler
Farr

Faran
(American) sincere
Fahran, Faren, Faron, Feren, Ferren

Fargo
(American) jaunty
Fargouh

Farley
(English) open
Farl, Farlee, Farleigh, Farlie, Farly, Farlye

Farnham
(English) windblown; field
Farnhum, Farnie, Farnum, Farny

Farquar
(French) masculine

Farr
(English) adventurer
Far

Farrar
(French) distinguished
Farr

Farrell
(Irish) brave
Farel, Farell, Faryl

Farren
(English) mover
Faran, Faron, Farrin, Farron

Farris
(Arabic) rider; (Irish) rock, reliable
Fare, Farice, Faris

Faulkner
(English) disciplinarian
Falcon, Falconner, Falkner, Falkoner

Faust
(Latin) lucky
Fauston

Favian, Favion
(Latin) knowing
Fav

Fawcett
(American) audacious
Fawce, Fawcet, Fawcette, Fawcie, Fawsie, Fowcett

Faysal
(Arabic) judgmental

Federico
(Spanish) peaceful and affluent
Federik

Fedrick
(American) form of Cedrick; wandering
Fed, Fedric, Fedrik

Felipe
(Spanish) horse-lover
Felepe, Filipe, Flippo

Felix
(Latin) joyful
Felixce, Filix, Phelix, Philix

Felman
(Last name as first name) smart
Fel, Fell

Fenner
(English) capable
Fen, Fenn, Fynner

Fenton
(English) nature-loving
Fen, Fenn, Fennie, Fenny

Fentress
(English) natural
Fentres, Fyntres

Feo
(Native American)
confident
Feeo, Feoh

Ferdinand
(German) adventurer
Ferdie, Ferdnand, Ferdy,
Fernand

Fergus
(Irish, Scottish)
topnotch
Feargus, Ferges, Fergie,
Fergis, Fergy

Ferguson
(Irish) bold; excellent
Fergie, Fergs, Fergus,
Fergusahn, Fergusen,
Fergy, Furgs, Furgus

Ferlin
(American) countrified
Ferlan

Fermin
(Spanish) strong-willed
Fer, Fermen, Fermun

Fernando
(Spanish) bold leader
Ferd, Ferdie, Ferdinando,
Ferdy, Fernand

Ferrell
(Irish) hero
Fere, Ferrel, Feryl

Festive
(American) word as
name; joyful
Fest, Festas, Festes

Festus
(Latin) happy
Festes

Fidel
(Latin) faithful
Fidele, Fidell, Fydel

Fidencio
(Spanish)
Fidence, Fidens, Fido

Field
(English) outdoorsman
Fields

Fielding
(English) outdoorsman;
working the fields

Fien
(American) elegant
Fiene, Fine

Fiero
(Spanish) fiery

Fife
(Scottish) bright-eyed
Fyfe, Phyfe

Fiji
(Place name) Fiji Islands;
islander
Fege, Fegee, Fijie

Fikry
(American) industrious
Fike, Fikree, Fikrey

Filbert
(English) genius
Fil, Filb, Bert, Phil

Filip
(Greek) horse-lover;
(Belgium) form of Philip
Fil, Fill

Filmer
(English) from Filmore;
famed
Fill, Filmar

Filmore
(English) famed
Fill, Fillie, Fillmore, Filly,
Fylmore

Finian
(Irish) fair
Fin, Finean, Finn, Fynian

Finley
(Irish) magical
Fin, Finny, Fynn, Fynnie

Finn
(Scandinavian) fair-
haired; from Finland
Fin, Finnie, Finny

Finnegan
(Irish) fair
Finegan, Finigan, Finn,
Finny

Finton
(Irish) magical, fair
Finn, Finny, Fynton

Fish, Fishel
(Hebrew) fish
Fysh

Fitz
(French) bright young man; son
Fitzy

Fitzgerald
(English) bright young man; Gerald's son

Fitzmorris
(Last name as first name) son of Morris
Fitz, Morrey, Morris

Fitzsimmons
(English) bright young man; Simmons's son

Flabia
(Spanish) light-haired
Flavia

Flag
(American) patriotic
Flagg

Flavean
(Flavian) form of Flavian

Flavian
(Greek) blond
Flovian

Flavio
(Italian) shining
Flav, Flavioh

Fleada
(American) introvert
Flayda

Flemming
(English) from Flanders; confident
Fleming, Flyming

Fletcher
(English) kind-hearted; maker of arrows
Fletch, Fletchi, Fletchie, Fletchy

Flint
(English) stream; nature-lover
Flinn, Flintt, Flynt, Flynnt

Florian
(Latin) flourishing
Florean, Florie

Floyd
(English) practical; hair of gray
Floid

Flynn
(Irish) brash
Flin, Flinn, Flinnie, Flinny, Flyne

Flynt
(English) flowing; stream
Flint, Flinte, Flinty, Flynte

Foley
(Last name as first name) creative
Folee, Folie

Folker
(German) watchful
Folke, Folko

Fontayne
(French) giving; fountain
Font, Fontaine, Fontane, Fountaine

Fonzie
(German) short for Alphonse
Fons, Fonsi, Fonz, Fonzi

For
(American) word as a name
Fore

Foran
(American) form of foreign; exotic
Foren, Forun

Forbes
(Irish) wealthy
Forb

Ford
(English) strong
Feord, Forde, Fyord

Fordan
(English) river crossing; inventive
Ford, Forday, Forden

Foreign
(American) word as name; foreigner
Foran

Forend
(American) forward
Fore, Foryn, Forynd

Forest
(French) nature-loving
Forrest, Fory, Fourast

Forester
(English) protective; of
the forest
Forrester, Forry

Fortune
(French) fortunate man
Fortounay, Fortunae

Fost
(Latin) form of Foster;
worthwhile
Foste, Fostee, Fosty

Foster
(Latin) worthy
Fauster, Fostay

Fowler
(English) hunter; traps
fowl
Fowller

Francesco
(Italian) flirtatious
*Fran, Francey, Frankie,
Franky*

Francis
(Latin) free spirit; from
France
*Fran, Frances, Franciss,
Frank, Franky, Frannkie,
Franny, Frans*

Francisco
(Spanish) free spirit;
from Latin Franciscus;
Frenchman
*Chuco, Cisco, Francisk,
Franco, Frisco, Paco,
Pancho*

Francista
(Spanish) from
Franciscus; Frenchman;
free
*Cisco, Cisto, Francisco,
Franciscus, Fransico*

Franco
(Spanish) defender;
spear
Francoh, Franko

Francois
(French) smooth;
patriot; Frenchman
*Frans, Franswaw, French,
Frenchie, Frenchy*

Frank
(English) short for
Franklin; outspoken;
landowner
*Franc, Franco, Frankee,
Frankey, Frankie, Franko,
Franky*

Frankie
(English) outspoken;
landowner
Frankee, Frankey, Franky

Franklin
(English) outspoken;
landowner
*Francklin, Franclin,
Frank, Frankie,
Franklinn, Franklyn,
Franklynn, Franky*

Frasier
(English) attractive; man
with curls
*Frase, Fraser, Fraze,
Frazer*

Fred
(German) short for
Frederick; plainspoken
leader
*Fredde, Freddo, Freddy,
Fredo*

Freddie
(German) short for
Frederick; plainspoken
leader
*Freddee, Freddey,
Freddi, Freddy*

Freddis
(German) from the name
Frederick; friendly
Freddus, Fredes, Fredis

Frederic
(French) peaceful king
Fred, Freddy

Frederick
(German) plainspoken
leader; peaceful
*Fred, Freddy, Frederic,
Fredrich, Fredrik*

Freeman
(English) free man
Free, Freedman, Freman

Frieder
(German) peaceful
leader
*Frie, Fried, Friedrich,
Friedrick*

Friederich, Friedrich .
(German) form of
Frederick; leader of
peace
Fridrich

Frisco
(American) short for
Francisco; free
Cisco, Frisko

Fritz
(German) short for
Frederick and Friedrich
*Firzie, Firzy, Frits, Fritts,
Fritzi, Fritzie, Fritzy*

Frost
(English) cold; freeze

Fructuoso
(Spanish) fruitful
Fru, Fructo

Fuddy
(Origin unknown) bright-
eyed
Fuddie, Fudee, Fudi

Fulbright
(German) brilliant; full of
brightness
Fulbrite

Fuller
(English) tough-willed
Fuler

Fullerton
(English) strong
Fuller, Fullerten

Fulton
(English) fresh mind;
field by the town

Funge
(Last name as first
name) stodgy
Funje, Funny

Furlo
(American) macho
Furl

Gabbana
(Italian) creative
Gabi

Gabe
(Hebrew) short for
Gabriel; devout
*Gabbee, Gabbi, Gabby,
Gabi, Gabie, Gaby*

Gabino
(Spanish) strong
believer
Gabby, Gabi

Gable
(French) dashing

Gabriel
(Hebrew) God's hero;
devout
*Gabby, Gabe, Gabi,
Gabreal, Gabrel,
Gabriele, Gabrielle,
Gabryel*

Gad
(Hebrew) lucky;
audacious
Gadd

Gaddis
(American) hard to please; picky
Gad, Gaddes, Gadis

Gael
(English) speaks Gaelic; independent

Gaetano
(Italian) from the city of Gaeta; Italian
Gaetan, Geitano, Guytano

Gagan
(French) form of Gage; dedicated
Gage

Gage
(French) dedicated

Gailen
(French) healer; physician
Galan, Galen, Galun

Galbraith
(Irish) sensible
Gal

Galbreath
(Irish) practical man
Galbraith, Gall

Gale
(English) cheerful
Gael, Gail, Gaile, Gaille, Gayle

Galen
(Greek) calming; intelligent
Gaelin, Gailen, Gale, Galean, Galey, Gaylen

Galileo
(Italian) from Galilee; inventor
Galilayo

Gallagher
(Irish) helpful
Galagher, Gallager, Gallie, Gally

Gallant
(American) word as a name; savoir-faire
Gael, Gail, Gaila, Gaile, Gayle

Gallman
(Last name as first name) lively
Galman

Galo
(Spanish) enthusiastic
Gallo

Galloway
(Irish) outgoing
Gallie, Gally, Galoway, Galway

Gamberro
(Spanish) hooligan
Gami

Gamble
(Scandinavian) mature wisdom
Gam, Gamb, Gambel, Gambie, Gamby

Gammon
(Last name as first name) game
Gamen, Gamon, Gamun

Ganon
(Irish) fair-skinned
Gannon, Ganny

Ganso
(Spanish) goose; goofy
Gans, Ganz

Ganya
(Russian) strong

Garcia
(Spanish) strong
Garce, Garcey, Garsey

Gard
(English) guard
Garde, Gardey, Gardi, Gardie, Gardy, Guard

Gardner
(English) keeper of the garden
Gar, Gard, Gardener, Gardie, Gardiner, Gardnyr, Gardy

Gareth
(Irish) kind, gentle
Gare

Garfield
(English) armed
Gar, Garfeld

Garin
(American) form of
Darin; kind
Gare, Gary

Garland
(French) adorned
*Gar, Garlan, Garlend,
Garlind, Garlynd*

Garn
(American) prepared
Gar, Garnie, Garny, Garr

Garner
(French) guard
Gar, Garn, Garnar, Garnir

Garnett
(English) armed; spear
Gar, Garn, Garnet, Garny

Garon
(American) gentle
Garonn, Garonne

Garonzick
(Last name as first
name) secure
*Gare, Garon, Garons,
Garonz*

Garr
(English) short for
Garnett and Garth;
giving
Gar

Garrett
(Irish) brave; watchful
*Gare, Garet, Garitt,
Garret, Garritt, Gary,
Gerrot*

Garrick
(English) ruler with a
spear; brave
*Garey, Garic, Garick,
Garik, Garreck, Gary,
Gerrick, Gerrieck*

Garrison
(French) prepared
*Garris, Garrish, Garry,
Gary*

Garth
(Scandinavian) sunny;
gardener
*Gar, Gare, Garry, Gart,
Garthe, Gary*

Garthay
(Irish) from Gareth;
gentle
Garthae

Garv
(English) peaceful
Garvey, Garvy

Garvy
(Irish) peacemaker
Garvey

Garwood
(English) natural
*Garr, Garwode,
Garwoode, Woody*

Gary
(English) strong man
Gare, Garrey, Garri

Gaspare
(Italian) treasure-holder
Casper, Gasp, Gasparo

Gaston
(French) native of
Gascony; stranger
Gastawn, Gastowyn

Gate
(English) open
Gait

Gaudy
(American) word as
name; colorful
Gaudin, Gaudy

Gavard
(Last name as first
name) creative
Gav, Gaverd

Gavin
(English) alert; hawk
*Gav, Gaven, Gavinn,
Gavon, Gavvin, Gavyn*

Gawain
(Hebrew) archangel
*Gawaine, Gawayne,
Gwayne*

Gaylin
(Greek) calm
*Gaelin, Gayle, Gaylen,
Gaylon*

Gaylord
(French) high-energy
Gallerd, Galurd, Gaylar, Gayllaird, Gaylor

Gaynor
(Irish) spunky
Gainer, Gaye, Gayner

Gayton
(Irish) fair
Gayten, Gaytun

Geary
(English) flexible
Gearey

Genaro
(Latin) dedicated
Genaroe, Genaroh

Gene
(Greek) noble
Geno, Jene, Jeno

General
(American) military rank as name; leader

Geno
(Italian) spontaneous

Genoah
(Place name) Genoa, Italy
Genoa, Jenoa, Jenoah

Genovese
(Italian) spontaneous; from Genoa, Italy
Genno, Geno, Genovise, Genovize

Gent
(American) short for gentleman; mannerly
Gynt, Jent, Jynt

Gentil
(Spanish) charming
Gentilo

Gentry
(American) high breeding
Genntrie, Gent, Gentree, Gentree, Gentrie

Geo
(Greek) form of George; good
Gee

Geoff
(English) short for Geoffrey; peaceful
Jeff

Geoffrey
(English) peaceful
Geffry, Geoff, Geoffie, Geoffry, Geoffy, Geofry, Jeff

George
(Greek) land-loving; farmer
Georg, Georgi, Georgie, Georgy, Jorg, Jorge

Georgio
(Italian) earth-worker
Giorgio, Jorgio, Jorjeo, Jorjio

Georgios
(Greek) land-loving

Georgy
(Greek) short for George
Georgee, Georgi, Georgie

Gerald
(German) strong; ruling with a spear
Geralde, Gerrald, Gerre, Gerry

Gerard
(French) brave
Gerord, Gerr, Gerrard

Gerber
(Last name as first name) particular
Gerb

Gere
(English) spear-wielding; dramatic
Gear

Gerhard
(German) forceful
Ger, Gerd

Germain
(French) growing; from Germany
Germa, Germaine, Germane, Germay, Germayne, Jermaine

German
(German) from Germany

Gerod
(English) form of Gerard; brave
Garard, Geraldo, Gerard, Gerarde, Gere, Gererde, Gerry, Gerus, Giraud, Jerade, Jerard, Jere, Jerod, Jerott, Jerry

Geronimo
(Italian, Native American) wild heart
Geronimoh

Gerry
(English) short for Gerald
Gerr, Gerre, Gerree, Gerrey, Gerri, Gerrie

Gershom
(Biblical) exile

Gervaise
(French) man of honor
Gerv, Gervase, Gervay

Gervasio
(Spanish) aggressive
Gervase, Gervaso, Jervasio

Gervis, Jervis
(German) honored
Gerv, Gervace, Gervaise, Gervey, Jervaise

Geter
(Origin unknown) hopeful
Getterr, Getur

Ghalby
(Origin unknown) winning
Galby

Ghassan
(Arabic) in the prime of life

Giacomo
(Italian) replacement; musical
Como, Gia

Giancarlo
(Italian) combo of Gian and Carlo; magnetic
Carlo, Carlos, Gia, Gian, Giannie, Gianny

Giann
(Italian) believer in a gracious God
Ghiann, Giahanni, Gian, Gianni, Giannie, Gianny

Gianni
(Italian) calm; believer in God's grace
Giannie, Gianny

Gibbs
(English) form of Gibson; spunky
Gib, Gibb, Gibbes

Gibson
(English) smiling
Gib, Gibb, Gibbie, Gibbson, Gibby, Gibsan, Gibsen, Gibsyn

Gid
(Hebrew) form of Gideon; warrior; Bible distributor
Gidd, Giddee, Giddi, Giddy

Gideon
(Hebrew) power-wielding
Giddy, Gideone, Gidion, Gidyun

Gidney
(English) strong
Gidnee, Gidni

Giglio
(Italian) form of the word gigolo
Gig

Gifford
(English) generous-hearted
Giff, Gifferd, Giffie, Giffy

Gilbert
(English) intelligent
Gil, Gilber, Gilburt, Gill, Gilly

Gilberto
(Spanish) bright
Bertie, Berty, Gil, Gilb, Gilburto, Gillberto, Gilly

Gilby
(Irish) blond
Gilbie, Gill, Gillbi

Gilchrist
(Irish) open
Gill

Gildo
(Italian) macho
Gil, Gill, Gilly

Giles
(French) protective
Gile, Gyles

Gilford
(English) kind-hearted
Gill, Gillford, Guilford

Gill
(Hebrew) happy man
Gil, Gilli, Gillie, Gilly

Gilles
(French) miraculous
Geal, Zheal, Zheel

Gillespie
(Irish) humble
Gilespie, Gill, Gilley, Gilli, Gilly

Gilley
(American) countrified
Gill, Gilleye, Gilli, Gilly

Gillian
(Irish) devout
Gill, Gilley, Gilly, Gillyun

Gilman
(Irish) serving well
Gilley, Gilli, Gillman, Gillmand, Gilly, Gilmand, Gilmon

Gilmer
(English) riveting
Gelmer, Gill, Gillmer, Gilly

Gilmore
(Irish) riveting
Gill, Gillmore, Gilmohr

Gilon
(Hebrew) joyful
Gill

Ginder
(American) form of gender; vivacious
Gin, Gind, Gindyr, Jind, Jinder

Gino
(Italian) of good breeding; outgoing
Geeno, Geino, Ginoh

Giordano
(Italian) delivered
Giorgie, Jiordano

Giorgio
(Italian) earthy; creative
George, Georgeeo, Georgo, Jorge, Jorgio

Giovanni
(Italian) jovial; happy believer
Geovanni, Gio, Giovani, Giovannie, Giovanny, Vannie, Vanny, Vonny

Gitel
(Hebrew) good

Giulio
(Italian) youth

Giuseppe
(Italian) capable
Beppo, Giusepe, Gusepe

Given
(Last name as first name) gift
Givens, Gyvan, Gyven, Gyvin

Gizmo
(American) playful
Gis, Gismo, Giz

Glad
(American) happy
Gladd, Gladde, Gladdi, Gladdie, Gladdy

Gladwyn
(English) friend who has a light heart
Glad, Gladdy, Gladwin, Gladwynn

Glancy
(American) form of Clancy; ebullient
Glance, Glancee, Glancey, Glanci

Glanville
(French) serene

Glasgow
(Place name) city in Scotland

Glenard
(Irish) from a glen;
nature-loving
Glen, Glenerd, Glenn,
Glennard, Glenni,
Glennie

Glen
(Irish) natural wonder
Glenn

Glendon
(Scottish) fortified in
nature
Glen, Glend, Glenden,
Glenn, Glynden

Glenn
(Irish) natural wonder
Glen, Glenni, Glennie,
Glenny, Glynn, Glynny

Gloster
(Place name) form of
Gloucester, city area in
England

Gobi
(Place name) audacious
Gobee, Gobie

Gobind
(Sanskrit) the name of a
Hindi deity
Govind

Gockley
(Last name as first
name) peaceful
Gocklee

Goddard
(German) staunch in
spirituality
Godard, Godderd,
Goddird

Godfrey
(Irish) peaceful
Godfree, Godfrie, Godfry

Godwin
(English) close to God
Godwinn, Godwyn,
Godwynn

Gohn
(African-American)
spirited
Gon

Goldo
(English) golden
Golo

Goliath
(Hebrew) large
Goliathe

Gomer
(English) famed fighter
Gomar, Gomher, Gomor

Gong
(American) forceful

Gonz
(Spanish) form of
Gonzalo; wild wolf
Gons, Gonz, Gonza,
Gonzales, Gonzalez

Gonzales
(Spanish) feisty
Gonzalez

Gonzalo
(Spanish) feisty wolf
Gonz, Gonzoloh

Goode
(English) good
Good, Goodey, Goody

Goran
(Croatian) good

Gordon
(English) nature-lover;
hill
Gord, Gordan, Gorden,
Gordi, Gordie, Gordy

Gordy
(English) short for
Gordon
Gordee, Gordi, Gordie

Gore
(English) practical; pie-
shaped land

Gorgon
(Place name) form of
Gorgonzola, Italy
Gorgan, Gorgun

Gorham
(English) sophisticated;
name of a silver
company
Goram

Gorky
(Place name) amusement park in Russia in the novel *Gorky Park*; mysterious
Gork, Gorkee, Gorkey, Gorki

Gorman
(Irish) small man
Gormann, Gormen

Grady
(Irish) hardworking
Grade, Gradee, Gradey

Graham
(English) wealthy; grand house
Graeham, Graeme, Grame

Granbel
(Last name as first name) grand and attractive
Granbell

Granderson
(Last name as first name) grand
Grand, Grander

Grange
(French) lonely; on the farm
Grainge, Granger, Grangher

Granison
(Last name as first name) son of Gran; grandiose
Gran, Grann

Granite
(American) rock; hard
Granet

Grant
(English) expansive
Grandt, Grann, Grannt

Granville
(French) grandiose
Grann, Granvel, Granvelle, Gravil

Gravette
(Origin unknown) grave
Gravet

Gray
(English) hair of gray
Graye, Grey

Graylon
(English) gray-haired
Gray, Grayan, Graylan, Graylin

Grayson
(English) son of man with gray hair
Gray, Grey, Greyson

Graz
(Place name) city in Austria

Graziano
(Italian) dearest
Graciano, Graz

Greenlee
(English) outdoorsy
Green, Greenlea, Greenly

Greeley
(English) careful
Grealey, Greel, Greely

Greenwood
(English) untamed; forest
Greene, Greenwoode, Greenwude, Grenwood

Greg
(Latin) short for Gregory; vigilant
Gregg, Greggie, Greggy

Gregoire
(French) watchful
Gregorie

Gregor
(Greek) cautious
Greger, Gregors, Greig

Gregorio
(Greek) careful

Gregory
(Greek) cautious
Greg, Greggory, Greggy, Gregori, Gregorie, Gregry

Grenville
(New Zealand) outdoorsy
Granville, Gren

Griffin
(Latin) unconventional
Greffen, Griff, Griffee,
Griffen, Griffey, Griffie,
Griffon, Griffy

Griffith
(Welsh) able leader
Griff, Griffee, Griffey,
Griffie, Griffy

Grigori
(Russian) watchful
Grig, Grigor

Grimm
(English) grim; dark
Grim, Grym

Gris
(German) gray
Griz

Griswald
(German) bland
Greswold, Gris, Griswold

Grover
(English) thriving
Grove

Gruver
(Origin unknown)
ambitious
Gruever

Guerdon
(English) combative

Guido
(Italian) guiding
Guidoh, Gwedo, Gweedo

Guillermo
(Spanish) attentive
Guilermo, Gulermo

Gundy
(American) friendly
Gundee

Gunn
(Scandinavian) macho;
gunman
Gun, Gunner

Gunnar
(Scandinavian) bold
Gunn, Gunner, Gunnir

Guntersen
(Scandinavian) macho;
gunman
Gun, Gunth

Gunther
(Scandinavian) able
fighter
Funn, Gunnar, Gunner,
Guntar, Gunthar,
Gunthur

Gunyon
(American) tough;
gunman
Gunn, Gunyun

Gus
(Scandinavian) short for
Gustav
Guss, Gussi, Gussy,
Gussye

Gustachian
(American) pretentious
Gus, Gussy, Gust

Gustaf
(German) armed; vital
Gus, Gusstof, Gustav,
Gustovo

Gustav, Gustave
(Scandinavian) vital
Gus, Gussie, Gussy,
Gusta, Gustaf, Gustaff,
Gusti, Gustof, Gustoff

Gustavo
(Spanish) vital; gusto
Gus, Gustaffo, Gustav

Gusto
(Spanish) pleasure
Gusty

Gustus
(Scandinavian) royal
Gus, Gustaf, Gustave,
Gustavo

Guth
(Irish) short for Guthrie;
in the wind
Guthe, Guthry

Guthrie
(Irish) windy; heroic
Guthree, Guthry

Guy
(French) assertive;
(German) leader
Guye

Guwayne
(American) combo of
Guy and Wayne
Guwain, Guwane, Guy,
Gwaine, Gwayne

Guzet
(American) bravado
Guzz, Guzzett, Guzzie

Gweedo
(Invented) form of Guido

Gwent
(Place name)

Gwill
(American) dark-eyed
Gewill, Guwill

Gwynn
(Welsh) fair
Gwen, Gwyn

Gyth
(American) capable
Gith, Gythe

Habib
(Arabic) well loved
Habeeb

Habie
(Origin unknown) jovial
Hab

Hackman
(German) fervent; hacks wood
Hackmann

Haddy
(English) short for Hadley; sylvan
Had, Haddee, Haddey, Haddi

Hadley
(English) lover of nature; meadow with heather
Haddleye, Hadlee, Hadlie, Hadly

Hagan
(German) defender
Hagen, Haggan, Haggin

Hakim, Hakeem
(Arabic) brilliant
Hakeam, Hakym

Hal
(English) home ruler

Haldane
(German) fierce; person who is half Danish
Haldayn, Haldayne

Hale
(English) heroic
Halee, Haley, Hali

Halen
(Swedish) portal to life
Hailen, Hale, Haley, Hallen, Haylen, Haylin

Haley
(Irish) innovative
Hail, Hailee, Hailey, Hale, Halee, Hayley

Hall
(English) solemn

Halmer
(English) robust

Halse
(English) on the island
Halce, Halsi, Halsy, Halzee, Halzie

Halsey
(English) isolated; island

Halwell
(English) special
Hallwell, Halwel, Halwelle

Hamaker
(Last name as first name) industrious
Ham

Hamid
(Arabic) grateful
Hameed

Hamidi
(Arabic and African) praiseworthy
Ham, Hamedi, Hameedi, Hamm, Hammad

Hamil
(English) rough-hewn
Hamel, Hamell, Hamill, Hamm

Hamilton
(English) benefiting
Hamelton, Hamil, Hammilton

Hamlet
(German, French) conflicted; small village; Shakespearean hero
Ham, Hamlette, Hamlit, Hamm

Hamlin
(German) homebody
Hamaline, Hamelin, Hamlen, Hamlyn

Hammond
(English) ingenious
Ham, Hamm, Hammon, Hamond

Hamp
(American) fun-loving
Ham, Hampton

Hampton
(English) distinctive
Ham, Hamm, Hamp, Hampt

Hank
(English) short for Henry; ruler; cavalier
Hankey, Hanks, Hanky

Hanley
(English) natural; meadow high
Han, Hanlee, Hanleigh, Hanly

Hannes
(Scandinavian) short form of Johannes; giving
Hahnes

Hannibal
(Slavic) leader
Hanibal, Hanibel, Hann

Hans
(Scandinavian) believer; warm
Hahns, Hanz, Hons

Hansa
(Scandinavian) traditional; believer in a gracious Lord
Hans

Hansel
(Scandinavian) gullible; open
Hans, Hansie, Hanzel

Hansen
(Scandinavian) warm; Hans's son
Han, Handsen, Hans, Hansan, Hanson, Hanssen, Hansson, Hanz

Hardin
(English) lively; valley of hares
Hardee, Harden

Harding
(English) fiery
Harden, Hardeng

Harean
(African) aware

Harford
(English) jolly
Harferd

Hargrove
(English) fruitful

Hark
(American) word as name; behold
Harko

Harlan
(English) army land; athletic
Hal, Harl, Harlen, Harlon, Harlynn

Harlemm
(African-American) from Harlem; dancer
Harl, Harlam, Harlem, Harlems, Harlum, Harly

Harley
(English) wild-spirited
Harl, Harlee, Harly

Harlow
(English) bold
Harlo, Harloh

Harmon
(German) dependable
Harm, Harman, Harmen

Harold
(Scandinavian) leader of
an army
*Hal, Harald, Hareld,
Harry*

Harper
(English) artistic and
musical; harpist
Harp

Harpo
(American) jovial
Harpoh, Harrpo

Harris
(English) dignified
Haris, Harriss

Harrison
(English) Harry's son;
adventurer
*Harrey, Harrie, Harris,
Harrisan, Harrisen, Harry*

Harrod
(Hebrew) victor
Harod, Harry

Harry
(English) home ruler
*Harree, Harrey, Harri,
Harrie, Harye*

Hart
(English) giving
Harte

Hartley
(English) wilderness
wanderer
*Hartlee, Hartleigh,
Hartly*

Hartman
(German) strong-willed
*Hart, Hartmann,
Harttman*

Hartsey
(English) lazing on the
meadow; sylvan
Harts, Hartz

Harun
(Arabic) highly regarded

Harv
(German) able
combatant
Har

Harvey
(German) fighter
*Harv, Harvi, Harvie,
Harvy*

Harwin
(American) safe
Harwen, Harwon

Hasan
(Arabic) attractive

Hasani
(African) good

Hashim
(Arabic) force for good
Hasheem

Hask
(Hebrew) from Haskell,
form of Ekekial; smart
Haske

Haskell
(Hebrew) ingratiating
*Hask, Haskel, Haskie,
Hasky*

Hassan
(Arabic) good-looking
Hasan

Hastings
(English) leader
Haste

Haswell
(English) dignified
Has, Haz

Hattan
(Place name) from
Manhattan; sophisticate
Hatt

Havard
(American) form of
Harvard; guardian
Hav

Haven
(English) sanctuary
Haiv, Hav

Hawke
(English) watchful;
falcon
Hauk, Hawk

Hayden
(English) respectful
Haden, Hadon, Hay,
Haydyn

Hayes
(English) open
Haies, Hay, Haye

Hayman
(English) hedging
Hay

Hayne
(English) working
outdoors
Haine, Haines, Haynes

Hayward
(English) creative; good
work ethic
Hay

Hayword
(English) open-minded
Haword, Hayward,
Haywerd

Hearn
(English) optimistic
Hearne, Hern

Heath
(English) place name;
open space; natural
Heathe, Heith, Heth

Heathcliff
(English) mysterious

Heaton
(English) high-principled
Heat, Heatan, Heaten

Hector
(Greek) loyal
Hec, Heco, Hect, Hectar,
Hecter, Tito

Hedley
(English) natural

Heinrich
(German) form of Henry;
leader
Hein, Heine, Heinrick,
Heinrik

Heinz
(German) advisor
Heinze

Helgi
(Scandinavian) happy
Helge

Helio
(Hispanic) bright

Heller
(German) brilliant

Hellerson
(German) brilliant one's
son; smart
Helley

Helmar
(German) protected;
smart
Helm, Helmer, Helmet,
Helmut

Helmut
(German, Polish)
brave

Hender
(German) ruler;
illustrious
Hend

Henderson
(English) reliable
Hender, Hendersen,
Hendersyn

Hendrik
(German) home ruler
Heinrich, Hendrick,
Henrick, Hindrick

Henley
(English) surprising
Henlee, Henly, Henlye,
Hinley

Henning
(Scandinavian) ruler

Henrik
(Norwegian) leader
Henric, Henrick

Henry
(German) leader
Hank, Harry, Henree,
Henri

Herb
(German) energetic
Herbi, Herbie, Herby,
Hurb

Herbert
(German) famed warrior
*Herb, Herbart, Herberto,
Herbie, Herbirt, Herby,
Hurb, Hurbert*

Hercule
(French) strong
*Hercuel, Harekuel,
Herkuel*

Hercules
(Greek) grand gift
Herc, Herk, Herkules

Heriberto
(Spanish)
Herbert, Heribert

Herman
(Latin) fair fighter
*Herm, Hermahn,
Hermann, Hermie,
Hermon, Hermy*

Hermes
(Greek) courier of
messages
Hermez

Hermod
(Scandinavian)

Hernando
(Spanish) bold
Hernan

Herndon
(English) nature-loving
Hern, Hernd

Hershall
(Hebrew) from Hershel;
deer; swift
*Hersch, Herschel, Hersh,
Herzl, Heshel, Hirschel,
Hirsh, Hirshel*

Herschel, Hershel
(Hebrew) fast; deer
*Hersch, Hersh, Hershell,
Hershelle, Herzl, Hirchel,
Hirsch, Hirshel*

Hershey
(Hebrew) deer; swift;
sweet
Hersh, Hershel, Hirsh

Hertzel
(Hebrew) form of
Herschel; deer; swift
Hert, Hertsel, Hyrt

Hervey
(American) form of
Harvey; ardent and
studious
Herv, Herve, Hervy

Herzon
(American) from
Hershel; fast
Herz, Herzan, Herzun

Hesperos
(Greek) evening star
Hesperios, Hespers

Hess
(Last name as first
name) bold
Hes, Hys

Hewitt
(German) smart
*Hew, Hewet, Hewett,
Hewie, Hewit, Hewy,
Hugh*

Hiawatha
(Native American)
Iroquois chief
Hia

Hickok
(American) Wild Bill
Hickok, U.S. marshal

Hieronymos
(Greek) alternate of
Jerome
Heronymous

Hilarion
(Greek) cheery; hilarious
Hilary, Hill

Hilary
(Latin) joyful
*Hilaire, Hill, Hillarie,
Hillary, Hillery, Hilly,
Hilorie*

Hildebrand
(German) combative;
sword
Hill, Hilly

Hillel
(Hebrew) praised;
devout
Hilel, Hill

Hillery
(Latin) form of Hilary;
pleasant
Hill

Hilliard
(German) brave;
settlement on the hill
*Hill, Hillard, Hillierd,
Hilly, Hillyerd, Hylliard*

Hilton
(English) sophisticated
*Hillton, Hiltawn, Hiltyn,
Hylton*

Hines
(Last name as first
name) strong
Hine, Hynes

Hippocrates
(Greek) philosopher
Hipp

Hiram
(Hebrew) most admired
Hi, Hirom, Hirym

Hiro
(Japanese) giving

Hirsh
(Hebrew) deer; swift
*Hersh, Hershel, Hirschel,
Hirshel*

Hitchcock
(English) creative;
spooky
Hitch

Hobart
(German) haughty
Hobb, Hobert, Hoebard

Hobson
(English) helpful backer
*Hobb, Hobbie, Hobbson,
Hobby, Hobsen*

Hodge
(English) form of Roger;
vibrant
Hodges

Hodgie
(English) nickname for
Hodge
Hodgy

Hogan
(Irish) high-energy;
vibrant
Hogahn, Hoge, Hoghan

Hogue
(Last name as first
name) youth
Hoge

Hojar
(American) wild spirit
Hobar, Hogar

Hoke
(Origin unknown)
popular

Holbrook
(English) place name;
educated
*Brooke, Brookie, Brooky,
Holb, Holbrooke*

Holden
(English) quiet; gracious
Holdan, Holdin, Holldun

Holder
(English) musical
Hold, Holdher, Holdyer

Holegario
(Spanish) superfluous
Holegard

Hollis
(English) flourishing
*Hollace, Hollice, Hollie,
Holly*

Holloway
(Last name as first
name) jovial
Hollo, Hollway, Holoway

Hollywood
(Place name) cocky;
showoff
Holly, Wood

Holm
(English) natural;
woodsy
Holms

Holmes
(English) safe haven
Holmm, Holmmes

Holt
(English) shaded view
Holte, Holyte

Homer
(Greek) secure
*Hohmer, Home, Homere,
Homero*

Honchy
(American) form of
honcho; leader
*Honch, Honchee,
Honchey, Honchi*

Hondo
(African) warring

Honesto
(Spanish) truthful
Honesta, Honestoh

Honorato
(Spanish) full of honor
Honor, Honoratoh

Honoré
(Latin) man who is
honored
Honor, Honoray

Hood
(Last name as first
name) easygoing; player
Hoode, Hoodey

Hoolihan
(American) hooligan
Hool, Hoole, Hooli

Hoop
(American) ball player
Hooper, Hoopy

Hopper
(Last name used as first
name) creative

Horace
(Latin) poetic
Horaace, Horase, Horice

Horatio
(Latin) poetic; dashing
Horate, Horaysho

Horst
(German) deep; thicket
Hurst

Horstman
(German) profound
*Horst, Horstmen,
Horstmun*

Horston
(German) thicket; sturdy
Horst

Horton
(English) brash
Horten, Hortun

Hosea
(Hebrew) prophet

Hosie
(Hebrew) from Hosea;
prophet
Hosaya, Hose

Houston
(English) Texas city;
rogue; hill town
Houst, Hust, Huston

How
(American) word as a
name
Howe, Howey, Howie

Howard
(English) well-liked
*How, Howerd, Howie,
Howurd, Howy*

Howart
(Origin unknown)
admired
Howar

Howe
(German) high-minded
How, Howey, Howie

Howell
(Welsh) outstanding
*Howel, Howey, Howie,
Howill*

Howlan
(English) living on a hill;
high

Hoyt
(Irish) spirited
Hoit, Hoye

Huang
(Chinese) rich

Hubbard
(German) fine
Hubberd, Hubert, Hubie

Hubert
(German) intellectual
*Bert, Bertie, Burt,
Hubart, Huberd, Hue,
Huebert, Hugh*

Hubie
(English) short for
Hubert
*Hube, Hubee, Hubey,
Hubi*

Ingmer
(Scandinavian) short for
Ingemar; famed
*Ing, Ingamar, Ingemar,
Ingmar*

Ingra
(English) short for
Ingram; kind-hearted
Ingie, Ingrah, Ingrie

Ingram
(English) angelic; kind
*Ing, Ingraham, Ingre,
Ingrie, Ingry*

Innad
(Syrian)
Inad

Innis
(Irish) isolated
Ines, Inis, Innes

Ira
(Hebrew) cautious
Irae, Irah

Iram
(English) smart
Irem, Irham, Irum

Iranga
(Sri Lanken) special

Irv
(English) short for Irving

Irvin
(English) attractive
Irv, Irvine

Irving
(English) attractive
Irv, Irve, Irveng, Irvy

Irwin
(English) practical
*Irwen, Irwhen, Irwie,
Irwinn, Irwy, Irwynn*

Isaac
(Hebrew) laughter
*Isaak, Isack, Izak, Ize,
Izek, Izzy*

Isadore
(Greek) special gift
*Isador, Isedore, Isidore,
Issy, Izzie, Izzy*

Isai
(Hebrew) believer

Isaiah
(Hebrew) saved by God
*Isa, Isay, Isayah, Isey,
Izaiah, Izey*

Isak
(Scandinavian) laughter
Isac

Ishmael
(Hebrew) outcast son of
Abraham in the Bible
Hish, Ish, Ishmel, Ismael

Isidore
(Greek, French) gift
Isi, Izzie

Isidoro
(Spanish) gift
*Cedro, Cidro, Doro,
Izidro, Sidro, Ysidor*

Isidro
(Greek) gift
Isydro

Israel
(Hebrew) God's prince;
conflicted
Israyel, Issy, Izzy

Isser
(Slavic) creative

Ivan
(Russian) believer in a
gracious God; reliable
one
Ivahn, Ive, Ivey, Ivie

Ivar
(Scandinavian) Norse
god

Ive
(English) able
Ivee, Ives, Ivey, Ivie

Ives
(American) musical
Ive

Ivor
(Scandinavian)
outgoing; ready
Ivar, Ive, Iver, Ivy

Izaak
(Polish) full of mirth

Izac
(Slavic) spicy; happy
*Isaac, Izak, Izie, Izze,
Izzee*

Izador
(Spanish) gift
*Dorrie, Dory, Isa, Isador,
Isadoro, Isidoros,
Isodore, Iza, Izadoro*

Izzy
(Hebrew) friendly
Issie, Issy, Izi, Izzee, Izzie

Jabal
(Place name) short for Japalpur (city in India); attractive
Jabari
(African-American) brave
JaBee
(American) combo of Jay and B
J.B., Jabee, Jaybe, Jaybee
Jaber
(American) form of Arabic Jabir; comforting
Jabar, Jabe, Jabir
Jabir, Jabbar
(Arabic) supportive
Jabon
(American) wild
Jabonne
Jace
(American) audacious
Jase, Jhace

Jacee
(American) combo of Jay and C
J.C., Jacey, JayC, Jaycee, Jaycie, Jaycy
Jacek
(Polish) hyacinth; growing
Jack, Yahcik
Jacett
(Invented) jaunty
Jaycett
Jacinto
(Spanish) hyacinth; fragrant
Jacint
Jack
(Hebrew) believer in a gracious God; personality-plus
Jackee, Jackie, Jacko, Jacky, Jax
Jackie
(English) personable
Jackee, Jackey, Jacki, Jacky, Jaki
Jackson
(English) Jack's son; full of personality
Jackee, Jackie, Jacks, Jacsen, Jakson, Jax, Jaxon

Jacob
(Hebrew) replacement;
best boy
Jaccob, Jacobe, Jacobee,
Jake, Jakes, Jakey, Jakob

Jacobo
(Spanish) warm
Jake, Jakey

Jacques
(French) romantic;
ingenious
Jacquie, Jacue, Jaques,
Jock, Jok

Jadaan
(Last name as first
name)
Jada, Jadan, Jade, Jay

Jadall
(Invented) punctual
Jada, Jade

Jade
(Spanish) valued (jade
stone)
Jadee, Jadie, Jayde

Jadee
(American) combo of Jay
and D
J.D., Jadee, JayD, Jaydy

Jadney
(Last name as first
name)
Jad

Jadon, Jadyn
(American) devout; ball-
of-fire
Jade, Jadin, Jadun,
Jaeden, Jaiden, Jaydie,
Jaydon

Jaegel
(English) salesman
Jaeg, Jaeger, Jael

Jaeger
(German) outdoorsman
Jaegir, Jagher, Jagur

Jael
(Hebrew) climber

Jaffey
(English) form of Jaffe
Jaff

Jagan, Jago
(English) confident
Jagen, Jagun

Jagger
(English) brash
Jagar, Jager, Jaggar, Jagir

Jaggerton
(English) brash
Jag, Jagg

Jagit
(Invented) brisk
Jaggett, Jaggit, Jagitt

Jaguar
(Spanish) fast
Jag, Jagg, Jaggy, Jagwar,
Jagwhar

Jai
(American) adventurer
Jay

Jaime
(Spanish) follower
Jaimey, Jaimie, Jamee,
Jaymie

Jair
(Hebrew) teacher
Jairo

Jairo
(Origin unknown)
Jaero, Jairoh

Jaison
(American) form of Jason
Jaizon

Jaja
(African) praise-worthy

Jakar
(Place name) from
Jakarta, Indonesia
Jakart, Jakarta, Jakarte

Jake
(Hebrew) short for Jacob
Jaik, Jakee, Jakey, Jakie

Jakob
(Hebrew) form of Jacob
Jakab, Jake, Jakeb, Jakey,
Jakie, Jakobe, Jakub

Jaleel, Jalil
(Arabic) handsome

Jalen
(American) vivacious
Jalon, Jaylen, Jaylin, Jaylon

Jamail
(Arabic) good-looking
Jahmil, Jam, Jamaal, Jamahal, Jamal, Jamil, Jamile, Jamy

JaMarcus
(African-American) combo of Jay and Marcus; attractive
Jamarcus, Jamark, Jamarkus

Jamari
(African-American) attractive

Jamarr
(African-American) attractive; formidable
Jam, Jamaar, Jamar, Jammy

Jamel
(Arabic) form of Jamal
Jameel, Jamele, Jimelle

James
(English) dependable; steadfast
Jaimes, Jamsey, Jamze, Jaymes, Jim, Jimmy

Jameson
(English) able; James's son
Jamesan, Jamesen, Jamesey, Jamison, Jamsie

Jamie
(English) short for James
Jaimie, Jamee, Jamey, Jay, Jaymsey

Jamin
(Hebrew) favored son
Jamen, James, Jamie, Jamon, Jaymon

Jamisen
(American) form of James/Jamie; lively
Jami, Jamie, Jamis, Jamison

Jan
(Dutch) form of John; believer
Jaan, Jann, Janne

Jan-Erik
(Slavic) combo of Jan and Erik; reliable
Jan-Eric

Janson
(Scandinavian) Jan's son; hardworking
Jan, Janne, Janny, Jansahn, Jansen, Jansey

Jantz
(Scandinavian) short for Jantzen
Janson, Janssen, Janz, Janzon

Janus
(Latin) Roman god of beginnings and endings; optimistic; born in January
Jan

Jaquawn
(African-American) rock
Jakka, Jaquan, Jaquie, Jaqwen, Jock

Jard
(American) form of Jared; longlasting
Jarra, Jarrd, Jarri, Jerd, Jord

Jared
(Hebrew) descendant; giving
Jarad, Jarod, Jarode, Jarret, Jarrett, Jerod, Jerrad, Jerrod

Jarek
(Slavic) fresh
Jarec

Jarell
(Scandinavian) giving
Jare, Jarelle, Jarey, Jarrell, Jerrell

Jaren
(Hebrew) vocal
Jaron, Jayrone, J'ron

Jarenal
(American) form of
Jaren; longlasting
*Jaranall, Jaret, Jarn,
Jaronal, Jarry, Jerry*

Jareth
(American) open to
adventure
Jarey, Jarith, Jarth, Jary

Jarred
(Hebrew) form of Jared
*Jared, Jere, Jerod, Jerred,
Jerud*

Jarrell
(English) jaunty
*Jare, Jarell, Jarrel, Jarry,
Jerele, Jerrell*

Jarrett
(English) confident
*Jare, Jaret, Jarret, Jarry,
Jerot, Jerret, Jerrett,
Jurett, Jurette*

Jarrod
(Hebrew) form of Jared
Jare, Jarod, Jarry, Jerod

Jarvey
(German) celebrated
*Garvey, Garvy, Jarvee,
Jarvi, Jarvy*

Jarvis
(German) athletic
*Jarv, Jarvee, Jarves,
Jarvey, Jarvhus, Jarvie,
Jarvus, Jarvy*

Jary
(Spanish) form of Jerry;
leader
Jaree

Jashon
(African-American)
combo of Jason and the
letter h

Jason
(Greek) healer; man on a
quest
*Jace, Jacey, Jaisen, Jase,
Jasen, Jasey, Jasyn,
Jayson, Jaysun*

Jason-Joel
(American) combo of
Jason and Joel; popular
Jasonjoel, Jason Joel

Jasper
(English) guard; country
boy
*Jasp, Jaspur, Jaspy,
Jaspyr*

Jaster
(English) form of Jasper;
vigilant
Jast

Jathan
(Invented) combo of
Jake and Nathan;
attractive
*Jae, Jath, Jathe, Jathen,
Jathun, Jay*

Javaris
(African-American) ready
Javares, Javarez

Javier
(Spanish) affluent;
homeowner
Havyaire, Javey, Javiar

Javon
(Hebrew) hopeful
*Javan, Javaughn, Javen,
Javonn, Javonte*

Javonte
(African-American)
jaunty
*Javaughantay, Javawnte,
Ja-Vonnetay, Ja-Vontae*

Jawon
(African-American) shy
*Jawaughn, Jawaun,
Jawuane, Jowon*

Jax
(American) form of
Jackson; fun
Jacks

Jay
(English) short for a
name starting with J;
colorful
Jai, Jaye

Jaya
(American) jazzy
Jay, Jayah

Jaydon
(American) bright-eyed
*Jayde, Jayden, Jaydey,
Jaydi, Jaydie, Jaydun,
Jaydy*

Jaylin
(American) combo of Jay
and Lin

Jaymes
(American) form of
James
Jaimes, James

JayR
(American) actor
J.R.

Jayson
(Greek) form of Jason

Jazz
(American) jazzy
Jazze, Jazzee, Jazzy

Jean
(French) form of John;
kind
Jeanne, Jeannie, Jene

Jean-Baptiste
(French) combo of Jean
and Baptiste; John the
Baptist; religious
John-Baptiste

Jean-Claude
(French) combo of Jean
and Claude; gracious

Jean-Francois
(French) combo of Jean
and Francois; smooth

Jean-Michel
(French) combo of Jean
and Michel; godly

Jean-Paul
(French) combo of Jean
and Paul; small and
giving

Jean-Philippe
(French) combo of Jean
and Philippe; handsome

Jean-Pierre
(French) combo of Jean
and Pierre; giving and
dependable

Jeb
(Hebrew) jolly
Jebb, Jebby

Jebediah
(Hebrew) close to God
*Jeb, Jebadiah, Jebby,
Jebedyah*

Jecori
(American) exuberant
Jekori

Jed
(Hebrew) helpful
Jedd, Jeddy, Jede

Jediah
(Hebrew) God's help
Jedi, Jedyah

Jedidiah
(Hebrew) close to God
*Jed, Jeddy, Jeddyah,
Jedidyah*

Jeevan
(African-American) form
of Jevon; lively
Jevaughn, Jevaun

Jeff
(English) short for Jeffrey
or Jefferson
Geoff, Jeffie, Jeffy

Jefferson
(English) dignified
*Jeff, Jeffarson, Jeffersen,
Jeffursen, Jeffy*

Jeffery
(English) alternate for
Jeffrey; peaceful
Jeffrey, Jeffrie, Jeffry, Jefry

Jeffrey
(English) peaceful
*Geoffrey, Jeff, Jeffree,
Jeffrie, Jeffry, Jeffy, Jefree*

Jelani
(African-American)
trendy
Jelanee, Jelaney, Jelanne

Jem
(English) short for James
*Jemmi, Jemmy, Jemmye,
Jemy*

Jemarr
(African-American) worldly
Jemahr

Jemonde
(French) man of the world
Jemond

Jenkins
(English) from the surname
Jenkin, Jenks, Jenky, Jenx, Jinx

Jep
(American) easygoing
Jepp

Jerald
(English) form of Gerald; merry
Jere, Jereld, Jerold, Jerrie, Jerry

Jeramy
(Hebrew) exciting
Jeramah, Jeramie, Jere, Jeremy

Jere
(Hebrew) short for Jeremy
Jeree, Jerey

Jeremiah
(Hebrew) prophet uplifted by God; farsighted
Jeramiah, Jere, Jeremyah, Jerome, Jerry

Jeremie
(Hebrew) loquacious
Jeremee, Jeremy

Jeremy
(English) talkative
Jaramie, Jere, Jeremah, Jereme, Jeremey, Jerrey, Jerry

Jericho
(Arabic) nocturnal
Jerako, Jere, Jerico, Jeriko

Jerick
(American) form of Jericho; tenacious
Gericho, Jereck, Jerik, Jero, Jerok, Jerrico

Jeril
(American) form of Jarrell; leader
Jerill, Jerl, Jerry

Jerma
(American) form of Germain; man of Germany
Jermah, Jermane, Jermayne

Jermain, Jerman
(French) from Germany
German, Germane, Germanes, Germano, Germanus, Jermaine, Jermane, Jermayn, Jermayne

Jermaine
(German) form of Germaine
Germain, Germaine, Jere, Jermain, Jermane, Jermene, Jerry

Jermey
(American) short for Jermaine; friendly
Jermy

Jermon
(African-American) dependable
Jermonn

Jernigan
(Last name as first name) spontaneous
Jerni, Jerny

Jero
(American) jaunty
Jeroh, Jerree, Jerri, Jerro, Jerry

Jerod
(Hebrew) form of Jerrod and Jarrod

Jerome
(Latin) holy name; blessed
Jarome, Jere, Jerohm, Jeromy, Jerree, Jerrome, Jerry, Jirome

Jerone
(English) hopeful
Jere, Jerohn, Jeron, Jerrone

Jeronimo
(Italian) form of Gerome; Geronimo, Apache Indian chief; excited
Gerry, Jero, Jerry

Jerral
(American) form of Gerald/Jerald; exciting
Jeral, Jere, Jerry

Jerrell
(American) exciting
Jarell, Jerre, Jerrel, Jerrie, Jerry

Jerrett
(Hebrew) form of Jarrett
Jeret, Jerete, Jerod, Jerot, Jerret

Jerry
(German) strong
Gerry, Gery, Jerre, Jerri, Jerrie, Jerrye

Jerse, Jersey
(Place name) calm; rural
Jerce, Jercey, Jerzy

Jesmar
(American) from Jesse; Biblical
Jess, Jessie, Jezz, Jezzie

Jesper
(American) easygoing
Jesp, Jess

Jesse, Jessie
(Hebrew) wealthy
Jess, Jessee, Jessey, Jessi, Jessye

Jessup
(Last name as first name) rich
Jess, Jessa, Jessie, Jessy

Jesuan
(Spanish) devout

Jesus
(Hebrew) saved by God
Hesus, Jesu, Jesuso, Jezus

Jesus-Amador
(Spanish) combo of Jesus and Amador; loving the Lord
Jesusamador, Jesus Amador

Jesus-Angel
(Spanish) combo of Jesus and Angel; angel of God
Jesusangel, Jesusangelo

Jetal
(American) zany
Jetahl, Jetil, Jett, Jettale, Jetty

Jethro
(Hebrew) fertile
Jeto, Jett, Jetty

Jeton
(French) a chip for gamblers; wild spirit
Jet, Jetawn, Jets, Jett, Jetty

Jett
(American) wild spirit
Jet, Jets, Jetty, The Jet

Jettie
(American) from mineral name Jett; wild spirit
Jette, Jettee, Jetti

Jevan
(African-American) spirited
Jevaughn, Jevaun, Jevln, Jevon

Jevon
(African-American) spirited
Jevaun

Jhonatan
(African) spiritual
Jhon, Jon

Ji
(Chinese) organized; orderly

Jim
(Hebrew) short for James
Jem, Jihm, Jimi, Jimmee, Jimmy

Jimbo
(American) cowhand;
endearment for Jim
Jim, Jimb, Jimbee,
Jimbey, Jimby

Jimbob
(American) countrified
Gembob, Jim Bob,
Jim-Bob, Jymbob

Jimmy
(English) short for James
Jim, Jimi, Jimmey, Jimmi,
Jimmye, Jimy

Jimmydee
(American) combo of
Jimmy and Dee;
southern boy
Jimmy D, Jimmy Dee,
Jimmy-Dee

Jimmy-John
(American) country boy
Jimmiejon, Jimmyjohn,
Jimmy-Jon, Jymmejon

Jin
(Chinese) golden

Jinan
(Place name) city in China
Jin

Jing
(Chinese) unblemished;
capital

Joab
(Hebrew) praising God;
hovering
Joabb

Joachim
(Hebrew) a king of
Judah; powerful;
believer
Akim, Jakim, Yachim,
Yakim

Joaquin
(Spanish) bold; hip
Joakeen, Joaquin,
Juakeen, Jwaqueen

Job
(Hebrew) patient
Jobb, Jobe, Jobi, Joby

Joby
(Hebrew) patient; tested
Job, Jobee, Jobi

Jock
(Hebrew) grace in God;
athlete
Jockie, Jocky

Jody
(Hebrew) believer in
Jehovah; combo of Joe
and Dee
Jodee, Jodey, Jodie,
Jodye, Joe

Joe
(Hebrew) short for Joel
and Joseph
Jo, Joey, Joeye, Joie

Joebob
(American) combo of Joe
and Bob
J.B., Jobob, Joe-Bob

Joedan
(American) combo of Joe
and Dan
Jodan, Jodin, Jodon,
Joe-Dan, Joedanne

Joel
(Hebrew) prophet in the
Bible
Joelie, Joell, Jole, Joly

Joemac
(American) combo of Joe
and Mac
J.M., Joe-Mac, Joe-Mack,
Jomack

Joey
(Hebrew) short for Joel
and Joseph
Joee, Joie

Johann
(German) spiritual
musician
Johan, Johane, Yohann,
Yohanne, Yohon

Johannes
(Hebrew) form of John,
the Biblical name
Johan, Jon

John
(Hebrew) honorable;
Biblical name
Jahn, Jhan, Johne,
Johnne, Johnni, Johnnie,
Johnny, Johnnye, Jon

Johnnie, Johnny
(Hebrew) endearment
for John; honorable man
*Gianni, Johnie, Jonni,
Jonny*

Johnny-Dodd
(American) country
sheriff
*Johnniedodd, Johnny
Dodd*

Johnpaul
(American) combo of
John and Paul
*John Paul, John-Paul,
Jonpaul*

Johnny-Ramon
(Spanish) renegade
*Johnnyramon, Johnny
Ramon*

Johnson
(English) John's son;
credible
*Johnsen, Johnsonne,
Jonsen, Jonson*

JoJo
(American) friendly;
popular
Jo-Jo

Jomar
(African-American)
helpful
Joemar, Jomarr

Jon
(Hebrew) alternative for
John
Jonni, Jonnie, Jonny, Jony

Jonah
(Hebrew) peacemaker
Joneh

Jonas
(Hebrew) capable; active
Jon

Jonathan, Johnathan
(Hebrew) gracious
Johnathon, Jonathon

Jordahno
(Invented) form of
Giordano

Jordan
(Hebrew) descending
*Jorden, Jordon, Jordun,
Jordy, Jordyn*

Jon-Eric
(American) combo of Jon
and Eric
*Joneric, Jon Eric, John-
Eric*

Jon-Jason
(American) combo of Jon
and Jason
*Johnjace, John-Jaison,
John-Jazon, Jon Jason,
Jonjason, Jon-Jayson*

Jonjay
(American) combo of Jon
and Jay; jaunty; believer
Jonjae, Jon Jay, Jon-Jay

Jonmarc
(American) combo of Jon
and Marc
*Jon Marc, Jon-Marc, John
Mark*

Jonnley
(American) form of Jon;
believer
Jonn, Jonnie

Jordy
(Hebrew) from Jordan

Jorge
(Spanish) form of
George; farmer
Jorje, Quiqui

Jorgen
(Scandinavian) farmer
Jorgan

Jos
(Place name) city in
Nigeria

José
(Spanish) asset; favored
*Joesay, Jose, Pepe,
Pepito*

Josef, Joseph
(Hebrew) asset;
supported by Jehovah
*Jodie, Joe, Joey, Josep,
Josephe, Jozef, Yusif*

Josh, Joshua
(Hebrew) saved by the Lord; devout
Joshuam, Joshyam, Josue, Jozua

Joshuah
(Hebrew) devout

Josia
(Hebrew) form of Josiah; supported by the Lord
Josea

Josiah
(Hebrew) Jehovah bolsters
Josyah

Joss
(English) form of Joseph; cool
Josslin, Jossly

Josue
(Spanish) devout

Jourdain
(French) flowing
Jordane, Jorden

Jovan
(Slavic) gifted
Jovahn, Jovohn

Jovani, Jovanni
(Italian) Roman god Jove; jovial
Jovani, Jovanni, Jovanny, Jovany

Jove
(Mythology) Roman sky god

Juanantonio
(Spanish) combo of Juan and Antonio; believer in a gracious God
Juan Antonio, Juan-Antonio

Jozef
(Polish) supported by Jehovah; asset
Joe, Joze

Juan
(Spanish) devout; lively
Juann, Juwon

Juancarlos
(Spanish) combo of Juan and Carlos; debonair

Juan-Fernando
(Spanish) combo of Juan and Fernando; believer in a gracious God
Juanfernand, Juanfernando, Juan Fernando

Juanjose
(Spanish) combo of Juan and Jose; active

Juanmiguel
(Spanish) combo of Juan and Miguel; hopeful

Juanpablo
(Spanish) combo of Juan and Pablo; believer
Juan Pablo, Juan-Pablo

Jubilo
(Spanish) rejoicing; jubilant
Jube

Judas
(Latin) Biblical traitor

Judd, Jud
(Latin) secretive

Jude
(Latin) form of Judas; disloyal
Judah

Judge
(English) judgmental
Judg

Judson
(Last name as first name) mercurial
Judsen

Judule
(American) form of Judah; judicious
Jud, Judsen, Judsun

Jules
(Greek) young Adonis
Jewels, Jule

Julian
(Greek) gorgeous
Juliane, Julien, Julyon, Julyun

Julio
(Spanish) handsome;
youthful
Huleeo, Hulie, Julie

Julius
(Greek) attractive
Juleus, Jul-yus, Jul-yuz

Ju-Long
(Chinese) powerful

Jumbe
(African) strong
Jumbey, Jumby

Juneau
(Place name) capital of
Alaska
Juno, Junoe

Junior
(Latin) young son of the
father, senior
Junnie, Junny, Junyer

Junius
(Latin) youngster
Junie, Junnie, Junny

Jupiter
(Roman) god of thunder
and lightning; guardian
Jupe

Jura
(Place name) mountain
range between France
and Switzerland
Jurah

Jurass
(American) from Jurassic
Period of dinosaurs;
daunting
Jurases, Jurassic

Jus
(French) just
Just, Justice, Justis

Juste
(French) law-abiding
Just, Zhuste

Justice
(Latin) just
*Jusees, Just, Justice,
Justiz, Justus, Juztice*

Justie
(Latin) honest; fair
Jus, Justee, Justey, Justi

Justin
(Latin) fair
*Just, Justan, Justen,
Justun, Justyn, Justyne*

Justino
(Spanish) fair
Justyno

Justiz
(American) judging; fair
Justice, Justis

Juvenal
(Latin) young
Juve

Juventino
(Spanish) young
*Juve, Juven, Juvey, Tino,
Tito*

Juwon
(African-American) form
of Juan; devout; lively
Jujuane, Juwan, Juwonne

Kacy
(American) happy
K.C., Kace, Kacee, Kase,
Kasee, Kasy, Kaycee

Kade
(American) exciting
Cade, Caden, K.D.
Kadey, Kaid, Kayde,
Kydee

Kadeem
(Arabic) servant
Kadim

Kaden
(American) exciting
Cade, Caden, Kadan,
Kadon, Kadyn, Kaiden

Kaeto
(American)
Cato, Cayto, Caytoe,
Kato

Kahil
(Turkish) ingénue;
(Arabic) friend; (Greek)
handsome
Cahill, Kaleel, Kalil,
Kayhil, Khalil

Kai
(Hawaiian, African)
attractive

Kaid
(English) round; happy
Caiden, Cayde, Caydin,
Kaden, Kadin, Kaid

Kailin
(Irish) sporty
Kailyn, Kale, Kalen,
Kaley, Kalin, Kallen,
Kaylen

Kale
(American) healthy;
vegetable
Kail, Kayle, Kaylee,
Kayley, Kaylie

Kalgan
(Place name) city in
China
Kal

Kalunga
(African) watchful; the
personal god of the
Mbunda of Angola

Kamal, Kamil
(Arabic) perfect
Kameel

Kamau
(African) quiet soldier
Kamall

Kameron
(Scottish) form of
Cameron
Kameren, Kammeron,
Kammi, Kammie,
Kammy, Kamran, Kamrin,
Kamron

Kamon
(American) form of
Cayman; place name:
Cayman Islands;
alligator
Cayman, Caymun, Kame,
Kammy, Kayman,
Kaymon

Kance
(American) combo of
Kane and Chance;
attractive
Cance, Cance, Cans,
Kaince, Kans, Kanse,
Kaynce

Kane
(American, English)
sterling spirit
Kain, Kaine, Kaney,
Kanie, Kayne

Kang
(Korean) healthy

Kaniel, Kanel
(Hebrew) confident;
supported by the Lord;
hopeful
Kane, Kan-El, Kanelle,
Kaney

Kano
(Place name) city in
Nigeria
Kan, Kanoh

Kant
(German) philosopher
Cant

Kaper
(American) capricious
Cape, Caper, Kahper,
Kape

Kapp
(Greek) short for the
surname Kaparos
Kap, Kappy

Kareem
(Arabic) generous
Karehm, Karem, Karim,
Karreem, Krehm

Karey
(Greek) form of Cary
or Carey
Karee, Kari, Karrey, Karry

Karl
(German) manly; forceful
Karll, Karlie

Karolek
(Polish) form of Charles;
grown man
Karol

Karr
(Scandinavian)
Carr

Kasey
(Irish) form of Casey
Kasi, Kasie

Kasper
(German) reliable
Caspar, Casper, Kasp,
Kaspar, Kaspy

Kass
(German) standout
among men
Cass, Kasse

Kassidy
(Irish) form of Cassidy
Kass, Kassidi, Kassidie,
Kassie

Kavan
(Irish) good-looking
Cavan, Kaven, Kavin

Kay
(Greek) joyful
Kai, Kaye, Kaysie, Kaysy

Kayle
(Hebrew) faithful
Kail, Kayl

Kayven
(Irish) handsome
Cavan, Kavan, Kave

Kazan
(Greek) creative
Kaz

Kazimierz
(Polish) practical
Kaz

Keane
(German) attractive
Kean, Keen, Keene,
Kiene

Keanu (Hawaiian) cool
breeze over mountains
Keahnu

Kearn
(Irish) outspoken
Kearny, Kern, Kerne,
Kerney

Kearney
(Irish) sparkling
Kearn, Kearns, Kerney,
Kirney

Keaton
(English) nature-lover
Keaten, Keats, Keatt,
Keatun, Keton

Keats
(Literature) poetic
Keatz

Kecalf
(American) inventive
Keecalf

Kechel
(African-American)
Kach, Kachelle

Kedrick
(American) form of
Kendrick
Ked, Keddy, Kedric,
Kedrik

Kee-Bun
(Taiwanese)
Keebun

Keefe
(Irish) handsome
Keaf, Keafe, Keef, Kief

Keegan
(Irish) ball-of-fire
Keagin, Kegan, Kege, Keghun

Keeley
(Irish) handsome
Kealy, Keelee, Keelie, Keely, Keilie

Keen
(German) smart
Kean, Keane, Keene, Keeney, Kene

Keenan
(Irish) bright-eyed
Kenan

Keeney
(American) incisive
Kean, Keane, Keaney, Keene, Kene

Keirer
(Irish) dark
Kerer

Keiron
(Irish) dark
Keiren, Keronn

Keith
(English) witty
Keath, Keeth, Keithe

Keithen
(Scottish) gentle
Keith

Kel
(Irish) fighter; energetic
Kell

Kelby
(English) snappy; charming
Kel, Kelbey, Kelbi, Kelbie, Kelbye, Kell, Kelly

Kelcy
(English) helpful
Kelci, Kelcie, Kelcye, Kelsie

Kell
(English) fresh-faced
Kel, Kelly

Kellen
(Irish) strong-willed
Kel, Kelen, Kelin, Kell, Kellan, Kellin, Kelly, Kelyn

Keller
(Last name as first name) bountiful
Kel, Keler, Kelher, Kell, Kylher

Kelly
(Irish) able combatant
Keli, Kellee, Kelley, Kelli

Kelsey
(Scandinavian) unique among men
Kel, Kells, Kelly, Kels, Kelsi, Kelsie, Kelsye, Kelzie, Kelzy

Kelts
(Origin unknown) energetic
Kel, Kelly, Kelse, Kelsey, Keltz

Kelvin
(English) goal-oriented
Kelvan, Kelven, Kelvun, Kelvynn, Kilvin

Kemper
(American) high-minded
Kemp, Kempar

Ken
(Scottish) short for Kenneth; cute
Kenn, Kenny, Kinn

Kendall
(English) shy
Ken, Kend, Kendahl, Kendal, Kendoll, Kendy, Kindal

Kendan
(English) strong; serious
Ken, Kend, Kenden

Kenel
(Invented) form of Kendall; hopeful
Kenele

Kenlee
(American) combo of
Ken and Lee

Kenley
(English) distinguished
Kenlee, Kenlie, Kenly

Kennard
(English) courageous;
selfless
*Ken, Kenard, Kennar,
Kenny*

Kennedy
(Irish) leader
Kennedie, Kennidy

Kenner
(English) capable
Kennard

Kennet
(Scandinavian) good-
looking
Kenet, Kennete

Kenneth
(Scottish) handsome;
(Irish) good-looking
*Ken, Keneth, Kenith,
Kennath, Kennie, Kenny*

Kenny
(Scottish) short for
Kenneth
*Kennee, Kenney, Kenni,
Kennie*

Kent
(English) fair-skinned

Kentlee
(Last name as first
name) dignified
*Ken, Kenny, Kent,
Kentlea, Kentleigh,
Kently*

Kenton
(English) from Kent

Kenyon
(Irish) dear blond boy
*Ken, Kenjon, Kenny,
Kenyawn, Kenyun*

Keon
(American) unbridled
enthusiasm
Keonne

Keontay
(African-American)
outrageous
Keon, Keontae, Keontee

Kerm
(Irish) form of Kermit;
guileless
Kurm

Kermit
(German) droll
*Kerm, Kermee, Kermet,
Kermey, Kermi, Kermie,
Kermy*

Kernis
(Invented) dark;
different
Kernes

Kerr
(Scandinavian) serious
Kerre, Kurr

Kerry
(Irish) dark
Kere, Keri, Kerrey, Kerrie

Kerstie
(American) spunky
Kerstee, Kersty

Kerwyn
(Irish) energetic
*Kerwen, Kerwin, Kerwun,
Kir, Kirs, Kirwin*

Keshawn
(African-American)
friendly
*Kesh, Keshaun,
Keyshawn, Shawn*

Keshon
(African-American)
sociable
Kesh

Keshua
(African-American) form
of the girl name Kesha
Keshe

Kesley
(American) derivative of
Lesley; active
Keslee, Kesli, Kezley

Kesse
(American) attractive
*Kessee, Kessey, Kessi,
Kessie*

Ketchum
(Place name) city in Idaho
Catch, Ketch, Ketcham, Ketchim

Kevin
(Irish) handsome; gentle
Kev, Kevahngn, Kevan, Keven, Kevvie, Kevvy

Key
(English) key
Keye, Keyes

Keyohtee
(Invented) form of Quixote

Khalid
(Arabic) everlasting
Khalead, Khaled, Khaleed

Khalil
(Arabic) good friend

Khambrel
(American) articulate
Kambrel, Kham, Khambrell, Khambrelle, Khambryll, Khamme, Khammie, Khammy

Khevin
(American) form of Kevin; good-looking
Khev

Khouri
(Arabic) spiritual
Couri, Khory, Khourae, Kori

Khyber
(Place name) pass on border of Pakistan and Afghanistan
Kibe, Kiber, Kyber

Kibo
(Place name) mountain peak (highest peak of Kilimanjaro); spectacular
Kib

Kiefer
(American) talented
Keefer, Kefer

Kiel
(Place name) city in North Germany

Kieran
(Irish) handsome brunette
Keiran, Kier, Kieren, Kierin, Kiers, Kyran

Kiev
(Place name) capital city of Ukraine

Killi
(Irish) form of Killian; fighter
Killean, Killee, Killey, Killyun

Killian
(Irish) effervescent
Killee, Killi, Killie, Killyun, Kylian

Kim
(English) enthusiastic
Kimmie, Kimmy, Kimy, Kym

Kimball
(Greek) inviting
Kim, Kimb, Kimbal, Kimbie, Kymball

Kincaid
(Scottish) vigorous
Kincaide, Kinkaid

King
(English) royal leader

Kingsley
(English) royal nature
King, Kings, Kingslea, Kingslee, Kingsleigh, Kingsly, Kins

Kingston
(English) gracious
King, Kingstan, Kingsten

Kinsey
(English) affectionate; winning
Kensey, Kinsie

Kip
(English) focused
Kipp, Kippi, Kippie, Kippy

Kipling
(Literature) adventurous
Kiplen

Kirby
(English) brilliant
*Kerb, Kirb, Kirbee,
Kirbey, Kirbie, Kyrbee,
Kyrby*

Kirk
(Scandinavian) believer
Kirke, Kurk

Kirkwood
(English) heavenly
Kirkwoode, Kurkwood

Kirvin
(American) form of
Kevin; good-looking
*Kerven, Kervin, Kirv,
Kirvan, Kirven*

Kit
(Greek) mischievous
Kitt

Klaus
(German) wealthy
Klaes, Klas, Klass

Klay
(English) form of Clay;
reliable
Klaie, Klaye

Kleber
(Last name as first
name) serious
Klebe

Klev
(Invented) form of Cleve
Kleve

Knight
(English) protector
Knighte, Nighte

Knoll
(American) flamboyant
Noll

Knowles
(English) outdoorsman
Knowlie, Knowls, Nowles

Knox
(English) bold

Knut
(Scandinavian)
aggressive
Knute

Kobe
(Hebrew) cunning
*Kobee, Kobey, Kobi,
Koby*

Kody
(English) brash
*Kodee, Kodey, Kodi,
Kodye*

Kohler
(Origin unknown)

Kolton
(Origin unknown)

Komic
(Invented) funny
Com, Comic, Kom

Konnor
(Irish) another spelling
of Connor
Konnar, Konner

Konrad
(German) bold advisor
*Khonred, Kon, Konn,
Konny, Konraad,
Konradd, Konrade*

Konstantin
(Russian) forceful
*Kon, Konny, Kons,
Konstance, Konstantine,
Konstantyne*

Konstantinos
(Greek) steadfast
*Constance, Konstance,
Konstant, Tino, Tinos*

Korey
(Irish) lovable
Kori, Korrey, Korrie

Kornelius
(Latin) another spelling
of Cornelius
*Korne, Kornellius,
Kornelyus, Korney,
Kornnelyus*

Korrigan
(Irish) another spelling
of Corrigan
*Koregan, Korigan, Korre,
Korreghan, Korri,
Korrigon*

Kort
(German) talkative

Kory
(Irish) another spelling
for Corey
*Kori, Korre, Korrey,
Korrye*

Koshy
(American) jolly
Koshee, Koshey, Koshi

Koster
(American) spiritual
*Kost, Kostar, Koste,
Koster*

Kraig
(Irish) another spelling
for Craig
Krag, Kragg, Kraggy

Kricker
(Last name as first
name) reliable
Krick

Kris
(Greek) short for Kristian
and Kristopher
Krissy, Krys

Krishna
(Hindi) pleasant
Krishnah

Krister
(Scandinavian) religious

Kristian
(Greek) another form of
Christian
Kris, Krist, Kristyan

Kristo
(Greek) short for
Kristopher

Kristopher
(Greek) bearer of Christ
*Kris, Krist, Kristo,
Kristofer*

Krystyn
(Polish) Christian
Krys, Krystian

Krzysztof
(Polish) bearing Christ
Kreestof

Kubrick
(Last name as first
name) creative
Kubrik

Kurt
(Latin) wise advisor
Curt, Kurty

Kurtis
(Latin) form of Curtis
*Kurt, Kurtes, Kurtey,
Kurtie, Kurts, Kurtus,
Kurty*

Kutty
(English) knife-wielding
Cutty

Kwame
(African) Saturday's
child
Kwamee, Kwami

Kwintyn
(Polish) fifth child
Kwint, Kwintin, Kwynt

Kyan
(Japanese)
Kyann

Kyle
(Irish) serene
*Kiel, Kiyle, Kye, Kyl,
Kyley, Kylie, Kyly*

Kyle-Evan
(American) combo of
Kyle and Evan
Kyle Evan

Kyler
(English) peaceful
Kieler, Kiler, Kye

Kylerton
(American) form of Kyle
Kylten

Kyzer
(American) wild spirit
Kaizer, Kizer, Kyze

Labarne
(American) form of
Laban; (Hebrew) white
Labarn

Labaron
(French) the baron
LaBaron, LaBaronne

LaBryant
(African-American) son
of Bryant; brash
*Bryant, La Brian, La
Bryan, Labryan,
Labryant*

Lachlan
(Scottish) feisty
*Lacklan, Lackland,
Laughlin, Lock, Locklan*

Ladarius
(Origin unknown)

Ladd
(English) helper; smart
Lad, Laddee, Laddey

Laddie
(English) youthful
*Lad, Ladd, Laddee,
Laddey, Laddy*

Ladisiao
(Spanish) helpful
Laddy

Lael
(Hebrew) Jehovah's
Lale

Lafaye
(American) cheerful
*Lafay, Lafayye, Laphay,
Laphe*

Lafayetta
(Spanish) from the
French name Lafayette;
bold
Lafay

Lafayette
(French) ambitious
Lafayet, Lafayett

Lafe
(American) punctual
Laafe, Laife, Laiffe

Lagos
(Place name) city in
Nigeria
Lago

Lagrand
(African-American) the
grand
Grand, Grandy, Lagrande

Laird
(Scottish) rich
Layrd, Layrde

Lalo
(Latin) singer of a lullaby
Laloh

Lamalcom
(African-American) son
of Malcolm; kingly
*LaMalcolm, LaMalcom,
Mal, Malcolm, Malcom*

Lamar
(Latin) renowned
Lamahr, Lamarr

Lamber
(German) form of
Lambert; ingratiating
Lambur

Lambert
(German) bright
*Lamb, Lamber, Lambie,
Lamburt, Lammie,
Lammy*

Lamond
(French) worldly
*Lamon, Lamonde,
Lemond*

Lamont
(Scandinavian) lawman
Lamon

Lance
(German) confident
Lanse, Lantz, Lanz

Lancelot
(French) romantic
*Lance, Lancelott,
Launcelot, Launcey*

Lander
(English) landed
Land

Landers
(English) wealthy
*Land, Landar, Lander,
Landor*

Landis
(English) owning land;
earthy
*Land, Landes, Landice,
Landise, Landly, Landus*

Lando
(American) masculine
Land

Landon
(English) place name;
plain; old-fashioned
Land, Landan, Landen

Landry
(French) entrepreneur
Landré, Landree

Lane
(English) secure
*Laine, Laney, Lanie,
Lanni, Layne*

Lang
(English) top
Lange

Langdon
(English) longwinded
Lang, Langden, Langdun

Langford
(English) healthy
Lanford, Langferd

Langham
(Last name as first
name) long
Lang

Langley
(English) natural
*Lang, Langlee, Langli,
Langly*

Langston
(English) longsuffering
*Lang, Langstan,
Langsten*

Langton
(English) long
Lange

Lanny
(American) popular
*Lann, Lanney, Lanni,
Lannie*

Lansing
(Place name) city in
Michigan
Lance, Lans

Laramie
(French) pensive
Laramee

Lare
(American) wealthy
Larre, Layr

Largel
(American) intrepid
Large

Lariat
(American) word as
name; roper
Lare, Lari

Larkin
(Irish) brash
*Lark, Larkan, Larken,
Larkie, Larky*

Larndell
(American) generous
*Larn, Larndelle, Larndey,
Larne*

Larne
(Place name) district in
Northern Ireland
Larn, Larney, Larny

Larnell
(American) giving
Larne

Laron
(American) outgoing
Larron, Larrone

Larrmyne
(American) boisterous
*Larmie, Larmine, Larmy,
Larmyne*

Larry
(Latin) extrovert
*Lare, Larrey, Larri, Larrie,
Lary*

Lars
(Scandinavian) short for
Lawrence and Laurens
Larrs, Larse, Larsy

Lashaun
(African-American)
enthusiastic
Lashawn, La-Shawn,
Lashon, Lashond

Lasisch
(Origin unknown)

Laskey
(Last name as first
name) jovial
Lask, Laski

Lassen
(Place name) a peak in
California in the Cascade
Range
Lase, Lasen, Lassan,
Lassun

Lassit
(American) broad-
minded
Lasset, Lassitte

Lassiter
(American) witty
Lassater, Lasseter,
Lassie, Lassy

Lathrop
(English) home-loving
Lathrap, Latrope, Laye,
Laythrep

Latimer
(English) interprets;
philanthropic
Latymer

Latorris
(African-American)
notorious
LaTorris

Latravious
(African-American)
healthy
Latrave

Latty
(English) giving
Lat, Latti, Lattie

Laurence
(Latin) glorified
Larence, Laurance,
Laurans, Laure, Lorence

Laurens
(German) brilliant
Larrie, Larry, Laure,
Laurins, Lorens, Lors

Laurent
(French) martyred
Laurynt

Lavaughn
(African-American) perky
Lavan, Lavon, Lavonn,
Levan, Levaughn

Lavaughor
(African-American)
laughing
Lavaugher, Lavawnar

Lawford
(English) dignified
Laford, Lauford, Lawferd

Lawrence
(Latin) honored
Larrie, Larry, Laurence,
Lawrance, Lawrunce

Lawson
(English) Lawrence's
son; special
Law, Laws, Lawsan,
Lawsen

Layshaun
(African-American) merry
Laysh, Layshawn

Laysy
(Last name as first
name) sophisticated
Lay, Laycie, Laysee

Layt
(American) fascinating
Lait, Laite, Late, Layte

Layton
(English) musical
Laytan, Laytawn, Layten

Lazar
(Hebrew) from Lazarus;
helped by God
Lazare, Lazaro, Lazear,
Lazer

Lazarus
(Greek) renewed
Lasarus, Lazerus,
Lazoros

Leamon
(American) powerful
Leamm, Leamond,
Leemon

Leand
(Greek) from Leander;
leonine
Leander

Leander
(Greek) ferocious;
lion-like
Anders, Leann, Leannder

Lear
(Greek) royal
Leare, Leere

Learly
(Last name as first
name) terrific
Learley

Leather
(American) word as
name; tough
Leath

Leavery, Leautry
(American) giving
*Leautree, Leautri, Levry,
Lo, Lotree, Lotrey, Lotri,
Lotry*

Lectoy
(American) form of
Lecter and Leroy; good-
old-boy
Lec, Lecto, Lek

Lee
(English) loving
Lea, Lee, Leigh

Leeander
(Invented) form of
Leander

Leenoris
(African-American) form
of Lenore; respected
Lenoris

Leeodis
(African-American)
combo of Lee and Odis;
carefree
Lee-Odis, Leotis

Leeron
(African-American)
combo of Lee and Ron
Leerawn

Leibel
(Hebrew) lion

Leif
(Scandinavian) loved
one
Laif, Leaf, Leife

Leighton
(Last name as first
name) hearty
*Laytan, Layton,
Leighten, Leightun*

Leland
(English) protective
*Leeland, Leighlon,
Leiland, Lelan, Lelond*

Leldon
(American) form of
Eldon; bookish
Leldun

Lemar
(American) form of
Lamar; famed landowner
Lemarr

Lemetrias
(African-American) form
of Lemetrius
Lem

Lemon
(American) fruit; tart
Lemonn, Lemun, Limon

Len
(German) short for
Leonard
Lennie, Lynn

Lenard
(American) form of
Leonard; heart of a lion
Lenerd

Lennart
(Scandinavian) brave
Lenn, Lenne

Lennon
(Irish) renowned; caped
Lenn, Lennan, Lennen

Lennox
(Scottish) authoritative
*Lennix, Lenocks, Lenox,
Linnox*

Lenny
(German) short for
Leonard
*Lenn, Lenney, Lenni,
Lennie, Leny, Linn*

Lenton
(American) religious
Lent, Lenten, Lentun

Lenvil
(Invented) typical
Lenval, Level

Leo
(Latin) lion-like; fierce

Leocadio
(Spanish) lion-hearted
Leo

Leoliver
(American) combo of Leo
and Oliver; audacious
Leo

Leon
(Greek) tenacious
Lee, Leo, Leone, Leonn

Leonard
(German) courageous
*Lee, Leo, Leonar,
Leonerd, Leonord, Lynar,
Lynard, Lynerd*

Leonardo
(Italian) lion-hearted
Leo

Leoncio
(Spanish) lion-hearted
Leon, Leonce, Leonse

Leondras
(African-American)
lionine
*Leon, Leondre,
Leondrus, Leonid*

Leonidus
(Latin) strong
*Leon, Leone, Leonidas,
Leonydus*

Leopaul
(American) combo of Leo
and Paul; brave; calm
Leo-Paul

Leopold
(German) brave
Lee, Leo

Leoti
(American) outdoorsy
Lee, Leo

Leovardo
(Spanish) form of
Leonardo; brave
Leo, Leovard

Lepoldo
(Spanish) form of
Leopold; brave
Lee, Lepold, Poldo

Lerey
(American) form of Larry
Lerrie, Lery

Leroy
(French) king; royal
*Leeroy, Leroi, Le-Roy,
Roy, Roye*

Les
(English) short for Leslie
Lez, Lezli

Leshawn
(African-American)
cheery
*Lashawn, Leshaun,
Le-Shawn*

Leslie
(Scottish) fortified
*Lee, Les, Lesley, Lesli,
Lezlie, Lezly*

Lesner
(Last name as first
name) serious
Les, Lez, Lezner

Lester
(American) large
persona
Les, Lestor

Lev
(Russian) lionine

Levar
(American) softspoken
Levarr

Levi
(Hebrew) harmonious
Lev, Levey, Levie, Levy

Levonne
(African-American)
forward-thinking
Lavonne, Leevon, Levon

Lew
(Polish) lion-like
Leu

Leward
(French) contentious
Lewar, Lewerd

Lew-Gene
(American) combo of
Lew and Gene;
renowned fighter
Lou-Gene

Lewie
(French) form of Louie
Lew, Lewee, Lewey, Lewy

Lewis
(English) different
spelling for Louis
*Lew, Lewey, Lewie,
Lewus, Lewy*

Lex
(English) short for
Alexander; mysterious
*Lexa, Lexe, Lexi, Lexie,
Lexy*

Li
(Chinese) strong man

Liam
(Irish) protective;
handsome
Leam, Leeam, Leeum

Liang
(Chinese) good man

Liberio
(Spanish) liberated
Libere, Lyberio

Liberty
(American) freedom-
loving
Lib

Librada
(Italian, Spanish) free

Lictor
(Invented) form of
Lecter; disturbed
Lec, Lek

Lidon
(Hebrew) judge

Lieven
(Belgium)
Lieve

Lillo
(American) triple-threat
talent
Lilo

Limo
(Invented) from the word
limousine; sporty
Lim

Linc, Link
(English) short for
Lincoln; leader
Links

Lincoln
(English, American)
quiet
Linc, Link

Lindberg
(German) blond good
looks
*Lin, Lind, Lindburg,
Lindie, Lindy, Lyndberg,
Lyndburg*

Linden
(Botanical) tree
Lindun

Lindoh
(American) sturdy
Lindo, Lindy

Lindsay, Lindsey
(English) natural
*Lind, Lindsee, Linz,
Linzee, Lyndsey, Lyndzie,
Lynz, Lynzie*

Lindy
(German) form of
Lindberg; daring
Lind

Linley
(English) open-minded
*Lin, Linlee, Linleigh,
Lynlie*

Linnard
(German) form of
Leonard; bold
Linard, Lynard

Lino
(American) form of Linus
Linus

Linus
(Greek) blond
Linas, Line, Lines

Linwood
(American) open

Lionel
(French) fierce
Li, Lion, Lionell, Lye,
Lyon, Lyonel, Lyonell

Lister
(Origin unknown)
intelligent

Litton
(English) centered
Lyten, Lyton, Lytton

Livingston
(English) comforting
Liv, Livey, Livingstone

Llano
(Place name) river in
Texas; flowing
Lano

Llewellyn
(Welsh) fiery; fast
Lew, Lewellen, Lewellyn

Lloyd
(Welsh) spiritual; joyful
Loy, Loyd, Loydde, Loye

Lobo
(Spanish) wolf
Loboe, Lobow

Lochlain
(Irish) assertive
Lochlaine, Lochlane,
Locklain

Lock
(English) natural
Locke

Lodge
(English) safe haven

Loey
(American) daring
Loie, Lowee, Lowi

Lofton
(Last name as first
name) lofty
Loften

Logan
(Irish) eloquent
Logen, Loggy, Logun

Lombardi
(Italian) winner
Bardi, Bardy, Lom,
Lombard, Lombardy

London
(English) ethereal;
capital of Great Britain
Londen

Lonnie
(Spanish) short for
Alonzo
Lonney, Lonni, Lonny

Loocho
(Invented) form of Lucho

Lorance
(Latin) form of
Lawrence; longsuffering;
patient
Lorans, Lorence

Lord
(English) regal
Lorde

Lordlee
(English) regal
Lordly, Lords

Loredo
(Spanish) smart cowboy
Lorado, Loredoh, Lorre,
Lorrey

Loren
(Latin) hopeful; winning
Lorin, Lorrin

Lorens
(Scandinavian) form of
Laurence

Lorenzo
(Spanish, Italian)
bold and spirited
Larenzo, Loranzo, Lore,
Lorence, Lorenso,
Lorentz, Lorenz, Lorrie,
Lorry

Loring
(German) brash
Looring, Lorrie, Louring

Lorne
(Latin) grounded
Lorn, Lorny

Lorry
(English) form of Laurie
Lore, Lorri, Lorrie, Lorry,
Lory

Lot
(Hebrew) furtive
Lott

Lothario
(German) lover
Lotario, Lothaire,
Lotherio, Lothurio

Lou
(German) short for Louis
Lew

Louie, Louey
(German) short for Louis

Louis
(German, French)
powerful ruler
Lew, Lewis, Lou, Louie,
Lue, Luie, Luis

Loundis
(American) visionary
Lound, Loundas,
Loundes, Lowndis

LouVon
(American) combo of
Lou and Von; searching
Lou Von, Louvaughan,
Louvawn, Lou-Von

Lovell
(English) brilliant
Lovall, Love, Lovelle

Lovett
(Last name as first
name) loving
Lovat, Lovet

Low
(American) word as a
name; lowkey
Lowey

Lowell
(English) loved
Lowall, Lowel

Lowry
(Last name as first
name) leader
Lowree, Lowrey

Loys
(American) loyal
Loyce, Loyse

Luc
(French) light; laidback
Lucca, Luke

Luca
(Italian) light-hearted
Louca, Louka, Luka

Lucas
(Greek) patron saint of
doctors/artists; creative
Lucca, Luces, Luka,
Lukas, Luke, Lukes,
Lukus

Lucho
(Spanish) lucky; light

Lucian
(Latin) soothing
Lew, Luciyan, Lushun

Luciano
(Italian) light-hearted
Luca, Lucas, Luke

Lucious
(African-American) light;
delicious
Luceous, Lushus

Lucius
(Latin) sunny
Lucca, Luchious, Lushus

Lucky
(American) lucky
Luckee, Luckey, Luckie

Ludie
(English) glorious
Ludd

Ludlow
(German) respected
Ludlo, Ludloe

Ludovic
(Slavic) smart; spiritual
Luddovik, Lude, Ludovik,
Ludvic, Vick

Ludwig
(German) talented
Ludvig, Ludweg,
Ludwige

Luigi
(Italian) famed warrior
Lui, Louie

Luis
(Spanish) outspoken
Luez, Luise, Luiz

Lujo
(Spanish) luxurious
Luj

Luka, Luca
(Italian, Croatian)
easygoing
Luke

Lukah
  (Invented) form of Luca
Lukas
  (Greek) light-hearted;
  creative
  Lucus
Luke
  (Latin) worshipful
  Luc, Lucc, Luk, Lukus
Lumer
  (American) light
  Lumar, Lume, Lumur
Luna
  (Spanish) moon
Lunn
  (Irish) smart and brave
  Lun, Lunne
Lusk
  (Last name as first
  name) hearty
  *Lus, Luske, Luskee,
  Luskey, Luski, Lusky*
Luther
  (German) reformer
  Luthar, Luth, Luthur
Luthus
  (American) form of
  Luther; prepared and
  armed
  Luth, Luthas
Lyal
  (English) form of Lyle;
  islander
  Lye

Lyle
  (French) unique
  Lile, Ly, Lyle
Lyman
  (English) meadow-man;
  sportsman
Lyndall
  (English) nature-lover
  Lynd, Lyndal, Lyndell
Lyndon
  (English) verbose
  *Lindon, Lyn, Lynd,
  Lyndonn*
Lynge
  (Scandinavian) sylvan
  nature
Lynn
  (English) water-loving
  Lin, Linn, Lyn, Lynne
Lynshawn
  (African-American)
  combo of Lyn and
  Shawn; helpful
  *Linshawn, Lynnshaw,
  Lynshaun*
Lyon
  (Place name) in France
  Lyone
Lysande
  (Greek) freewheeling
  Lyse
Lysander
  (Greek) lover
  Lysand

Lyulf
  (German) haughty;
  combative
  Lyulfe, Lyulff

Mac, Mack
(Irish, Scottish) short for
"Mc" or "Mac" surname;
friendly
*Mackee, Macki, Mackie,
Macky*

Macaffie
(Scottish) charming
*Mac, Mack, Mackey,
McAfee, McAffee,
McAffie*

Macario
(Spanish) blessed
Macareo, Makario

Macarlos
(Spanish) manly
Carlos

Macauley
(Scottish) righteous;
dramatic
*Mac, Macaulay,
McCauley*

Macbey
(American) form of
Mackey
*Mackbey, Makbee,
Makbi*

Mackenzie
(Irish) giving
*Mackenzy, Mackinsey,
Makinzie, McKenzie*

Maclain
(Irish) natural wonder
*McLain, McLaine,
McLean*

Macon
(Place name) creative;
southern
Makon

Macy
(French) lasting; wealthy
*Mace, Macee, Macey,
Macye*

Madan
(Hindi) god of love;
loving

Maddox
(English) giving
*Maddocks, Maddy,
Madox*

Madhav
(Hindi) sweet
Madhu

Madison
(English) good
*Maddison, Maddy,
Madisan, Madisen, Son*

Madock
(American) giving
*Maddock, Maddy,
Madoc*

Madras
(Place name) city in
India

Magee
(Irish) practical; lively
Mackie, Maggy, McGee

Magic
(American) magical
Majic

Magnus
(Latin) outstanding
Maggy, Magnes

Maguire
(Irish) subtle
Macky, Maggy, McGuire

Mahan
(American) cowboy
*Mahahn, Mahand,
Mahen, Mayhan*

Mahir
(Arabic) skilled

Mahmud
(Arabic) remarkable

Main
(Place name) river in
Gemany; leader
Mainess, Mane, Maness

Majeed
(Arabic) majestic
Majid

Majid
(Arabic) glorious

Major
(Latin) leading
Mage, Magy, Majar,
Maje, Majer

Makale
(Invented) form of
Mikhail

Maks
(Russian) short for
Maksimilian

Maksimilian
(Russian) competitor
Maksim

Makya
(Native American)
hunter

Malachi
(Hebrew) angelic;
magnanimous
Malachy, Malakai,
Malaki, Maleki

Malcolm
(Scottish) peaceful
Mal, Malkalm, Malkelm,
Malkolm

Maldon
(French) strong and
combative
Maldan, Malden

Malfred
(German) feisty
Malfrid, Mann

Malik
(Arabic) angelic
Malic

Malla-Ki
(Invented) form of
Malachi

Mallin
(English) rowdy warrior
Malen, Malin, Mallan,
Mallen, Mallie, Mally

Mallory
(French) wild spirit
Mal, Mallie, Malloree,
Mallorie, Mally, Malory

Maloney
(Irish) religious
Mal, Malone, Malonie,
Malony

Malvin
(English) open-minded
Mal, Malv, Malven,
Malvyne

Mandell
(German) tough; almond
Mandee, Mandel,
Mandela, Mandie,
Mandy

Manfred
(English) peaceful
Manferd, Manford,
Mannfred, Mannie,
Manny, Mannye

Manfredo
(Italian) strong
peacefulness

Manila
(Place name) capital of
Philippines
Manilla

Maninder
(Hindi) masculine;
potent

Manley
(English) virile; haven
Man, Manlee, Manlie,
Manly

Manning
(English) heroic
Man, Maning, Mann

Mannix
(Irish) spiritual
Manix, Mann, Mannicks

Manny
(Spanish) short for
Manuel
Manney, Manni, Mannie

Manolo
(Spanish) from Spanish
shoe designer Manolo
Blahnik; cutting-edge

Mansfield
(English) outdoorsman
Manesfeld, Mans,
Mansfeld

Manu
(Hindi) father of people;
masculine

Manuel
(Hebrew, Spanish) gift from God
Mann, Mannuel, Manny, Manual, Manuelle

Manus
(American) strong-willed
Manes, Mann, Mannas, Mannes, Mannis, Mannus

Manvel
(French) great town; hardworking
Mann, Manny, Manvil, Manville

Marc, Mark
(French) combative
Markee, Markey, Markeye, Markie Mark, Markie, Marko, Marky

Marc-Anthony
(French) combo of Marc and Anthony
Marcantony, Mark-Anthony, Markantony

Marcel
(French) singing God's praises
Marcell, Mars, Marsel

Marcellus
(Latin) romantic; persevering
Marcel, Marcelis, Marcey, Marsellus, Marsey

Marcial
(Spanish) martial; combative
Mars

Marco
(Italian) tender
Marc, Mark, Markie, Marko, Marky

Marconi
(Italian) inventive; tough

Marcos
(Spanish) outgoing
Marco, Marko, Markos, Marky

Marco-Tulio
(Spanish) fighter; substantial
Marco Tulio, Marcotulio

Marcoux
(French) aggressive; manly
Marce, Mars

Marcus
(Latin) combative
Marc, Mark, Markus, Marky

Marcus-Anthony
(Spanish) valuable; aggressive
Marc Anthony, Marc-Antonito, Marcus-Antoneo, Marcusantonio, Markanthony, Taco, Tonio, Tono

Marek
(Polish) masculine

Marguez
(Spanish) noble
Marguiz

Mariano
(Italian) combative; manly
Mario

Marin
(French) ocean-loving
Maren, Marino, Maryn

Mario
(Italian) masculine
Marioh, Marius, Marrio, Morio

Marion
(Latin) suspicious
Mareon, Marionn

Marjuan
(Spanish) contentious
Marhwon, Marwon, Marwond

Markell
(African-American) personable
Markelle

Markham
(English) homebody
Marcum, Markhum, Markum

Markos
(Greek) warring;
masculine
Marc, Mark

Marl
(English) rebel
Marley, Marli

Marley
(English) secretive
Marlee, Marleigh, Marly

Marlin
(English) opportunistic;
fish
Marllin

Marlo, Marlow
(English) hill by a lake;
optimistic
Mar, Marl, Marlowe

Marlon
(French) wizard; strange
Marlan, Marlen, Marlin,
Marly

Marmaduke
(English) haughty
Duke, Marmadook,
Marmahduke

Marmion
(French) famed
Marmeonne, Marmyon

Marq
(French) noble
Mark, Marque, Marquie

Marquise
(French) noble
Mark, Markese, Marky,
Marq, Marquese,
Marquie, Marquis

Mars
(Latin) warlike (god of
war)
Marrs, Marz

Marsdon
(English) comforting
Marr, Mars, Marsden,
Marsdyn

Marsh
(English) handsome
Marr, Mars, Marsch,
Marsey, Marsy

Marshall
(French) giving care
Marsh, Marshal,
Marshel, Marshell,
Marsy

Marston
(English) personable
Mars, Marst, Marstan,
Marsten

Martin
(Latin) combative; from
Mars
Mart, Marten, Marti,
Martie, Marton, Marty

Marty
(Latin) short for Martin
Mart, Martee, Martey,
Marti, Martie, Martye

Marv
(English) short for
Marvin; good friend
Marve, Marvy

Marvin
(English) steadfast
friend
Marv, Marven, Marvy

Masa
(African) centered

Mashawn
(African-American)
vivacious
Masean, Mashaun,
Mayshawn

Maslen
(American) promising
Mas, Masline, Maslyn

Mason
(French) ingenious;
reliable; stonemason
Mace, Mase

Masood
(Iranian)

Massey
(English) doubly
excellent
Maccey, Masey, Massi

Massimo
(Italian) great
Masimo, Massey,
Massimmo

Mateo
(Italian) gift
Mateus
(Italian) God's gift
Mathau
(American) spunky
Mathou, Mathow,
Mathoy
Mather
(English) leader; army;
strong
Mathar
Mathias
(German) form of
Matthew; dignified
Mathies, Mathyes, Matt,
Matthias, Matty
Matias
(Spanish) gift from God
Mathias, Matios, Mattias
Matlock
(American) rancher
Lock, Mat, Matt
Matson
(Hebrew) son of
Matthew
Matsan, Matsen, Matt,
Matty
Matt
(Hebrew) short for
Matthew
Mat, Matte

Matthew
(Hebrew) God's gift
Math, Matheu, Mathieu,
Matt, Mattie, Mattsy,
Matty
Matti
(Scandinavian) form of
Matthias; God's gift
Mat, Mats
Matts
(Swedish) gift from God
Matty
(Hebrew) short for
Matthew
Mattey, Matti
Mauri
(Latin) short for
Maurice; dark
Maurice
(Latin) dark
Maur, Maurie, Maurise,
Maury, Moorice, Morice,
Morrie, Morry
Mauricio
(Italian) dark
Mari, Mauri, Maurizio
Maurizio
(Italian) dark
Marits, Miritza, Moritz,
Moritza, Moritzio
Maury
(Latin) short for
Maurice; dark
Mauree, Maurey

Maverick
(American)
unconventional
Mav, Mavarick,
Mavereck, Mavreck,
Mavvy
Mavis
(French) bird; thrush;
free
Mavas, Mavus
Max
(Latin) best
Mac, Mack, Macks,
Maxey, Maxie, Maxx,
Maxy
Maxime
(French) greatest
Max, Maxeem, Maxim
Maximilian
(Latin) most wonderful
Max, Maxemillion,
Maxie, Maxima,
Maximillion,
Maxmyllyun, Maxy
Maximino
(Spanish) maximum;
tops
Max, Maxem, Maxey,
Maxi, Maxim, Maxy
Maxinen
(Spanish) maximum
Max, Maxanen, Maxi

Maxwell
(English) full of
excellence
Maxe, Maxie, Maxwel,
Maxwill, Maxy

Mayer
(Hebrew) smart
Mayar, Maye, Mayor,
Mayur

Maynard
(English) reliable
Mayne, Maynerd

Mayo
(Irish) nature-loving
Maio, Maioh, May,
Mayes, Mayoh, Mays

Mayon
(Place name) volcano in
the Phillpplnes
May, Mayan, Mays,
Mayun

Maz
(Hebrew) aid
Maise, Maiz, Mazey,
Mazi, Mazie, Mazy

McCoy
(Irish) jaunty; coy
Coye, MacCoy

McDonald
(Scottish) open-minded
Mac-D, Macdonald

McFarlin
(Last name as first
name) son of Farlin;
confident
Far, Farr

McGowan
(Irish) feisty
Mac-G, Mcgowan

McGregor
(Irish) philanthropic
Macgregor

McKinley
(Last name as first
name) son of Kinley;
holding his own
Kin, Kinley, McKInlee

McLin
(Irish) careful
Mac, Mack

Mead
(English) outdoorsman
Meade, Meede

Meallan
(Irish) sweet
Maylan, Meall

Medford
(French) natural; comical
Med, Medfor

Meir
(Hebrew) teacher
Mayer, Myer

Mel
(Irish) short for Melvin
Mell

Melbourne
(Place name) city in
Australia; serene
Mel, Melborn, Melbourn,
Melburn, Melburne

Melburn
(English) sylvan;
outdoorsy
Mel, Melbourn,
Melburne, Milbourn,
Milburn

Meldon
(English) destined for
fame
Melden, Meldin, Meldyn

Meldric
(English) leader
Mel, Meldrik

Melecio
(Spanish) cautious
Melesio, Melezio, Mesio

Melroy
(American) form of Elroy
Mel

Melton
(English) nature; natural
Mel, Meltan

Melville
(French) mill town
Mel, Mell, Melvil, Melvill

Melvin
(English) friendly
Mel, Melvine, Melvon,
Melvyn, Milvin

Melvis
(American) form of Elvis;
songbird
Mel, Melv

Memphis
(Place name) city in
Tennessee
Memphus

Mercer
(English) affluent
Merce, Mercur, Murcer

Meredith
(Welsh) protector
Merdith, Mere,
Meredyth, Meridith,
Merrey

Merlin
(English) clever
Merl, Merlan, Merle,
Merlinn, Merlun, Murlin

Merrick
(English) bountiful
seaman
Mere, Meric, Merik,
Merrack, Merrik

Merrie
(English) giving
Merey, Meri, Merri

Merrill
(French) renowned
Mere, Merell, Merill,
Merrell, Merril, Meryll

Merritt
(Latin) worthy
Merid, Merit, Merret,
Merrid

Merv
(Irish) short for Mervin;
bold
Murv

Mervin
(Irish) bold
Merv, Merven, Mervun,
Mervy, Mervyn, Murv,
Murvin

Meshach
(Hebrew) fortunate
Meeshak, Meshack,
Meshak

Mesquite
(American) rancher;
spiny shrub
Meskeet

Meyer
(Hebrew) brilliant
Maye, Meier, Mye, Myer

Meyshaun
(African-American)
searching
Maysh, Mayshaun,
Mayshawn, Meyshawn

Michael
(Hebrew) spiritual
patron of soldiers
Mical, Michaelle, Mickey,
Mikael, Mike, Mikey,
Mikiee, Miko

Michel
(French) fond
Mich, Michelle, Mike,
Mikey

Michelangelo
(Italian) God's
angel/messenger;
artistic
Michel, Michelanjelo,
Mikalangelo, Mike,
Mikel, Mikelangelo

Michon
(French) form of Michel;
God-like
Mich, Michonn, Mish,
Mishon

Mickel
(American) form of
Michael; friend
Mick, Mikel

Mickey
(American) enthusiastic
Mick, Micki, Mickie,
Micky, Miki, Myck

Mickey-Lee
(American) friendly
Mickey Lee, Mickeylee,
Mickie-Lee

Miga
(Spanish) persona; essence

Miguel
(Spanish) form of Michael
Megel, Migel, Migelle

Miguelangel
(Spanish) angelic
Miguelanjel

Mihir
(Hindi) sunny

Mika
(Hebrew) form of Micah
Mikah, Mikie, Myka, Mykie, Myky

Mikael
(Scandinavian) warrior
Michael, Mikel, Mikkel

Mike
(Hebrew) short for Michael
Meik, Miik, Myke

Mikhail
(Russian) god-like; graceful
Mika, Mikey, Mikkail, Mykhey

Mikolas
(Greek) form of Nicholas; bright
Mick, Mickey, Mickolas, Mik, Miko, Mikolus, Miky

Milagros
(Spanish) miracle
Milagro

Milam
(Last name as first name) uncomplicated
Mylam

Milan
(Place name) city in Italy; smooth
Milano

Milburn
(Scottish) volatile
Milbyrn, Milbyrne, Millburn

Miles
(German) forgiving
Mile, Miley, Myles, Myyles

Miley
(American) reliable; forgiving
Mile, Miles, Mili, Mily, Myles, Myley

Milford
(English) from a calm (mill) setting; country
Milferd, Milfor

Millard
(Latin) old-fashioned
Milard, Mill, Millerd, Millurd, Milly

Miller
(English) practical
Mille, Myller

Mills
(English) safe
Mill, Milly, Mylls

Milo
(German) soft-hearted
Miles, Milos, Mye, Mylo

Milos
(Slavic) kind
Mile, Miles, Myle, Mylos

Milton
(English) innovative
Melton, Milt, Miltey, Miltl, Mlltle, Milty, Mylt, Mylton

Mimi
(Greek) outspoken
Mims

Miner
(Last name as first name) hard-working; miner
Mine, Miney

Mingo
(American) flirtatious
Ming-O, Myngo

Mirlam
(American) great
Mir, Mirsam, Mirtam

Misael
(Hebrew) godlike

Misha
(Russian) short for
Mikhail
Mitchell
(English) optimistic
*Mitch, Mitchel,
Mitchelle, Mitchie,
Mitchill, Mitchy, Mitshell,
Mytchil*
Modesto
(Spanish) modest
Modysto
Modred
(Greek) unafraid
Modrede, Modrid
Moe
(American) short for
names beginning with
Mo or Moe; easygoing
Mo
Moey
(Hebrew) easygoing
Moe, Moeye
Mohammad
(Arabic) praiseworthy
*Mohamad, Mohamid,
Mohamud, Muhammad*
Mohan
(Hindi) compelling
Mohana
(Sanskrit) handsome
Mohann

Mohawk
(Place name) river in
New York
Mohsen
(Austrian)
Mosen
Moises
(Hebrew) drawn from
the water
Moe
Mojave
(Place name) desert in
California; towering man
Mohave, Mohavey
Moline
(American) narrow
Moleen, Molene
Momo
(American) rascal
Monahan
(Irish) believer
*Mon, Monaghan,
Monehan, Monnahan*
Money
(American) word as
name; popular
Muney
Monico
(Spanish) form of
Monaco; player
Mon

Monroe
(Irish) delightful;
presidential
*Mon, Monro, Munro,
Munroe*
Montague
(French) forward-
thinking
*Mont, Montagew,
Montagu, Montegue,
Monty*
Montana
(Spanish) U.S. state;
sports icon
*Mont, Montane,
Montayna, Monty*
Monte
(Spanish) short for
Montgomery and
Montague; handsome
*Mont, Montee, Monti,
Monts, Monty*
Monteague
(African-American)
combo of Monty and
Teague; creative
*Mont, Montegue, Monti,
Monty*
Montgomery
(English) wealthy
*Mongomerey, Monte,
Montgomry, Monty*

Montraie
(African-American) fussy
Mont, Montray, Montraye, Monty

Montrel
(African-American) popular
Montrell, Montrelle, Monty

Montrose
(French) high-and-mighty
Mont, Montroce, Montros, Monty

Monty
(English) short for Montgomery and Montague
Monte, Montee, Montey, Monti

Moody
(American) expansive
Moodee, Moodey, Moodie

Moon
(African) dreamer

Mooney
(American) dreamer
Moon, Moonee, Moonie

Moore
(French) dark-haired
Mohr, Moores, More

Mooring
(Last name as first name) centered
Moring

Moose
(American) large guy
Moos, Mooz, Mooze

Mordecai
(Hebrew) combative
Mord, Morde, Mordekai, Morducai, Mordy

Morell
(French) secretive
More, Morelle, Morey, Morrell, Mourell, Murell

Morey
(Latin) dark
Morrie, Morry

Morgan
(Celtic) confident seaman
Morg, Morgen, Morghan

Morlen
(English) outdoorsy
Morlan, Morlie, Morly

Moroni
(Place name) city in Comoros; joyful
Maroney, Maroni, Marony, Moroney, Morony

Morris
(Latin) dark
Maurice, Moris, Morse, Mouris

Morrley
(English) outdoors-loving
More, Morlee, Morley, Morly, Morrs

Morse
(English) bright code-maker
Morce, Morcey, Morry, Morsey

Mortimer
(French) deep
Mort, Mortemer, Mortie, Morty, Mortymer

Morton
(English) sophisticated
Mort, Mortan, Mortun, Morty

Moses
(Hebrew) appointed for special things
Mosa, Mose, Mosesh, Mosie, Mozes, Mozie

Moshe
(Hebrew) special
Mosh, Moshie

Moss
(Irish) giving
Mossy

Motee
(Paskistani)

Motor
(American) word as name; speedy; active
Mote

Mottel
(Hebrew) from Max; fighter
Mozam
(Place name) from Mozambique
Moze
Mudge
(Last name as first name) friendly
Mud, Mudj
Muhammad
(Arabic) form of Mohammed; praised
Muhamed, Muhammed
Mukul
(Hindi) bird; beginnings
Mundo
(Spanish) short for Edmundo; prosperous
Mun, Mund
Mungo
(Scottish) loved; congenial
Mongo, Mongoh, Munge, Mungoh
Murcia
(Place name) region in Spain
Mursea
Murdoch
(Scottish) rich
Merdock, Merdok, Murd, Murdock, Murdok, Murdy

Murfain
(American) bold spirit
Merfaine, Murf, Murfee, Murfy, Murphy
Murff
(Irish) short for Murphy; feisty
Merf, Murf
Murl
(English) nature-lover; sea
Murphy
(Irish) fighter
Merph, Merphy, Murfie, Murph
Murray
(Scottish) sea-loving; sailor
Mur, Muray, Murrey, Murry
Murrell
(English) nature-lover; sea
Mycheal
(African-American) devoted
Mysheal
Myles
(German) form of Miles
Mylos
(Slavic) kind
Milos

Myrle
(American) able
Merl, Merle, Myrie, Myryee
Myron
(Greek) notable
Mi, Miron, My, Myrayn
Myrzon
(American) humorous
Merzon, Myrs, Myrz

Nabil
(Arabic) of noble birth;
honored
Nabeel, Nobila

Nada
(Arabic) morning dew;
giver
Nadah

Nadir
(Arabic) rare man

Nahir
(Hebrew) light
Nahor

Nando
(Spanish) short for
Fernando

Nanson
(American) spunky
*Nance, Nanse, Nansen,
Nansson*

Napoleon
(German) lion of Naples;
domineering
*Nap, Napo, Napoleone,
Napolion, Napolleon,
Nappy*

Narciso
(Spanish) form of Greek
Narcissus, who fell in
love with his reflection;
vain
Narcis

Narcissus
(Greek) self-loving; vain
*Narciss, Narcissah,
Narcisse, Nars*

Nasario
(Spanish) dedicated to
God
*Nasar, Nasareo,
Nassario, Nazareo,
Nazarlo, Nazaro, Nazor*

Nash
(Last name as first
name) exciting
Nashe, Nashey

Nasser
(Arabic) winning
*Nasir, Nassar, Nasse,
Nassee, Nassor*

Nat
(Hebrew) short for
Nathaniel
Natt, Natte, Nattie, Natty

Nate
(Hebrew) short for
Nathan and Nathaniel
Natey

Natividad
(Spanish) a child born at
Christmastime

Nathan
(Hebrew) short for
Nathaniel;
magnanimous
*Nat, Nate, Nathen,
Nathin, Natthaen,
Natthan, Natthen, Natty*

Nathaniel
(Hebrew) God's gift to
mankind
*Nat, Nate, Nathan,
Nathaneal, Nathanial,
Nathe, Nathenial*

Nation
(American) patriotic

Nato
(American) gentle
Nate, Natoe, Natoh

Navarro
(Spanish) place name;
wild spirit
*Navaro, Navarroh,
Naverro*

Neal
(Irish) winner
*Nealey, Neall, Nealy,
Neel, Neelee, Neely, Nele*

Neander
(Greek) from
Neanderthal
Ander, Nean, Neand

Nebraska
(Place name) U.S. state
Neb

Ned
(English) short for
Edward; comforting
Neddee, Neddie, Neddy

Nedrun
(American) difficult
*Ned, Nedd, Neddy,
Nedran, Nedro*

Neely
(Scottish) winning
Neel, Neels

Nehemiah
(Hebrew) compassionate
Nehemyah, Nemo

Nellie
(English) short for
Nelson; singing
*Nell, Nellee, Nelli, Nells,
Nelly*

Nelson
(English) broad-minded
*Nell, Nels, Nelsen,
Nelsun, Nilsson*

Neptune
(Latin) god of the sea
*Neptoon, Neptoone,
Neptunne*

Nero
(Latin) unyielding
Neroh

Nery
(Spanish) daring
*Neree, Nerey, Nerrie,
Nerry*

Nesto
(Greek) adventurer
Nestoh, Nestoro

Nestor
(Greek) wanderer
*Nest, Nester, Nestir,
Nesto, Nesty*

Netar
(African-American)
bright
Netardas

Netzer
(American) form of
Nestor
Net

Nevada
(Place name) U.S. state
Nev, Nevadah

Neville
(French) innovator
*Nev, Nevil, Nevile,
Nevvy, Niville*

Newbie
(American) novice
New, Newb

Newell
(English) fresh face in
the hall
*New, Newall, Newel,
Newy, Nywell*

Newlin
(Welsh) able; new pond
Newl, Newlynn, Nule

Newman
(English) attractive
young man
*Neuman, New,
Newmann*

Newt
(English) new

Newton
(English) bright; new
mind
New, Newt

Neyman
(American) son of Ney;
bookish
Ney, Neymann, Neysa

Nicah
(Greek) victorious
Nik, Nike

Nicholas
(Greek) winner; the
people's victor
*Nichelas, Nicholus, Nick,
Nickee, Nickie, Nicklus,
Nickolas, Nicky, Nikolas,
Nyck, Nykolas*

Nichols
(English) kind-hearted
Nicholes, Nick, Nicky,
Nikols

Nick
(English) short for
Nicholas
Nic, Nik

Nicklaus
(Greek) form of Nicholas
Nicklaws, Niklus

Nicky
(Greek) short for
Nicholas
Nick, Nickee, Nickey,
Nicki, Nik, Nikee, Nikki

Nico
(Italian) victor

Nicolas
(Italian) form of
Nicholas; victorious
Nic, Nico, Nicolus

Niels
(Scandinavian)
victorious
Neels

Nigel
(English) champion
Nigie, Nigil, Nygelle

Nike
(Greek) winning
Nykee, Nykie, Nyke

Nikita
(Russian) not yet won
Nika

Niklas
(Scandinavian) winner
Niklaas, Nils, Klaas

Nikolai
(Russian) winning
Nika

Nikolas
(Greek) form of Nicholas
Nik, Nike, Niko, Nikos,
Nyloas

Nikos
(Greek) victor
Nicos, Niko, Nikolos

Niles
(English) smooth
Ni, Nile, Niley, Nyles,
Nyley

Nimrod
(Hebrew) renegade
Nimrodd, Nymrod

Nino
(Spanish) child; young
boy

Ninyun
(American) spirited
Ninian, Ninion, Ninyan,
Nynyun

Nissan
(Hebrew) omen
Nisan, Nissyn

Niven
(Last name as first
name) smooth

Nix
(American) negative
Nicks, Nixy

Nixon
(English) audacious
Nickson, Nixen, Nixun

Noah
(Hebrew) peacemaker
Noa, Noe, Nouh

Noam
(Hebrew) sweet man
Noahm, Noe

Noble
(Latin) regal
Nobe, Nobee, Nobel,
Nobie, Noby

Noe
(Spanish) quiet;
(Polish) comforter
Noeh, Noey

Noel
(French) born on
Christmas
Noelle, Noelly, Nole,
Nollie

Noey
(Spanish) form of Noah;
he who wanders
Noe, Noie

Nolan
(Irish) outstanding;
noble
*Nole, Nolen, Nolline,
Nolun, Nolyn*

Nolden
(American) noble
Nold

Nolly
(Scandinavian) hopeful
*Nole, Noli, Noll, Nolley,
Nolleye, Nolli, Nollie*

Norb
(Scandinavian)
innovative
*Noberto, Norbie, Norbs,
Norby*

Norbert
(German) bright north
Norb, Norbie, Norby

Nordin
(Nordic) handsome
*Nord, Nordan, Norde,
Nordee, Nordeen, Nordi,
Nordun, Nordy*

Norman
(English) sincere; man of
the North
*Norm, Normen, Normey,
Normi, Normie, Normon,
Normun, Normy*

Norshawn
(African-American)
combo of Nor and
Shawn
*Norrs, Norrshawn,
Norshaun*

North
(American) directional
Norf, Northe

Norton
(English) dignified man
of the North
Nort, Nortan, Norten

Norval
(English) from the North
Norvan

Norville
(French) resident of a
northern village; warm-
hearted
*Norvel, Norvil, Norvill,
Norvyl*

Norshell
(African-American) brash
Norshel, Norshelle

Norwin
(English) friendly
*Norvin, Norwen,
Norwind, Norwinn*

Nowell
(Last name as first
name) dependable
Nowe

Nowey
(American) knowing
Nowee, Nowie

Nueces
(Place name) Nueces
River

Nuell
(American) form of
Newell (last name); in
charge
Nuel

Nuey
(Spanish) short for
Nueva
Nui, Nuie

Nunry
(Last name as first
name) giving
Nunri

Nuys
(Place name) from Van
Nuys, California
Nies, Nyes, Nys

Nye
(Welsh) focused
Ni, Nie, Nyee

Nyle
(American) form of
Niles/Nile; smooth
Nyl, Nyles

Oak
(English) sturdy
Oake, Oakie

Oakley
(English) sturdy; strong
Oak, Oakie, Oakly, Oklie

Obadiah
(Hebrew) serving God
Obadyah, Obediah, Obee, Obie, Oby

Obbie
(Biblical) from Biblical prophet Obadiah; serving God
Obey, Obi, Obie

Obedience
(American) strict
Obie

Oberon
(German) strong-bearing
Obaron, Oberahn, Oberone, Oburon

Obey
(American) short for Obadiah
Obe, Obee, Obie, Oby

Ocean
(Greek) ocean; child born under a water sign
Oceane

Ocie
(Greek) short for Ocean
Osie

Octavio
(Latin) eight; able
Octavioh

Ode
(Greek) poetry as a name; poetic
Odee, Odie

Odell
(American) musical
Dell, Odall, Ode, Odey, Odyll

Oder
(Place name) river in Europe
Ode

Odin
(Scandinavian) Norse god of magic; soulful
Odan, Oden

Odisoose
(Invented) form of Odysseus
Ode

Odysseus
(Greek) wanderer
Ode, Odey, Odie

Ogdon
(English) literate
Og, Ogdan, Ogden

Ogle
(American) word as name; leer; stare
Ogal, Ogel, Ogll, Ogul

Ojay
(American) brash
O.J., Oojai

Okan
(Turkish)
Oke

Okie
(American) man from Oklahoma
Okey, Okeydokey

Olaf
(Scandinavian) watchful
Olay, Ole, Olef, Olev, Oluf

Olajuwon
(Arabic) honorable
Olajuwan, Olujuwon

Olan
(Scandinavian) royal ancestor
Olin, Ollee

Olav
(Scandinavian) traditional
Ola, Olov, Oluf

Ole
(Scandinavian) watchful
Olay

Oleg
(Russian) holy; religious
Olag, Ole, Olig

Oliver
(Latin) loving nature
Olaver, Olive, Ollie, Olliver, Olly, Oluvor

Olivier
(French) eloquent
Oliveay

Ollie
(English) short for Oliver
Olie, Ollee, Olley, Olly

Omaha
(Place name) city in Nebraska

Omar
(Arabic) spiritual
Omahr, Omarr

Omie
(Italian) homebody
Omey, Omi, Omye

Onesimo
(Spanish) number one
Onie

Onofrio
(German) smart
Ono, Onofreeo, Onofrioh

Oo
(Korean)

Oren
(Hebrew) from Owen; sturdy (tree)

Orenthiel
(American) sturdy as a pine
Ore, Oren

Orenthiem
(American) sturdy as a pine
Orenth, Orenthe

Orestes
(Greek) leader
Oresta, Oreste, Restie, Resty

Oriol
(Spanish) best
Orioll

Orion
(Greek) fiery hunter
Oreon, Ori, Orie, Ory

Orlando
(Spanish) famed; distinctive
Orl, Orland, Orlie, Orlondo, Orly

Orme
(English) kind
Orm

Ormond
(English) kind-hearted
Ormand, Ormande, Orme, Ormon, Ormonde, Ormund, Ormunde

Orran
(Irish) green-eyed
Ore, Oren, Orin

Orrick
(English) sturdy as an oak
Oric, Orick, Orreck, Orrik

Orrie
(American) short for Orson; solid
Orry

Orson
(Latin) strong as a bear
Orsan, Orsen, Orsey, Orsun

Orth
(English) honest
Orthe

Orval
(American) form of Orville; bold
Orvale

Orville
(French) brave
Orv, Orvelle, Orvie, Orvil

Orway
(American) kind
Orwaye

Osborne
(English) strong-spirited
Osborn, Osbourne, Osburn, Osburne, Ossie, Oz, Ozzie, Ozzy

Osburt
(English) smart
Osbart, Osbert, Ozbert, Ozburt

Oscar
(Scandinavian) divine
Ozkar

Oscard
(Greek) fighter
Oscar, Oskard

Osgood
(English) good man
Osgude, Ozgood

Osiel
(Spanish)

Oslo
(Place name) capital of
Norway
Os, Oz

Osman
(Spanish) verbose
*Os, Osmen, Osmin,
Ossie, Oz, Ozzie*

Osmond
(English) singing to the
world
*Os, Osmonde, Osmund,
Ossie, Oz, Ozzy*

Osrec
(Scandinavian) leader
Os, Ossie

Ossie
(Hebrew) powerful
Os, Oz, Ozzy

Osvaldo
(German) divine power
Osvald, Oswaldo

Oswald
(English) divine power
*Oswalde, Oswold,
Oswuld, Oszie, Oz*

Othell
(African-American)
thriving
Oth, Othey, Otho

Othello
(Spanish) bold
Otello, Othell

Otis
(Greek) intuitive
*Oates, Odis, Otes, Ottes,
Ottis*

Otoniel
(Spanish) fashionable
Otonel

Otto
(German) wealthy
Oto, Ott, Ottoh

Ottway
(German) fortunate
Otwae, Otway

Overton
(Last name as first
name) leader
Ove, Overten

Ovidlo
(Spanish) from Ovid
(Roman poet); creative
Ovido

Owen
(Welsh) well-born; high-
principled
Owan, Owin, Owwen

Ox
(American) animal;
strong
Oxy

Oxford
(English) scholar; ox
crossing
Fordy, Oxferd, Oxfor

Oz
(Hebrew) courageous;
unusual

Ozell
(English) strong
Ozel

Oziel
(Spanish) strong

Ozzie
(English) short for
Oswald
Oz, Ozzee, Ozzey, Ozzy

Pablo
(Spanish) strong;
creative
Pabel, Pabo, Paublo
Packer
(Last name as first
name) orderly
Pack
Paco
(Spanish) energetic
*Pak, Pakkoh, Pako,
Paquito*
Paddy
(Irish) short for Patrick;
noble; comfortable
*Paddey, Paddi, Paddie,
Padee*
Page
(French) helpful
Pagey, Paige, Payg
Pago
(Place name) Pago Pago
Pay

Palladin
(Greek) confrontational;
wise
*Palidin, Palladyn,
Palleden, Pallie, Pally*
Palmer
(English) open
*Pallmar, Pallmer, Palmar,
Palmur*
Pampa
(Place name) city in
Texas
Pan
(Greek mythology) god
of forest and shepherds
Pann
Panama
(Place name) canal
connecting North and
South America; rounder
Pan
Pancho
(Spanish) short for
Francisco; jaunty
Panchoh, Ponchito
Pantaleon
(Spanish) pants;
trousers; manly
Pant, Pantalon
Paolo
(Italian) form of Paul;
small and high-energy
Paoloh, Paulo

Paquito
(Spanish) dear Paco
Paris
(English) lover; France's
capital
Pare, Paree, Parris
Park
(English) calming
Parke, Parkey, Parks
Parker
(English) manager
Park, Parks
Parnell
(French) ribald
Parne, Parnel, Parnelle
Parnelli
(Italian) frisky
Parnell
Paros
(Place name) Greek
island; charming
Par, Paro
Parr
(English) protective
Par, Parre
Parrish
(French) separate and
unique; district
Parry
(Welsh) young son
Parrie, Pary

Parryth
(American)
up-and-coming
Pareth, Parre, Parry,
Parythe

Pascal
(French) boy born on
Easter or Passover;
spiritual
Pascalle, Paschal,
Paskalle, Pasky

Pasquale
(Italian) spiritual
Pask, Paskwoll, Pasq,
Pasquell, Posquel

Pastor
(English) clergyman
Pastar, Paster

Pat
(English) short for
Patrick; noble
Pattey, Patti, Patty,
Pattye, Pattee

Patrick
(Irish) aristocrat
Paddy, Patric, Patrik,
Patriquek, Patryk, Pats,
Patsy

Patriot
(American) patriotic

Patterson
(English) intellectual
Paterson, Pattersen,
Pattersun, Pattersund

Patton
(English) brash warrior
Patten, Pattun, Patun,
Peyton

Paul
(Latin) small; wise
Pauley, Paulie, Pauly

Pauli
(Italian) dear Paul
Paulee, Pauley, Paulie,
Pauly

Paulo
(Spanish) form of Paul

Paulos
(Greek) small

Paulus
(Latin) small
Paul, Paulie, Paulis,
Pauly

Pavel
(Russian) inspired
Pasha

Pawel
(Polish) believer
Pawl

Pax
(Latin) peace-loving
Paks, Paxy

Payne
(Latin) countryman
Paine, Payn

Payton
(English) soldier's town
Pate, Payten, Paytun,
Peyton

Peader
(Scottish) rock or stone;
reliable
Peder, Peter

Pearson
(English) dark-eyed
Pearse, Pearsen,
Pearsun, Peerson

Pecos
(Place name) Pecos
River in Texas; cowboy
Peck, Pekos

Pedro
(Spanish) audacious
Pedra, Pedrin, Pedroh

Pelly
(English) happy
Peli, Pelley, Pelli

Pelon
(Spanish) joyful

Pembroke
(French) sophisticated
Brookie, Pemb,
Pembrooke, Pimbroke

Penn
(German) strong-willed
Pen, Pennee, Penney,
Pennie, Penny

Pepin
(German) ardent
Pepen, Pepi, Pepp,
Peppi, Peppy, Pepun

Pepper
(Botanical) livewire
Pep, Pepp, Peppy

Per
(Scandinavian) secretive

Percival
(French) mysterious
Parsival, Percey, Percy, Perseval, Purcival, Purcy

Percy
(French) short for Percival
Percee, Percey, Perci, Percie

Perfecto
(Spanish) perfect
Perfek

Pericles
(Greek) fair leader
Periklees, Perry

Perine
(Latin) adventurer
Perrin, Perrine, Perry, Peryne

Perk
(American) perky
Perkey, Perki, Perky

Perkins
(English) political
Perk, Perkens, Perkey

Peron
(Spanish)

Perry
(English) tough-minded
Parry, Perr, Perrey, Perri, Perrie

Perryman
(Last name as first name) nature-lover
Perry

Perth
(Place name) capital of Western Australia
Purth

Perun
(Hindi) from the name Perunkulam

Pete
(English) easygoing
Petey, Petie

Peter
(Greek) dependable; rock
Per, Petar, Pete, Petee, Petey, Petie, Petur

Petra
(Place name) city in Arabia; dashing

Peyton
(English) form of Payton
Pey, Peyt

Pharis
(Irish) heroic
Farres, Farrus, Pharris

Phelps
(English) droll
Felps, Filps

Phex
(American) kind
Fex

Phil
(Greek) short for Phillip
Fill, Phill

Philander
(Greek) lover of many; infidel
Filander, Phil, Philandyr

Philemon
(Greek) kisser
Filemon, Philamon

Philip
(Greek) outdoorsman; horse-lover
Felipe, Filipp, Flippo, Phil, Phillie, Phillippe, Philly

Philippe
(French) form of Philip
Felipe, Filippe, Philipe

Philo
(Greek) lover
Filo

Phineas
(English) far-sighted
Fineas, Finny, Pheneas, Phineus, Phinny

Phoenix
(Greek) bird of
immortality; everlasting
Fee, Feenix, Fenix, Nix

Pierce
(English) insightful;
piercing
*Pearce, Peerce, Peers,
Peersey, Percy, Piercy,
Piers*

Pierre
(French) socially adroit
Piere

Pietro
(Italian) reliable
Pete

Pilar
(Spanish) basic
Pilarr

Pin
(Vietnamese) joyful

Pincus
(American) dark
Pinchas, Pinchus, Pinkus

Pinechas
(Hebrew) form of Paul;
dark

Piney
(American) living among
pines; comfortable
Pine, Pyney

Pinkston
(Last name as first
name) different
Pink, Pinky

Pio
(Italian) pious

Pip
(German) ingenious
*Pipp, Pippin, Pippo,
Pippy*

Pitch
(American) word as
name; musical

Pitt
(English) swerving
dramatically

Pittman
(English) blue-collar
worker

Placid
(Latin) calm
Plasid

Placido
(Italian) serene songster
*Placeedo, Placidoh,
Placydo*

Plato
(Greek) broad-minded
Plata, Platoh

Playtoh
(Invented) form of Plato

Plutarco
(Greek) nefarious

Pluto
(Greek) universal

Poet
(American) writer
Poe

Pollard
(German) close-minded
Pollar, Pollerd, Polley

Polo
(Greek) adventurer
Poloe, Poloh

Ponce
(Spanish) fifth; wanderer
Poncey, Ponse

Ponnuswamy
(Hindl)

Pontius
(Latin) the fifth

Pony
(Scottish) dashing
Poney, Ponie

Poogie
(American) snuggly
*Poog, Poogee, Poogi,
Poogs, Pookie*

Poole
(Place name) area in
England
Pool

Pope
(Greek) father
Po

Porter
(Latin) decisive
Poart, Port, Portur, Porty
Powder
(American) cowboy
Powd, Powe
Powell
(English) ready
Prairie
(American) rural man or
rancher
*Prair, Prairey, Prairi,
Prairy*
Preemoh
(Invented) form of Primo
Prentice
(English) learning
*Prenticce, Prentis,
Prentiss, Printiss*
Presley
(English) songbird;
meadow of the priest
Preslee, Preslie, Presly
Preston
(English) spiritual
Prestyn
Price
(Welsh) vigorous
Pricey, Pryce
Priestley
(English) cottage of
the priest
*Priestlea, Priestlee,
Priestly*

Primerica
(American) form of
America; patriotic
Prime
Primitivo
(Spanish) primitive
Primi, Tito, Tivo
Primo
(Italian) topnotch
*Preemo, Primoh,
Prymo*
Prince
(Latin) regal leader
*Preenz, Prins, Prinz,
Prinze*
Prop
(American) word as
name; fun-loving
Propp
Prosper
(Italian) having good
fortune
Pros
Pryor
(Latin) spiritual director
Pry, Prye
Purvin
(English) helpful
Pervin
Purvis
(French) provider
Pervis, Purviss

Putnam
(English) fond of water
*Puddy, Putnum, Puttie,
Putty*

Quaddus
(African-American)
bright

Quannell
(African-American)
strong-willed
*Kwan, Kwanell,
Kwanelle, Quan,
Quanelle, Quannel*

Quaronne
(African-American)
haughty
*Kwarohn, Kwaronne,
Quaronn*

Quashawn
(African-American)
tenacious
*Kwashan, Kwashaun,
Kwashawn, Quasha,
Quashie, Quashy*

Quenby
(English) giving
*Quenbee, Quenbie,
Quenbey*

Quentin
(Latin) fifth
*Kwent, Quent, Quenton,
Quint, Quintin, Quinton,
Qwent, Qwentin,
Qwenton*

Quick
(American) fast;
remarkable

Quiessencia
(Spanish) essential;
essence
Quiess, Quiessence

Quigley
(Irish) loving nature
Quiglee, Quiggly, Quiggy

Quincy
(French) fifth; patient
*Quensie, Quincee,
Quinci, Quincie*

Quinn
(Irish) short for Quinton;
bright
*Kwen, Kwene, Quenn,
Quin*

Quintavius
(African-American) fifth
child
Quint

Quintin
(Latin) planner
Quenten, Quint, Quinton

Quintus
(Spanish) fifth child
Quin, Quinn, Quint

Quiqui
(Spanish) friend; short
for Enrique
Kaka, Keke

Quito
(Spanish) lively
Kito

Quoitrel
(African-American)
equalizer
Kwotrel, Quoitrelle

Quon
(Chinese) bright; light

Rabbit
(Literature) character in
Rabbit Run; fast
Rab

Rad
(Scandinavian) helpful;
confident
Radd

Raddy
(Slavic) cheerful
*Rad, Radde, Raddie,
Radey*

Radford
(English) helpful
*Rad, Raddey, Raddie,
Raddy, Radferd*

Radimir
(Polish) joyful

Radley
(English) sways with the
wind
Radlea, Radlee, Radleigh

Rady
(Filipino)

Raekwon
(African-American)
proud
Raykwonn

Rael
(African)

Rafael
(Hebrew, Spanish)
renewed
*Rafaelle, Rafayel,
Rafayelle, Rafe, Raphael,
Raphaele*

Rafe
(Irish) tough
Raff, Raffe, Raif

Rafferty
(Irish) wealthy
*Rafarty, Rafe, Raff,
Raferty, Raffarty,
Raffertie, Raffety*

Rafi
(Arabic) musical; friend
Rafee, Raffy

Raheem
(Arabic) having empathy
Rahim

Rahman
(Arabic) full of
compassion
Raman, Rahmahn

Rahn
(American) form of Ron;
kind
*Rahnney, Rahnnie,
Rahnny*

Rain
(English) helpful; smart
*Raine, Rainey, Rainey,
Raini, Rains, Raney,
Rayne*

Rainer
(German) advisor
Rainor, Rayner, Raynor

Rainey
(German) generous
*Rain, Raine, Raney,
Raynie*

Rainier
(Place name)
distinguished

Raj
(Sanskrit) with stripes
Rajiv

Rajab
(Arabic) glorified

Rajoseph
(American) combo of
Ra and Joseph
Raejoseph

Rakesh
(Hindi) king

Raleigh
(English) jovial
*Ralea, Ralee, Raleighe,
Rawlee, Rawley, Rawlie*

Ralf
(American) form of Ralph
Raulf

Ralph
(English) advisor to all
Ralf, Ralphie, Ralphy,
Raulf, Rolf

Ralphie
(English) form of Ralph
Ralphee, Ralphi

Ram
(Sanskrit) compelling;
pleasant
Ramm

Rambo
(Movie name) daring;
action-oriented
Ram

Ramiro
(Spanish) all-knowing
judge
Rameero, Ramero,
Ramey, Rami

Ramone
(Spanish) wise
advocate; romantic
Ramond, Raymond,
Romon

Ramp
(American) word as
name; hyper
Ram, Rams

Rams
(English) form of
Ramsey; boisterous;
strong
Ramm, Ramz

Ramsey
(English) savvy
Rams, Ramsay, Ramsy,
Ramz, Ramzee, Ramzy

Rance
(American) renegade
Rans, Ranse

Rancye
(American) form of
Rance
Rancel, Rancy

Rand
(Place name) ridge of
gold-bearing rock in
South Africa

Randal
(English) secretive
Randahl, Randel,
Randey, Randull, Randy

Randolph
(English) protective
Rand, Randolf,
Randolphe, Randy

Randy
(English) short for
Randall or Randolph
Randee, Randey, Randi,
Randie

Rangarajan
(Hindi) charming

Ranger
(French) vigilant
Rainge, Range, Rangur

Rani
(Hebrew) joyful
Ran, Ranie, Rannie

Rank
(American) word as
name
Ran

Ransom
(Latin) wealthy
Rance, Ranse, Ransome,
Ransum, Ransym

Raoul
(Spanish) confidant
Raul, Raulio

Raphael
(Hebrew) archangel in
the Bible; painter
Rafael, Rafe, Rapfaele

Rashad
(Arabic) wise
Rachad, Rashaud,
Rashid, Rashod, Roshad

Rasheed
(Arabic) intelligent

Rashid
(Arabic) focused

Rasputin
(Russian) a Russian
mystic
Rasp

Raudel
(African-American)
rowdy
Raudell, Rowdel

Raul
(French) sensual
Rauly, Rawl

Raven
(American) bird; dark and mysterious
Rave, Ravey, Ravy, Rayven

Ravi
(Hindi) sun god
Ravee

Rawle
(French) form of Raul; sensitive

Rawleigh
(American) form of Raleigh
Rawlee, Rawli

Ray
(French) royal; king
Rae, Raye, Rayray

Rayce
(American) form of Raymond; advisor
Rays, Rayse

Rayfield
(English) woodsy; capable
Rafe, Ray, Rayfe

Raymond
(English) strong
Ramand, Ramond, Ray, Raymie, Raymonde, Raymun, Raymund, Raymy

Raymont
(American) combo of Ray and Mont; distinguished
Raemon, Raymon, Raymonte

Raynaldo
(Spanish) form of Renaldo; innovative
Ray, Rayni, Raynie, Raynoldo

Raynard
(French) judge; sly
Ray, Raynaud, Renard, Renaud, Rey, Reynard, Reynaud

Rayner
(French) form of Raymond; counselor
Ray, Rayne

Rayshan
(African-American) inventive
Ray, Raysh, Raysha, Rayshun

Rayshawn
(African-American) combo of Ray and Shawn
Raeshaun, Rayshaun, Rayshie, Rayshy

Reace, Rhys
(Welsh) passionate
Reece, Rees, Rees, Reese

Read
(English) red-haired
Reade, Reed, Reid

Reagan
(Irish) kingly
Ragan, Raghan, Reagen, Reegan, Regan

Reaner
(Last name as first name) even-tempered
Rean, Rener

Rebel
(American) outlaw
Reb, Rebbe, Rebele

Red
(English) man with red hair
Redd, Reddy

Redford
(English) handsome man with ruddy skin
Readford, Red, Reddy, Redferd, Redfor

Redmon
(German) protective
Redd, Reddy, Redmond, Redmun, Redmund

Reece
(Welsh) vivacious
Rees, Reese, Reez

Reed
(English) red-haired
Read, Reede, Reid

Rees
(Welsh) form of the
name Rhys; ardor
Reece, Reese, Reez, Rez

Reese
(Welsh) vivacious
Reis, Rhys

Reeves
(English) giving
Reave, Reaves, Reeve

Regal
(American) debonair
Regall

Regent
(Latin) word as name;
royal; grand

Reggie
(English) short for
Reginald; wise advisor
*Reg, Reggey, Reggi,
Reggye*

Reginald
(English) wise advisor
*Reg, Reggie, Reginal,
Regineld*

Regine
(French) artistic
Regeen

Regis
(Latin) king; gilded
talker
Reggis

Reid
(English) red-haired
Reide

Reilly
(Irish) daring
Rilee, Riley, Rilie

Reinhart
(German) brave-hearted
*Reinhar, Reinhardt,
Rhinehard, Rhinehart*

Remi
(French) fun-loving
*Remee, Remey, Remmy,
Remy*

Remington
(Last name as first
name) intellectual
Rem, Remmy

Remuda
(Spanish) herd of
horses, or changing
horses (a relay); rancher
Rem, Remmie, Remmy

Remus
(Latin) fast
*Reemus, Remes,
Remous*

Renard
(French) smart
Renardt

Renato
(Italian) born again
Renata, Renate

Renaud
(English) powerful
Renny

René
(French) born again
*Renee, Rennie, Renny,
Re-Re*

Renfro
(Welsh) calm
*Renfroe, Renfrow,
Renphro, Rinfro*

Renny
(French) able
Renney, Renni, Rennye

Reno
(Place name)
Reen, Reenie, Renoh

ReShard
(African-American)
rough
Reshar, Reshard

Resugio
(Spanish) form of
Refugio
Resuge

Rett
(Literature) form of
Rhett, from *Gone With
the Wind*
Rhett

Reuben
(Hebrew) religious;
(Spanish) creative
*Rube, Rubey, Rubie,
Rubin, Ruby, Rubyn*

Rev
(Invented) ramped up
Revv

Revin
(American) distinctive
Revan, Revinn, Revun

Rex
(Latin) kingly
Rexe

Rexford
(American) form of Rex;
noble
*Rex, Rexferd, Rexfor,
Rexy*

Rey
(Spanish) short for
Reynaldo
Ray, Reye, Reyes

Reynard
(French) brilliant
*Raynard, Rayne,
Renardo*

Reynold
(English) knowledgeable
tutor
*Ranald, Ranold, Reinold,
Renald, Renalde, Rey,
Reye, Reynolds*

Reza
(Iranian) content

Rhene
(American) smiley
Reen, Rheen

Rhett
(American) romantic
Rhet, Rhette

Rhodes
(Greek) lovely
Rhoades, Rodes

Rhodree
(Welsh) ruler
Rodree, Rodrey, Rodry

Rhyon
(American) form of Ryan
Rhyan, Rhyen

Ricardo
(Spanish) snappy
*Recardo, Ric, Riccardo,
Ricky*

Rice
(English) rich
Ryes

Rich
(English) affluent
Richie, Ritchie

Richard
(English) wealthy leader
*Rich, Richerd, Richey,
Richi, Richie, Rickie,
Ricky, Ritchie*

Richardean
(American) combo of
Richard and Dean;
unusual
*Richard Dean, Richard-
Dean, Richardene*

Richey
(German) ruler
*Rich, Richee, Richie,
Ritch, Ritchee, Ritchee,
Ritchey*

Richie
(English) short for
Richard
*Richey, Richi, Ritchey,
Ritchie*

Richmond
(German) rich and
protective
*Rich, Richie, Richmon,
Richmun, Ricky,
Ritchmun*

Richter
(Last name as first
name) hopeful
Rick, Ricky, Rik, Rikter

Rick
(German) short for
Richard; friendly
*Ric, Rickey, Ricki, Rickie,
Ricky, Rik*

Rico
(Italian) spirited; ruler
*Reco, Reko, Ricko,
Rikko, Riko*

Ricotoro
(Spanish) combo of Rico
and Toro; brave bull
*Ricky, Rico-Toro,
Rikotoro, Toro*

Ridge
(English) on the ridge;
risk-taker

Ridley
(English) ingenious
Redley, Rid, Ridley, Ridlie, Ridly, Rydley

Rigby
(English) high-energy
Rigbie, Rigbye, Rygby

Rigoberto
(Spanish) strong
Bert, Berto, Rigo

Rike
(American) form of Nike; high-spirited
Rikee, Rykee, Rykie, Ryky

Rilee
(American) form of Riley
Rilea, Rileigh

Rileigh
(American) form of Riley
Ryleigh

Riley
(Irish) brave
Reilly, Rylee, Ryley, Rylie, Ryly

Ringo
(English) funny
Ring, Ringgoh, Ryngo

Rio
(Spanish) water-loving
Reeo

Rione
(Spanish) flowing
Reo, Reone, Rio

Rio Grande
(Spanish) a river in Texas
Rio, Riogrande

Rip
(English) serene
Ripp, Rippe

Ripley
(English) serene
Riplee

Ris
(English) outdoorsman; smart
Rislea, Rislee, Risleigh, Riz, Rizlee

Risley
(English) smart and quiet
Rislee, Risleye, Rizlee, Rizley

Ritch
(American) leader
Rich, Richee, Richey, Ritch, Ritchal, Ritchee, Ritchi

Ritchie
(English) form of Richie
Ritchee, Ritchey, Ritchy

Rito
(American) spunky
Reit

Ritt
(German) debonair
Rit, Rittie, Rittly

Ritter
(German) debonair
Riter, Rittyr

River
(Place name) hip
Riv, Ryver

Roam
(American) wanderer
Roamey, Roamy, Roma, Rome

Roarke
(Irish) ruler
Roark, Rork, Rourke

Rob
(English) short for Robert; smart
Robb

Robbie
(English) short for Robert; smart
Robbee, Robbey, Robbi, Robby

Robert
(English) brilliant; renowned
Bob, Bobbie, Bobby, Rob, Robart, Robbie, Robby, Roberto, Robs, Roburt

Roberto
(Spanish) form of Robert; bright and famous
Berto, Rob, Robert, Tito

Roberts
(Last name as first name) luminous
Rob, Robards, Robarts, Roburts

Robert-Lee
(American) patriotic
Bobbylee, Robby Lee, Robert Lee, Robert-E-Lee, Robertlee

Robeson
(English) Rob's son; bright
Roberson, Robison

Robin
(English) gregarious
Robb, Robbin, Robby, Robyn

Roble
(Last name as first name) divine
Robel, Robl, Robley

Robson
(English) sterling character
Robb, Robbson, Robsen

Rocco
(Italian) tough
Roc, Rock, Rockie, Rocko, Rocky, Rok, Rokee, Rokko, Roko

Rochester
(English) guarded
Roche

Rock
(American) hardy
Roc, Rocky, Rok

Rocket
(American) word as a name; snappy
Rokket

Rockleigh
(English) dependable; outdoorsy
Rocco, Rock, Rocklee, Rockley, Rocky, Roklee

Rockwell
(American) spring of strength
Rock, Rockwelle, Rocky

Rocky
(English) hardy; tough
Rocco, Rock, Rockee, Rockey, Rocki, Rockie

Rod
(English) brash
Rodd, Roddy

Rodas
(Spanish) Spanish name for the Rhone River in France
Rod, Roda

Roddy
(German) short for Roderick; effective
Roddee, Roddi, Roddie

Rodel
(American) generous
Rodell, Rodey, Rodie

Rodeo
(Spanish) roundup; cowboy
Rodayo, Roddy, Rodyo

Roderick
(German) effective leader
Roddy, Roddyrke, Roderic, Roderik, Rodreck, Rodrick, Rodrik

Rodger
(German) form of Roger
Rodge, Roge

Rodman
(German) hero
Rodmin, Rodmun

Rodney
(English) open-minded
Rod, Roddy, Rodnee, Rodni, Rodnie

Rodolfo
(Spanish) spark
Rod, Rudolfo, Rudolpho

Rodree
(American) leader
Rodrey, Rodri, Rodry

Rodrigo
(Spanish) feisty leader
Rod, Roddy, Rodrego, Rodriko

Rodriguez
(Spanish) hot-blooded
Rod, Roddy, Rodreguez,
Rodrigues

Roe
(English) deer

Rogelio
(Spanish) aggressive
Rojel, Rojelio

Roger
(German) famed warrior
Rodge, Rodger, Roge,
Rogie, Rogyer

Roi
(French) form of Roy

Roland
(German) renowned
Rolend, Rollan, Rolland,
Rollie, Rollo, Rolund

Rolando
(Spanish) famous
Rolan

Role
(American) word as
name; brash
Roel, Roll

Rolf
(German) kind advisor
Rolfee, Rolfie, Rolfy,
Rolph

Rollie
(English) short for
Roland
Rollee, Rolley, Rolli,
Rolly

Rollins
(German) form of
Roland; dignified
Rolin, Rolins, Rollin,
Rolyn

Roman
(Latin) fun-loving
Romen, Romey, Romi,
Romun, Romy

Rome
(Place name)
Romeo

Romeo
(Italian) romantic lover
Romah, Rome, Romeoh,
Romero, Romey, Romi,
Romy

Romer
(American) form of Rome
Roamar, Roamer

Romney
(Welsh) roamer
Rom, Romnie

Romulo
(Spanish) man from
Rome
Romo

Romulus
(Latin) presumptuous
Rom, Romules, Romulo

Ron
(English) short for
Ronald; kind
Ronn

Ronald
(English) helpful
Ron, Ronal, Ronel,
Ronney, Ronni, Ronnie,
Ronuld

Rondel
(French) poetic
Ron, Rondal, Rondell,
Rondie, Rondy

Ronford
(English) distinguished
Ronferd, Ronnforde

Roni
(Hebrew) joyful
Rone, Ronee

Ronnie
(English) short for
Ronald
Ronnee, Ronney, Ronni,
Ronny

Roone
(Irish) distinctive; bright
face
Rooney, Roune

Rooney
(Irish) man with red hair
Rooni, Roony

Roose
(Last name as first
name) high-energy
Rooce, Roos, Rooz, Ruz

Roosevelt
(Dutch) strong leader
Rooseveldt, Rosevelt,
Rosy, Velte

Rooster
(American) animal as name; loud
Roos, Rooz

Roper
(American) roper
Rope

Rory
(German) strong
Roree, Rorey, Roreye, Rorie

Rosano
(Italian) rosy prospects; romantic

Roscoe
(English) woods; nature-loving
Rosco, Roskie, Rosko, Rosky

Roser
(American) redhead; outgoing
Rozer

Roshaun
(African-American) loyal
Roshawn

Rosk
(American) swift
Roske

Rosling
(Scottish) redhead; explosive
Roslin, Rosy, Rozling

Ross
(Latin) attractive
Rossey, Rossie, Rossy

Rossa
(American) exuberant
Ross, Rosz

Rossain
(American) hopeful
Rossane

Roswell
(English) fascinating
Roswel, Roswelle, Rosy, Rozwell, Well

Roth
(German) man with red hair
Rothe, Rauth

Roupen
(American) quiet
Ropan, Ropen, Ropun

Rover
(English) wanderer
Rovar, Rovey, Rovur, Rovy

Rowan
(English) red-haired; adorned
Rowe, Rowen

Rowdy
(English) athletic; loud
Roudy, Rowdee, Rowdi, Rowdie

Rowe
(English) outgoing
Roe, Row, Rowie

Rowell
(English) rocker
Roll, Rowl

Roy
(French) king
Roi

Royal
(French) king
Roy, Royall, Royalle, Roye

Royalton
(French) king
Royal, Royallton

Royce
(English) affluent
Roy, Royse

Roycie
(American) form of Royce; kind
Rory, Roy, Royce, Royse, Roysie

Royden
(English) outdoors; regal
Roy, Roydin

Rube
(Spanish) short for Ruben
Rubino

Ruben
(Spanish) form of Reuben
Rubens, Rube, Ruby

Rudeger
(German) friendly
*Rudger, Rudgyr, Rudigar,
Rudiger, Rudy*

Rudo
(African) loving

Rudolf
(German) wolf
Rodolf, Rudy

Rudolph
(German) wolf
*Rodolf, Rodolph, Rud,
Rudee, Rudey, Rudi,
Rudolpho, Rudy*

Rudow
(German) lovable

Rudy
(German) short for
Rudolph
*Rude, Rudee, Rudey,
Rudi*

Rudyard
(English) closed off
Rud, Rudd, Ruddy

Rueban
(American) form of
Ruben; talented
Ruban

Rufino
(Spanish) redhead

Rufus
(Latin) redhead
*Fue, Rufas, Rufes, Ruffie,
Ruffis, Ruffy, Rufous*

Rugby
(English) braced for
contact
*Rug, Rugbee, Rugbie,
Ruggy*

Rulon
(Native American)
spirited
Rulonn

Runako
(African) attractive

Rune
(German) secretive
Roone, Runes

Rush
(English) loquacious
Rusch

Rusk
(Spanish) innovator
Rusck, Ruske, Ruskk

Russ
(French) short for
Russell; dear

Russell
(French) man with red
hair; charmer
*Russ, Russel, Russy,
Rusty*

Rustin
(English) redhead
Rustan, Ruston, Rusty

Rusty
(French) short for
Russell
Rustee, Rustey, Rusti

Rutherford
(English) dignified
*Ruthe, Rutherfurd,
Rutherfyrd*

Rutilio
(Spanish)

Rutledge
(English) substantial
Rutlidge

Ryan
(Irish) royal; good-
looking
*Rhine, Rhyan, Rhyne,
Ryane, Ryann, Ryanne,
Ryen, Ryun*

Ryder
(English) outdoorsy
(man who rides horses)
Rider, Rye

Ryerson
(English) fit
outdoorsman
Rye

Ryland
(English) excellent
Rilan, Riland, Rye, Rylan

Rylandar
(English) farmer
Rye, Rylan, Ryland

Ryne
(Irish) form of Ryan;
royal
Rine, Ryn, Rynn

Ryszard
(Polish) courageous
leader
Reshard

Sabene
(Latin) optimist
*Sabe, Sabeen, Sabin,
Sabyn, Sabyne*

Saber
(French) armed; sword
Sabar, Sabe, Sabre

Saddam
(Arabic) powerful ruler
Saddum

Sadler
(English) practical
*Sadd, Saddle, Sadlar,
Sadlur*

Sae
(American) talkative
Saye

Saeed
(African) lucky

Sagaz
(Spanish) clever
Saga, Sago

Sage
(Botanical) wise
Saje

Saginaw
(Place name) city in
Michigan
Sag, Saggy

Saied
(Arabic) fortunate

Sal
(Italian) short for
Salvador and Salvatore
Sall, Sallie, Sally

Salado
(Spanish) funny
Sal

Salehe
(Africa) good

Salford
(Place name) city in
England

Salim
(Arabic) safe; peaceful
Saleem

Salt
(American) word as
name; salt-of-the-earth
Salty

Salute
(American) patriotic

Salvador
(Spanish) savior;
spirited
Sal, Sally, Salvadore

Salvatore
(Italian) rescuer; spirited
*Sal, Sallie, Sally,
Salvatori, Salvatorre*

Sam
(Hebrew) short for
Samuel; wise
Samm, Sammey, Sammi,
Sammy

Sami
(Lebanese) high

Samir
(Arabic) special
Sameer, Samere

Sammy
(Hebrew) wise
Samie, Sammee, Sammi,
Sammie, Samy

Samos
(Place name) casual

Samson
(Hebrew) strong man
Sam, Sampson

Samuel
(Hebrew) man who
heard God; prophet
Sam, Samael, Sammeul,
Sammie, Sammo,
Sammuel, Sammy,
Samual

Sanborn
(English) one with
nature
Sanborne, Sanbourn,
Sandy

Sancho
(Latin) genuine
Sanch, Sanchoh

Sander
(Greek) savior of
mankind; nice
Sandor

Sanders
(English) kind
Sandars, Sandors,
Saunders

Sandy
(English) personable
Sandee, Sandey, Sandi

Sanford
(English) negotiator
Sandford, Sandy,
Sanferd, Sanfor

Sanorelle
(African-American)
honest
Sanny, Sano, Sanorel,
Sanorell

Sansone
(Italian) strong

Santana
(Spanish) saintly
Santa, Santanah,
Santanna, Santee

Santiago
(Spanish) sainted;
valuable
Sandiago, Santego,
Santiagoh, Santy, Tago

Santos
(Italian) holy; blessed
Sant, Santo

Sarday
(American) extrovert
Sardae, Sardaye

Sargent
(French) officer/leader
Sarge, Sergeant

Sasha
(Russian) helpful
Sacha, Sash

Sasson
(Hebrew) happy

Satchel
(American) unique
Satch

Saunder
(English) defensive;
focused
Saunders

Saul
(Hebrew) gift
Sawl, Saulie, Sol, Solly

Savage
(Last name as first
name) wild
Sav

Saville
(French) stylish
Savelle, Savile, Savill

Savoy
(Place name) region in
France
Savoe

Sawyer
(English) hardworking
Saw, Sawyrr

Saxe
(English) short for Saxon
Sax, Saxee, Saxey, Saxie

Saxon
(English) swordfighter;
feisty
*Sackson, Sax, Saxan,
Saxe, Saxen*

Sayre
(Welsh) skilled
Saye, Sayer, Sayers

Scafell
(Place name) mountain
in England

Scanlon
(Irish) devious
*Scan, Scanlin, Scanlun,
Scanne*

Scant
(American) word as
name; too little
Scanty

Scardino
(Italian)

Schaffer
(German) watchful
Schaffur, Shaffer

Schelde
(Place name) river in
Europe; calm
Shelde

Schmidt
(German) hardworking;
blacksmith
Schmit

Schneider
(German) stylish; tailor
Sneider, Snider

Schuyler
(Dutch) protective
Skylar, Skyler

Scorpio
(Latin) lethal
Scorp, Scorpioh

Scott
(English) from Scotland;
happy
Scot, Scotty

Scotty
(English) happy
Scottee, Scottey, Scotti

Scully
(Irish) vocal
Scullee, Scullie

Seabrook
(English) outdoorsy
Seabrooke

Seamus
(Gaelic) replacement;
bonus
Seemus, Semus

Sean
(Hebrew, Irish) grace in
God
*Seann, Shaun, Shaune,
Shawn*

Searcy
(English) fortified
Searcee, Searcey

Searles
(English) fortified
*Searl, Searle, Serles,
Serls*

Sebastian
(Latin) dramatic;
honorable
*Bastian, Seb, Sebashun,
Sebastion, Sebastuan,
Sebo*

Sebe
(Latin) short for
Sebastian
*Seb, Sebo, Seborn,
Sebron, Sebrun*

Sedg
(American) classy
Sedge

Seger
(English) singer
*Seager, Seeger, Sega,
Segur*

Segundo
(Spanish) second child

Sekani
(African) laughing

Selestino
(Spanish) heavenly
*Celeste, Celestino, Celey,
Sele, Selestyno*

Selvon
(American) gregarious
Sel, Selman, Selv,
Selvaughn, Selvawn

Sender
(Hebrew) form of
Alexander; protective

Senior
(French) older
Sennyur, Senyur, Sinior

Sennen
(English) old

Seraphim
(Hebrew) full of fire
Sarafim, Saraphim,
Serafim, Serephim

Sergeant
(French) officer; leader
Sarge, Sargent

Sergei
(Russian) handsome
Serg, Serge, Sergie,
Sergy, Surge

Sergio
(Italian) handsome
Serge, Sergeeo, Sergeoh

Seth
(Hebrew) chosen
Sethe

Seven
(American) dramatic;
seventh child
Sevene, Sevin

Several
(American) word as
name; multiplies
Sevral, Sevrull

Severo
(Italian) unbending;
severe

Sevester
(American) form of
Sylvester
Seveste, Sevy

Seward
(English) guarding the
sea
Sew, Sewerd, Sward

Sexton
(English) church-loving
Sextan, Sextin, Sextown

Seymour
(French) prayerful
Seamore, See, Seye,
Seymore

Shade
(English) mysterious
Shadee, Shadey, Shady

Shadow
(English) mystique
Shade

Shadrach
(Biblical) Godlike; brave
Shad, Shadd, Shadrack,
Shadreck, Shadryack

Shakir
(Arabic) appreciative
Shakee, Shakeer

Shalom
(Hebrew) peaceful
Sholem, Sholom

Shaman
(Russian) mystical
Shamain, Shamon,
Shayman

Shamus
(Irish) seizing
Shamuss

Shance
(American) form of
Chance; open
Shan, Shanse

Shand
(English) loud
Shandy

Shandee
(English) noisy
Shandi, Shandy

Shane
(Irish) easygoing
Shain, Shay, Shayne

Shannon
(Irish) wise
Shana, Shanan, Shane,
Shann, Shannen,
Shanon

Shaq
(Arabic) short for
Shaquille
Shack, Shak

Shaquille
(Arabic) handsome
Shak, Shakeel, Shaq,
Shaquil, Shaquill

Sharif
(Arabic) truthful
Shareef, Sheref

Shaun
(Irish) form of Sean
Seanne, Shaune,
Shaunn

Shaw
(English) safe; in a tree
grove
Shawe

Shawn
(Irish) form of Sean
Shawnay, Shawne,
Shawnee, Shawney

Shawnell
(African-American)
talkative
Shaunell

Shawner
(American) form of
Shawn

Shawon
(African-American)
optimistic
Shawan, Shawaughn,
Shawaun

Shay
(Irish) short for Shamus;
bolstering
Shai

Shayde
(Irish) confident
Shaedy, Sheade

Shaykeen
(African-American)
successful
Shay, Shaykine

Shayshawn
(American) combo of
Shay and Shawn; able
Shaeshaun, Shaeshawn,
Shayshaun

Shea
(Irish) vital
Shay

Sheehan
(Irish) clever
Shehan, Shihan

Sheen
(English) bright and
shining; talented
Shean, Sheene

Shelby
(English) established
Shel, Shelbee, Shelbey,
Shelbie, Shell, Shelly

Sheldon
(English) quiet
Shel, Sheld, Shelden,
Sheldin, Shell, Shelly

Shem
(Hebrew) famous

Shen
(Chinese) introspective

Sheng
(Chinese) winning

Shep
(English) watchful
Shepp, Sheppy

Sheridan
(Irish) wild-spirited
Sharidan, Sheridon,
Sherr, Sherrey, Shuridun

Sherlock
(English) fair-haired;
smart
Sherlocke, Shurlock

Sherm
(English) worker; shears
Shermy

Sherman
(English) tough-willed
Cherman, Shermann,
Shermy, Shurman

Sherwood
(English) bright options
Sherwoode, Shurwood,
Woodie, Woody

Shevon
(African-American) zany
Shavonne, Shevaughan,
Shevaughn

Shiloh
(Hebrew) gift from God; charmer
Shile, Shilo, Shy, Shye

Shipley
(English) meadow of sheep
Ship

Shiva
(Hindi) of great depth and range; life/death
Shiv

Shon
(American) form of Shawn
Sean, Shaun, Shonn

Shontae
(African-American) hopeful
Shauntae, Shauntay, Shawntae, Shontay, Shontee, Shonti, Shontie, Shonty

Shorty
(American) small in stature
Shortey, Shorti

Shuu
(Japanese) responsible

Si
(Hebrew) short for Simon
Sy

Sid
(French) short for Sidney
Cyd, Siddie, Siddy, Syd

Sidney
(French) attractive
Ciddie, Cidnie, Cyd, Cydnee, Sidnee, Sidnie, Syd, Sydney

Sidor
(Russian) gifted
Isidor, Sydor

Siegfried
(German) victor
Siegfred, Sig, Sigfred, Sigfrid, Siggee, Siggie, Siggy

Sierra
(Spanish) dangerous
See-see, Serra, Siera, Sierrah

Sig
(German) short for Sigmund and Siegfried
Siggey, Siggi, Sigi, Syg

Sigga
(Scandinavian) from Siegfried; peaceful; winning
Sig

Sigmund
(German) winner
Siegmund, Sig, Siggi, Siggy, Sigi, Sigmon, Sigmond

Silas
(Latin) saver
Si, Siles, Silus

Silous
(American) form of Silas; brooding
Si, Silouz

Silvano
(Latin) of the woods; unique
Silvan, Silvani, Silvio, Sylvan

Silver
(Spanish) form of Silva; outgoing
Sylver

Simcha
(Hebrew) joyful

Simeon
(French) listener
Si, Simone, Sy

Simms
(Hebrew) good listener
Sims

Simon
(Hebrew) good listener; thoughtful
Si, Siman, Simen, Simeon, Simmy, Sye, Symon, Syms

Simpson
(Hebrew) simplistic
Simpsen, Simpsun, Simson

Sinclair
(French) prayerful
Clair, Sinc, Sinclare, Synclaire

Sindbad
(Literature) daring
Sinbad

Singer
(Last name as first
name) vocalist
Synger

Sisto
(American) cowboy

Sisyphus
(Greek) in mythology,
a cruel king

Six
(American) number as
name
Syx

Skeeter
(English) fast
Skeater, Skeet, Skeets

Skeetz
(American) zany
Skeet, Skeeter, Skeets

Skilling
(English) masterful
Skillings

Skip
(American) short for
Skipper
Skipp, Skyp, Skyppe

Skippy
(American) fast
*Skippee, Skippie,
Skyppey*

Skye
(Dutch) goal-oriented
Sky

Skylar
(Dutch) protective
*Skilar, Skye, Skyeler,
Skylir*

Slade
(English) quiet child
Slaid, Slayd, Slayde

Sladkey
(Slavic) glorious
Sladkie

Slam
(American) friendly
Slams, Slamz

Slavek
(Polish) smart; glorious
Slavec, Slavik

Slawomir
(Slavic) great glory;
famed
Slavek, Slavomir

Sloan
(Irish) sleek
Sloane, Slonne

Slocum
(Last name as first
name) happy
Slo, Slocom, Slocumb

Slover
(Last name as first
name)
Slove

Smith
(English) crafty;
blacksmith
*Smid, Smidt, Smit,
Smitt, Smitti, Smitty*

Smokey
(American) smokin'
Smoke, Smokee, Smoky

Snake
(Place name) U.S. river

So
(Vietnamese) smart

Socorro
(Spanish) helpful
Sokorro

Socrates
(Greek) philosophical;
brilliant
*Socratez, Socratis,
Sokrates*

Sol
(Hebrew) short for
Solomon
Solly

Solly
(Hebrew) short for
Solomon
*Sollee, Solley, Solli,
Sollie*

Solomon
(Hebrew) peaceful and
wise
*Salamon, Sol, Sollie,
Solly, Soloman*

Somerset
(English) talented
Somer, Somers,
Sommerset, Summerset

Sommar
(English) summer
Somer, Somers, Somm,
Sommars, Sommer

Son
(English) boy
Sonni, Sonnie, Sonny

Sonny
(English) boy
Son, Sonney, Sonni,
Sonnie

Sonteeahgo
(Invented) form of
Santiago

Soren
(Scandinavian) good
communicator
Soryn

Sorrel
(French) reddish-brown
horse; horse lover
Sorre, Sorrell, Sorrey

Sound
(American) word as a
name; dynamic

Spanky
(American) outspoken;
stubborn
Spank, Spankee,
Spankie

Sparky
(Latin) ball of fire; joyful
Spark, Sparkee, Sparkey,
Sparki, Sparkie

Speers
(English) good with
spears; swift-moving
Speares, Spears, Spiers

Spence
(English) short for
Spencer
Spens, Spense

Spencer
(English) giver; provides
well
Spence, Spencey,
Spenser, Spensor,
Spensy

Spider
(American) scary
Spyder

Spike
(American) word as
name
Spiker

Spiker
(English) go-getter
Spike, Spikey, Spyk

Spiro
(Greek) breath of fresh
air
Spi, Spiroh, Spiros, Spy,
Spyro

Springer
(English) fresh
Spring

Sprague
(French) high-energy

Spud
(English) energetic

Spurgeon
(Botanical) from the
shrub spurge; natural
Spurge

Spunk
(American) spunky;
lively
Spunki, Spunky

Spurs
(American) boot devices
used to spur horses;
cowboy
Spur

Squire
(English) land-loving
Squirre, Skwyre

Stacey
(English) hopeful
Stace, Stacee, Stacy,
Stase, Stasi

Stafford
(English) dignified
Staff, Staffard, Stafferd,
Staffi, Staffie, Staffor,
Staffy

Stamos
(Greek) reasonable
Stammos, Stamohs

Stan
(Latin) short for Stanley

Standish
(English) farsighted
Standysh

Stanford
(English) dignified
Stan, Stanferd, Stann

Stanislaus
(Latin) glorious
*Staneslaus, Stanis,
Stanislus, Stann, Stanus*

Stanislav
(Russian) glory in
leading
Slava, Stasi

Stanley
(English) traveler
*Stan, Stanlea, Stanlee,
Stanli, Stanly*

Stanton
(English) stone-hard
Stan

Stark
(German) high-energy
Starke, Starkey

Starling
(English) singer; bird
Starlling

Starr
(English) bright star
*Star, Starri, Starrie,
Starry*

Stavros
(Greek) winner
Stavrohs, Stavrows

Steadman
(English) landowner;
wealthy
*Steadmann, Sted,
Stedmann*

Steele
(English) hardworking
Steel, Stille

Stefan
(Scandinavian) crowned;
(German) chosen one
*Stefawn, Steff, Steffan,
Steffie, Steffon, Steffy,
Stefin, Stephan*

Stefano
(Italian) crowned
*Stef, Steffie, Steffy,
Stephano, Stephanos*

Stehlin
(Last name as first
name) genius
Staylin, Stealan, Stehlan

Steinbeck
(Last name as first)

Stellan
(Swedish)

Sten
(Scandinavian) stone
Stene, Stine

Steph
(English) short for
Stephen; victorious
Stef, Steff, Steffy

Stephan
(Greek) form of Stephen;
victorious

Stephanos
(Greek) crowned; martyr
*Stef, Stefanos, Steph,
Stephanas*

Stephen
(Greek) victorious
*Stephan, Stephon,
Stevee, Steven, Stevey,
Stevi, Stevie, Stevy*

Stephene
(French) form of
Stephen; wearing a
crown
Stef, Steff, Steph

Sterling
(English) worthwhile

Stern
(German) bright; serious
Stearn, Sterns

Stetson
(American) cowboy
*Stetsen, Stetsun,
Stettson*

Steubing
(Last name as first name)
Steuben, Stu, Stuben, Stubing

Steve
(Greek) short for Steven and Stephen; victorious
Stevie

Steven
(Greek) victorious
Stevan, Steve, Stevey, Stevie

Stevie
(English) short for Steven, Stephen
Stevee, Stevey, Stevi, Stevy

Stewart
(English) form of Stuart; steward or keeper
Stewert, Stu, Stuie

Stig
(Scandinavian) upwardly mobile
Stigg, Styg, Stygg

Stiles
(English) practical
Stile, Stiley, Styles

Sting
(English) spike of grain

Stobart
(German) harsh
Stobe, Stobey, Stoby

Stock
(American) macho
Stok

Stockard
(English) dramatic
Stock, Stockerd, Stockord

Stocker
(English) foundation
Stock

Stoli
(Russian) celebrant

Stone
(English) athletic
Stonee, Stoney, Stonie, Stony

Stonewall
(English) fortified
Stone, Stoney, Wall

Stoney
(American) form of Stone; friendly
Stonee, Stoni, Stonie

Storm
(English) impetuous; volatile
Storme, Stormy

Stowe
(English) secretive
Stow, Stowey

Strato
(Invented) strategic
Strat, Stratt

Stratton
(Scottish) home-loving
Straton, Strattawn

Stretch
(American) easygoing
Stretcher

Strike
(American) word as name; aggressive
Striker

Strom
(German) water-lover
Strome, Stromm

Strother
(Irish) strict
Strothers, Struther, Struthers

Struther
(Last name as first name) flowing
Strother, Strothers, Struthers

Stu
(English) short for Stuart
Stew, Stue, Stuey

Stuart
(English) careful; watchful
Stewart, Stu, Stuey

Studs
(American) cocky
Studd, Studds

Sture
(Scandinavian) difficult
Sturah

Styles
(English) practical
Stile, Stiles, Style

Stylianos
(Greek) stylish
Styli

Sugar-Ray
(American) strong
Sugar Ray

Sullivan
(Irish) dark-eyed; quiet
*Sullavan, Sullie,
Sullivahn, Sully*

Sully
(Irish) melancholy; quiet
*Sull, Sullee, Sulley,
Sullie*

Sultan
(American) bold
Sultane, Sulten, Sultin

Sumney
(American) ethereal
*Summ, Summy, Sumnee,
Sumnie*

Sutherland
(Scandinavian) sunny;
southerner
Southerland

Sutter
(English) southern
Sutt, Suttee, Sutty

Sutton
(English) sunny;
southerner

Sven
(Scandinavian) young
boy
Svein, Svend, Swen

Swain
(English) rigid; leading
the herd
Swaine, Swayne

Sweeney
(Irish) hero
Schwennie, Sweeny

Swift
(English) fast
Swifty

Swindell
(English) polished
*Schwindell, Swin,
Swindel*

Sy
(Latin) short for Silas,
Sylas, *Si*

Sydney
(French) form of Sidney
Cyd, Syd, Sydie

Sylvain
(Latin) reclusive
Syl

Sylvan
(Spanish) nature-loving
*Silvan, Syl, Sylvany,
Sylvin*

Sylvester
(Latin) forest dweller;
heavyduty
Sil, Silvester, Sly, Syl

Symms
(Last name as first
name) landowner

Symotris
(African-American) lucky
*Sym, Symetris,
Symotrice, Syms*

Tab
(German) intelligent
Tabbey, Tabby

Tad
(Greek) short for
Thaddeus
*Taddee, Taddey, Taddie,
Taddy*

Tadeusz
(Polish) praise-worthy
Tad, Taduce

Taff
(American) sweet
*Taf, Taffee, Taffey, Taffi,
Taffy*

Taft
(English) flowing
Tafte, Taftie, Taffy

Tahoe
(Place name) Lake
Tahoe, Nevada
Taho

Taj
(Sanskrit) royal;
crowned

Tal
(Hebrew) worrier
Tallee, Talley, Talli, Tally

Talbot
(French) skillful
Tal, Talbott, Tally

Talmadge
(English) natural; living
by lakes
Tal, Tally, Tamidge

Talon
(French) wily
*Tallie, Tallon, Tally,
Tawlon*

Tam
(Hebrew) truthful
Tammy

Tamarius
(African-American)
stubborn
*Tam, Tamerius, Tammy,
T'Marius*

Tammy
(English) short for
Thomas and Tamarius
*Tammee, Tammie,
Tammey*

Tan
(Japanese) high achiever

Tane
(Polynesian) sky god;
fertile
Tain

Tankie
(American) big
Tank, Tankee, Tanky

Tanner
(English) tanner of skins
*Tan, Tann, Tannar, Tanne,
Tannor, Tanny*

Tannie
(English) tanner of skins
Tann, Tanney, Tanny

Taos
(Place name) town in
New Mexico
Tao, Tayo

Tap
(American) word as
name
Tapp, Tappi, Tappy

Tariq
(African-American)
conquerer
Tarik

Tarleton
(English) stormy
Tally, Tarlton

Tarrance
(Latin) smooth
Terance, Terrance, Terry

Tarri
(American) form of Terry
Tari, Tarree, Tarrey, Tarry

Taryll
(American) form of
Terrell
Tarell

Tate
(English) happy
Tait, Tatey, Tayt

Tatry
(Place name) mountains
in Poland
Tate, Tatree, Tatri

Taurean
(African-American)
reclusive; quiet
Taureen

Taurus
(Astrological sign)
macho
Tar, Taur, Tauras, Taures

Tavares
(African-American)
hopeful
Tavarus

Tavarius
(African-American)
fun-loving
*Tav, Taverius, Tavurius,
Tavvy*

Tavish
(Scottish) upbeat
Tav, Taven, Tavis

Tay
(Scottish) river in
Scotland; jaunty
Tae, Taye

Taylor
(English) tailor
*Tailor, Talor, Tayler,
Tayley*

Tayton
(American) form of
Payton
*Tate, Taye, Tayte, Tayten,
Taytin*

Teague
(Irish) bard; poet
Teaguey, Tege

Ted
(English) short for
Theodore
*Teddee, Teddey, Teddi,
Teddy*

Teddy-Blue
(American) smiley
*Blu, Blue, Teddie-Blue,
Teddy, Teddyblu,
Teddy-Blu, Teddyblue*

Tedrick
(African-American) form
of Cedrick
Ted, Tedrik

Tedshawn
(American) combo of Ted
and Shawn
Teddshawn, Tedshaun

Tedwayne
(American) combo of Ted
and Wayne; friendly
Ted Wayne, Ted-Wayne

Tegan
(Irish) form of Teague;
literary figure
*Tege, Tegen, Tegun,
Teige*

Teller
(English) relates stories;
storytelling
Tellie, Telly

Telvis
(American) form of Elvis
Telly

Tempest
(French) stormy; volatile
Tempie, Tempy, Tempyst

Temple
(Latin) spiritual
Tempie, Templle, Tempy

Templeton
(English) from religious
place
*Temp, Tempie, Temple,
Temps*

Ten
(American) word as
name; tenth

Tennant
(American) capable
Tenn

Tennessee
(Native American) able
fighter; U.S. state
Tenns, Tenny

Tennyson
(English) storyteller
*Tenie, Tenn, Tenneyson,
Tenny, Tennysen*

Teodoro
(Spanish) God's gift
Tedoro, Teo, Teodore, Theo

TeQuarius
(African-American) secretive
Teq, Tequarius, Tequie

Terard
(Invented) form of Gerard
Terar, Tererd, Terry

Termell
(Invented) form of Terrell; militant
Termel

Terrance
(Latin) calm
Terance, Terence, Terre, Terree, Terrence, Terrie, Terry

Terrelle
(German) thunderous; outspoken
Terel, Terele, Terell, Teril, Terille, Terral, Terrale, Terre, Terrel, Terril, Terrill, Terrille, Terry, Tirill, Tirrill, Tyrel, Tyril

Terry
(English) short for Terrence
Terree, Terrey, Terri, Terrie

Teva
(Hebrew) natural
Tevah

Tevaughn
(African-American) tiger
Tev, Tevan, Tevaughan, Tivan, Tivaughan

Tevey
(Hebrew) good
Tev, Tevi, Tevie

Tevin
(African-American) outgoing
Tev, Tevan, Tivan

Tevis
(American) flamboyant
Tev, Tevas, Teves, Teviss, Tevy

Tex
(American) from Texas; cowboy
Texas, Texx

Texas
(American) from Texas; cowboy
Tex

Thad
(Greek) short for Thaddeus; brave
Thadd, Thaddy

Thaddeus
(Greek) brave
Thad, Thaddius, Thaddy, Thadeus, Thadius

Thady
(Irish) thankful
Thad, Thaddee, Thaddie, Thaddy, Thads

Thane
(English) protective
Thain, Thayn

Thanus
(American) landowner; wealthy
Thainas, Thaines

Thatcher
(English) practical
Thatch, Thatchar

Thayer
(English) protected; sheltered
Thay, Thayar

Themba
(African) hopeful

Theo
(Greek) Godlike

Theodore
(Greek) God's gift; a blessing
Teddy, Theeo, Theo, Theodor, Theos

Theodoros
(Greek) God's gift
Theo, Theodor

Theophilos
(Greek) loved by God
Theo

Therman
(Scandinavian)
thunderous
Thur, Thurman, Thurmen

Theron
(Greek) industrious
Therron, Theryon

Thierno
(American) humble
Therno, Their

Thomas
(Greek) twin; lookalike
*Thom, Thomes, Thommy,
Thomus, Tom, Tomas,
Tommi, Tomus*

Thompson
(English) prepared
*Thom, Thompsen,
Thompsun, Thomson,
Tom, Tommy*

Thor
(Scandinavian)
protective; god of
thunder
Thorr, Tor

Thorin
(Scandinavian) form of
Thor; god of thunder
Thorrin, Thors

Thorne
(English) complex
*Thorn, Thornee, Thorney,
Thornie, Thorny*

Thornston
(Scandinavian)
protected
Thornse, Thors

Thornton
(English) difficult
Thorn, Thornten

Thorpe
(English) homebody
Thor, Thorp

Thrace
(Place name) region in
southeast Europe
Thrase

Thurman
(Last name as first
name) popular
*Thurmahn, Thurmen,
Thurmie, Thurmy*

Thurmond
(Norse) sheltered
Thurman, Thurmon

Thurston
(Scandinavian) thunders
*Thor, Thors, Thorst,
Thorsten, Thur, Thurs,
Thursten, Torsten,
Torston*

Thurstron
(Scandinavian) volatile
*Thorst, Thorsten,
Thorstin, Thurs,
Thurstran*

Tiago
(Hispanic) brave
Ti, Tia

Tige
(American) easygoing
Tig, Tigg

Tiger
(American) ambitious;
strong
*Tig, Tige, Tigur, Tyg,
Tyge, Tyger, Tygur*

Tillery
(German) ruler
Till, Tiller

Tilton
(English) prospering
Till, Tillie, Tylton

Tim
(Greek) short for
Timothy
Timmy, Tym

Timber
(American) word as
name
*Timb, Timby, Timmey,
Timmi, Timmy*

Timmy
(Greek) truthful
*Timi, Timmee, Timmey,
Timmie*

Timon
(Literature) from
Shakespeare's *Timon of
Athens*; wealthy man
Tim

Timothy
(Greek) reveres God
Tim, Timathy, Timmie,
Timmy, Timothey,
Timothie, Timuthy

Tinks
(American) coy
Tink, Tinkee, Tinki,
Tinky, Tynks, Tynky

Tino
(Spanish) respected
Tyno

Tinsley
(English) personable
Tensley, Tins, Tinslee,
Tinslie, Tinsly

Tip
(American) small boy
Tipp, Tippee, Tippey,
Tippi, Tippy, Typp

Tisa
(African) ninth child

Titan
(Greek) powerful giant
Titun, Tityn

Tito
(Latin) honored
Teto, Titoh

Titus
(Latin) heroic
Titas, Tite, Tites

Tobes
(Hebrew) form of Tobias;
believing the Lord is
good
Tobee, Tobi, Tobs

Tobias
(Hebrew) believing the
Lord is good
Tobi, Toby, Tobyas, Tovi

Tobin
(Hebrew) form of Tobias;
believing the Lord is
good
Toban, Toben, Tobun,
Toby, Tobyn

Toby
(Hebrew) short for
Tobias; believing the
Lord is good
Tobe, Tobee, Tobey,
Tobie, Toto

Todd
(English) sly; fox
Tod, Toddy

Todros
(Hebrew) gifted;
treasure
Todos

Togo
(Place name) country in
West Africa; jaunty

Toks
(American) carefree

Tolan
(American) studious
Tolen, Toll

Tolbert
(English) bright
prospects
Talbart, Talbert, Tolbart,
Tolburt, Tollee, Tolley,
Tollie, Tolly

Toledo
(Place name) city in
Ohio; casual
Tol, Tolly

Tom
(English) short for
Thomas; twin
Thom, Tommy

Tomas
(Spanish) form of
Thomas

Tomasso
(Italian) doubter
Maso, Tom

Tommie
(Hebrew, English) short
for Thomas
Tomee, Tommee,
Tommey, Tommi, Tomy

Toni
(Greek, Italian,
American, English)
soaring
Tonee, Toney, Tonie

Tor
(Scandinavian) thunder; brash
Thor, Torr, Torri, Torrie, Torry

Tord
(Dutch) peaceful

Toribio
(Spanish) strong; bullish

Torkel
(Scandinavian) protective

Torn
(Last name as first name) whirlwind
Torne, Tornn

Toro
(Spanish) bull

Toronto
(Place name) jaded
Torontoe

Torq
(Scandinavian) form of Thor, god of thunder
Tork

Torr
(English) tower; tall
Torre

Torrence
(Latin) smooth
Torence, Torey, Tori, Torr, Torrance, Torrie, Tory

Torri
(English) calming
Toree, Tori, Torre, Torree, Torrey, Torry

Tova
(Hebrew) good
Tov

Townie
(American) jovial
Townee, Towney, Towny

Toyah
(Place name) town in Texas; saucy
Toy, Toya, Toye

Trace
(French) careful
Trayse

Tracy
(French) spunky
Trace, Tracee, Tracey, Traci

Trae
(American) form of Trey; third

Trahan
(English) handsome
Trace, Trahahn, Trahain, Trahane, Trahen

Trampus
(American) talkative
Amp, Tramp, Trampy

Trap
(American) word as name; masculine
Trapp, Trappy

Traves
(American) traversing different roads
Trav, Travus, Travys

Travers
(English) helpful

Travis
(English) conflicted
Tavers, Traves, Travess, Travey, Travus, Travuss

Travon
(African-American) brash
Travaughn

Trayton
(English) third
Tray, Trey

Tremayne
(French) protector
Tramaine, Treemayne, Trem, Tremain, Tremaine, Tremane, Tremen

Trent
(Latin) quick-minded
Trente, Trenty, Trint, Trynt

Trenton
(Latin) fast-moving
Trent, Trentan, Trenten, Trentin

Treva
(Irish) wise
Trevan

Trevan
(African-American) outgoing
Trevahn, Trevann

Trevon
(African-American) studious
Trevaughan

Trevor
(Irish) wise
Trever, Trevur, Treve

Trey
(English) third-born; creatively brilliant
Trae, Tray, Tre, Treye

Trigg
(American) short for Trigger; horse or trigger-finger
Trig, Trygg

Trinee
(Spanish) musical
Triney, Trini

Trinity
(Latin) triad
Trinitie

Trip
(English) wanderer
Tripe, Tripp

Tripsy
(English) dancing
Trippsie, Tryppsi

Tristan
(English) impulsive
Trestan, Trestyn, Trist, Tristen, Tristie, Triston, Tristy, Tristyn

Triste
(French) sad love affair
Tristan

Trivett
(Last name as first name)
Trevett, Triv

Trivin
(American) form of Devin; clever
Trevin

Trocky
(American) manly
Trockey, Trockie

Troy
(French) good-looking
Troi, Troye, Troyie

Troylane
(American) combo of Troy and Lane
Troy Lane, Troy-Lane

Trudell
(English) remarkable for honesty
Trude, True

True
(English) truthful
Tru

Truitt
(English) honest
Tru, True, Truett, Truitte

Truk
(Place name) islands in the West Pacific; tough
Truck

Truman
(English) honest man
Tru, True, Trueman, Trumann

Trusdale
(English) truthful
Dale, Tru, True

Tu
(Vietnamese) fourth

Tucker
(English) stylish
Tuck, Tucky, Tuckyr

Tucks
(English) short for Tucker; fanciful
Tuk

Tullis
(Latin) important
Tull, Tullice, Tullise, Tully

Tully
(Irish) short for Tullis; interesting
Tull, Tulley, Tulli, Tullie

Tulsa
(Place name) cowboy;
rancher
Tune
(American) dancer;
musical
Toone, Tuney
Tung
(Chinese, Vietnamese)
dignified; wise
Turk
(English) tough
Terk, Turke
Turone
(African-American) form
of Tyrone
Ture, Turrey, Turry
Turner
(Latin) skilled
Turn
Tut
(Arabic) brave
Tuttie, Tutty
Tuvia
(Hebrew) good
Tuvyah
Twain
(English) dual-faceted
Twaine, Tway, Twayn
Ty
(English) short for Tyler
Ti, Tie, Tye
Tyce
(American) lively
Tice

Tygie
(American) energetic
Tygee, Tygey, Tygi
Tyler
(English) industrious
*Tile, Tiler, Ty, Tye, Tylar,
Tyle, Tylir, Tylor*
Tyonne
(African-American) feisty
Tye, Tyon
Typhoon
(Weather name) volatile
*Tifoon, Ty, Tyfoon,
Tyfoonn*
Tyr
(Scandinavian) Norse
god; daring warrior
Tyre
(English) thunders
Tyr
Tyree
(African-American)
courteous
Ty, Tyrae, Tyrie, Tyry
Tyreece
(African-American)
combative
Tyreese
Tyrell
(African-American)
personable
*Trelle, Tyrel, Tyrelle, Tyril,
Tyrrel*

Tyron
(African-American) self-
reliant
Tiron, Tyronn
Tyrone
(Greek) self-starter;
autonomous
*Terone, Tirone, Tirus, Ty,
Tyronne, Tyroon, Tyroun*
Tyroneece
(African-American) ball-
of-fire
Tironeese, Tyronnee
Tys
(American) fighter
*Thysen, Tyes, Tys, Tyse,
Tysen*
Tyson
(French) son of Ty
*Tison, Tyse, Tysen,
Tysson, Tysy*

Udall
(English) certain; valley of trees
Eudall, Udahl, Udawl, Yudall

Ugo
(Italian) bright mind

Ukel
(American) player
Ukal, Uke, Ukil

Ukraine
(Place name) republic

Ulan
(Place name) city in Russia, Ulan Ude
Ulane

Uldarico
(Spanish)

Ulff
(Scandinavian) wolf; wild
Ulf, Ulv

Ulices
(Latin) form of Ulysses; wanderer
Uly

Ulissus
(Invented) form of Ulysses

Ulrich
(German) ruling; powerful
Ulrek, Ulriche, Ulrick

Ulysses
(Latin) forceful
Ule, Ulesses, Ulises, Ulisses

Umi
(African) life

Unique
(American)
Uneek, Unik

Upton
(English) highbrow writer
Uppton, Uptawn, Upten, Uptown

Urban
(Latin) city dweller
Urb, Urbain, Urbaine, Urbane, Urben, Urbin, Urbun, Urby

Uri
(Hebrew) short for Uriel; light

Uriah
(Hebrew) bright; led by God
Uri, Urie, Uryah

Urias
(Hebrew) Lord as my light; old-fashioned
Uri, Uria, Urius

Uriel
(Hebrew) light; God-inspired

Urvano
(Spanish) city boy
Urbano

Urvine
(Place name) form of Irvine, California
Urveen, Urvene, Urvi

Ury
(Hispanic) God-loving

Usher
(Latin) decisive

Utah
(Place name) U.S. state

Vadim
(French) creative
Vadeem

Vaduz
(Place name) city in
Germany

Vail
(English) serene
Vaile, Vale, Valle

Val
(Latin) short for Valery
and Valentine; strong
Vall

Valenti
(Italian) strong; romantic
*Val, Valence, Valentin,
Valentyn*

Valentin
(Russian) healthy;
strong
Val, Valeri

Valentine
(Latin) robust
Val, Valentyne, Valyntine

Valentino
(Italian) strong; healthy
Val

Valeri
(Russian) athletic;
strong
*Val, Valerian, Valerio,
Valry*

Van
(Dutch) from the family
of...
Vann

Vance
(English) brash
Vans, Vanse

Vander
(Greek) short for
Evander
Vand

Vandiver
(American) quiet
*Van, Vand, Vandaver,
Vandever*

Vandwon
(African-American)
covert
Vandawon, Vandjuan

Vanya
(Russian) right
Van, Yard, Yardy

Varkey
(American) boisterous

Varlan
(American) tough
Varland, Varlen, Varlin

Varma
(Hindi) fruitful

Varner
(Last name as first
name) formidable
Varn

Vas
(Slavic) protective
Vaston, Vastun, Vasya

Vashon
(American) delightful
Vashaun, Vashonne

Vassil
(Bulgarian) king
Vass

Vaughn
(Welsh) compact
Vaughan, Vaunie, Von

Veejay
(American) talkative
V.J., Vee-Jay, Vejay

Vegas
(Place name) from Las
Vegas, Nevada
Vega

Vejis
(Invented) form of Regis;
outgoing
*Veejas, Veejaz, Vejas,
Vejes*

Velle
(American) tough
Vell, Velley, Velly, Veltree

Velvet
(American) smooth
Vel, Velvat, Velvit

Venancio
(Spanish)

Ventura
(Spanish) good fortune

Vergel
(Spanish) writer
Vergele, Virgil

Verile
(German) macho
*Verill, Verille, Verol,
Verrill*

Vern
(Latin) short for Vernon
Verne, Vernie, Verny

Vernados
(Greek) hearty

Verner
(German) resourceful
*Vern, Verne, Vernir,
Virner*

Verniamln
(Greek) form of
Benjamin; son of the
right hand

Vernon
(Latin) fresh and bright
Verne, Vernen, Verney

Verona
(Italian) man of Venice
Verone

Vic
(Latin) short for Victor
Vick, Vickey, Vik

Vicente
(Spanish) winner
Vic, Vicentay, Visente

Victor
(Latin) winner
*Vic, Vickter, Victer, Vikki,
Viktor, Vitorio*

Vidalo
(Spanish) vibrant
Vidal

Viggo
(Scandinavian)
exuberant
Viggoa, Vigo

Vigile
(American) vigilant
Vegil, Vigil

Vilmos
(Italian) happy
Villmos

Vin
(Italian) short for
Vincent
*Vinn, Vinney, Vinni,
Vinnie*

Vince
(English) short for
Vincent
Vee, Vence, Vlns, Vinse

Vincent
(Latin) victorious
*Vencent, Vincente,
Vinciente, Vinn, Vinny*

Vincenzo
(Italian) conquerer
Vincenze, Vinnie, Vinny

Vinson
(English) winning
attitude
*Venson, Vince, Vinny,
Vins*

Virgil
(Latin) holding his own
*Verge, Vergil, Virge,
Virgie, Virgy*

Vitale
(Italian) vital

Vitas
(Latin) lively
Vidas, Vite

Vito
(Italian) short for
Vittorio; lively; victor
Veto, Vite

Vittorio
(Italian) victorious
*Vite, Vito, Vitor, Vitorio,
Vittore*

Vivar
(Greek) alive
Viv

Vlad
(Russian) short for
Vladimir

Vladimir
(Russian) glorious leader
Vlada, Vladameer, Vladamir, Vlademar, Vlakimar

Vladja
(Russian) short for Vladislav

Volf
(Hebrew) form of Will; bold

Volker
(German) prepared to defend
Volk

Von
(German) bright
Vaughn, Vonn, Vonne

Vonzie
(American) form of Fonzie; personable
Vons, Vonze, Vonzee, Vonzey, Vonzi

Waclaw
(Polish) glorified

Wade
(English) mover; crossing a river
Wadie, Wayde

Wadell
(English) southerner
Waddell, Wade

Waden
(American) form of Jaden; fun
Wade, Wedan

Wadsworth
(English) homebody
Wadswurth

Wagner
(German) musical; practical
Wagg, Waggner, Waggoner, Wagnar, Wagnur

Wagon
(American) conveyance
Wag, Wagg, Waggoner

Wait
(American) word as name; patient
Waite

Wake
(Place name) island in the Marshall Islands

Waldemar
(German) famous leader
Valdemar

Walden
(English) calming
Wald, Waldan, Waldin, Waldo, Waldy

Waldo
(German) short for Oswald; zany
Wald, Waldoh, Waldy

Walenty
(Polish) strong

Wales
(English) from Wales in England
Wails, Wale, Waley, Wali, Waly

Walker
(English) distinctive
Walk, Wally

Wallace
(English) from Wales; charming
Wallas, Walley, Walli, Wallice, Wallie, Wally

Walls
(American) walled
Walen, Wally, Waltz, Walz

Wally
(English) short for Walter
Wall, Walley, Walli, Wallie

Walsh
(English) inquisitive
Walls, Welce, Welch, Wells, Welsh

Walter
(German) army leader
Walder, Wallie, Wally, Walt, Waltur, Walty

Walton
(English) shut off; protected
Walt, Walten, Waltin

Ward
(English) vigilant; alert
Warde

Warden
(English) watchful
Warde, Wardie, Wardin, Wardon

Ware
(English) aware; cautious
Warey, Wary

Waring
(English) dashing
Wareng, Warin, Warring

Wark
(American) watchful

Warner
(German) protective
Warne

Warren
(German) safe haven
Waren, Warron, Warry, Worrin

Warwen
(American) defensive
Warn, Warwun, Warwun

Warwick
(English) lavish
War, Warweck, Warwyc, Warwyck, Wick

Washburn
(English) bountiful
Washbern, Washbie, Washby

Washington
(English) leader
Wash, Washe, Washing

Watkins
(English) able
Watkens, Wattie, Wattkins, Watty

Watson
(English) helpful
Watsen, Watsie, Watsun, Watsy, Wattsson

Wave
(American) word as a name
Waive, Wave, Wayve

Waverley
(Place name) city in New South Wales
Waverlee, Waverli, Waverly

Way
(English) landed; smart
Waye

Wayling
(English) the right way
Waylan, Wayland, Waylen, Waylin

Waylon
(English) country boy
Way, Wayland, Waylen, Waylie, Waylin, Waylond, Waylun, Wayly

Wayman
(English) traveling man
Way, Waym, Waymon, Waymun

Waymon
(American) knowing the way
Waymond

Wayne
(English) wheeler-dealer
Wain, Way, Wayn, Waynne

Webb
(English) intricate mind
Web, Webbe

Weber
(German) intuitive
Webb, Webber

Webster
(English) creative
Web, Webstar, Webstur

Weebie
(American) wily
Weebbi

Weido
(Italian) bright;
personable
Wedo

Welby
(German) astute
*Welbey, Welbi, Welbie,
Wellby*

Welford
(English) unusual
Walferd, Wallie, Wally

Wellington
(English) nobility
Welling

Wells
(English) place name;
unique
Well, Wellie, Welly

Welsh
(English) form of Walsh
Welch, Wellsh

Wendell
(German) full of
wanderlust
*Wend, Wendall, Wendel,
Wendey, Wendie,
Wendill, Wendull, Wendy*

Went
(American) ambitious
Wente, Wentt

Wes
(English) short for
Wesley
Wess, Wessie, Wessy

Wesley
(English) bland
*Wes, Weslee, Weslie,
West, Westly, Wezlee,
Wezley*

Wesson
(American) from the
West
Wess, Wessie

West
(English) westerner
Weste, Westt

Westie
(American) capricious
*West, Westee, Westey,
Westt, Westy*

Westleigh
(English) western
Westlea, Westlie, Wezlee

Westoll
(American) open
West, Westall

Weston
(English) good neighbor
*West, Westen, Westey,
Westie, Westy, Westin*

Wether
(English) light-hearted
*Weather, Weth, Wethar,
Wethur*

Wheat
(Invented) fair-haired
*Wheatie, Wheats,
Wheaty, Whete*

Wheel
(American) important
player
Wheele

Wheeler
(English) likes cars;
wheel maker
*Weeler, Wheel, Wheelie,
Wheely*

Wheeless
(English) off track
Whelus

Wheelie
(American) bigwig
*Wheeley, Wheels,
Wheely*

Whistler
(English) melodic
*Whis, Whistlar, Whistle,
Whistlerr*

Whit
(English) short for
Whitman
Whitt, Wit

Whitey
(English) fair-skinned
White

Whitman
(English) man with white hair
Whit, Whitty, Witman

Whitney
(English) likes white spaces
Whit, Whitnee, Whitnie, Whitt, Whittney, Witt

Whitson
(English) son of Whit
Whitt, Witt

Whittaker
(English) outdoors-loving
Whitaker, Whitt, Witaker, Wittaker

Wick
(American) burning
Wic, Wik, Wyck

Wilbert
(German) smart
Wilburt

Wilbur
(English) fortified
Wilbar, Wilber, Willbur

Wilburn
(German) brilliant
Bernie, Wil, Wilbern, Will

Wilder
(English) wild man
Wildar, Wilde, Wildey

Wiles
(American) tricky
Wyles

Wiley
(English) cowboy
Wile, Willey, Wylie

Wilfred
(German) peacemaker
Wilferd, Wilford, Will, Willfred, Willfried, Willie, Willy

Wilfredo
(Italian) peaceful

Wilhelm
(German) resolute; determined
Wilhem

Wilkins
(English) affectionate
Welkie, Welkins, Wilk, Wilkie, Willkins

Will
(English) short for William; likable
Wil, Wyll

Willard
(German) courageous
Wilard, Willerd

William
(English) staunch protector
Will, Willeam, Willie, Wills, Willy, Willyum, Wilyam

Willie
(German) short for William; protective
Will, Willey, Willeye, Willi, Willy

Willis
(German) youthful
Willace, Willece, Willus

Wilmer
(German) resolute; ambitious
Willmer, Wilmyr, Wylmer

Wilson
(English) extraordinary
Willson, Wilsen, Wilsun

Wilt
(English) talented
Wiltie

Wilton
(English) practical and open
Wilt, Wiltie, Wylten, Wylton

Winchell
(English) meandering
Winchie, Winshell

Wind
(American) word as name; breezy
Windy

Windell
(German) wanderer
Windelle, Windyll

Windsor
(English) royal
Win, Winnie, Winny,
Winsor, Wyndsor,
Wynser

Wings
(American) soaring; free
Wing

Winkel
(American) bright;
conniving
Wink, Winky

Winlove
(Filipino) winning favor

Winslow
(English) friendly
Winslo, Wynslo,
Wynslow

Winsome
(English) gorgeous;
winsome
Wins, Winsom, Winz

Winston
(English) dignified
Win, Winn, Winnie,
Winny, Winstan,
Wynsten, Wynston

Winter
(English) born in winter
Win, Winnie, Winny,
Wintar, Wintur, Wynter,
Wyntur

Winthrop
(English) winning; stuffy
Win, Winn, Winnie,
Winny, Wintrop

Wintle
(French)

Wiss
(American) carefree
Wissie, Wissy

Witold
(Polish) lively

Witt
(Slavic) lively
Witte

Witty, Witte
(American) humorous
Wit, Witt, Wittey, Wittie

Wize
(American) smart
Wise, Wizey, Wizi, Wizie

Wladymir
(Polish) famous ruler

Wladyslaw
(Polish) good leader
Slaw

Wohn
(African-American)

Wojtek
(Polish) comforter;
warrior

Wolf
(German) short for
Wolfgang
Wolff, Wolfy

Wolfe
(German) wolf; ominous
Wolf, Wolff, Wulf, Wulfe

Wolfgang
(German) talented; a
wolf walks
Wolf, Wolff, Wolfy,
Wulfgang

Wolley
(American) form of Wally
Wolly

Wood
(English) short for
Woodrow
Woode, Woody

Woodery
(English) woodsman
Wood, Wooderree,
Woodree, Woodri,
Woodry, Woods,
Woodsry, Woody

Woodfin
(English) attractive
Wood, Woodfen,
Woodfien, Woodfyn,
Woodie, Woody

Woodrow
(English) special
Wood, Woodrowe,
Woody

Woodward
(English) watchful
Wood, Woodie,
Woodwerd, Woody

Woody
(American) jaunty
Woodey, Woodi, Woodie

Woolsey
(English) leader
Wools, Woolsi, Woolsie, Woolsy

Worcester
(English) secure

Word
(American) word as name; talkative
Words, Wordy, Wurd

Worden
(American) careful
Word, Wordan, Wordun

Wordsworth
(English) poetic
Words, Worth

Worsh
(American) from the word worship; religious
Wor

Worth
(English) deserving
Werth, Worthey, Worthie, Worthy, Wurth

Worthington
(English) fun; worthwhile
Worth, Worthey, Worthing, Worthingtun, Wurthington

Wrangle
(American) cowboy
Wrang, Wrangler, Wrangy

Wren
(American) leader of men
Ren, Rin, Rinn, Wrenn

Wright
(English) clear-minded; correct
Right, Rite, Wrighte, Write

Wulf
(Hebrew) wolf
Wolf

Wyatt
(French) ready for combat
Wy, Wyat, Wyatte, Wye

Wyclef
(American) trendy
Wycleff

Wycliff
(English) edgy
Cliffie, Cliffy, Wicliff, Wyclif, Wycliffe

Wydee
(American) form of Wyatt; fighter
Wy, Wydey, Wydie

Wylie
(English) charmer
Wiley, Wye, Wylee

Wymann
(English) contentious
Wimann, Wye, Wyman

Wynne
(English) dear friend
Winn, Wynn

Wyshawn
(African-American) friendly
Shawn, Shawny, Why, Whysean, Wieshawn, Wye, Wyshawne, Wyshie, Wyshy

Wyton
(English) fair-haired crowd-pleaser
Wye, Wytan, Wyten, Wytin

Wyze
(American) sizzle; capable
Wise, Wye, Wyse

Xander
(Greek) short for
Alexander
*Xan, Xande, Xandere,
Xandre*

Xanthus
(Greek) golden-haired
child

Xavier
(Arabic) shining
Zavey, Zavier

Xaxon
(American) happy
Zaxon

Xen
(African-American)
original
Zen

Xeno
(Greek) gracious
*Xenoes, Zene, Zenno,
Zenny, Zeno, Zenos*

Xerxes
(Persian) leader
*Xerk, Xerky, Zerk, Zerkes,
Zerkez*

Xyle
(American) helpful
Zye, Zyle

Xyshaun
(African-American) zany
*Xye, Zye, Zyshaun,
Zyshawn*

Yadon
(Last name as first
name) different
Yado, Yadun

Yael
(Hebrew) teacher
Yail, Yaley, Yalie

Yancy
(American) vivacious
*Yanci, Yancie, Yancy,
Yanzie*

Yank
(American) Yankee
Yanke

Yannis
(Greek) believer in God
Yannie

Yarden
(Hebrew) flowing
*Yard, Yardan, Yarde,
Yardene, Yardun*

Yardley
(English) adorned;
separate
*Yard, Yarde, Yardie,
Yardlea, Yardlee, Yardly,
Yardy*

Yash
(Hindi)
Yates
(English) smart; closed
Yate, Yattes, Yeats
Yeats
(English) gates
Yen
(Chinese) calming;
capable
Yeoman
(English) helping
Yeomann, Yo, Yoeman,
Yoman, Yoyo
Yimer
(Scandinavian) giant
Yoav
(Hebrew) form of Joab
Yoel
(Hebrew) form of Joel
Yohann
(German) form of Johann
Yohan, Yohn
Yonah
(Hebrew) form of Jonah
York
(English) affluent
Yorke, Yorkee, Yorkey,
Yorki, Yorky
Yorker
(English) rich
York, Yorke, Yorkur
Yosef
(Hebrew) form of Joseph
Yose, Yoseff, Yosif

Young
(English) fledgling
Jung, Younge
Yovan
(Slavic) form of Jovan
Yu
(Chinese) shiny; smart
Yuan
(Chinese) circle
Yuke
(American) short for
Yukon
Yukon
(Place name)
individualist
Yule
(English) Christmas-born
Yuel, Yuley, Yulie
Yuma
(Place name) city in
Arizona; cowboy
Yumah
Yuri
(Russian) dashing
Yurah, Yure, Yurey, Yurie,
Yurri, Yury
Yuris
(Latin) farmer
Yures, Yurus
Yves
(French) honest;
handsome
Eve, Ives

Yvonn
(French) attractive
Von, Vonn, Yvon

Z

Zab
(American) slick
Zabbey, Zabbi, Zabbie, Zabby

Zac
(Hebrew) short for Zachariah; Lord remembers
Zacary, Zach, Zachary, Zachry

Zacary
(Hebrew) form of Zachary
Zac, Zacc, Zaccary, Zaccry, Zaccury

Zaccheus
(Hebrew) unblemished
Zac, Zacceus, Zack

Zace
(American) pleasure-seeking
Zacey, Zacie, Zase

Zach
(Hebrew) short for Zachary
Zac, Zachy

Zachariah
(Hebrew) Lord remembers
Zac, Zacaryah, Zachary, Zachey, Zachi, Zachie, Zachy, Zack, Zechariah, Zhack

Zacharias
(Hebrew) devout
Zacharyas

Zachary
(Hebrew) spiritual
Zacary, Zacchary, Zach, Zackar, Zackarie, Zak, Zakari, Zakri, Zakrie, Zakry

Zack
(Hebrew) short for Zachary
Zacky, Zak

Zade
(Arabic) flourishing; trendy
Zaid

Zadok
(Hebrew) unyielding
Zadek, Zaydie, Zadik, Zayd

Zain
(American) zany
Zane, Zayne

Zakary
(Hebrew) form of Zachary

Zaki
(Arabic) virtuous
Zak

Zale
(Greek) strong
Zail, Zaley, Zalie

Zander
(Greek) short for Alexander
Zande, Zandee, Zandey, Zandie, Zandy

Zandy
(American) high-energy
Zandee, Zandi

Zane
(English) debonair
Zain, Zay, Zayne, Zaynne

Zano
(American) unique
Zan

Zappa
(American) zany
Zapah, Zapp

Zartavious
(African-American) unusual
Zar, Zarta

Zashawn
(African-American) fiery
Zasean, Zash, Zashaun, Zashe, Zashon, Zashone

Zavier
(Arabic) form of Xavier

Zbignlew
(Polish) free of malice;
calming
Zeb
(Hebrew) short for
Zebediah
Zebe
Zebby
(Hebrew) believer;
rambunctious
Zabbie, Zeb, Zebb,
Zebbie
Zebediah
(Hebrew) gift from God
Zeb, Zebadia, Zebb,
Zebbie, Zebby, Zebi,
Zebidiah
Zechariah
(Hebrew) form of
Zachariah
Zeke
Zed
(Hebrew) energetic
Zedd, Zede
Zedekiah
(Hebrew) believing in a
just God
Zed, Zeddy, Zedechia,
Zedechiah
Zeevy
(American) sly
Zeeve, Zeevi, Zeevie
Zeffy
(American) explosive
Zeff, Zeffe, Zeffi, Zeffie

Zeke
(Hebrew) friendly;
outgoing
Zeek, Zekey, Zeki
Zelig
(Hebrew) holy; happy
Zel
Zen
(Japanese) spiritual
Zeno
(Greek) philosophical;
stoic
Zeney, Zenie, Zenno,
Zeny
Zenon
(Greek, Polish)
godlike
Zent
(American) zany
Zynt
Zephyr
(Greek) breezy
Zefar, Zefer, Zeffer, Zefur
Zero
(Arabic) nothing
Zeroh
Zerond
(American) helpful
Zerre, Zerrie, Zerry,
Zerund
Zeshon
(African-American) zany
Zeshaune, Zeshawn

Zeus
(Greek) vibrant
Zues
Zevi
(Hebrew) brisk
Zevie
Zhivago
(Russian) dashing;
romantic
Vago
Zhong
(Chinese) middle
brother; loyal
Zia
(Hebrew) in motion
Zeah, Zlah
Zie
(American) compelling
Zye, Zyey
Ziggy
(American) zany
Zigmand
(American) form of
Sigmund
Zig, Ziggy
Zikomo
(African) grateful
Zino
(Greek) philosopher
Zeno
Zion
(Hebrew) sign
Zeione, Zi, Zione, Zye

Ziv
(Hebrew) energetic
Zeven, Zevy

Ziven
(Polish) lively
Ziv

Ziya
(Turkish)

Zol
(American) jaunty
Zoll

Zoma
(American) loquacious
Zome

Zorba
(Greek) pleasure seeker
Zorbah, Zorbe

Zorby
(Greek) tireless
Sorby, Zorb, Zorbie

Zorshawn
(African-American) jaded
*Zahrshy, Zorsh, Zorshie,
Zorshon, Zorshy*

Zuberi
(African) powerful

Zvon
(Croatian) short for
Zvonimir
Zevon, Zevonn

Zyke
(American) high-energy
Zykee, Zyki, Zykie, Zyky

part five

Girls

Aaliyah
 (Hebrew) moving up
 Aliya

Aamori
 (African) good

Abay
 (Native American)
 growing
 *Abai, Abbay, Abey,
 Abeye*

Abayomi
 (African) giving joy

Abby
 (English) happy
 *Abbee, Abbey, Abbie,
 Abbye*

Abella
 (French) vulnerable;
 capable
 *Abela, Abele, Abell,
 Bela, Bella*

Abery
 (Last name as first
 name) supportive
 *Abby, Aberee, Abrie,
 Abry*

Abia, Abiah
 (Arabic) excellent
 Ab, Aba, Abbie

Abigail
 (Hebrew, English, Irish)
 joyful
 *Abagail, Abbegayle,
 Abbey, Abbie, Abby,
 Abegail, Abey, Abigal,
 Abigayle, Gail, Gayle*

Abilene
 (Place name) Texas
 town; southern girl
 *Abalene, Abi, Abiline,
 Aby*

Abiola
 (Spanish) God-loving
 Abby, Abi, Biola

Abra
 (Hebrew) form of
 Abraham; strong and
 exemplary
 *Aba, Abbee, Abbey,
 Abbie, Abby*

Abrianna
 (American) insightful
 Abryanna, Abryannah

Abrielle
 (American) form of
 Abigail; rejoices
 *Abby, Abree, Abrey,
 Abrie, Abriella, Abryelle*

Acacia
 (Greek) everlasting; tree
 *Akaysha, Cacia, Cacie,
 Case, Casey, Casha,
 Casia, Caysha, Kassy,
 Kaykay*

Accalia
 (Latin) stand-in
 *Accal, Accalya, Ace,
 Ackie*

Achantay
 (African-American)
 reliable
 Achantae, Achanté

Ada
 (German) noble; joyful
 *Adah, Addah, Adeia,
 Aida*

Adaani
 (French) pretty; noble
 *Adan, Adane, Adani,
 Daani, Dani*

Adabelle
 (American) combo of
 Ada and Belle; noble
 beauty
 *Ada, Adabel, Addabel,
 Belle*

Adaeze
 (African) prepared
 Adaese

Adair
(Scottish) innovative
*Ada, Adare, Adayr,
Adayre, Adda*

Adalia
(Spanish) spunky
*Adahlia, Adailya,
Adallyuh, Adaylia*

Adara
(Greek) lovely
Adarah, Adrah

Addison
(English) awesome
*Addeson, Addie,
Addison, Addy, Addyson,
Adeson, Adison*

Addy
(English) nickname for
Addison; distinctive;
smiling
*Addee, Addie, Addy,
Addye, Adie, Ady*

Adeen
(American) decorated
*Addy, Adeene, Aden,
Adene, Adin*

Adelaide
(German) calming;
distinguished
*Ada, Adalaid, Adalaide,
Adelade, Adelaid, Laidey*

Adeline
(English) sweet
*Adaline, Adealline,
Adelenne, Adelina,
Adelind, Adlin, Adline*

Adelita
(Spanish) form of Adela;
noble
*Adalina, Adalita,
Adelaina, Adelaine,
Adeleta, Adey, Audilita,
Lita, Lite*

Adelka
(German) form of
Adelaide; noble
*Addie, Addy, Adel,
Adelkah, Adie*

Adelle
(German) giving
Adel, Adell, Addy

Adelpha
(Greek) beloved sister
Adelfa, Adelphe

Adena
(Hebrew) precious
*Ada, Adenna, Adina,
Adynna, Deena, Dena*

Adia
(African) God's gift

Adina
(Hebrew) high hopes
*Addy, Adeen, Adeena,
Adine, Deena, Dena,
Dina*

Adisa
(Hispanic) friendly
Adesa, Adissa

Adiva
(Arabic) gracious

Adjanys
(Hispanic) lively
Adjanice, Adjanis

Adline
(German) reliable
*Addee, Addie, Addy,
Adleen, Adlene, Adlyne*

Adonia
(Greek) beauty
*Adona, Adonea,
Adoniah, Adonis*

Adora
(Latin) adored child
*Adorae, Adoray, Dora,
Dore, Dorey, Dori,
Dorree, Dorrie, Dorry*

Adra
(Greek) beauty

Adria
(Latin) place name
Adrea

Adrianna
(Greek, Latin) rich;
exotic
*Addy, Adree, Adriana,
Adrie, Adrin, Anna*

Adrienne
(Latin) wealthy
*Adreah, Adreanne,
Adrenne, Adriah, Adrian,
Adrien, Adrienn, Adrin,
Adrina*

Aereale
(Hebrew) form of Ariel;
light and sprite
Aereal, Aeriel, Areale

Aeronwenn
(Welsh) white; aggressor
Awynn

Afton
(English) confident
Aft, Aftan, Aften, Aftie

Africa
(Place name) continent
Afrika

Afua
(African) baby born on
Friday
Afuah

Agafi
(Greek) form of Agnes;
pure
*Ag, Aga, Agafee, Agaffi,
Aggie*

Agapi, Agape
(Greek) love
Agapay, Agappe

Agasha
(Greek) form of Agatha;
longsuffering
Agashah, Agashe

Agate
(English) gemstone;
precious girl
*Agatte, Aget, Aggey,
Aggie*

Agatha
(Greek) kind-hearted
*Agath, Agathah, Agathe,
Aggey, Aggie, Aggy*

Agatta
(Greek) form of Agatha;
honorable and patient
*Ag, Agata, Agathi,
Aggie, Agi, Agoti, Agotti*

Agave
(Botanical) strong-
spined; genus of plants
*Ag, Agavay, Aggie,
Agovay*

Agentina
(Spanish) form of
Argentina; colorful
Agen, Agente, Tina

Aggie
(Greek) kind-hearted
Aggee, Aggy

Agnes
(Greek) pure
*Ag, Aggie, Aggnes,
Aggy, Agnas, Agnes,
Agness, Agnie, Agnus,
Nessie*

Ahvanti
(African) focused
Avanti

Aida
(Arabic) gift
Aeeda, Ayeeda, Ieeda

Aidan
(Irish) from the male
name Aidan; fiery
Aden, Aiden

Aileen
(Irish, Scottish) fair-
haired beauty
*Aleen, Alene, Alenee,
Aline, Allee, Alleen,
Allene, Allie, Ally*

Ailey
(Irish) form of Aileen;
light and friendly
*Aila, Ailee, Ailie, Ailli,
Allie*

Aimee
(French) beloved
*Aime, Aimey, Aimme,
Amee, Amy*

Aimee-Lynn
(American) combo of
Aimee and Lynn; lovable
*Aimee Lynn, Aimeelin,
Aimeelynn*

Aimer
(German) leader; loved
Aimery, Ame, Amie

Ainsley
(Scottish) meadow;
outdoorsy
*Ainslea, Ainslee,
Ainsleigh, Ainslie, Anes,
Anslie, Aynslee, Aynsley*

Aintre
(Irish) joyous estate
*Aintree, Aintrey, Antre,
Antry*

Aisha
(Arabic, African) life;
lively
*Aeesha, Aiesha,
Aieshah, Ayeesha,
Ayisha, Ieashia, Ieeshah,
Iesha*

Aislinn
(Irish) dreamy
Aisling, Aislyn, Aislynn

Alabama
(Place name) western
Bama

Alaine
(Gaelic) lovely
*Alaina, Alaiyne, Alenne,
Aleyna, Aleyne, Allaine,
Allayne*

Alala
(Roman mythology)
sister of Mars; protected
Alalah

Alana
(Scottish) pretty girl
*Alahna, Alahnah, Alaina,
Alainah, Alanah, Alanna,
Alannah, Allana, Allie,
Ally*

Alanis
(French) shining star
Alannis

Alason
(German) form of Alison;
noble; bright
Ala, Alas

Alaygrah
(Invented) form of
Allegra; frisky
Alay, Allay

Alaytheea
(Invented) form of
Aleithea; honest
Alay, Thea, Theea

Alberta
(French) bright-eyed
*Alb, Albertah, Albie,
Albirta, Alburta, Bertie,
Berty*

Albertine
(English) form of Albert;
bright
*Albertyne, Albie,
Albyrtine, Teeny*

Albie
(American) casual
Albee, Albey, Alby, Albye

Alcina
(Greek) magical; strong-
willed
*Alcee, Alcie, Als, Alsena,
Alsie. Cina, Seena, Sina*

Aldona
(American) sweet
Aldone

Alea
(Arabic) excellent
*Alaya, Aleah, Aleeah,
Alia, Ally*

Aleah
(American) combo of
Allie and Leah
Alayah, Alayja

Aleeza, Aliza
(Hebrew) joy

Alegria
(Spanish) beautiful
movement
Allegria

Aleksandra
(Polish, Russian) helpful

Alessa
(Italian) helper
Alesa

Alessandra
(Italian) defender of
mankind
Aless, Alessa

Alessia, Allyshia
(Italian) nice
Alesha, Alyshia

Alethea

(Greek) truthful
Alathea, Aleethia, Aletha, Aletie, Altheia, Lathea, Lathey

Aletta

(Greek) carefree
Aleta, Aletta, Eletta, Letti, Lettie, Letty

Alexa

(Greek) short for Alexandra
Alecksa, Aleksah, Alex, Alexia

Alexakai

(American) combo of Alexa and Kai; merry
Alexikai, Lexi, Kai

Alexandra

(Greek, English, Scottish, Spanish) regal protector
Alejandra, Alejaundro, Alex, Alexandrah, Alexandria, Alexis, Alezandra, Allesandro, Ally, Lex, Lexi, Lexie

Alexandrine

(French) helpful
Alexandrie, Alex, Ally, Lexi, Lexie

Alexia

(Greek) helpful, bright
Alexea, Alexiah, Alixea, Lex, Lexey, Lexie, Lexy

Alexis

(Greek) short for Alexandra; helpful; pretty
Aleksus, Alexius, Alexus, Alexys, Lex, Lexey, Lexi, Lexie, Lexis, Lexus

Alfonsith

(German) aggressive
Alf, Alfee, Alfey, Alfey, Alfie, Alfonsine, Allfrie, Alphonsine, Alphonsith

Alfre

(English) short for Alfreda; seer
Alfree

Alfreda

(English) wise advisor
Alfi, Alfie, Alfred, Alfredah, Alfrede, Alfredeh, Freda, Freddy

Ali

(Greek) short for Alexandra; defending
Aley, Allee, Alley, Ally

Alianet

(Spanish) honest; noble
Alia, Aliane

Alice

(Greek) honest
Alece, Alicea, Alise, Alliss, Ally, Allys, Alyse, Alysse, Lisie, Lisy, Lysse

Aliceann

(American) combo of Alice and Ann; well-born; southern feel
Alice Ann, Alicean, Alice-Ann

Alicia

(Greek) delicate; lovely
Alisha

Alida

(Greek) stylish
Aleda, Aleta, Aletta, Alidah, Alita, Lee, Lida, Lita, Lyda

Alina

(Scottish, Slavic) fair-haired
Alene, Aline, Allene, Allie, Ally, Allyne, Lena, Lina

Alisa

(Hebrew) happy
Alissa, Allisa, Allissah, Alyssa

Alisha

(Greek) happy; truthful
Aleesha, Alesha, Alicia, Ally, Allyshah, Lesha, Lisha

Alison

(Scottish) noble
Alisen

Alissa
(Greek) pretty
Alesa, Alessa, Alise,
Alissah, Allee, Allie, Ally,
Allyssa, Alyssea

Alita
(Native American)
sparkling

Alka
(Polish) distinctive
Alk, Alkae

Allegra
(Italian) snappy
Aligra, All, Allagrah,
Allie, Alligra, Ally

Allena
(Greek) outstanding
Alena, Alenah, Allana,
Allie, Ally

Allene
(Greek) wonderful
Alene, Alyne

Allessandra
(Italian) kind-hearted
Allesandra

Allie
(Greek) smiling
Ali, Allee, Alli, Ally, Allye

Allison
(English) kind-hearted
Alison, Allie, Allisan,
Allisen, Allisun, Ally,
Allyson, Sonny

Allura
(Hispanic) alluring
Alura

Allyson
(English) another form of
Allison
Alisaune, Allysen,
Allysun, Alyson

Allysse
(Greek) smooth
Allice, Allyce, Allyss

Alma
(Latin) good; soulful
Almah, Almie, Almy

Almeria
(Arabic) princess
Alma, Almara, Almaria,
Almer, Almurea, Als

Almirah, Almira
(Spanish, Arabic)
princess
Allmeerah, Elmira, Mira

Alodie
(Origin unknown)
thriving
Alodee

Aloha
(Hawaiian) love

Alona
(Jewish) sturdy oak
Allona

Alondra
(Spanish) bright
Alond, Alondre, Alonn

Alouette
(French) birdlike
Allie, Allo, Allou,
Allouetta, Alou, Alowette

Aloyse, Aloise
(German) renowned
Aloice, Aloyce

Alpha
(Greek) first; superior
Alf, Alfa, Alfie, Alph,
Alphah, Alphie

Alston
(English) a place for a
noble
Allie, Ally, Alstan, Alsten,
Alstun

Alta
(Latin) high place; fresh

Altea
(Polish) healer

Althaea
(Latin, Italian) healing

Althea
(Greek, English) demure;
healer
Althe, Althey, Althia,
Althie, Althy, Thea, They

Alva
(Spanish) fair; bright
Alvah

Alvada
(American) evasive
Alvadah, Alvayda

Alverna
(English) truthful friend
(elf friend)
Alver, Alverne,
Alvernette

Alvernise
(English) form of
Alverne; honest (elf
friend)
Alvenice

Alvina
(English) beloved;
friendly
Alvee, Alveena, Alvie,
Alvine, Alvy

Alvita
(Latin) charismatic

Alyda
(French) soaring
Aleda, Alida, Alita, Lida,
Lyda

Alysia
(Greek) compelling
Aleecia, Alesha, Alicia,
Alish, Alycia

Alyssa
(Greek) flourishing
Alissa, Allissa, Allissae,
Ilyssah, Lissa, Lyssa,
Lyssy

Amabe
(Latin) loved
Ama

Amabelle
(American) loved
Amabel, Amahbel

Amada
(Latin, Spanish) loved
one
Ama, Amadah

Amal
(Arabic) optimistic
Amahl

Amalina
(German) worker
Am, Ama, Amaleen,
Amaline, Amalyne

Amanda
(Latin, English, Irish)
lovable
Amand, Amandah,
Amandy, Manda,
Mandee, Mandi, Mandy

Amandra
(American) variant of
Amanda; lovely
Amand, Mandee, Mandi,
Mandra, Mandree,
Mandry, Mandy

Amara
(Greek, Italian) unfading
beauty
Am, Amarah, Amareh,
Amera, Amura, Mara

Amarillo
(Place name) a city in
Texas; cowgirl
Ama, Amari, Amarilla,
Amy, Rillo

Amaris
(Hebrew) beloved;
dedicated
Amares

Amaryllis
(Greek) fresh flower
Ama, Amarillis

Amber
(French) gorgeous and
golden; semiprecious
stone
Ambar, Amberre, Ambur,
Amburr

Amber-Dee
(American) combination
of Amber and Dee;
golden jewel;
spontaneous
Amber D, Amber Dee

Amberkalay
(American) combo of
Amber and Kalay;
beautiful energy
Amber-Kalé, Amber-Kalet

Amberlee
(American) combo of
Amber and Lee
Amberlea, Amberleigh,
Amberley, Amberli,
Amberly, Amburlee

Amberlyn
(American) combo of
Amber and Lyn
Amberl, Amberlin,
Amberlynn, Amlynn

Amboree
(Last name as first
name) precocious
Ambor, Ambree

Ambrosette
(Greek) eternal
Amber, Ambie, Ambro,
Ambrosa, Ambrose

Ambrosia
(Greek) eternal
Ambroze, Ambrozeah,
Ambrozia

Amelia
(German) industrious
Amalee, Amaylyuh,
Amele, Ameleah, Ameli,
Amelie, Amelya, Amilia

Amera
(Arabic) of regal birth
Ameera, Amira

America
(American) patriotic
Amer, Amerca, Americah,
Amerika, Amur

Amethyst
(Greek) precious gem
Amathist, Ameth

Amica
(Latin) good friend
Ameca, Ami, Amika

Amici
(Italian) friend
Amicie, Amie, Amisie

Amiga
(Spanish) friend
Amigah

Amina
(Arabic) trustworthy
Amena, Amine

Amity
(Latin) a good friend
Amitee, Amitey, Amiti

Amor
(Spanish) love
Amora, Amore

Amora
(Spanish) love

Amorelle
(French) lover
Amoray, Amore, Amorel,
Amorell

Amoretta
(French) little love

Amorita
(Spanish) loved

Amy
(Latin) loved one
Aimee, Amey, Ameyye,
Ami, Amie, Amye, Amye

Amykay
(American) combo of
Amy and Kay
Amikae

Amylynn
(American) combo of
Amy and Lynn
Ameelyn, Amilynn,
Amylyn

Amyrka
(Spanish) lively
Amerka, Amurka, Amyrk,
Amyrrka

Anabelle, Anabella
(American) combo of
Ana and Belle; lovely
Anabel, Anabell,
Annabelle

Anabril
(Spanish) merciful;
pretty
Anabrelle, Anna,
Annabril

Anais
(French) variant of Anne;
graceful

Anala
(Hindi) fiery

Analia
(Hebrew) gracious;
hopeful
Ana, Analea, Analeah,
Analiah, Analya

Analeese
(Scandinavian) gracious
Analece, Analeece,
Annaleese

Analicia
(Spanish) combo of Ana and Licia; gracious sweetheart
Analice, Analicea, Analisha, Licia

Analisa
(American) combo of Ana and Lisa; lovely
Analise, Annalisa, Anna-Lisa

Analy
(American) graceful; gracious
Analee, Anali

Analynne
(American) combo of Ana and Lynne
Analinn, Analynn, Annalinne, Annalynn

Anand
(Hindi) joyful; profound
Anan, Ananda

Anastasiya
(Greek, Russian) reborn; royal
Anastasia, Anastasya

Anastay
(Greek) born again; renewed
Ana, Anastae, Anastie

Anatola, Anatole
(Greek, French) dawn
Anatol

Anayancy
(Spanish) combo of Ana and Yancy; buoyant
Ana Yancy, Anayanci, Anayancie, Ana-Yancy

Anders
(Scandinavian) stunning
Andars, Andie, Andurs, Andy

Andi
(English) casual
Andee, Andie

Andraa
(Greek, French) feminine
Andrah

Andrea
(Greek) feminine
Andee, Andi, Andie, Andra, Andrae, Andre, Andreah, Andreena

Andreanne
(American) combo of Andrea and Anne
Andreane, Andrie, Andry

Andree
(Greek) strong woman
Andrey, Andrie, Andry

Andrenna
(Scottish) pretty; gracious
Andreene, Adrena

Andrianna
(Greek) feminine
Andree, Andy

Andromeda
(Greek) beautiful star
Andromedah

Anemone
(Greek) breath of fresh air

Anewk
(Invented) form of Anouk

Angel
(Latin) sweet; angelic
Angelle, Angie, Anjel, Annjell

Angela
(Greek) divine; angelic
Angelena, Angelica, Angelina, Angelle, Angie, Gela, Nini

Angelia
(American) angelic messenger
Angelea, Angeliah

Angelica
(Latin) angelic messenger
Angie, Anjeleka, Anjelica, Anjelika, Anjie

Angelina
(Latin) angelic
Ange, Angelyna, Angie, Anje, Anjelina, Anjie

Angeline
(American) angelic
Angelene, Angelline

Angelique
(Latin, French) angelic
*Angel, Angeleek,
Angelik, Angie, Anjee,
Anjel, Anjelique*

Angelle
(Latin) angelic
*Ange, Angell, Anje,
Anjell, Anjelle,*

Angie
(Latin) angelic
*Angey, Angi, Angye,
Anjie*

Aniece
(Hebrew) gracious
*Ana, Anesse, Ani, Anice,
Annis, Annissa*

Aniela
(Polish) sent by God
Ahneela

Anik, Anika
(Hebrew) hospitable
*Anec, Anecca, Aneek,
Aneeka, Anic, Anica,
Annlka*

Anissa
(Greek) a completed
spirit
*Anisa, Anise, Anyssa,
Anysse*

Anita
(Spanish) gracious
Aneda, Aneeta, Anitta

Anitra
(Invented, from
literature) combo of
Anita and Debra
Anetra, Anitrah, Annitra

Anjali
(Hindi) pretty; honored
Anjaly

Anjana
(Hindi) merciful; pretty
Anjann

Anjelica
(Latin) angelic
Anjelika

Anjeliett
(Spanish) little angel
*Anjel, Anjeli, Jelette,
Jeliett, Jeliette, Jell, Jelly*

Anjul
(French) jovial
*Angie, Anjewel, Anji,
Anjie, Anjool*

Ann
(Hebrew) loving;
hospitable
*Aine, An, Ana, Anna,
Anne, Annie, Ayn*

Ann-Dee
(American) variant of
Andy; graceful
*Andee, Andey, Andi,
Andy, Ann Dee, Anndi*

Anna
(English, Italian,
German, Russian,
Polish) gracious
*Ana, Anae, Anah, Annah,
Anne, Anuh*

Annalrls
(American) combo of
Anna and Iris; sweet
*Anairis, Ana-Iris, Anna
Iris*

Annamaria
(Italian) combo of Anna
and Maria; merciful and
holy
*Anamaria, Anna-Maria,
Annamarie*

Anna-Pearl
(American) Anna and
Pearl; dated
*Anapearl, Anna Pearl,
Annapearl*

Anneliese
(Scandinavian) gracious;
(German) religious
Aneliece, Aneliese

Annella
(Scottish) graceful
Anell, Anella, Anelle

Annemarie
(German) combo of Anne
and Marie
*Anmarie, Ann Marie,
Anne-Marie, Annmarie*

Annette
(American) vivacious;
giving
*Anette, Ann, Anne,
Annett, Annetta, Annie,
Anny*

Anne-Louise
(American) combo of
Anne and Louise; sweet
*Anlouise, Ann Louise,
Annelouise, Annlouise,
Ann-Loweez*

Annie
(Hebrew, Irish) gracious;
hip
*Ann, Annee, Anney,
Anni, Anny*

Annika
(Scandinavian) gracious
Anika

Anninka
(Russian) gracious;
graceful

Annissa
(Greek) gracious;
complete
*Anissa, Anni, Annie,
Annisa*

Anouk
(French) form of Ann

Anshaunee
(African-American)
combo of Ann and
Shaunee; happy
*Annshaunee,
Anshawnee*

Ansley
(English) happy in the
meadow
*Annesleigh, Ans, Anslea,
Anslee, Ansleigh, Ansli,
Anslie*

Anstass
(Greek) resurrected;
eternal
*Ans, Anstase, Stace,
Stacey, Stass, Stassee*

Anstice
(Greek) everlasting
*Anst, Steece, Steese,
Stice*

Antigone
(Greek) impulsive;
defiant

Antique
(Word as name) old soul
Anteek, Antik

Antoinette
(Latin) quintessential;
(French) feminine form
of Antoine
*Antoine, Antoinet,
Antwanett, Antwonette,
Antwonette, Toinette,
Tonette*

Antonia
(Latin) perfect
*Antone, Antonea,
Antoneah*

Antonian
(Latin) valuable
*Antoinette, Antonetta,
Toni, Tonia, Tonya*

Antwanette
(African-American) form
of Antoinette; prized
Antwan, Antwanett

Anya
(Russian) grace

Aphra
(Hebrew) earthy;
sentimental
*Af, Affee, Affey, Affy,
Afra, Aphree, Aphrie*

Aphrodite
(Greek) goddess of love
and beauty
Afrodite, Aphrodytee

Apolinaria
(Spanish) form of Greek
god Apollonia; martyr
Apolinara

Apollonia
(Greek) sun goddess
*Apolinia, Apolyne,
Appollonia*

Apple
(Botanical) fruit; quirky
Apel, Appell

April
(Latin) month of the
year; springlike
*Aprel, Aprile, Aprille,
Apryl*

Aqua
(Spanish) colorful
Akwa

Arabella
(Latin) answer to a
prayer; beauty
*Arabel, Arabelle, Arbel,
Arbella, Bella, Belle,
Orabele, Orabella*

Araceli
(Latin) heavenly
Ara, Aracelli, Ari

Aracelle
(Spanish) flamboyant;
heavenly
*Ara, Aracel, Aracell,
Araseli, Celi*

Arachne
(Greek) weaver; spider

Araminta
(English) unique;
precious dawn
*Ara, Arama, Aramynta,
Minta*

Araylia
(Latin) golden
Araelea, Aray, Rae, Ray

Arbra
(American) form of Abra;
sensitive
Arbrae

Arcelia
(Spanish) treasured
*Arcey, Arci, Arcilia, Arla,
Arlia*

Arcelious
(African-American)
treasured
*Arce, Arcel, Arcelus, Arcy,
Arselious*

Archon
(American) capable
*Arch, Archee, Archl,
Arshon*

Ardath
(Hebrew) ardent
*Ardee, Ardie, Ardith,
Ardon*

Ardele
(Latin) enthusiastic;
dedicated
*Ardell, Ardella, Ardelle,
Ardine*

Arden
(Latin) ardent; sincere
*Ardan, Ardena, Ardin,
Ardon*

Ardiana
(Spanish) ardent
Ardi, Ardie, Diana

Ardie
(American) enthusiastic;
special
Ardee, Ardi

Areika
(Spanish) pure
*Areka, Areke, Arika,
Arike*

Arekah
(Greek) virtuous; loving

Arelie
(Latin) golden girl
Arelee, Arely, Arlea

Aretha
(Greek) virtuous;
vocalist

Aretta
(Greek) virtuous
Arette, Arie

Argentina
(Place name) confident;
land of silver
*Arge, Argen, Argent,
Argenta, Argie, Tina,
Tinee*

Arianda
(Greek) helper
Ariand

Aridatha
(Hebrew) flourishing
Ar, Arid, Datha

Arisca
(Greek) form of Arista;
best; delight
Ariska, Ariske, Arista

Argosy
(French) bright
Argosee, Argosie
Argus
(Greek) bright
Arguss
Argyle
(French, American)
complicated
*Argie, Argile, Argy,
Argylle*
Aria
(Italian) melody; solo
Ariah
Ariadne
(Greek) faithful
*Ariadna, Aryana,
Aryanna*
Ariana
(Greek) devout;
(Welsh) treasured silver
*Ana, Ari, Aria, Arianah,
Arianna, Arri, Arriannah*
Ariane
(Greek) very gracious
Arianne, Aryahn
Arianne
(French) kind
Ana, Ari, Ariann
Ariel
(French, Hebrew)
heavenly singer
Aeriel, Airey, Arielle

Aries
(Latin) zodiac sign of the
ram; contentious
Arees
Arista
(Greek) wonderful
Aristelle
(Greek) wonder
Aristela, Aristella
Aritha
(Greek) virtuous
Arete, Aretha
Arizona
(Place name) cowgirl
Zona
Arketta
(Invented) outspoken
Arkett, Arkette, Arky
Arlea
(Greek) heavenly
*Airlea, Arlee, Arleigh,
Arlie, Arly*
Arleana
(American) form of
Arlene; dedicated
Arlena, Arlina
Arlena
(Irish) dedicated
*Arlana, Arlen, Arlenna,
Arlie, Arlina, Arlyna,
Arrlina, Lena, Lina,
Linney*

Arlene
(Irish) dedicated
*Arlee, Arleen, Arlie,
Arline, Arlyne, Arlynn,
Lena, Lina*
Arlette
(French) loyal
Arlet
Armanda
(French) disciplined
Armani, Armonie
(French) fashionable
*Armanee, Armanie,
Armond, Armonee,
Armoni*
Armida
(Latin) armed; prepared
Armi, Armid, Army
Arnette
(English) little eagle;
observant
*Arn, Arnee, Arnet,
Arnett, Ornette*
Arosell
(Last name as first
name) loyal
Arosel
Arpine
(Romanian) dedicated
Arpyne
Arthlese
(Irish) rich
Arth, Arthlice, Artis

Artriece
(Irish) stable
Artee, Artreese, Arty

Arvis
(American) special
*Arvee, Arvess, Arvie,
Arviss, Arvy*

Asabi
(African) outstanding

Asha, Ashra
(Hebrew) lucky
Ashah

Ashandra
(African-American)
dreamer
Ashan, Ashandre

Ashanti
(African) place name;
graceful
Ashantay, Anshante

Ashantia
(American) outgoing
Ashantea, Ashantiah

Asharaf
(Hindi) wishful
Asha, Ashara

Ashby
(English) farm of ash
trees
Ashbee

Ashland
(Irish) dreamlike
*Ashelyn, Ashlan,
Ashleen, Ashlin, Ashlind,
Ashline, Ashlinn*

Ashlei
(English) variant of
Ashley; pretty
*Ashee, Ashie, Ashly,
Ashy*

Ashley
(English) woodland
sprite; meadow of ash
trees
*Ash, Ashie, Ashlay,
Ashlea, Ashlee,
Ashleigh, Ashli, Ashlie,
Ashly*

Ashlyn
(English) natural

Ashonika
(African-American)
pretty
Ashon, Ashoneka, Shon

Ashton
(English) place name;
from an eastern town;
sassy
*Ashe, Ashten, Ashtun,
Ashtyn*

Asia
(Greek) reborn;
continent
*Ashah, Asiah, Asya,
Aysia, Azhuh*

Asma
(Arabic) exalted; loyal

Asmay
(Origin unknown) special
Asmae, Asmaye

Asp
(Greek) short for
Aspasia; witty

Aspasia
(Greek) witty
Aspashia

Aspen
(Place name) earth
mother
Azpen

Asra
(Hindi) pure
Azra

Astera
(Greek) star-like
*Asteria, Astra, Astree,
Astrie*

Astra
(Greek) star
Astrah, Astrey

Aylee
(Hebrew) light
Ayleen
(Hebrew) light-hearted
Aylene
Aylin
(Spanish) strong
Aylen
Aylwin
(Welsh) beloved
Ayle, Aylwie
Aynona
(Hebrew) form of Anne;
graceful
Ayn, Aynon, Aynonna,
Aynonne
Azenet
(Spanish) sungod's gift
Aza, Azey
Azucena
(Spanish) lily pure
Azu, Azuce, Azucina
Azura, Azure
(French) blue-eyed
Azuhre, Azzura

Babe
(Latin) little darling;
baby
Babette
(French) little Barbara
Babianne
(American) combo of
Babi and Anne; fun-
loving
Babi, Babiane, Babyann,
Biann, Bianne
Babs
(American) short for
Barbara; lively
Bachi
(Japanese) happy
Bachee, Bachey, Bachie,
Bochee
Baden, Boden
(German) friendly
Bodey
Badger
(Irish) badger
Badge
Baek
(Origin unknown)
mysterious

Bagent
(Last name as first
name) baggage
Bage
Bagula
(German) enthused
Baggy
Bahama
(Place name) sun-loving
Baham
Bahati
(African) lucky girl
Baha, Bahah
Bahir
(Arabic) striking
Bah, Baheer, Bahi
Bai
(Chinese) outgoing
Baiben
(Irish) sweet; exotic
Babe, Babe, Bai, Baib,
Baibe, Baibie, Baibin
Bailey
(English) bailiff
Bailee, Baylee, Baylie
Bailon
(American) variant of
Bailey; dancing; happy
Bai, Baye, Baylon
Bain
(American) thorn; pale
Baine, Bane, Bayne
Baird
(Irish) ballad singer
Bayrde

Baldree
(German) brave;
loquacious
Baldry

Bali
(Place name) exotic

Ballou
(American) outspoken
Bailou, Balou

Balvino
(Spanish) powerful
Balvene, Balveno

Bambi
(Italian) childlike; baby
girl
*Bambee, Bambie,
Bamby*

Bamp
(American) vivid
Bam, Bampy

Banessa
(American) combo of B
and Vanessa; hopeful
*B'Nessa, Banesa,
Benessa*

Bano
(Persian) bride
*Bannie, Banny, Banoah,
Banoh*

Bao
(Chinese) adorable;
creative

Bao-Jin
(Chinese) precious gold

Baptista
(Latin) one who baptizes
Battista

Barb
(Latin) short for Barbara

Barbara
(Greek, Latin)
unusual stranger
*Babette, Babina, Babs,
Barb, Barbie, Barbra,
Bobbie, Bobi*

Barbro
(Swedish) extraordinary
Bar, Barb, Barbar

Barcelona
(Place name) exotic
Barce, Lona

Barcie
(American) sassy
Barsey, Barsi

Barrett
(Last name as first
name) happy girl
*Bari, Barret, Barrette,
Barry, Berrett*

Barrie
(Irish) markswoman
Feminine form of the
masculine Barry
Bari, Barri, Barry

Barron
(Last name as first
name) bright
*Bare, Baron, Barrie,
Beren, Beron*

Basey
(Last name as first
name) beauty
Bacie, Basi

Baseylea
(American) combo of
Basey and Lee; pretty
*Basey, Basilea, Basilee,
Leelee*

Basimah
(Arabic) smiling

Bastienna
(French) from male name
Bastien; clever
Bastee, Bastienne

Bathsheba
(Hebrew) beautiful
daughter of Sheba
Sheba

Bathshira
(Arabic) happy; seventh

Batia, Batya
(Hebrew) daughter of
God
Batea

Batice
(American) warrior;
attractive
*Bateese, Batese,
Batiece, Batty*

Bay
(Vietnamese) Saturday's child; patient; unique
Bae, Baye

Bayo
(African) bringing joy

Baynes
(American) from male name Baines; confident
Bain, Baines, Bayne

Bayonne
(Greek) joyful victor
Bay, Baye, Bayonn, Bayonna, Bayunn

Bea
(American) short for Beatrice

Beata
(German) blessed
Bayahta

Beatrice
(Latin) blessed woman, joyful
Beat, Beata, Beatrise, Bibi, Treece, Trice

Beatrix
(Latin) happy

Beatriz
(American) joy

Bebe
(French) baby
Babee, Baby, Bebee

Becca
(Hebrew) short for Rebecca; lively
Bekka

Bechet
(French)

Becky
(English) short for Rebecca; spunky
Becki, Beki

Bedelia
(Irish) form of Bridget; powerful

Beegee
(American) laidback; calm
B.G., Begee, Be-Gee

Bee-Sun
(Filipino) nature-loving; glad
Bee Sun

Bego
(Hispanic) spunky
Beago

Begonia
(Botanical) flower

Behorah
(Invented) friend
Be, Behi, Behie, Behora

Beige
(American) simple; calm
Bayge

Beige-Dawn
(American) clear morning
Bayge-Dawn, Beige Dawn

Beila
(Spanish) beautiful

Beilarosa
(Spanish) combo of Beila and Rosa; beautiful rose
Beila, Beila-Rosa, Beila-Rose, Beiliarose, Rose

Bela
(Czech) white
Belah

Belanie
(Invented) combo of B and Melanie; lovely
Bela, Belan, Belanee, Belaney, Belani, Belle

Belann, Belan
(Spanish) pretty
Bela, Belana, Belane, Belanna

Belem
(Spanish) pretty
Bel, Beleme, Bella

Belgica
(American) white
Belgika, Belgike, Belgyke, Bellgica

Belia
(Spanish) beauty
Belea, Beliano, Belya, Belyah

Belicia
(Spanish) believer
Belia

Belinda
(Latin, Spanish)
beautiful serpent
Belynda

Belita
(Spanish) pretty little
one; (French) beauty

Bella
(Italian) beautiful

Bellace
(Invented) pretty
Bellase, Bellece, Bellice

Belle
(French) beautiful
Bele, Bell

Bellina
(French) beautiful

Belva
(Latin) beautiful view

Belvia
(Invented) practical
*Bell, Belva, Belve,
Belveah*

Bendite
(Latin) well blessed
*Ben, Bendee, Bendi,
Bennie, Benny, Binni*

Benecia
(Latin) short for Benedicta

Benedicta
(Latin) woman blessed
Benna, Benni

Beneva
(American) combo of
Ben and Eva; kind
*Benevah, Benna, Benni,
Bennie, Benny, Bineva*

Bening
(Filipino) blessing

Benita
(Latin, Spanish) lovely
Benetta

Benni
(Latin) short for
Benedicta; blessed
Bennie, Binny

Bente
(Latin) blessed

Berdina
(German) bright; robust
*Berd, Berdie, Berdine,
Berdyne, Burdine,
Burdynne, Dina, Dine*

Bergen
(American) pretty
Berg, Bergin

Berget
(Irish) form of Bridget
Bergette

Berit
(Scandinavian) glorious
Beret, Berette

Berkley
(American) smart
*Berkeley, Berkie, Berklie,
Berkly*

Berlynn
(English) combo of
Bertha and Lynn
Berla, Berlinda, Berlyn

Bermuda
(Place name) personable
Bermudoh

Bernadette
(French) form of
Bernadine
Berna, Berneta

Bernadine
(German) brave;
(English) feminine form
of Bernard
*Bernadene, Berni,
Bernie*

Bernice
(Greek) victorious
Berneta, Berni

Berry
(Nature name) tiny;
succulent
Berree, Berrie

Bersaida
(American) sensitive
*Bersaid, Bersaide,
Bersey, Bersy, Sada,
Saida*

Bertha
(German) bright
*Barta, Berta, Berte,
Berthe, Bertie, Bertita,
Berty*

Bertie
(German) bright
*Bert, Bertee, Bertey,
Berty*
Bertina
(German) shining bright;
feminine form of
masculine Bert
Berule
(Greek) bright; pure
Berue, Berulle
Beryl
(Greek) bright and
shining gem
*Berlie, Berri, Beryle,
Beryn*
Bess
(Hebrew) form of
Elizabeth
Bessie
Bet
(Hebrew) daughter
Beth
(Hebrew) form of
Elizabeth
Betha
(Welsh) devoted to God
Bethah, Bethanne
Bethann
(English); combo of Beth
and Ann; devout
*B-Anne, Bethan, Beth-
ann, Bethanne*

Bethany
(Hebrew) God's disciple
*Beth, Bethani, Bethania,
Bethanie, Betheny,
Bethina*
Beti
(English) small woman
Betriss
(Welsh) blessed
Betrys
Betsy
(Hebrew) form of
Elizabeth
*Bet, Betsey, Betsi,
Betsie, Betts*
Bette
(French) lively; God-
loving
Bettina
(Spanish) combo of Beth
and Tina
Betina, Betti, Bettine
Betty
(Hebrew) God-loving;
form of Elizabeth
Bett, Betti, Bettye
Betula
(Hebrew) dedicated;
religious
Bee , Bet, Bett, Betulah
Beulah
(Hebrew) married
Beula, Bew, Bewla

Bev
(English) short for
Beverly; friendly
Beverly
(English) beaver stream;
friendly
*Bev, Beverlee, Beverley,
Beverlie, Bevvy, Verly*
Bevina
(Irish) vocalist
*Beavena, Bev, Beve,
Beven, Bevena, Bevy,
Bovana*
Bevinn
(Irish) royal
Bevan
Bianca
(Italian) white
*Beonca, Beyonca,
Biancha, Biancia,
Bionca, Blanca*
Bibi
(Arabic, Latin, French)
girl; lively
Bebe
Bijou
(French) saucy
*Bejeaux, Bejou, Bejue,
Bidge, Bija, Bijie, Bijy*
Bik
(Chinese) jade
Bikini
(Place name) fun-loving
Bikinee

Billie
(German) form of
Wilhelmina; (English)
strong-willed
Billa, Billee, Billy, Billye

Billie-Jean
(American) combo of
Billie and Jean
Billie Jean, Billijean

Billie-Jo
(American) combo of
Billie and Jo
Billie Jo, Billyjo

Billie-Sue
(American) combo of
Billie and Sue
Billie Sue, Billysue

Billina
(English) from male
name Bill; kind
*Belli, Bill, Billee, Billie,
Billy*

Billings
(American) bright
*Billey, Billie, Billing, Billy,
Billye, Billyngs, Byllings*

Bina
(Hebrew) perceptive
woman

Binase
(Hebrew) bright
*Beanase, Benace, Bina,
Binah, Binahse*

Bionda
(Italian) black
Beonda, Biondah

Bird
(English)
Birdy

Birdie
(English) bird
Birdee, Birdi

Birgit
(Scandinavian)
spectacular
*Bergette, Berit, Birgetta,
Birgite, Britta, Byrget,
Byrgitt*

Birgitta
(Swedish) excellent
splendor
*Birgette, Brita, Byrgetta,
Byrgitta*

Birte
(Scandinavian) form of
Bridget; powerful
*Berty, Birt, Birtey, Byrt,
Byrtee*

Bishop
(Last name as first
name) loyal
Byshop

Bitsie
(American) small
*Bitsee, Bitzee, Bitzi,
Bytsey*

Bitta
(Scandinavian) variant of
Bridget; excellent
Bit, Bitt, Bittey

Bivona
(African-American) feisty
*BeBe, Biv, Bivon,
Bivonne*

Bjork
(Icelandic) unique
Byork

Blaine
(Irish) thin
Blane, Blayne

Blair
(Scottish) plains-dweller
Blaire

Blaise
(Latin, French)
stammerer
Blaize, Blase, Blaze

Blake
(English) dark

Blakely
(English) dark
*Blakelee, Blakeley,
Blakeli*

Blanca
(Spanish) white
*Blancah, Blonka,
Blonkah*

Blanche
(French) white
*Blanca, Blanch,
Blanchette*

Blanda
(Latin) seductive
Bless
(American) blessed
Blessie
Bleu
(French) blue
Blue
Bliss
(English) blissful girl
Blondie
(American) blonde
Blondee
Blondelle
(French) fair of hair
Blondie
Blossom
(English) flower
Bluebell
(Flower name) pretty
*Belle, Blu, Blubel,
Blubell, Blue*
Blush
(American) pink-cheeked
Blushe
Bly
(American) soft; sensual
Blye
Blythe
(English) carefree
Blithe, Blyth
Bo
(Chinese) precious girl

Boanah
(American) good
*Boana, Bonaa, Bonah,
Bonita*
Bobbi
(American) form of
Barbara
*Bobbie, Bobby, Bobbye,
Bobi*
Bobbiechristine
(American) combo of
Bobbie and Christine
*BobbiChris,
Bobbichristine, Bobbie-
Christine*
Bobbi-Ann
(American) combo of
Bobbi and Ann
*Bobbiann, Bobbyann,
Bobbyanne*
Bobbi-Jo
(American) combo of
Bobbi and Jo
*Bobbiejo, Bobbijo,
Bobijo*
Bobbi-Lee
(American) combo of
Bobbi and Lee
Bobbilee, Bobbylee
Bobby-Kay
(American) combo of
Bobby and Kay
Bobbikay

Bobby-Sue
(American) combo of
Bobby and Sue
Bobbisue, Boby-Sue
Bogdana
(Polish) gift from God
Bogda, Bogna
Bola
(Origin unknown) clever
Bolo
Bona
(Latin, Italian, Polish,
Spanish) good
Bonah, Bonna
Bonda
(Spanish) good
Bona
Bonita
(Spanish) good; pretty
Bona, Bonitah
Bonn
(Place name) satisfied
Bon, Bonne
Bonnevie
(Scandinavian) good life
Bonnie, Bonny
(English, Scottish) pretty
face
Boni, Bonnee, Bonni
Bonnie-Bell
(American) combo of
Bonnie and Belle; lovely
*Bonnebell, Bonnebelle,
Bonnibelle*

Bootsey
(American) cowgirl
Boots, Bootsie

Bors
(Latin) foreign
Borse

Boston
(American) courteous
Boste, Bosten, Bostin

Boswell
(Last name as first
name) intellectual
Boz, Bozwell

Bowdy
(American) outgoing
*Bow, Bowdee, Bowdey,
Bowdie*

Braisly
(American) cautious
*Braise, Braislee, Braize,
Braze*

Brandy
(Dutch) after-dinner
drink; fun-loving
*Bran, Brande, Brandea,
Brandee, Brandeli,
Brandi, Brandye,
Brandyn, Brani*

Brandy-Lynn
(American) combo of
Brandy and Lynn
*Brandelyn, Brandilynn,
Brandlin, Brandy-Lyn*

Branka
(Czech) glory
*Bran, Branca, Bronca,
Bronka*

Brayden
(American) humorous
*Braden, Brae, Braeden,
Bray, Brayd, Braydan,
Braydon*

Breana
(Irish) form of Briana
Bre-Anna, Breeana

Breann
(Irish) form of Briana
*Bre-Ann, Bree, Breean,
Breeann*

Breck
(Irish) freckled

Bree
(Irish) upbeat
Brea, Brie

Breena
(Irish) glowing
Brena

Breeshonna
(African-American)
happy-go-lucky
Bree, Brie, Brieshona

Breezy
(American) easygoing
Breezee, Breezie

Brehea
(American) self-
sufficient
Breahay, Brehae, Brehay

Bren
(American) short for
Brenda
Breyn

Brenda
(Irish) royal; glowing
*Brenna, Brinda, Brindah,
Brinna*

Brenda-Lee
(American) combo of
Brenda and Lee
*Brandalee, Brindlee,
Brinlee*

Brendette
(French) small and royal

Brendie
(American) form of
Brenda
Brendee, Brendi

Brendelle
(American) distinctive

Brendolyn
(Invented) combo of
Brenda and Madolyn;
intelligent
*Brend, Brendo,
Brendolynn, Brendy*

Brenna
(Irish) form of Brenda;
dark-haired
Bren, Brenn, Brenie

Brett
(Latin) jolly
Bret, Bretta, Brette

Breyawna
(African-American)
variant of Brianna
Bryawn, Bryawna,
Bryawne

Bria
(Irish) short for Briana;
pure; spirited

Briana
(Irish) virtuous; strong
Breana, Breann, Bria,
Brianna, Briannah, Brie-
Ann, Bryanna

Brianne
(Irish) strong
Briane, Brienne, Bryn

Briar
(French) heather
Brear, Brier

Briar-Rose
(Literature: *Sleeping*
Beauty) princess
Briar, Rose

Brice
(English) quick

Briceidy
(English) precocious
Brice, Bricedi, Briceidee,
Briceidey

Bridey
(Irish) wise
Bredee, Breedee, Bride,
Bryde

Bridget
(Irish) powerful
Birgitt, Bridge,
Bridgette, Bridgey,
Briget, Brigette, Brigid,
Brijette, Brygett

Brie
(French) from Rozay-en-
Brie, a town in France
known for its cheese
Bree, Brielle

Brielle
(Invented) combo of Bri
and Elle
Briell, Bryelle

Briesha
(African-American)
giving
Bri, Brieshe

Brigidine
(Invented) combo of
Brigit and Dine (from
Geraldine)
Brige, Brigid

Bril
(American) strong
Brill

Briley
(Last name as first
name) popular
BeBe, Bri, Brile

Brina
(Latin) short for Sabrina

Brinlee
(American) sweetheart
Brendlie, Brenlee, Brenly

Brionna
(Irish) happy
Breona, Briona

Brinkelle
(American) independent
nature
Binkee, Binky, Brinkee,
Brinkel, Brinkell, Brinkie

Brisa
(Spanish) beloved; In
mythology, the loved
one of Achilles
Breza, Brissa

Brisco
(American) high-energy
woman
Briscoe, Briss, Brissie,
Brissy

Brissellies
(Spanish) happy
Briselle, Briss, Brisse,
Brissel, Brissell, Brissey,
Brissi, Brissies

Britaney
(English) place name
Britanee, Britani,
Briteny, Brittaney,
Brittenie, Britnee,
Britney, Britni

Britt
(Latin) from Britain
Brit

Britta
(Swedish) strong woman
Brita

Brittany
(English) place name;
trendy
Briteney, Britni,
Brittaney

Bronte
(Literature) romantic
Brontae, Brontay

Bronwyn
(Welsh) white-breasted
Bron, Bronwen,
Bronwhen, Bronwynn

Brook
(English) sophisticated
Brooke, Brooky

Brooklyn
(Place name) combo of
Brook and Lynn
Brookelyn, Brookelynn,
Brooklynn, Brooklynne

Browning
(LIterature) romantic

Bruenetta
(French) brown-haired
Bru, Brunetta

Bruneita
(German) brown-haired
Broon, Brune, Bruneite,
Brunny

Brunella
(German) intelligent
Brun, Brunela, Brunilla,
Brunne

Brunhilda
(German) warrior
Brunhilde, Hilda

Bryanna
(Gaelic) powerful female
Breanna, Brianna,
Bryana

Bryanta
(American) form of male
name Bryan; strong
Brianta, Bryan, Bryianta

Bryce
(American) happy
Brice

Bryleigh
(English) spinoff of
Brittany; jovial
Brllee, Briley, Brily,
Brilye, Brylee, Brylie

Bryn
(Welsh) hopeful;
climbing a hill
Brenne, Brynnie

Brynn
(Welsh) hopeful
Brenn, Brinn, Brynne

Brynna
(Welsh) optimistic
Brinn, Brinna

Bryonie
(Latin) clinging vine
Breeonee, Brioni, Bryony

Bua
(Vietnamese) fortunate
Boo, Bu

Bubbles
(American) saucy
Bubb

Buffy
(American) plains-
dweller
Buffee, Buffey, Buffie

Bukola
(Origin unknown)
Bucola

Bunard
(American) good
Bunerd, Bunn, Bunny

Bunny
(English) little rabbit;
bouncy
Bunnee, Bunnie

Burgundy
(French) red wine;
unique
Burgandi, Burgandy

Burke
(American) loud
Berk, Burk, Burkie

Burns
(Last name as first name) presumptuous
Bernes, Berns, Burn, Burnee, Burnes, Burney, Burni, Burny

Butter
(American) sweet
Budter

Buzzie
(American) spirited
Buzz, Buzzi

Bwyana
(African-American) smart
Bwya, Bwyanne

Byronae
(American) form of Byron; smart
Byrona, Byronay

Cabriole
(French) adorable
Cabb, Cabby, Cabriolle, Kabriole

Cachay
(African-American) distinctive

Cachet
(French) fetching
Cache, Cachee

Cade
(American) precocious
Kade, Kaid

Cadence
(American) hip
Kadence

Cady
(English) fun-loving
Cadee, Cadey, Cadye, Caidee, Caidy, Kadee, Kady

Cai
(Chinese) wealthy; girlish

Cailin
(American) happy
Cayleen, Caylin, Caylyn, Caylynne

Cairo
(Place name) Egypt's capital; confident
Kairo, Kiero

Cait
(Greek) purest
Cate, Kate

Caitlin
(Irish) virginal
Cailin, Caitleen, Caitlinn, Caitlyn, Catlin, Catlyn, Catlynne

Cala, Calla
(Arabic) strong
Callah

Calandra
(Greek) lark
Calendra, Kalandra

Calantha
(Greek) gorgeous flower
Calanth, Calanthe, Calli

Cale
(Latin) respected
Kale

Caledonia
(Latin) from Scotland; worthy
Kaledonia

Caley
(American) warm
Caleigh, Kaylee

Calhoun
(Last name as first name) surprising

California
(Place name) hip; cool
Callie, Kalifornia, Kallie

Calinda
(American) combo of Cal and Linda
Cal, Calenda, Calli, Callie, Cally, Kalenda, Kalinda

Caliopa
(Greek, Spanish) singing beautifully
Kaliopa

Calista
(Greek) most beautiful
Calysta, Kali, Kalista, Kalli, Kallista

Calla
(Greek) beautiful
Cala, Callie, Cally

Callie
(Greek) beautiful
Caleigh, Callee, Calley, Calli, Cally, Kali, Kallee, Kallie

Calliope
(Greek) muse; poetic
Kalliope

Callison
(American) combo of Calli and Allison; pretty offspring
Cal, Calli, Callice, Callis, Callisen, Callisun

Calypso
(Greek mythology) sea nymph who held Odysseus captive

Cam
(American) short for Cameron
Cami, Camie, Cammie

Cambay
(Place name) saucy
Cambaye, Kambay

Camber
(American) spinoff of Amber; has potential
Cambie, Cambre, Cammy, Kamber

Cambree
(Place name) from Cambria, Wales; ingenious
Cambrie, Cambry, Cambry, Kambree, Kambrie

Camden
(American) glorious face
Cam, Camdon, Cammi, Cammie, Cammy

Cameka
(African-American) form of Tameka/Tamika
Cammey, Cammi, Cammy, Kameka, Kammy

Camellia
(Italian) flower
Camelia, Kamelia

Camelot
(English) elegant
Cam, Cami, Camie, Camy

Cameo
(French) piece of jewelry; singular
Cameoh, Cammie, Kameo

Camera
(Word as name) stunning
Kamera

Camerino
(Spanish) unblemished
Cam, Cammy

Cameron
(Scottish) popular (crooked nose)
Cameran, Camren, Camryn, Kameron, Kamryn

Cami
(French) short for
Camille, Camilla,
Cameron
Camey, Camie, Cammie,
Cammy

Camilla
(Latin, Italian) wonderful
Camila, Camillia

Camille
(French) swift runner;
great innocence
Camila, Cammille,
Cammy, Camylle, Kamille

Camp
(American) hip
Cam, Campy

Campbell
(Last name as first
name) amazing
Cam, Cambell, Camey,
Cami, Camie, Camy

Camrin
(American) variant of
Cameron
Camren, Camryn

Canada
(Place name) decisive
Cann, Kanada

Candace
(Greek) glowing girl
Candice, Candis, Candys,
Kandace

Candelara
(Spanish) spiritual
Cande, Candee,
Candelaria, Candi,
Candy, Lara

Candida
(Latin) white

Candra
(Latin) she who glows
Candria, Kandra

Candy
(American) short for
Candace
Candee, Candi, Candie

Cannes
(French) place name
Can, Kan

Cantara
(Arabic) bridge
Canta, Kanta, Kantara

Capelta
(American) fanciful
Capeltah, Capp, Cappy

Caplice
(American) spontaneous
Capleece, Capleese,
Kapleese

Capri
(Italian) island off coast
of Italy
Caprie, Kapri

Caprice
(Italian) playful;
capricious
Caprece, Capreese,
Capricia, Caprise

Capucine
(French) cloak
Cappy

Car
(American) zany
Carr, Kar, Karr

Cara
(Latin, Italian) dear one
Carah, Kara

Caramia
(Italian) my dear
Cara Mia, Cara-Mia

Cardia
(Spanish) giving
Candi, Kardia

Carenleigh
(American) combo of
Caren and Leigh
Caren-Leigh

Carey
(Welsh) by a castle; fond
Caree, Cari, Carrie, Cary

Caridad
(Spanish) giving
Cari

Carina
(Greek, Italian) dearest
Careena, Carena, Carin,
Carine, Kareena, Karina

Carissa
(Greek, Italian) beloved
Carisa, Karessa, Karissa

Carita
(Latin) giving; loved
Caritta, Karita

Caritina
(Spanish) combo of Cari
and Tina; dearest
Cari, Cartine, Tina

Carla
(German) feminine of
Charles, Carl, Carlo
Carlah, Carlia, Karla

Carlee
(German) darling
*Carleigh, Carley, Carli,
Carly, Karlee, Karley*

Carlene
(American) sweet
Carleen

Carlanda
(American) darling
*Carlan, Carland,
Carlande, Carlee, Carlie,
Carly, Karlanda*

Carlett
(Spanish) affectionate
*Carle, Carlet, Carletta,
Carlette, Carley, Carli*

Carlin
(Latin, German) winner
Caline, Carlan, Carlen

Carlisle
(Place name) sharp
Carlile, Carrie, Karlisle

Carlisa
(Italian) combo of Carla
and Lisa; fond of friends
*Carlie, Carlissa, Carly,
Carlysa, Karlese, Karlisa*

Carlissa
(American) pleasant
Carleeza, Carlisse

Carlotta
(Italian, Spanish)
feminine form of Carlo
and Carlos; sweetheart
Karlotta

Carly
(German) darling
*Carlee, Carley, Carli,
Carlie, Karlee*

Carma
(Hebrew) short for
Carmel; special garden
*Car, Carmee, Carmi,
Carmie, Karma*

Carmel
(Hebrew) place name;
garden
*Carmela, Carmella,
Karmel*

Carmela
(Hebrew, Italian) fruitful
*Carmalla, Carmel,
Carmella, Carmie,
Carmilla*

Carmen
(Hebrew) crimson
*Carma, Carman,
Carmela, Carmelinda,
Carmita, Carmynne,
Chita, Mela, Melita*

Carmensita
(Spanish) dear girl
*Carma, Carmens,
Carmense, Karmence*

Carmine
(Italian) sexy
Carmyne, Karmine

Carminia
(Italian) dearest
*Carma, Carmine,
Carmynea, Karm,
Karminia, Karmynea*

Carnation
(Latin) flower
*Carn, Carna, Carnee,
Carney, Carny*

Carnethia
(Invented) fragrant
*Carnee, Carney,
Carnithia, Karnethia*

Carnie
(American) happy
Carni, Karni, Karnie

Carody
(American) humorous
*Caridee, Caridey,
Carodee, Carodey,
Carrie, Karodee, Karody*

Carol
(English) feminine;
(French) joyful song;
(German) farming
woman
*Carole, Carroll, Caryl,
Karol, Karrole*

Carolanne
(American) combo of
Carol and Anne
Carolane, Carolann

Carole
(French) a joyous song
Karol, Karole

Carolina
(Italian) feminine
Carrolena, Karolina

Caroline
(German) petite woman
*Caraline, Carilene,
Cariline, Caroleen,
Carolin, Karalyn, Karoline*

Carolyn
(English) womanly
*Carilyn, Carilynn,
Carolyne, Carolynn,
Karolyn*

Caron
(Welsh) giving heart
Carron, Karon

Caronsy
(American) form of
Caron; sweet
*Caronnsie, Caronsi,
Karonsy*

Carrelle
(American) lively
Carrele

Carrie
(French, English) joyful
song
*Carey, Cari, Carri, Carry,
Kari*

Carson
(Nordic) dramatic
*Carse, Carsen, Carsun,
Karrson, Karsen, Karson*

Carylan
(American) combo of
Caryl and An; soft
*Carolann, Caryland,
Carylanna, Karylan*

Caryn
(Danish) form of Karen
*Caren, Carrin, Caryne,
Carynn*

Carys
(Welsh) love

Casey
(Greek, Irish) attentive
female
*Casie, Cassee, Cassey,
Casy, Caysee, Caysie,
Caysy, Kasey*

Cashonya
(African-American)
monied; lively
Kashonya

Casielee
(American) combo of
Casie and Lee; popular
*Caseylee, Casie Lee,
Casielea, Casie-Lee,
Casieleigh*

Casilde
(Spanish) combative
*Casilda, Casill, Cass,
Cassey, Cassie*

Cason
(Greek) seer; spirited
Case, Casey, Kason

Cassandra
(Greek) insightful
*Casandra, Casandria,
Cass, Cassie, Cassondra,
Kassandra*

Cassia
(Greek) spicy; cinnamon

Cassidy
(Irish) clever girl
*Casadee, Cass,
Cassidee, Cassidi,
Kassidy*

Cassie
(Greek) short for
Cassandra; tricky
Cassey, Cassi

Cassiopeia
(Greek) starry-eyed
*Cass, Cassi, Kass,
Kassiopia*

Catalina
(Spanish) pure
*Catalena, Katalena,
Katallna*

Catarina
(Greek, Italian) pure
Katarina

Cather
(Literature) earthy
Kather

Catherine
(Greek, Irish, English)
pure
*Cartharine, Cathrine,
Cathryn, Katherine*

Cathleen
(Irish) pure
*Cathelin, Cathleyn,
Cathlinne, Cathlyn,
Cathy*

Cathresha
(African-American) pure;
outspoken
*Cathrisha, Cathy,
Kathresha, Resha*

Cathryn
(Greek) pure female;
form of Catherine

Cathy
(Greek) pure
*Cathee, Cathey, Cathie,
Kathy*

Catline
(Irish) form of Caitlin;
virtuous
*Cataleen, Catalena,
Catleen, Catlen, Katline*

Catrice
(Greek) form of
Catherine; wholesome
*Catrece, Catreece,
Catreese, Katreece,
Katrice*

Catrina
(Greek) pure
*Catreena, Catreene,
Catrene, Katrina*

Cavender
(American) emotional
*Cav, Cavey, Kav,
Kavender*

Cayenne
(Spice name) peppery

Caykee
(American) combo of
Cay and Kee; lively
*Caycay, Caykie, Kaykee,
Kee*

Cayla
(Hebrew) unblemished
*Cailie, Calee, Cayley,
Caylie, Kayla*

Cayley
(American) joyful
*Caelee, Caeley, Cailey,
Cailie, Caylea, Caylee,
Cayleigh*

Caylisa
(American) combo of
Cay and Lisa;
lighthearted
*Cayelesa, Cayl, Cay-Lisa,
Caylise, Kayl, Kaylisa*

Cayman
(Place name) the
islands; islander spirit
*Caman, Caymanne,
Kayman*

Cayne
(American) generous
Cain, Kaine

Ceaskarshenna
(African-American)
ostentatious
*Ceaskar, Karshenna,
Shenna*

Ceci
(Latin) short for Cecilia;
dignity
Cecile
(Latin) short for Cecilia;
genteel
Cecily
Cecilia
(Latin, Polish) blind;
dim-sighted
*Cacelia, Cece, Cecelia,
Ceil, Celia, Cice, Cicilia,
Cilley, Secilia, Sissy*
Cedrice
(American) form of male
name Cedric; feisty
Ced, Cedrise
Ceil
(Latin) blythe
Ceel, Ciel
Celand
(Latin) heavenward
Cel, Cela, Celanda, Celle
Celebration
(American) word as
name; celebrant
Cela, Sela
Celena
(Greek) heavenly; form
of Selena
Celeena, Celene
Celery
(Food name) refreshing
*Cel, Celeree, Celree,
Celry, Sel, Selery, Selry*

Celeste
(Latin) gentle and
heavenly
Celest, Celestial, Seleste
Celestia
(Latin) heavenly
*Celeste, Celestea,
Celestiah, Seleste,
Selestia*
Celestyna
(Polish) heavenly
*Cela, Celeste,
Celesteenah, Celestinah,
Celestyne*
Celina
(Greek) loving; form of
Celena
Selina, Celena
Celine
(Greek) lovely
Celeen, Celene
Celka
(Latin) celestial
*Celk, Celkee, Celkie,
Selk, Selka*
Celkee
(Latin) form of Celeste;
sweet
*Celkea, Celkie, Cell,
Selkee*
Cena
(English) special
Cenna, Sena

Cera
(French) colorful
Cerea
(Greek) thriving
Serea
Ceres
(Latin) joyful
Cerise
(French) cherry red
*Cerese, Cerice, Cerrice,
Ceryce*
Cesary
(Polish) outspoken
Cesarie, Cezary, Ceze
Cesia
(Spanish) celestial
Cesea, Sesia
Chablis
(French) white wine
Chabli
Chacita
(Spanish) lively girl
*Chaca, Chacie, Chaseeta,
Chaseta*
Chadee
(French) goddess
Shadee
Chaemarique
(Invented) combo of
Chae and Marique;
pretty
*Chae, Chaemareek,
Marique, Shaymarique*

Chafin
(Last name as first name) sure-footed
Chaffin, Shafin

Chai
(Hebrew) life-giving
Chae, Chaeli

Chaka-Khan
(Invented) singer

Chakra
(Sanskrit) energy
Chak, Chaka, Chakara, Chakyra

Chala
(African-American) exuberant
Chalah, Chalee, Chaley, Chalie

Chalette
(American) good taste
Chalett, Challe, Challie, Shalette

Chalice
(French) a goblet; toasting
Chalace, Chalece, Chalyse, Chalyssie

Chaline
(American) smiling
Chacha, Chaleen, Chalene

Chalis
(African-American) sunny disposition
Chal, Chaleese, Chalise

Chalissa
(African-American) optimistic
Chalisa, Chalysa, Chalyssa

Challie
(American) charismatic
Challee, Challi, Chally

Chalondra
(African-American) pretty
Chacha, Chalon, Chalondrah, Cheilonndra, Chelondra

Chalsey
(American) variation of Chelsea
Chalsea, Chalsee, Chalsi, Chalsie, Chalsie

Chambray
(French) fabric; hardy
Chambree

Champagne
(French) wine; luxurious

Chana
(Hindi) moon-like

Chanah
(Hebrew) graceful
Chanach, Channah

Chanal
(American) moon-like

Chanda
(Hindi) moon goddess
Chandi, Chandie, Shanda

Chandelle
(French) candle-lighter
Chandal, Shandalle, Shandel

Chandler
(English) romantic; candle-maker
Chandlee, Shandler

Chandra
(Hindi) of the moon
Chandre, Shandra, Shandre

Chanel
(French) fashionable; designer name
Chan, Chanell, Chanelle, Channel, Shanel, Shanell, Shanelle

Chanelle
(American) stylish
Shanell, Shanelle

Chaney
(English) short for Chandler; cute
Chanie, Chaynee, Chayney

Chanicka
(African-American) loved
Chaneeka, Chani, Chanika, Nicka, Nika, Shanicka

Chanise
(American) adored
Chanese, Shanise

Channing
(Last name as first
name) clever
Chanon
(American) shining
Chanen, Chann, Chanun
Chansanique
(African-American) girl
singing
*Chansan, Chansaneek,
Chansani, Chansanike,
Shansanique*
Chantal
(French) singer of songs
*Chandal, Chantale,
Chantalle, Chante,
Chantee, Chantel,
Chantell, Chantelle,
Chantile, Chantille,
Chawntelle, Shanta,
Shantel, Shawntel,
Shontelle*
Chantee
(American) singer
*Chantey, Chanti,
Chantie, Shantee,
Shantey*
Chanti
(American) melodious
Chantee, Chantie
Chantilly
(French) beautiful lace
Chantille, Shantilly

Chantrice
(French) singer of songs
Shantreece, Treece
Chanyce
(American) risk-taker
*Chance, Chancie,
Chaneese, Chaniece,
Chanycey*
Chaquanne
(African-American) sassy
*Chaq, Chaquann,
Shakwan*
Charanne
(American) combo of
Char and Anne;
charitable
Charann, Cherann
Charbonnet
(French) loving and
giving
*Charbonay, Charbonet,
Charbonnay, Sharbonet,
Sharbonnet*
Charde
(French) wine
*Charday, Chardea,
Shardae*
Chardonnay
(French) white wine
*Char, Chardonee,
Shardonnay*

Charille
(French) variant of
Charlotte; feminine;
delightful
*Char, Chari, Charill, Shar,
Sharille*
Charis
(Greek) graceful
Charice, Charisse
Charish
(American) cherished
Chareesh
Charisma
(American) charming
Char, Karismah
Charissa
(Greek) giving
*Char, Charesa, Charisse,
Charissey*
Charita
(Spanish) sweet
Cherita
Charity
(Latin) loving;
affectionate
*Carisa, Charis, Chariti,
Sharity*
Charla
(French) from Charlotte;
feminine
Char
Charlaine
(English) small woman;
form of Charlene
Charlane

Charlana
(American) form of Charlene; feminine
Chalanna

Charlene
(French) petite and beautiful
Charla, Charlaine, Charleen, Sharlene

Charlesetta
(German) form of Charles; royal
Charlesette, Charlsetta

Charlesia
(American) form of Charles; royal; womanly
Charlese, Charlisce, Charlise, Charlsie, Charlsy, Sharlesia

Charlesey
(American) expansive; generous
Charlesee, Charlie, Charlsie, Charlsy

Charlianne
(American) combo of Charlie and Anne
Charlann, Charleyann

Charlie
(American) easygoing
Charl, Charlee, Charley, Charli

Charlize
(American) pretty

Charlotte
(French) little woman
Carly, Charla, Charle, Charlott, Charolot

Charlottie
(French) small
Charlotty

Charlsheah
(American) happy

Charluce
(American) form of Charles; feminine; royal
Charl, Charla, Charluse

Charm
(Greek) short for Charmian; charming
Charma, Charmay, Sharm

Charmaine
(Latin) womanly; (French) singer
Charma, Charmagne, Charmane, Charmine, Charmyn, Sharmaine, Sharmane, Sharmayne, Sharmyne

Charmine
(French) charming
Charmen, Charmin

Charminique
(African-American) dashing
Charmineek

Charmonique
(African-American) charming
Charm, Charmi, Charmon, Charmoneek, Charmoni, Charmonik, Sharmonique

Charnee
(American) effervescent
Charney, Charnie, Charny

Charneeka
(African-American) obsessive
Charn, Charnika, Charny

Charnelle
(American) sparkling
Charn, Charnel, Charnell, Charney, Sharnell, Sharnelle

Charnesa
(African-American) noticed
Charnessa, Charnessah

Charo
(Spanish) flower
Charro

Charsetta
(American) form of Charlene; emotional
Charsee, Charsette, Charsey, Charsy

Chartra
(American) classy
Chartrah

Chartres
(French) planner
Chartrys

Charysse
(Greek) graceful girl
Charece, Charese,
Charisse

Chassie
(Latin) form of Chastity;
virtuous
Chass, Chassey, Chassi

Chastity
(Latin) pure woman
Chasta, Chastitie

Chaucer
(English) demure
Chauser, Chawcer,
Chawser

Chava
(Hebrew) life-giving
Chavah, Chave, Hava

Chaviva
(Hebrew) beloved

Chaya
(Jewish) living

Chayan
(Native American)
variant of Cheyenne;
tribe
Chay, Chayanne, Chi,
Shayan, Shy

Chea
(American) witty
Chea, Cheeah

Cheer
(American) joyful

Chekia
(Invented) cheeky
Chekie, Shekia

Cheletha
(African-American)
smiling
Chelethe, Cheley

Chelle
(American) short for
Chelsea; secure
Shell

Chelsea
(Old English) safe harbor
Chelcy, Cheli, Chellsie,
Chelse, Chelsee, Chelsey,
Chelsie, Kelsey, Shelsee

Chenille
(American) soft
Chenile, Chinille

Chenoa
(American) form of
Genoa
Cheney, Cheno

Cher
(French) dear
Sher

Cherelle
(French) dear
Charell, Cherrelle,
Sharelle

Cherie
(French) dear
Cherey, Cheri, Cherice,
Cherree, Cherrie, Cherry

Cherika
(French) form of Cherry;
kind; dear
Chereka, Cherikah

Cherilynn
(American) combo of
Cheryl and Lynn; kind-
hearted
Cheryl-Lynn, Cherylynne,
Sherilyn, Sherilynn,
Sherralin

Cherinne
(American) happy
Charinn, Cherin, Cherry

Cherise
(French) cherry
Cherece, Cherrise

Cherish
(French) precious girl
Charish, Cherishe,
Sherishe

Cherisha
(American) endearing
Cherishah, Cherishuh

Cherita
(Spanish) dearest
Cheritt, Cheritta, Cherrita

Cheritte
(American) held dear
Cher, Cherette, Cheritta

Cherly
(American) form of
Shirley; natural; bright
meadow
Cherlee, Sherly

Cherlyn
(American) combo of
Cher and Lyn; dear one
Cherlin, Cherlinn,
Cherlynn, Cherlynne

Cherokee
(Native American) Indian
tribe member

Cherron
(American) graceful
dancer
Cher, Cheron, Cherronne

Cherry
(Latin, French) cherry red
Cheree, Cherey, Cherrye,
Chery

Cherrylee
(French, American)
combo of Cherry and
Lee; lively
Charalee, Charralee,
Cheralee, Cherilea,
Cherilee, Cherileese,
Cher-Lea, Cherry-Lee,
Cherylee, Sharilee,
Sheralea, Sherryleigh

Cherry-Sue
(American) combo of
Cherry and Sue

Cheryl
(French) beloved
Charyl, Cherel, Cherelle,
Cheryll

Chesley
(English) pretty;
meadow
Ches, Cheslay, Cheslea,
Chesleigh

Chesna
(Slavic) peace
Ches, Chesnah

Chesney
(English) peacemaker
Chesnee, Chesni,
Chesnie, Chessnea

Chesskwana
(African-American)
evoker
Chesskwan,
Chessquana, Chessy

Chessteen
(American) needed
Ches, Chessy, Chesteen,
Chestene

Chet
(American) vivacious
Chett

Chevy
(American) funny
Chev, Chevee

Cheyenne
(Native American) Indian
tribe; capital of
Wyoming
Chayanne, Cheyan,
Cheyanna, Cheyene,
Chynne, Shayan,
Shayann, Sheyenne

Chiara
(Italian) bright and clear
Cheara, Chiarra, Kiara,
Klarra

Chica
(Spanish) girl
Chika

Chick
(American) fun-loving
Chicki, Chickie

Chickadee
(American) cute little girl
Chicka, Chickady,
Chickee, Chickey, Chicky

Chikira
(Spanish) dancer
Shakira

Childe
(American) literary
Child

Childers
(Last name as first
name) dignified
Chelders, Childie,
Chillders, Chylders

China
(Place name) unique
Chinnah, Chyna, Chynna

Chinadoll
(Invented) fun
*China Doll, China-Doll,
Chynadoll*

Chiquida
(Spanish) form of
Chiquita; small
Chiquide

Chiquita
(Spanish) small girl
*Chica, Chick, Chickie,
Chikita, Chiquitia,
Chiquitta, Shiquita*

Chirline
(American) variant of
Charline; sweet
*Chirl, Chirlene, Shirl,
Shirline*

Chivonne
(American) happy
*Chevonne, Chivaughan,
Chivaughn, Chivon,
Chivonn*

Chloe
(Greek) flowering
*Chloee, Clo, Cloee,
Cloey, Khloe, Kloe*

Chloris
(Greek) pale-skinned
Cloris, Kloris

Chris
(Greek) form of
Christina; best
Chrissie, Chrissy, Kris

Chrisana
(American) boisterous
Chris, Chrisanah, Crisane

Chrissa
(Greek) form of Christina
Crissa, Cryssa, Krissa

Chrissy
(English) short for
Christina
Chrissie, Krissy

Christa
(German, Greek)
loving
Crista, Krista

Christabelle
(American) combo of
Christa and Belle
Cristabel

Christal
(Latin) form of Crystal
*Christall, Christalle,
Christel*

Christalin
(American) combo of
Christa and Lin
Christalinn, Christalynn

Christanda
(American) smart
*Christandah,
Christawnda*

Christauna
(American) spiritual
*Christaun, Christawna,
Christown, Christwan*

Christen
(Greek) form of
Christina; Christian
*Christan, Christin,
Cristen, Kristen*

Christian
(Greek) Christian

Christiana
(Greek, German)
Christ's follower
*Christa, Christianna,
Christianne, Christie,
Chystyana, Crystianne,
Crysty-Ann, Kristiana*

Christie
(Greek) short for
Christina
Christi, Kristi, Kristie

Christina
(Greek, Scottish,
German, Irish) the
anointed one
*Chris, Chrissie, Christi,
Christiana, Chrystina,
Crista, Kristina*

Christine
(French, English, Latin)
faithful
*Christene, Christin,
Cristine, Kristine*

Christopher
(Greek) devout Christian
Kris, Krissie, Krissy,
Krista, Kristofer,
Kristopher

Christy
(Scottish) Christian
Christee, Christi, Christie

Chrysanthemum
(American) flower
Chrys, Chrysanthe,
Chrysie, Mum

Chrysanthum
(Invented) from flower
chrysanthemum;
flowering
Chrys, Chrysan,
Chrysanth

Chulisa
(Invented) clever
Chully, Ulisa

Ciara
(Irish) brunette
Cearra, Ciarah, Ciarra,
Keera, Keerah

Cicely
(Latin) form of Cecilia;
clever
Cicelie, Cici, Sicely

Cid
(American) fun
Cyd, Syd

Cidni
(American) jovial
Cidnee, Cidney, Cidnie

Cidrah
(American) unusual
Cid, Ciddie, Ciddy, Cidra

Cieara
(Spanish) dark
CiCi, Ciear, Sieara

Ciera
(Irish) dark
Cíera, Cia, Cieera, Cierra,
Cierre

Cilla
(Greek) vivacious
Cika, Sica, Sika

Cille
(American) short for
Lucille
Ceele

Cinderella
(French) imaginative;
hopeful
Cinda, Cindi, Cindie,
Cindy

Cindy
(Greek, Latin) moon
goddess;
Cindee, Cindi, Cyndee,
Cyndi, Cyndie, Sindee,
Syndi, Syndie, Syndy

Cinnamon
(Spice) sweet
Cenamon, Cinna,
Cinnammon,
Cinnamond, Cinamen,
Cynamon

Ciona
(American) steadfast
Cinonah, Cionna, Cyona

Ciprianna
(Italian) from Ciprus;
cautious
Cipri, Cipriannah,
Cypriana, Cyprianna,
Cyprianne, Sipriana,
Siprianna

Circe
(Greek) sorceress deity;
mysterious
Circee, Cirsey, Cirsie

Ciri
(Latin) regal
Ceree, Ceri, Seree, Siri

Cirila
(Latin) heavenly
Ceri, Cerila, Cerilla,
Cerille, Cerine, Ciria,
Cirine

Cissy
(American) sweet
Ciss, Cissey, Cissi, Sissi

Citare
(Greek) musical; variant
of the Indian lute sitar
Citara, Sitare

Claire
(Latin, French) smart
Clair, Clairee, Claireen,
Claireta, Clairy, Clare,
Clarette, Clarry, Klair

Clarieca
(Latin) bright
Claire, Clare, Clari,
Clarieka, Clary, Klarieca,
Klarieka

Clancey
(American)
devil-may-care
Clance, Clancee, Clancie,
Clancy

Clara
(Latin) bright one
Clarie, Clarine, Clary

Clarabelle
(Latin) combo of Clara
and Belle; bright lovely
woman
Claribel

Clarice
(Latin, Italian)
insightful
Clairece, Claireece,
Clairice, Clarece,
Clareece, Clariece,
Clarise

Clarissa
(Latin, Greek) smart
and clear-minded
Claressa, Clarisa,
Clerissa

Clarity
(American) clear-minded
Clare, Claritee, Claritie

Claudia
(Latin, German, Italian)
persevering
Claudelle, Claudie,
Claudina, Clodia,
Klaudia

Claudia-Rose
(American) combo of
Claudia and Rose

Claudette
(French) persevering
Claude, Claudee,
Claudet, Claudi, Claudie,
Claudy

Clea
(Invented) short for
Cleanthe and Cleopatra;
famed
Clia, Klea, Klee

Cleanthe
(English) famed
Clea, Klea, Kleanth

Clemence
(Latin) easygoing;
merciful
Clem, Clemense,
Clements, Clemmie,
Clemmy

Clementina
(Spanish) kind; forgiving
Clementyna,
Clymentyna, Klementina

Clementine
(Latin) gentle;
(German) merciful
Clemencie, Klementine,
Klementynne

Cleo
(Greek) short for
Cleopatra

Cleopatra
(Greek) Egyptian queen
Cleo, Clee, Kleeo, Kleo

Clio
(Greek) history muse
Kleeo, Klio

Cloe
(Greek) flourishing
Cloee, Cloey

Cloreen
(American) happy
Clo, Cloreane, Cloree,
Cloreene, Corean, Klo,
Klorean, Kloreen

Cloressa
(American) consoling
Cloresse, Kloressa

Clorinda
(Latin) happy
Cloee, Cloey, Clorinde,
Clorynda, Klorinda

Clory
(Spanish) smiling
Clori, Clorie, Kloree,
Klory

Closetta
(Spanish) secretive
Close, Closette, Klosetta, Klosette

Clotilda
(German) famed fighter
Tilda, Tillie, Tilly

Clotilde
(French) combative

Cloud
(Weather name) light-hearted
Cloudee, Cloudie, Cloudy

Clove
(Spice) distinctive
Klove

Clover
(Botanical) natural
Clove, Kloverr

Clydette
(American) form of Clyde
Clidette, Clydett, Clydie, Klyde, Klydette

Clytie
(Greek) excellent; in love with love
Cly, Clytee, Clytey, Clyty, Klytee, Klytie

Co
(American) jovial
Coco, Ko, Koko

Coby
(American) glad
Cobe, Cobey, Cobie

Coco
(Spanish) coconut
Koko

Cocoa
(Spanish) chocolate; spunky girl

Cody
(English) soft-hearted; pillow
Codi, Codie, Kodie

Coffey
(American) lovely
Cofee, Caufey

Coiya
(American) coquettish
Coyuh, Koya

Cokey
(American) intelligent
Cokie

Colby
(English) enduring
Cobie, Colbi, Kolbee

Cole
(Last name as first name) laughing
Coe, Colie, Kohl

Colemand
(American) adventurer
Colmyand

Colette
(French) spiritual; victorious
Coey, Collette, Kolette

Colina
(American) righteous
Colena, Colin, Colinn

Colisa
(English) delightful
Colissa, Collisa, Collissa

Colleen
(Irish) young girl
Coleen, Colene, Coley, Colleene, Collen, Colli, Kolene, Kolleen

Colley
(English) fearful; worrier
Col, Collie, Kolley

Colola
(African-American) combination of Co and Lola; victor
Co, Cola, Colo

Coloma
(Spanish) calm
Colo, Colom, Colome

Columbine
(Latin) dove; flower

Comfort
(American) comforting; easygoing
Komfort

Comfortyne
(French) comforting
Comfort, Comfortine, Comfurtine, Comfy

Concetta
(Italian) pure female

Conchetta
(Spanish) wholesome
Concheta, Conchette

Conchie
(Latin) conception
Conchee, Conchi, Konchey, Konchie

Conchita
(Spanish) girl of the conception
Chita, Concha, Conchi

Conchiteen
(Spanish) pure
Conchita, Conchitee, Connie

Concordia
(Latin) goddess of peace

Condoleezza
(American) smart
Condeleesa, Condilesa, Condolissa

Coneisha
(African-American) giving
Coneisha, Conisha, Conishah, Conniesha

Conesa
(American) free-flowing nature
Conisa, Connesa, Konesa

Conlee
(American) form of Connelly; radiant
Con, Conlee, Conley, Conlie, Conly, Conly, Connie, Konlee, Konlee, Konlie

Conner
(American) brave
Con, Coner, Coni, Connie, Connor, Conny, Conor

Connie
(Latin, English) short for Constance; constant
Con, Conni, Conny, Konnie

Connie-Kim
(Vietnamese) golden girl
Conni-Kim

Conradina
(German) form of Conrad; brave
Connie, Conradyna, Konnie, Konradina

Conroe
(Place name) small town in Texas
Conn, Connie, Konroe

Conroy
(Last name as first name) stately; literary
Conroi, Konroi, Konroy

Constance
(Latin) loyal
Con, Connie

Constantina
(Italian) loyal; constant
Conn, Connee, Conni, Connie, Conny, Constance, Constanteena, Constantinah

Constanza
(Hebrew) constant
Constanz, Connstanzah

Constanze
(German) unchanging
Con, Connie, Stanzi

Consuelo
(Spanish) comfort-giver
Chelo, Consolata, Consuela

Contessa
(Italian) pretty
Contesa, Contessah, Contesse

Cookie
(American) cute
Cooki

Copeland
(Last name as first name) good at coping
Copelan, Copelyn, Copelynn

Copper
(American) redhead
Coper

Coppola
(Italian) theatrical
Copla, Coppi, Coppo, Coppy, Kopla, Kopola, Koppola

Cora
(Greek) maid; giving girl
Corah, Corra, Kora

Coral
(Latin) nature name; small stone
Corall, Coraly, Core, Koral, Koraly

Coralee
(American) combo of Cora and Lee
Cora-Lee, Coralie, Koralie

Coralynn
(American) combo of Cora and Lynn
Coralene, Coralyn, Cora-Lyn, Cora-Lynn, Coralynne, Corline, Corlynn

Corazon
(Spanish) heart
Cora, Corrie, Zon, Zonn

Corday
(English) prepared; heart
Cord, Cordae, Cordie, Cordy, Korday

Cordelia
(Latin) warm-hearted woman
Cordi, Cordie, Cordilia, Kordelia, Kordey, Kordi

Cordelita
(Latin, Spanish) heartfelt
Cordelia, Cordelite, Cordella

Cordula
(Latin) heart; (German) jewel
Cord, Cordie, Cordoola, Cordoolah, Cordy

Corey
(Irish) perky
Cori, Corree, Corrie, Korey, Korri, Korrie

Corgie
(American) funny
Corgi, Korgee, Korgie

Cori
(Greek, Irish) caring person
Corey, Corri, Corrie, Cory

Corinna
(Greek) young girl
Corina, Corrinna, Corryna, Corynna

Corinne
(Greek) maiden; (French) protective
Coreen, Corina, Corine, Corinna, Corrina, Coryn, Corynn, Koreene, Korinne

Coris
(Greek) singer
Corris, Koris, Korris

Corissa
(Greek) kind-hearted
Korissa

Corky
(American) energetic
Corkee, Corkey, Corki, Corkie, Korkee, Korky

Corliss
(English) open-hearted
Corless, Corlise, Corly, Korlis, Korliss

Corly
(American) energetic
Corlee, Corli, Corlie, Korli, Korly

Corlyn
(American) innovative
Corlin, Corlinn, Corlynn, Corlynne, Korlin, Korlyn

Cormella
(Italian) fiery
Cormee, Cormela, Cormelah, Cormellia, Cormey, Cormie

Cornae
(Origin unknown)
Coma, Korna, Kornae
Cornelia
(Latin) practical
Carnelia, Corney, Corni
Cornelius
(Latin) realistic
Corneal, Corneelyus, Corney, Corny
Cornesha
(African-American) talkative
Cornee, Corneshah, Cornesia
Corona
(Spanish) crowned; name of a beer
Corone, Coronna, Korona
Correne
(American) musical
Coree, Coreen, Correen, Correna, Korrene, Korene
Corrianna
(American) joyful
Coreanne, Corey, Corianna, Corri, Corriana
Corrinda
(French) girlish
Corri, Corrin, Korin, Korinda

Cortanie
(American) variation on Courtney
Cortanny, Cortany
Cortland
(American) distinctive
Cortlan, Courte, Courtland, Courtlin
Cortlinn
(American) happy
Cortlenn, Cortlin, Cortlyn, Cortlynn
Corvette
(Car model) speedy, dark
Corv, Corva, Corve, Korvette
Cosette
(French) warm
Cossette
Cosima
(Greek, German, Italian) of the universe; in harmony
Coseema, Koseema, Kosima
Cosmee
(Greek) organized
Cos, Cosmi, Cosmie
Cossette
(French) winning
Coss, Cossie, Cossy, Kossee, Kossette

Costner
(American) embraced
Cosner, Cost, Costnar, Costnor, Costnur
Cotcha
(African-American) stylish
Kasha, Katcha, Katshay, Kotsha
Cotrena
(American) form of Katrina; pure
Catreena, Catrina, Catrine, Cotrene, Katrine, Kotrene
Cotton
(American) comforting
Cottie
Countess
(American) blueblood
Contessa
Cournette
(American) form of coronet; regal
Courney, Kournette
Courtney
(English) regal; (French) patient
Cortney, Courtenay, Courteney, Courtnay, Courtnee, Courtny, Kortnee, Kortney

Covin
(American)
unpredictable
Covan, Cove, Coven,
Covyn

Coy
(American) sly
Coye, Koi, Koy

Coyah
(American) singular
Coya, Coyia

Coyote
(American) wild
Coyo, Kaiote, Kaiotee

Cramer
(American) jolly
Cramar, Cramir, Kramer

Cramisa
(Invented) nice
Cramissa, Kramisa

Cree
(American) wild spirit
Crea, Creeah

Creed
(American) boisterous
Crede, Cree, Kreed

Crescente
(American) impressive
Crescent, Cresent, Cress,
Cressie

Cressa
(Greek) delicate (from
the name Cressida)
Cresa, Cressah, Cresse,
Cress, Kressa

Cressida
(Greek) infidel
Cresida, Cresiduh,
Cresside

Cressie
(American) growing;
good
Cress, Cressy, Kress,
Kressie

Creston
(American) worthy
Crest, Crestan, Creste,
Cresten, Crestey, Cresti,
Crestie

Cricket
(American) energetic
Kricket

Crimson
(American) deep
Cremsen, Crims,
Crimsen, Crimsonn,
Crimsun

Criselda
(Spanish) wild
Crisselda

Crishonna
(American) beautiful
Crishona, Crisshone,
Crissie, Crissy, Krishona,
Krishonna

Crisiant
(Welsh) crystal; clear
Cris, Crissie

Crispy
(Invented) fun-loving;
zany
Crispee, Krispy

Crista
(Italian) form of
Christina
Krista

Cristin
(Irish) dedicated
Cristen, Crystyn, Kristin,
Krystyn

Cristina
(Greek) form of
Christina; devout
Christina, Kristina

Cristos
(Greek) dedicated
Criss, Crissie, Christos

Cristy
(English) spiritual
Cristi, Crysti, Krystie,
Kristi

Crystal
(Latin) clear; open-
minded
Chrystal, Cristal,
Cristalle, Crys, Crystelle,
Krystal

Crystilis
(Spanish) focused
Chrysilis, Crys, Cryssi,
Cryssie, Crystylis

Cullen
(Irish) attractive
Cullan, Cullie, Cullun, Cully

Cumale
(American) open-hearted
Cue, Cuemalie, Cue-maly, Cumahli

Cumthia
(American) open-minded
Cumthea, Cumthee, Cumthi, Cumthie, Cumthy

Cupid
(American) romantic
Cupide

Curine
(American) attractive
Curina, Curinne, Curri, Currin

Curry
(American) languid
Curree, Currey, Curri, Currie

Cursten
(American) form of Kirsten
Curst, Curstee, Curstie, Curstin

Cushaun
(American) elegant
Cooshaun, Cooshawn, Cue, Cushawn, Cushonn, Cushun

Cyan
(American) colorful
Cyanne, Cyenna, Cyun

Cyanetta
(Greek) little blue
Cyan, Cyanette, Syan, Syanette

Cybill
(Latin) prophetess
Cybell, Cybelle, Cybil, Sibyl, Sibyle

Cydell
(American) country girl
Cydee, Cydel, Cydie, Cydile, Cydy

Cydney
(American) perky
Cyd, Cydni, Cydnie

Cylee
(American) darling
Cye, Cyle, Cylea, Cyli, Cylie, Cyly

Cylene
(American) melodious
Cylena, Cyline

Cymbeline
(Greek) Shakespearean play
Beline, Cymba, Cymbe, Cymbie, Cyme, Cymmie, Symbe

Cyn
(Greek) short for Cynthia
Cynnae, Cynnie, Syn

Cynder
(English) having wanderlust
Cindee, Cinder, Cindy, Cyn, Cyndee, Cyndie, Cyndy

Cyntanah
(American) singer
Cintanna, Cyntanna

Cynthia
(Greek, English) moon goddess
Cindy, Cyn, Cyndee, Cyndy, Cynthea, Cynthee, Cynthie

Cyntia
(Greek) variant of Cynthia; smiling goddess
Cyn, Cyntea, Cynthie, Cyntie, Syntia

Cyntrille
(African-American) gossipy
Cynn, Cyntrell, Cyntrelle, Cyntrie

Cypress
(Botanical) swaying
Cypres, Cyprice, Cypriss, Cyprus

Cyra
(American) willing
Cye, Cyrah, Syra

Cyreen
(American) sensual
Cyree, Cyrene, Cyrie

Cyrenian
(American) bewitching
Cyree, Cyren, Cyrenean,
Cyrey, Siren, Syrenian

Cyrenna
(American)
straightforward
Cyrena, Cyrennah,
Cyrinna, Cyryna, Cyrynna

Cyriece
(American) artistic
Cyreece, Cyree, Cyreese,
Cyrie

D'Anna
(Hebrew) special

Dacey
(Irish) a southerner
Dace, Dacee, Daci,
Dacie, Dacy, Daicie,
Daycee

Dae
(English) day
Day, Daye

Daelan
(English) aware
Dael, Daelan, Daelin,
Daely, Dale, Daley,
Daylan, Daylin, Daylind,
Dee

Daeshonda
(African-American)
combo of Dae and
Shonda
Daeshanda, Daeshawna,
Daeshondra

Daffodil
(Botanical) flower
Daffy

Dafnee
(Greek, American) form
of Daphne; pretty
Dafney, Dafnie

Dagmar
(German, Scandinavian)
glorious day
Dag, Dagmarr

Dahlia
(Scandinavian) flower
Dahl, Dollie

Dai
(Welsh, Japanese)
beloved one of great
importance

Daira
(American) outgoing
D'Aira, Daire, Dairrah,
Darrah, Derrah

Daisha
(American) sparkling
D'Aisha, Daish, Daishe,
Dasha, Dashah

Daisy
(English) flower and
day's eye
Daisee, Daisi, Daisie,
Daissy, Daizee, Daizi,
Daizy, Dasie, Daysy

Daisyetta
(American) combo of
Daisy and Etta; spunky;
the day's eye
Daiseyetta, Daizie,
Daiziette, Dasie,
Dazeyetta, Daziette

Daiton
(American) wondrous
Day, Dayten, Dayton

Daja
(American) intuitive
Dajah

Dajanae
(African-American)
persuasive
Daije, Daja, Dajainay,
Dayjanah

Dajon
(American) gifted
D'Jon, Dajo, Dajohn,
Dajonn, Dajonnay,
Dajonne

Dakara
(American) firebrand
Dacara, Dakarah,
Dakarea, Dakarra

Daking
(Asian) friendly

Dakota
(Native American) tribal
name; solid friend
Dacota, Dakohta,
Dakotah, Dakotta

Dalacie
(American) brilliant
Dalaci, Dalacy, Dalasie,
Dalce, Dalci, Dalse

Dalaina
(American) spirited
Dalana, Dalayna,
Delaina, Delaine,
Delayna

Dalaney
(American) hopeful
Dalanee, Dalaynee,
Dalayni

Dale
(English) valley-life
Dalena, Dayle

Daleah
(American) pretty
Dalea

Daley
(Irish) leader
Dailey, Dalea, Daleigh,
Dali, Dalie, Daly

Dalia
(Spanish) flower
Daliah, Dayliah, Doliah,
Dolliah, Dolya

Dalian
(Place name) joy
Dalean

Daliana
(American) joyful spirit
Daliane, Dalianna, Dilial,
Dollianna

Dalice
(American) able
Daleese, Dalleece

Dalila
(African) gentle

Dalin
(American) calm
Dalen, Dalenn, Dalun

Dalita
(American) smooth
Daleta, Daletta, Dalite,
Dalitee, Dalitta

Dallas
(Place name) confident
Dalis, Dalisse, Daliz,
Dallice, Dallis, Dallsyon,
Dallus, Dallys

Dallen
(American) outspoken
Dal, Dalin, Dallin, Dalen

Dallise
(American) gentle
Dalise, Dallece, Dalleece,
Dalleese

Dalondra
(Invented) generous
Dalandra, Dalon,
Dalondrah, Delondra

Dalonna
(Invented) generous
Dalohn, Dalona,
Dalonne

Dalphine
(French) form of
Delphine; delicate and
svelte
*Dal, Dalf, Dalfeen,
Dalfene, Dalphene*

Dalton
(American) smart
*Dallee, Dalli, Dallie,
Dallton, Dally, Daltawyn*

Daltrey
(American) quiet
Daltree, Daltri, Daltrie

Dalyn
(American) smart
*Dalin, Dalinne, Dalynn,
Dalynne*

Dama
(Hindi) temptress
Dam

Damalla
(Greek) fledgling; young;
calf
*Damala, Damalas,
Damalis, Damall*

Damaris
(Greek) calm
*Damalis, Damara,
Damares, Damaret,
Damrez*

Damecia
(Invented) sweet
*Dameisha, Damesha,
Demecia, Demisha,
Demeshe*

Dami
(Greek) short for Damia;
spirited
*Damee, Damey, Damie,
Damy*

Damia
(Greek) spirited
*Damiah, Damya,
Damyah, Damyen,
Damyenne, Damyuh*

Damianne
(Greek) one who
soothes
Damiana

Damica
(French) open-spirited
*Dameeka, Dameka,
Damika, Demica*

Damita
(Spanish) small woman
of nobility
Dama, Damah

Damon
(American) sprightly
Damoane, Damone

Damone
(American) mighty
Dame

Dana
(English) bright gift of
God
*Daina, Danah, Danna,
Dayna, Daynah*

Danae
(Greek) bright and pure
Dannae, Danays, Danee

Danala
(English) happy, golden
*Dan, Danalla, Danee,
Danela, Danney, Danny*

Danasha
(African-American)
combo of Dana and
Tasha; spirited
*Anasha, Danas, Danash,
Danashah, Daneash,
Danesha*

Danay
(American) happy
D'Nay, Dánay, Danaye

Dancel
(French) energetic
*Dance, Dancell,
Dancelle, Dancey,
Dancie, Danse, Dansel,
Danselle*

Dancie
(American) from the
word dancer
Dancy

Danelle
(Hebrew) kind-hearted;
combo of Dan and Nelle
*Danele, Dani, Dannele,
Danny*

Danelly
(Spanish) form of Daniel; judged by God
Daneli, Danellie, Dannelley, Dannelly

Danessa
(American) dainty
Danese, Danesse

Danette
(American) form of Danielle
Danett

Dangela
(Latin) form of Angela; angelic
Angee, Angelle, Angie, Dangelah, Dangelia, Dangey, Dangi, Dangie

Dani
(Hebrew) short for Danielle or Danelle
Danee, Danni, Dannie, Danny

Dania
(Hebrew) short for Danielle

Daniah
(Hebrew) judged
Dan, Dania, Danny, Danya

Danica
(Latin, Polish) star of the morning
Daneeka, Danika, Dannika

Daniele
(Hebrew, French) form of Daniel; judged by God alone
Danelle, Daniell, Danielle, Danniella, Danyel

Daniella
(Italian) form of Danielle
Danilla

Danir
(American) fresh
Daner

Danita
(American) combo of Dan and Anita; gregarious
Danni, Danny, Denita, Denny

Danna
(American) cheerful
D'Ana, D'Anna, Dannae, Danni, Danny

Daphiney
(Greek) form of Daphne; nymph
Daff, Daph

Daphne
(Greek) pretty nymph
Daphany, Daphiney, Daphnee, Daphney, Daphnie, Daphny, Daphonie, Daphy

Dara
(Hebrew) compassionate
Dahrah, Darah, Darra

Daralice
(Greek) beloved
Dara, Daraleese, Daraliece

Darby
(Irish) a free woman
Darb, Darbee, Darbi, Darbie, Darbye

Darcelle
(American) secretive
Darce, Darcel, Darcell, Darcey

Darci
(Irish) dark
Darce, Darcee, Darcie, Darcy, Dars, Darsey

Daria
(Greek, Italian) rich woman of luxury
Dare, Darea, Dareah, Dari, Darria

Darian
(Anglo-Saxon) precious
Dare, Darien, Darry, Derian, Derian

Darice
(English) contemporary
Dareese, Darese, Dari, Dariece, Darri, Darrie, Darry

Darielle
(French) rich
Darell, Darelle, Dariel,
Darrielle

Darilyn
(American) darling
Darilin, Darilinn,
Darilynn, Derilyn

Darionne
(American)
adventuresome
Dareon, Darion, Darionn,
Darionna

Dariya
(Russian) sweet
Dara, Darya

Darla
(English) short for
Darlene
Darl, Darli, Darlie

Darlee
(English) darling
Darl, Darley, Darli, Darlie

Darlene
(French) darling girl
Darlean, Darleen,
Darlena, Darlin, Darling

Darlie-Lynn
(American) combo of
Darlie and Lynn

Darling
(American) precious
Darline, Darly, Darlyng

Darlonna
(African-American)
darling
Darlona

Darnelle
(Irish) seamstress
Darnel

Daron
(Irish) great woman
Daren, Darun, Daryn

Darrow
(Last name as first
name) cautious
Darro, Darroh

Darryl
(French, English)
beloved
Darel, Darelle, Daril,
Darrell, Darrill, Daryl,
Daryll, Derel, Derrell

Darshelle
(African-American)
confident
Darshel, Darshell

Dart
(English) tenacious
Darte, Dartee, Dartt

Darva
(Invented) sensible
Darv, Darvah, Darvee,
Darvey, Darvi, Darvie

Daryn
(Greek, Irish) gift-giver
Darynn

Dash
(American) fast-moving
Dashee, Dasher, Dashy

Dasha
(Russian) darling
Dashah

Dashanda
(African-American)
loving
Dashan, Dashande

Dashawn
(African-American) brash
Dashawna, Dashay

Dashawntay
(African-American)
careful
Dash, Dashauntay

Dashea
(Hebrew) patient

Dasheena
(African-American)
flashy
Dashea, Dasheana

Dashelle
(African-American)
striking
Dachelle, Dashel,
Dashell, Dashy

Dashika
(African-American)
runner
Dash, Dasheka

Dashilan
(American) solemn
*Dashelin, Dashelin,
Dashlinne, Dashlyn,
Dashlynn, Dasialyn*

Dasmine
(Invented) sleek
*Dasmeen, Dasmin,
Dazmeen, Dazmine*

Dassia
(American) pretty
*Dasie, Dassea, Dasseah,
Dassee, Dassi, Dassie,
Deassiah*

Daureen
(American) darling
*Dareen, Daurean,
Daurie, Daury, Dawreen*

Daveena
(Scottish) form of David;
loved
*Daveen, Davena, Davey,
Davina, Davinna*

Davelyn
(Invented) combo of
Dave and Lynn; loved
*Davalin, Davalynn,
Davalynne, Dave, Davey,
Davie, Davilynn*

Davida
(Hebrew) beloved one
Daveeda, Daveta, Davita

Davina
(Hebrew) believer;
beloved
*Daveena, Davene,
Davida, Davita, Devina,
Devinia, Devinya*

Davincia
(Spanish) God-loving;
winner
Davince, Davinse, Vincia

Davinique
(African-American)
believer; unique
Davin, Davineek, Vineek

Davis
(American) boyish
Daves

Davisnell
(Invented) vivacious
Daviesnell, DavisNell

Davonne
(African-American)
splashy
*Davaughan, Davaughn,
Davion, Daviona, Davon,
Davone, Davonn*

Dawa
(Tibetan) girl born on
Monday

Dawanda
(African-American)
righteous
*Dawana, Dawand,
Dawanna, Dawauna,
Dawonda, Dawonna,
Dwanda*

Dawn
(English) dawn
Daun, Dawna, Dawne

Dawna
(English) eloquence of
dawn
*Dauna, Daunda, Dawn,
Dawnah, Dawny*

Dawnika
(African-American) dawn
*Dawneka, Dawneeka,
Dawnica, Donika*

Dawnisha
(African-American)
breath of dawn
*Daunisha, Dawnish,
Dawny, Nisa, Nisha*

Dawntelle
(African-American)
morning bright
*Dawntel, Dawntell,
Dontelle*

Dawona
(African-American) smart
Dawonna, Dawonne

Dayana
(American) variant of
Diana; darling
Dayannah, Dyana

Dayanara
(Spanish) form of
Deyanira; forceful;
destructive
*Day, Daya, Dayan,
Dianara, Diannare, Nara*

Daylee
(American) calm;
reserved
*Dailee, Day, Dayley,
Dayly*

Dayna
(English) variant of
Dana; bright gift of God
Daynah

Dayshanay
(African-American) saucy
*Daysh, Dayshanae,
Dayshannay, Dayshie*

Dayshawna
(American) laughing
*Dayshauna, Dayshona,
Dashonah*

Dayshay
(African-American)
lovable
Dashae, Dashay, Dashea

Dayton
(Place name) fast

Daytona
(American) speedy
Dayto, Daytonna

Dayvonne
(African-American)
careful
*Dave, Davey, Davonne,
Dayvaughn*

De
(Chinese) virtuous

Deacon
(Greek) joyful
messenger
*Deak, Deakon, Deecon,
Deke*

Dean
(English) practical
Deanie, Deanni

Deandra
(English) combo of
Deanna and Sandra;
pretty face
Andie, Andra, Dee

Deandralina
(American) combo of
Deandra and Lina; divine
seer
*Deandra-Lina, Deandra
Lina. Deanalina, Lina,
Deandra, Dee, DeeDee*

Deandria
(American) sweetheart
Deandreah, Deandriah

Deanie
(English) form of Dean;
from the valley
Deanee, Deaney, Deani

Deanna
(Latin, English)
divine girl
Deana, Deanne, Dee

Deanne
(Latin) from Diana;
moon goddess
Deann, Dee, Deeann

Dearon
(American) dear one
*Dear, Dearan, Dearen,
Deary*

Dearoven
(American) form of
Dearon
Derovan, Deroven

Debbie
(Hebrew) short for
Deborah
*Deb, Debbee, Debbi,
Debby, Debbye, Debi*

Debbie-Jean
(American) combo of
Debbie and Jean

Debbielou
(American) combo of
Debbie and Lou
Debilou

Debbie-Sue
(American) combo of
Debbi and Sue
Debbisue

Deborah
(Hebrew) prophetess
*Debbie, Deboreh,
Deborrah, Debra*

Debra
(Hebrew) prophetess
Debrah

Debray
(American) form of
Deborah; prophetess
*Dabrae, Deb, Debrae,
Debraye*

Debra-Jean
(American) combo of
Debra and Jean

DeChell
(Invented) combo of De
and Chell; quiet
Dechelle, Dee

Dedra
(American) spirited
*Dee, DeeDee, Deedra,
Deidra, Deirdre*

Dee
(English, Irish) lucky one
*Dedee, DeeDee, Dee-
Dee, Didee*

Deedee
(American) short for D
names; vivacious
*D.D., Dee Dee, DeeDee,
Dee-Dee*

DeErica
(African-American)
audacious
Dee-Erica

Deesha
(American) dancing
*Dedee, Dee, Deesh,
Deeshah, Deisha*

Deidra
(Irish) sparkling
Deedra, Deidre, Dierdra

Deighan
(American) exciting
Daygan, Deigan

Deiondra
(Greek) partier; wine-
loving
*Deandrah, Deann,
Deanndra, Dee, Deean,
Deeann, DeeDee,
Deondra*

Deirdre
(Irish) passionate
*Dedra, Dee, Deedee,
Deedrah, Deerdra,
Deerdre, Didi*

Deishauna
(African-American)
combo of Dei and
Shauna; pious; day of
God
*Dayshauna, Deisha,
Deishaun, Deishaune,
Shauna*

Deissy
(Greek) form of Desma;
sworn; loyal
*Deisi, Deissey, Deissie,
Desma, Desmee,
Desmer, Dessi*

Deitra
(Greek) goddess-like
Deetra

Deja
(French) already seen
D'Ja, Dejah

Deja-Marie
(American) combo of
Deja and Marie
Deja, Dejamarie

Delaine
(American) combo of D
and Elaine; smart
D'Laine, Delane

Delana
(German) protective
*Dalana, Daleena,
Dalena, Deedee*

Delanah
(American) wise
Delana, Dellana, Delano

Delandra
(American) outgoing
Delan, Delande

Delaney
(Irish) bouncy;
enthusiastic
*Dalanie, Delaine,
Delalney, Delane,
DeLayney, Dellie,
Dulaney*

Delcarmen
(Spanish) combo of Del
and Carmen; worldly
*Del, Del Carmen, Del-
Carmen, Delcee, Delcy*

Delcy
(American) friendly
Del, Delcee, Delci

Dele
(American) rash; noble
Del, Dell

Delfina
(Latin, Italian) flowering
Dellfina, Delphina

Delgadina
(Spanish) derivative of
Delgado; slender
Delga, Delgado

Delia
(Greek) lovely; moon
goddess
Deilyuh, Delya, Delyah

Delise
(Latin) delicious
*Del, Delice, Delicia,
Delisa, Delissa*

Delicia
(Latin, Spanish)
delicious; delightful
*Delisa, Delishea, Delisia,
Delysa*

Delilah
(Hebrew) beautiful
temptress
Dalia, Dalila, Delila, Lilah

Delinda
(American) form of
Melinda; pretty
Delin, Delinde, Delynda

Delite
(American) pleasure-
giving
Delight

Dell
(Greek) kind
Del

Della
(Greek) kind
Dee, Del, Dell

Dellana
(Irish) form of Delaney;
vibrant; delight
*Delaine, Delana, Dell,
Dellaina, Dellane,
Dellann*

Dell-Marie
(American) combo of
Dell and Marie; helpful;
gracious
*Dell Marie, Delmaria,
Delmarie*

Delma-Lee
(American) combo of
Delma and Lee;
uncomplicated
Delmalea, Delmalee

Delmee
(American) star
*Del, Delmey, Delmi,
Delmy*

Delmys
(American) incredible
Del, Delmas, Delmis

Delon
(American) musical
Delonn, Delonne

Delores
(Spanish) woman of
sorrowful leaning
Delore, Dolores, Deloris

Delos
(Greek) beautiful brunette; a small Aegean isle; stunning
Delas

Delpha
(Greek) from Delphi, or the flower delphinium; flourishing
Delfa

Delphine
(Latin) swimmer
Delfine, Delphene

Delta
(Greek) door; Greek alphabet letter; (American) land-loving
Del, Dell, Dellta, Delte

Deltrese
(African-American) jubilant
Del, Delltrese, Delt, Delta, Deltreese, Deltrice

Delwyn
(English, Welsh) beautiful friend
Delwen, Delwenne, Delwin

Demetress
(Greek) form of Demetria, corn goddess
Deme, Demetra, Demetres, Demetri, Demetria, Dimi, Tress, Tressie, Tressy

Demetria
(Greek) harvest goddess
Demeteria, Demetra, Demitra

Demi
(French) half
Demie

Dena
(English) laidback; valley
Deena, Denah

Denedra
(American) lively; natural
Den, Dene, Denney

Deneen
(American) from Hebrew Dena; absolved
Denean, Denene

Denes
(English) nature-lover
Denis, Denne, Denny

Denetria
(Greek) from God
Denitria, Denny, Dentria

Denetrice
(African-American) optimistic
Denetrise, Denitrise, Denny

Denise
(French) wine-lover
Danise, Denese, Deniece, Denni, Denny

Denisha
(American) jubilant
Danisha, Deneesha, Deneshea

Denton
(American) Texas town
Dent, Dentun, Denty, Dentyn

Denver
(English) born in a green valley
Denv, Denvie

Denz
(Invented) lively
Dens

Deoniece
(African-American) feminine
Dee, DeeDee, Deo, Deone, Deoneece, Deoneese

Dericka
(American) dancer
D'ericka, Derica, Dericca, Derika

Derie
(Hebrew) form of Derora; dear; bird
Derey, Drora , Drorah

Deronique
(African-American) unique girl
Deron, Deroneek

Derrona
(American) natural
Derona, Derone, Derry

Derry
(Irish) red-haired woman
Deri, Derrie

Desdemona
(Greek) a name from
Greek drama and
Shakespeare's *Othello*;
tragic figure
Des, Desde, Dez

Deshawna
(African-American)
vivacious
*Deshauna, Deshaune,
Deshawnna, Deshona,
Deshonna*

Deshette
(African-American) dishy
Deshett

Deshondra
(African-American)
vivacious
*Deshaundra,
Deshondrah, Deshondria*

Desi
(French) short for
Desiree
Dezi, Dezzie

Desire
(English) desired
Dezire

Desiree
(French) desired
*Des'ree, Desairee,
Desarae, Desaray,
Desaraye, Desaree,
Desarhea, Desary,
Deseri, Desree, Des-Ree,
Dezaray, Deziree, Dezray*

Destin
(American) destiny
Destinn, Destyn

Destina
(Spanish) destiny
Desteena, Desteenah

Destiny
(French) fated
*Destanee, Destanie,
Desteney, Destinay,
Destinee, Destinei,
Destini, Destinyi,
Destnay, Destney,
Destonie, Destony,
Destyni*

Destry
(American) well-fated;
western feel
Destrey, Destri, Destrie

Deterrion
(Latin) form of Detra;
blessed
*Deterr, Deterreyon,
Detra, Detrae*

Detra
(Latin) form of Detta;
blessed
Detraye

Deva
(Hindi) moon goddess;
wielder of power
Devi

Devalca
(Spanish) generous
Deval

Devan
(Irish) poetic
Devana, Devn

Devi
(Hindi) beloved goddess
*Devia, Deviann, Devian,
Devie, Devri*

Devin
(Irish) poetic
Devn, Devyn, Devynne

Devina, Devin
(Irish) divine; creative
*Davena, Devie, Devine,
Devy, Divine*

Devon
(English) place name;
poetic
*Dev, Devaughan,
Devaughn, Devie,
Devonne, Devy*

Devorah
(American) combo of
Devon and Deborah
Devora, Devore

Dew
(American) from the
word dew; fresh
Dewi, Dewie

Dewanna
(African-American) clingy
*D'Wana, Dewana,
Dewanne*

Dexter
(English) spunky;
dexterous
*Dex, Dexee, Dexey,
Dexie, Dext, Dextar,
Dextur, Dexy*

Deyanira
(Spanish) aggressor
*Deyan, Deyann, Dianira,
Nira, Nira*

Dharcia
(American) sparkler
Darch, Darsha, Dharsha

Dharika
(American) sad
Darica, Darika

Dharma
(Hindi) morality; beliefs
Darma, Darmah

Dhazalai
(African)
Dhaze, Dhazie

Dhelal
(Arabic) coy

Dhessie
(American) glowing
*Dhessee, Dhessey,
Dhessi, Dhessy*

Di
(Latin) short for Diane or
Diana
Didi, Dy

Dia
(Greek) shining
Di

Diaelza
(Spanish) divine; pretty
Diael, Dialza, Elza

Diah
(American) pretty
Dia

Diamantina
(Spanish) sparkling
*Diama, Diamante,
Mantina*

Diamond
(Latin) precious
gemstone
*Diamin, Diamon,
Diamonds, Diamun,
Diamyn, Diamynd,
Dyamond*

Diamondah
(African-American)
glowing
Diamonda, Diamonde

Diamondique
(African-American)
sparkling
Diamondik

Diamony
(American) gem
*Diamonee, Diamoney,
Diamoni, Diamonie*

Diana
(Latin) divine woman;
goddess of the hunt and
fertility
*Dee, Di, Diahana,
Diahna, Dianah,
Diannah, Didi, Dihanna,
Dyanna, Dyannah,
Dyhana*

Dianalynn
(American) combo of
Diana and Lynn
*Dianalin, Dianalinne,
Dianalyn*

Diandro
(American) special
*Diandra, Diandrea,
Diandroh*

Diane
(Latin) goddess-like;
divine
*Deedee, Di, Diahann,
Dian, Diann, Dianne,
Didi*

Dianette
(American) combo of
Diane and Ette; high-
spirited
*Di, Diane, Dianett, Didi,
Diette, Diyannette,
Dyan, Dyanette, Dyanne,
Dyenette*

Diantha
(Greek) flower; heavenly
Dianth

Diarah
(American) pretty
*Dearah, Di, Diara, Diarra,
Dierra*

Diavonne
(African-American) jovial
*Diavone, Diavonna,
Diavonni*

Dicey
(American) impulsive
*Di, Dice, Dicee, Dicy,
Dycee, Dycey*

Dicia
(American) wild
Desha, Dicy

Diedre
(Irish) variant of Deidre;
spunky
Diedra, Diedré

Diesha
(African-American) zany
*Diecia, Dieshah, Dieshie,
Dieshay*

Diggs
(American) tomboyish
Digs, Dyggs

Dihana
(American) natural
Dihanna

Dijonaise
(Invented) condiments;
combo of Dijon and
mayonnaise
*Deejonaise, Dijon,
Dijonais, Dijonaze, Naise*

Dijonnay
(American) fun-loving
*Dijon, Dijonae, Dijonay,
Dijonnae, Dijonnaie*

Dilan
(American) form of Dylan
Dillan, Dilon

Dillyana
(English) worshipful
*Diliann, Dilli, Dillianna,
Dilly*

Dilynn
(American) variant of
Dylan; loving the sea
*Di, Dilenn, Dilinn, Dilyn,
Lynn*

Dima
(American) high-spirited
Deemah, Dema

Dina
(Hebrew, Scottish) right;
royal

Dinah
(Hebrew) fair judge
*Dina, Dinah, Dinna,
Dyna*

Dinesha
(American) happy
*Dineisha, Dineshe,
Diniesha*

Dini
(American) joyful
Dinee, Diney, Dinie

Dinora
(Spanish) judged by God
Dina, Dino, Nora

Diona
(Greek) divine woman
*Dee, Di, Dion, Dionah,
Dionuh*

Dioneece
(American) daring
*Dee, DeeDee, Deon,
Deone, Deonece,
Deoneece, Dioniece,
Neece, Neecey*

Dionicia
(Spanish) vixen
*Di, Dione, Dionice,
Dionise, Nicia, Nise,
Nisee*

Dionndra
(American) loving
*Diondra, Diondrah,
Diondruh*

Dionne
(Greek) love goddess
Deona, Dion, Dione, Dionna
Dionshay
(African-American) combo of Dion and Shay; loving
Dionsha, Dionshae, Dionshaye
Dior
(French) stylish
Diora, Diore
Direll
(American) svelte
Di, Direl, Direlle
Dirisha
(African-American) outgoing
Di, Diresha, Direshe
Disa
(Scandinavian) goddess
Disha
(American) fine
Dishae, Dishuh
Dishawna
(African-American) special
Dishana, Dishauna, Dishawnah, Dishona, Dishonna
Divina
(American) divine

Divina, Divine
(Italian) divine
Divin, Divina
Divinity
(American) sweet; devout
Divinitee, Diviniti, Divinitie
Dix
(French) livewire
Dixann
(American) combo of Dixie and Ann
Dixan, Dixanne, Dixiana, Dixieanna
Dixie
(American) southern girl
Dixee, Dixi
D'Nicola
(American) combo of D and Nicola
D'nicole, Deenicola, Dnicola
Dnisha
(African-American) rejoicing
D'Nisha, Dnisa, Dnish, Dnishay, Dnishe
Dobie
(American) cowgirl
Dobee, Dobey, Dobi

Dodie
(Greek, Hebrew) short for Dorothy; beloved woman
Dodi, Dody
Doherty
(American) ambitious
Dhoertey, Dohertee, Dohertie
Dolcy
(American)
Dolcee, Dolcie, Dolsee
Dolly
(American) effervescent
Doll, Dollee, Dolli
Dolores
(Spanish) woman of sorrowful leaning
Delores
Dometria
(American) form of Greek Demetria; goddess; fruitful
Dome, Dometrea, Domi, Domini, Domitra
Domini
(Latin) form of Dominick
Dom, Dominee, Domineke, Dominey, Dominie, Dominika, Domino, Dominy

Dominica
(Latin) follower of God
Dominika, Domenika, Domineca, Dom

Dominique
(French) bright; masterful
Dom, Domenique, Domino, Domonik

Dona
(Italian) form of Donna; gracious

Donata
(Italian) celebrating
Donada, Donatah, Donni, Donnie, Donny

Donatella
(Latin, Italian) gift
Don, Donnie, Donny

Donava
(African) jubilant
Donavah

Donika
(African-American) stemming from Donna; home-loving
Donica

Donisha
(African-American) laughing; cozy
Daneesha, Danisha, Doneesha

Donna
(Italian) ladylike and genteel
Dom, Don, Dona, Dondi, Donnie, Donya

Donnata
(Latin) giving
Dona, Donata, Donni

Donnelly
(Italian) lush
Donally, Donelly, Donnell, Donnelli, Donnellie, Donni, Donnie, Donny

Donnis
(American) pleasant; giving
Donnice

Donserena
(American) dancer; giving
Donce, Doncie, Dons, Donse, Donsee, Donser, Donsey

Donyale
(African-American) form of Danielle; kind
Donyelle

Dora
(Greek) gift from God
Dori, Dorie

Dorat
(French) a gift
Doratt, Dorey, Dorie

Doreen
(Greek, Irish) capricious
Dorene, Dorine, Dory

Dorian
(Greek) happy
Dorean, Doreane, Doree, Doriane, Dorri, Dorry

Dorianne
(American) combo of Doris and Ann; sparkly

Dorika
(Greek) God's gift
Doreek, Dorike, Dory

Doris
(Greek) place name; sea-loving; sea nymph mother
Dor, Dorice, Dorise, Doriss, Dory

Dorit
(Greek) God's gift; shy
Dooritt

Dornay
(American) involved
Dorn, Dornae, Dornee, Dorny

Dorren
(Irish) sad-faced
Doren

Dortha
(Greek) God's gift; studious
Dorth, Dorthee, Dorthey, Dorthy

Dory

(French) gilded; gold hair

Dora, Dore, Dorie

Dorthe

(Scandinavian) God's gift

Dorothea

(Greek) open-armed

Dorothia

Dorothy

(Greek) God's gift

Do, Dorathy, Dori, Dorthy

Dossey

(Last name as first) rambunctious

Dosse, Dossi, Dossie, Dossy, Dozze

Dot

(Greek) spunky

Dottee, Dottie, Dotty

Douce

(French) sweet

Doucia, Dulce, Dulci, Dulcie

Dougiana

(American) combo of Dougi and Ana

Dougi

Dove

(Greek) dreamy

Draven

(American) loyal

Dravan, Dravin, Dravine

Draxy

(American) faithful

Drax, Draxee, Draxey, Draxi

Drea

(American) adorable

Dream, Dreama

(American) dreamgirl; misty

Dreamee, Dreamey, Dreami, Dreamie, Dreamy

Dree

(American) softspoken

Dreena

(American) cautious

Dreenah, Drina

Drew

(Greek) woman of valor

Dru, Drue

Drover

(American) surprising

Drovah, Drovar

Dru

(American) bright

Drew, Drue

Druanna

(American) bold

Drewann, Drewanne, Druanah, Druannah

Drucelle

(American) smart

Druce, Drucee, Drucel, Drucell, Drucey, Druci, Drucy

Drusilla

(Latin) strong

Dru, Drucilla

Dryden

(Last name as first name) special

Dydie

Dubethza

(Invented) sad

Dubeth

Duchess

(American) fancy

Duc, Duchesse, Ducy, Dutch, Dutchey, Dutchie, Dutchy

Duffy

(Irish) spunky

Dufvenius

(Swedish) lovely

Duf, Duff

Duhnell

(Hebrew) kind-hearted

Danee, Danny, Nell

Dulce-Maria

(Spanish) sweet Mary

Dulce, Dulcey

Dulcie, Dulcy

(Latin, Spanish) sweet one

Dee, Dulce, Dulcey

Dune

(American) summery

Doone, Dunah, Dunie

Dumia
   (Hebrew) quiet
   Dumi
Dunesha
   (African-American) warm
   Dunisha
Dupre
   (American) softspoken
   Dupray, Duprey
Dusanka
   (Slavic) soulful
   Dusan, Dusana, Dusank,
   Sanka
Duscha
   (Russian) happy
   Dusa
Dusky
   (Invented) dreamy
Dusky-Dream
   (Invented) dreamy
   Duskee-Dream
Dustine, Dustina
   (German) go-getter
   Dusteen, Dustene, Dusti,
   Dustie, Dusty
Dusty
   (American) southern
   Dustee, Dusti, Dustie,
   Dustey
Dwanda
   (American) athletic
   Dwana, Dwayna,
   Dwunda

Dyan
   (Latin) form of Diane;
   divine
   Dian, Dyana, Dyann
Dyandra
   (Latin) sleek
   Diandra, Dianndrah,
   Dyan, Dyandruh
Dylan
   (Welsh) creative; from
   the sea
   Dilann, Dyl, Dylane,
   Dylann, Dylanne, Dylen,
   Dylin, Dyllan, Dylynn
Dymond
   (American) variant of
   diamond
   Dymahn, Dymon,
   Dymonn, Dymund
Dyney
   (American) consoling
   others
   Diney, DiNey, Dy
Dyonne
   (American) marvelous
   Dyonn, Dyonna,
   Dyonnae
Dyronisha
   (African-American) fine
   Dyron
Dyshaunna
   (African-American)
   dedicated
   Dyshaune, Dyshawn,
   Dyshawna

Dywon
   (American) bubbly
   Diwon, Dywan, Dywann,
   Dywaughn, Dywonne

E

Eadrianne
(American) standout
Eddey, Eddi, Eddy,
Edreiann, Edrian, Edrie

Earla
(English) leader
Earlah, Erla, Erlene,
Erletta, Erlette

Earlean
(Irish) dedicated
Earlene, Earline, Erlenne

Early
(American) bright
Earlee, Earlie, Earlye,
Erly

Eartha
(English) earth mother

Easter
(American) born on
Easter; spring-like

Easton
(American) wholesome
Eastan, Easten, Eeston,
Eastun, Estynn

Eavan
(Irish) beautiful
Evaughn, Eevonne

Ebba
(English, Scandinavian)
strong
Eb, Eba, Ebbah

Ebban
(American) pretty;
affluent
Ebann, Ebbayn

Ebony
(Greek) hard and dark
Eb, Ebanie, Ebbeny,
Ebbie, Ebonea, Ebonee,
Eboney, Eboni, Ebonie,
Ebonni

Ebrel
(Cornish) from the
month April
Ebby, Ebrelle, Ebrie,
Ebrielle

Echo
(Greek) smitten
Eko

Ecstasy
(American) joyful
Ecstasey, Ecstasie, Stase

Edaena
(Irish) fiery; energetic
Ed, Eda, Edae, Edana,
Edanah, Edaneah, Eddi

Edalene
(German) refined
Eda, Edalyne, Edeline,
Ediline, Lena, Lene

Edana
(Irish) flaming energy
Edan, Edanna

Eddi
(English) form of
Edwina; spirited
brunette
Eddie, Eddy

Edel
(German) clever; noble
Edell, Eddi

Eden
(Hebrew) paradise of
delights
Edene, Edyn

Edenathene
(American) combo of
Eden and Athene

Edie
(English) short for Edith;
blessed
Edee, Edy, Eydie

Edith
(English) a blessed girl
who is a gift to mankind
Edy, Edyth, Edythe,
Eydie

Edju
(Origin unknown) giving
Eddju

Edlin
(German) noble;
sophisticated
Eddi, Eddy, Edlan,
Edland, Edlen

Edmee
(American) spontaneous
Edmey, Edmi, Edmy,
Edmye

Edmonda
(English) form of
Edmond; rich
Edmon, Edmond,
Edmund, Edmunda,
Monda

Edna
(Hebrew) youthful
Eddie, Ednah, Eydie

Edreanna
(American) merry
Edrean, Edreana,
Edreanne, Edrianna

Edrina
(American) old-
fashioned
Ed, Eddi, Eddrina,
Edrena, Edrinah

Edsel
(American) plain
Eds, Edsell, Edzel

Edshone
(American) wealthy
Ed, Eds, Edshun

Edwina
(English) prospering
female
Eddi, Eddy, Edwena,
Edwenna, Edwyna,
Edwynna

Effemy
(Greek and German)
good singer
Efemie, Efemy, Effee,
Effemie, Effey, Effie, Effy

Effie
(Greek) of high morals;
(German) good singer
Effi, Effy

Egan
(American) wholesome
Egen, Egun

Egypt
(Place name) exotic
Egyppt

Egzanth
(Invented) form of
Xanthe; beautiful blonde

Eileen
(Irish) bright and
spirited
Eilean, Eilee, Eileena,
Eileene, Elene, Ellie

Eireen
(Scandinavian)
peacemaker
Eirena, Erene, Ireen,
Irene

Eires
(Greek) peaceful
Eiress, Eres, Heris

Eirianne
(English) peaceful
Eirian, Eriann

Elaine
(French) dependable girl
Elane, Elayn, Elayne,
Ellaine

Elana
(Greek) pretty
Ela, Elanie, Lainie

Elata
(Latin) bright; well-
positioned
Ela, Elate, Elatt, Elle,
Elota

Elda
(Italian) protective

Eleacie
(American) forthright
Acey, Elea, Eleasie

Eldee
(American) light
El, Eldah, Elde

Eldora
(Spanish) golden spirit

Eleanor
(Greek) light-hearted
Elanore, Eleanora,
Eleonore, Ellie, Ellinor,
Ellinore, Lenore

Electra
(Greek) resilient and
bright
Elec, Elek, Elektra

Elegy
(American) lasting
Elegee, Eleggee, Elegie,
Eligey

Elek
(American) star-like
Elec, Ellie, Elly

Elena
(Greek, Russian, Italian,
Spanish) light and
bright; beautiful
*Elana, Eleena, Elene,
Ilena, Ilene, Lena, Leni,
Lennie, Lina, Nina*

Eleni
(Greek) sweet
Elenee

Eleonore
(Greek, German) light
and bright
Elenore, Elle, Elnore

Eleri
(Welsh) smooth
Elere, Eleree

Elettra
(Latin, Italian) shining

Elfin
(American) small girl
*El, Elf, Elfan, Elfee, Elfey,
Elfie, Elfun, Els*

Elfrida
(German) peaceful spirit
*Elfreeda, Elfreyda,
Elfryda*

Eliana
(Latin, Greek, Italian)
sunny
*Eliane, Elliana, Ellianne,
Ellie*

Eliane
(French) cheerful; sunny

Elisa
(English, Italian) God-
loving; grace
*Eleesa, Elesa, Elissa,
Elisse, Leese, Leesie,
Lisa*

Elisabet
(Hebrew, Scandinavian)
God as her oath
Bet, Elsa, Else, Elisa

Elisabeth
(Hebrew, French,
German) sworn to God
*Bett, Bettina, Elisa, Elise,
Els, Elsa, Elsie, Ilsa,
Ilyse, Liesa, Liese,
Lisbeth, Lise*

Elise
(French, English) soft-
mannered
*Elice, Elisse, Elle, Ellyse,
Lisie*

Elisha
(Greek) God-loving
*Eleasha, Elicia, Eliesha,
Ellie, Lisha*

Elite
(Latina) best
Elita

Eliza
(Irish) sworn to God
Elieza, Elyza

Elizabeth
(Hebrew) God-directed;
beauty
*Beth, Betsy, Elisabeth,
Elizebeth, Lissie, Liza*

Elke
(Dutch) distinguished

Elkie
(Dutch) variant of Elke;
distinguished
Elk, Elka

Ella
(Greek) beautiful and
fanciful
Elle, Ellie, Elly

Ella Bleu
(Invented) combo of Ella
and Bleu; gorgeous
daughter of fame
Ella-Bleu

Ellaina
(American) sincere
Elaina, Ellana, Ellanuh

Ellan
(American) coy
Elan, Ellane, Ellyn

Elle
(Scandinavian) woman
Ele

Ellen
(English) open-minded
El, Elen, Ellie, Ellyn, Elyn

Ellender
(American) decisive
*Elender, Ellander, Elle,
Ellie*

Elletra
(Greek, Italian) shining
Elletrah, Illetrah

Elli
(Scandinavian) aged
Ell, Elle, Ellie

Ellie
(English) candid
Ele, Elie, Elly

Ellyanne
(American) combo of Elly
and Anne
*Elian, Elianne, Ellyann,
Elyann*

Elma
(Turkish) sweet
El

Elmas
(Armenian) diamond-like
Elmaz, Elmes, Elmis

Elnora
(American) sturdy
Ellie, Elnor, Elnorah

Elodia
(Spanish) flowering
Elodi

Eloise
(German) high-spirited
Eluise, Luise

Elora
(American) fresh-faced
Elorah, Flory, Floree

Elpidia
(Spanish) shining
El, Elpey, Elpi, Elpie

Elrica
(German) leader
*Elrick, Elrika, Elrike,
Rica, Rika*

Elsa
(Hebrew, Scandinavian,
German) patient; regal
*Els, Elsah, Elseh, Elsie,
Ellsee*

Elsie
(German) hard-working
Elsee, Elsi

Elsiy
(Spanish) God-loving
*El, Els, Elsa, Elsee, Elsi,
Elsy*

Elspeth
(Scottish)
El, Elle, Els

Elton
(American) spontaneous
Elt, Elten, Eltone, Eltun

Elva
(English) tiny
Elvie, Elvina, Elvah

Elvia
(Latin) sunny
Elvea, Elviah, Elvie

Elvira
(Latin, German) light-
haired and quiet
Elva, Elvie

Elyanna
(American) good friend
*Elyana, Elyannah,
Elyunna*

Elyse
(English) soft-mannered
Elice, Elle, Elysee

Elyssa
(Greek) loving the
ocean; (English) lovely
and happy
*Elisa, Elissa, Elysa,
Illysa, Lyssa*

Elysia
(Latin) joyful
*Elyse, Elysee, Elysha,
Elyshia*

Emalee, Emaline
(German) thoughtful
*Emalea, Emaleigh,
Emaley, Emally, Emaly,
Emmalynn, Emmeline,
Emmelyne*

Emann
(American) softspoken
Eman

Ember
(American)
temperamental
Embere, Embre

Emberatriz
(Spanish) respected
Emb, Ember, Embera,
Emberatrice,
Emberatryce,
Embertrice, Embertrise

Emberli
(American) pretty
Em, Emb, Ember,
Emberlee, Emberley,
Emberly

Eme
(German) short for
Emma; strong
Emee, Emme, Emmee

Eme
(Hawaiian) loved
Em, Emee, Emm,
Emmee, Emmie, Emmy

Emelle
(American) kind
Emell

Emely
(German) go-getter
Emel, Emelee, Emelie

Emena
(Latin) of fortunate birth
Em, Emen, Emene,
Emina, Emine

Emerald
(French) bright as a
gemstone
Em, Emmie

Emestina
(American) form of
Ernestina; competitive
Emee, Emes, Emest, Tina

Emilee
(American) combo of
Emma and Lee

Emilia
(Italian) soft-spirited
Emila

Emily
(German) poised;
(English) competitor
Em, Emalie, Emilee,
Emili, Emilie, Emmi,
Emmie

Emma
(German, Irish) strong
Em, Emmah, Emme,
Emmie, Emmi, Emmot,
Emmy, Emmye, Emott

Emmalee
(American) combo of
Emma and Lee
Em, Emalee, Emliee,
Emma-Lee, Emmali,
Emmie

Emmaline
(French, German) form
of Emily
Em, Emaline, Emalyne,
Emiline, Emmie

Emmanuelle
(Hebrew, French)
believer
Em, Emmi, Emmie,
Emmy

Emmalise
(American) combo of
Emma and Lise; lovely
Emalise, Emmalisa,
Emmelise

Emme
(German) feminine
Em

Emmi
(German) pretty
Emmee, Emmey, Emmy

Emmylou
(American) combo of
Emmy and Lou
Emmilou, Emmi-Lou,
Emylou

Emylinda
(American) combo of
Emy and Linda; happy
and pretty
Emi, Emilind,, Emilynd,
Emy, Emylin, Emylynda

Ena
(Hawaiian) intense
Eana, En, Enna, Ina

Enchantay
(American) enchanting
Enchantee

Endah
(Irish) flighty
Ena, End, Enda

Endia
(American) variant of
India; magical
*Endee, Endey, Endie,
Endy, India, Ndia*

Enedina
(Spanish) praised,
spirited
Dina, Ened

Enid
(Welsh) lively
Eneid

Enore
(English) careful
Enoor, Enora

Enslie
(American) emotional
*Ens, Enslee, Ensley,
Ensly, Enz*

Enya
(Irish) fiery; musician
Enyah, Nya

Epifania
(Spanish) proof
*Epi, Epifaina, Epifanea,
Eppie, Pifanie, Piffy*

Eppy
(Greek) lively, always
"on"
*Ep, Eppee, Eppey, Eppi,
Eps*

Equoia
(African-American) great
equalizer
Ekowya

Eranth
(Greek) spring bloomer
*Erantha, Eranthae,
Eranthe*

Erasema
(Spanish) happy
Eraseme

Ercilia
(American) frank
Erci, Ercilya

Eres
(Greek) goddess of
chaos
Era, Ere, Eris

Erika
(Scandinavian)
honorable; leading
others
*Erica, Ericah, Ericca,
Ericka, Erikka, Eryka*

Erin
(Irish) peace-making
Eran, Erine, Erinne, Eryn

Erina
(American) peaceful
*Era, Erinna, Erinne,
Eryna, Erynne*

Erla
(Irish) playful

Erlind
(Hebrew) from Erlinda;
angelic
Erlinda, Erlinde

Erma
(Latin) wealthy
Erm, Irma

Ermelinda
(Spanish) fresh-faced
*Ermalinda, Ermelind,
Ermelynda*

Ermine
(Latin) rich
Ermeen, Ermie, Ermin

Erna
(English) short for
Ernestine; knowing;
earnest
Emae, Ernea, Ernie

Ernestine
(English) having a
sincere spirit
Ernestina, Ernestyne

Es
(American) short for
Estella
Esa, Essie

Esbelda
(Spanish) black-haired beauty
Es, Esbilda, Ezbelda

Esdey
(American) warm-hearted
Esdee, Esdy, Essdey

Eshah
(African) exuberant
Esha

Eshe
(African) life
Eshay

Eshey
(American) life
Es, Esh, Eshae, Eshay

Esmee
(French) much loved
Esme, Esmie

Esmeralda
(Spanish) emerald; shiny and bright
Es, Esmie, Esmirilda

Esne
(English) happy
Es, Esnee, Esney, Esny, Essie

Esperanza
(Spanish) hopeful
Es, Espe, Esperance

Essence
(American) ingenious
Esence, Essens, Essense

Essie
(English) shining
Es, Essy

Esta
(Hebrew) star
Es, Estah

Estee
(English) brightest
Esti

Estella
(French) star
Es, Estel, Estell, Estelle, Estie, Stell, Stella

Estelle
(French) star
Es, Estel, Estele, Estie

Estevina
(Spanish) adorned; wreathed
Estafania, Este, Estebana, Estefania, Estevan, Estevana

Esthelia
(Spanish) shining
Esthe, Esthel, Esthele, Esthelya

Esther
(Persian, English) shining star
Es, Essie, Ester

Estherita
(Spanish) bright
Estereta

Estime
(French) esteemed
Es

Estrella
(Latin) shining star
Estrell, Estrelle, Estrilla

Eta
(German) short for Henrietta
Etah

Etaney,
(Hebrew) focused
Eta, Etana, Etanah, Etanee

Ethel
(English) class
Ethyl

Ethelene
(American) form of Ethel; noble
Ethe, Etheline

Ethne
(Irish) blueblood
Eth, Ethnee, Ethnie, Ethny

Ethnea
(Irish) kernel; piece of the puzzle
Ethna, Ethnia

Etta
(German, English) short for Henrietta; energetic
Etti, Ettie, Etty

Eudlina
(Slavic) generous; afflent
Eudie, Eudlyna, Udie, Udlina

Eudocia
(Greek) fine
Eude, Eudocea, Eudosia

Eudora
(Greek) cherished

Eugenia
(Greek) regal and polished
Eugeneia, Eugenie, Eugina, Gee, Gina

Eula
(Greek) specific
Eulia

Eulala
(Greek) spoken sweetly
Eulalah

Eulalia
(Greek, Italian) spoken sweetly
Eula, Eulia, Eulie

Eulanda
(American) fair
Eudlande, Eulee, Eulie

Eulee
(Greek)
Eulie, Ulee, Uley

Eunice
(Greek) joyful; winning
Euniece, Eunise

Eupheme
(Greek) well-spoken
Eu, Euphemee, Euphemi, Euphemie

Euphemia
(Greek) respected
Eufemia, Euphie, Uphie

Eurydice
(Greek) adventurous
Euridice

Eustacia
(Greek) industrious
Eustace, Stacey, Stacy

Euvenia
(American) hardworking
Euvene, Euvenea

Eva
(Hebrew, Scandinavian) life
Evah

Evadne
(Greek) pleasing; lucky
Eva, Evad, Evadnee, Evadny

Evaline
(French) form of Evelyn; matter-of-fact
Evalyn, Eveleen

Evalouise
(American) combo of Eva and Louise; witty
Eva-Louise, Evaluise

Eva-Marie
(American) combo of Eva and Marie; generous

Evan
(American) bright; precocious
Evann, Evin

Evana, Evania
(Greek) lovely woman
Eve, Ivana, Ivanna

Evangelina
(Greek) bringing joy
Eva, Evangeline, Eve, Lina

Evania
(Irish) spirited
Ev, Evanea, Eve

Evanthie
(Greek) flowering well
Evanthe, Evanthee, Evanthi

Eve
(French, Hebrew)
Eva, Evie, Evvy

Evelina
(French) lively
Eve, Evelin, Evelinna, Evelyn

Evelina
(Russian) lively
Evalina, Evalinna

Evelyn
(English) optimistic
Aveline, Ev, Evaline, Evalenne, Evline

Ever
(Invented name) cool; vibrant
Ev

Everilde
(Origin unknown) hunter

Evette
(French) dainty
Evett, Ivette

Evonne
(French) form of Yvonne; sensual
Evanne, Eve, Evie, Yvonne

Ewelina
(Polish) life
Eva, Lina

Eydie
(American) endearing
Eidey, Eydee

Eyote
(Native American) great
Eyotee

Ezra
(Hebrew) happy; helpful
Ezrah, Ezruh

Ezza
(American) healthy
Eza

Faba
(Latin) bean; thin
Fabah, Fava

Fabia
(Latin) fabulous; special
Fabiann, Fabianna, Fabianne

Fabienne
(French) farming beans
Fabiola, Fabiole

Fabio
(Latin) fabulous
Fabeeo, Fabeo, Fabeoh

Faillace
(French) delicate beauty
Faill, Faillaise, Faillase, Falace

Faine
(English) happy
Fai, Fainne, Fay, Fayne

Fairlee
(English) lovely
Fair, Fairlea, Fairley, Fairly

Faith
(English) loyal woman
Fay, Fayth

Falesyia
(Hispanic) exotic
Falesyiah, Falisyia

Faline
(Latin, French) lively
Faleen, Falene

Fall
(Season name) changeable
Falle

Fallon
(Irish) fetching; from the ruling class
Falan, Fallen, Fallyn, Falyn

Falsette
(American) fanciful
Falcette

Fanchon
(French) from France
Fan, Fanchee, Fanchie, Fanny, Fran, Frannie, Franny

Fancy
(English) fanciful
Fanci, Fancie

Fane
(American) strict
Fain, Faine

Fanfara
(Last name as first name) fanfare; excitement
Fann, Fanny

Fang
(Chinese) pleasantly
scented

Fanny
(Latin) from France;
bold; buttocks
Fan, Fani, Fannie

Fantasia
(American) inventive
*Fantasha, Fantasiah,
Fantasya, Fantazia*

Fanteen
(English) clever
*Fan, Fannee, Fanney,
Fanny, Fantene, Fantine*

Faredah
(Arabic) special
Farida

Faris
(American) forgiving
*Fair, Farris, Pharis,
Pharris*

Farrah
(Arabic) beautiful;
(English) joyful
Fara, Farah

Farren
(American) fair
Faren, Farin

Farrow
(American) narrow-
minded
Farow, Farro

Faryl
(American) inspiring
Farel, Farelle

Fashion
(American) stylish
Fashon, Fashy, Fashyun

Fatima
(Arabic) wise woman;
(African) dedicated
Fatema, Fatimah, Fatime

Faulk
(American) respected
Falk

Fauna
(Roman mythology)
nature goddess
Faunah, Fawna, Fawnah

Faunee
(Latin) nature-loving
*Fauney, Fauneye,
Fawnae, Fawni, Fawny*

Faustene
(French, American)
envied
*Fausteen, Faustine,
Fausty, Fawsteen*

Faustiana
(Spanish) good fortune
*Faust, Fausti, Faustia,
Faustina*

Faustina
(Italian) lucky
*Fawsteena, Fostina,
Fostynna*

Favianna
(Italian) confident
Faviana

Fawn
(French) gentle
Faun, Fawne

Fawna
(French) softspoken
*Fawnna, Fawnah,
Fawnuh*

Faye
(English, French)
light-spirited
Fae, Fay, Fey

Fayette
(American) southern
*Fayet, Fayett, Fayetta,
Fayitte*

Fayleen
(American) quiet
*Faylene, Fayline, Falyn,
Falynn, Faye, Fayla*

Fayth
(American) form of Faith;
faithful
Falthe, Faythe

Feather
(Native American) svelte
Feathyr

Febe
(Polish, Greek) bright
Febee

February
(Latin) icy
Feb

Felder
(Last name as first
name) bright
Felde, Feldy

Felice
(Latin) happy
Felece, Felise

Felicia
(Latin) joyful
*Faleshia, Falesia, Felecia,
Felisha*

Felicie
(Latin) happy;
(German) fortunate
*Feliccie, Felicee, Felicy,
Felisie*

Felicita
(Spanish) gracious
*Felice, Felicitas, Felicitee,
Felisita*

Felicity
(Latin) happy girl
*Felice, Felicite, Felicitee,
Felisitee*

Felise
(German) joyful
Felis

Femay
(American) classy
Femae

Femi
(African) love-seeking
Femmi

Femise
(African-American)
asking for love
Femeese, Femmis

Fenn
(American) bright
Fen, Fynn

Feo
(Greek) God-given
Fee, Feeo

Feodora
(Greek) God-given girl
Fedora

Fern
(German, English) natural
Ferne

Fernanda
(German) bold
Ferdie, Fernnande

Fernilia
(American) successful
*Fern, Fernelia, Ferny,
Fyrnilia*

Feven
(American) shy
Fevan, Fevun

Fia
(Scandinavian) perky

Fiamma
(Italian) fiery spirit
*Feamma, Fee, Fia, Fiama,
Fiammette, Fifi*

Fidela
(Spanish) loyal
Fidele, Fidella, Fidelle

Fidelia
(Italian) faithful
Fidele

Fidelity
(Latin) loyal
Fidele, Fidelia

Fife
(American) dancing
eyes; musical
Fifer, Fifey, Fyfe

Fifi
(French) jazzy
Fifee

Fifia
(African) Friday's child
FeeFee, Fifeea

Filia
(Greek) devoted
Filea, Feleah, Filiah

Fillis
(Greek) form of Phyllis;
devoted
*Filis, Fill, Fillees, Filly,
Fillys, Fylis*

Finelle
(Irish) fair-faced
*Fee, Finell, Finn, Finny,
Fynelle*

Finesse
(American) smooth
Fin, Finese, Finess

Finn
(Irish) cool

Fion
(Irish) blonde
Fiona
(Irish) fair-haired
Fionna
Fiorella
(Irish) spirited
Fee, Feorella, Rella
Fire
(American) feisty
Firey, Fyre
Flair
(English) stylish
Flaire, Flairey, Flare
Flame
(Invented) sensual
Flanders
(Place name) creative
Fland, Flann
Flannery
(Irish) warm; red-haired
Flann
Flavia
(Latin) light-haired
Flavie
Flax
(Botanical) plant with
blue flowers
Flacks, Flaxx
Fleming
(Last name as first
name) adorable
*Flemma, Flemmie,
Flemming, Flyming*

Flemmi
(Italian) pretty
Flemmy
Fleur
(French) flower
*Fleura, Fleuretta,
Fleurette, Fleuronne*
Flirt
(Invented) flirtatious
Flyrtt
Flo
(American) short for
Florence
Flor
(Spanish) blooming
*Flo, Flora, Floralia,
Florencia, Florencita,
Florens, Florensia,
Flores, Floria, Floriole,
Florita, Florite*
Flora
(Latin, Spanish)
flowering
Floria, Florie
Floramaria
(American) combo of
Flora and Maria; spring;
Mary's flower
Flora Maria, Flora-Maria

Florence
(Latin, Italian) place
name; flourishing and
giving
*Flo, Flora, Florencia,
Florense, Florenze,
Florie, Florina, Flossie*
Florens
(Polish) blooming
Floren
Florent
(French) flowering
*Flor, Floren, Florentine,
Florin*
Florida
(Place name) flowered
Flora, Flory
Florine
(American) blooming
*Flo, Flora, Floren,
Floryne, Florynne*
Florizel
(Literature)
Shakespearean name;
in bloom
Flora, Flori, Florisel
Flower
(American) blossoming
beauty
Flo
Fluffy
(American) fun-loving
Fluff, Fluffi, Fluffie

Flynn
(Irish) red-haired
Flenn, Flinn, Flyn

Fog
(American) dreamy
Fogg, Foggee, Foggy

Fola
(African) honored
Folah

Fonda
(American) risk-taker
Fond

Fondice
(American) fond of
friends
Fondeese, Fondie

Fontaine
(French) fountain-like in
bounty
*Fontane, Fontanna,
Fontanne*

Fontenot
(French) special girl;
fountain of beauty
*Fonny, Fontay, Fonte,
Fonteno*

Ford
(Last name as first
name) confident
Forde

Fortune
(Latin) excellent fate;
prized

Fotine
(Greek) light-hearted
Foty, Fotyne

Fowler
(Last name as first
name) stylish
Fowla, Fowlar, Fowlir

Fran
(Latin) from France;
freewheeling
Frann, Franni, Frannie

France
(Place name) French girl
Frans, Franse

Frances
(Latin) free; of French
origin
*Fanny, Fran, Francey,
Franci, Francie, Franse*

Francesca
(Italian) form of Frances;
open-hearted
*Fran, Francessca,
Franchesca, Frannie*

Franchelle
(French) from France
*Franshell, Franchelle,
Franchey*

Franchesca
(Italian) smiling
*Cheka, Chekkie,
Francheska, Francheska,
Franchessca*

Francine
(French) form of Frances;
beautiful
*Fran, Franceen,
Francene, Francie*

Frankie
(American) a form of
Frances; tomboyish
Franki, Franky

Frannie
(English) friendly
Franni, Franny

Fransabelle
(Latin) beauty from
France
Fransabella, Franzabelle

Frea
(Scandinavian) noble;
hearty
Fray, Freas, Freya

Freddie
(English) short for
Frederica; spunky
Fredi, Freddy

Frederica
(German) peacemaking
*Federica, Fred, Freda,
Freddie, Fritze, Rica*

Free
(American) free; open

Freesia
(Botanical) fragrant
flower

Freida
(German) short for
Frederica and Alfreda;
graceful
Freda, Frida, Frieda

Frenchie
(French, American)
saucy
*French, Frenchee,
Frenchi, Frenchy*

Freya
(Scandinavian) goddess;
beautiful
Freja

Frida
(Scandinavian) lovely

Frieda
(German) happy
Freda

Frigg
(Scandinavian) loved
one
Frigga

Frigga
(Scandinavian) beloved
Fri, Friga, Frigg

Frond
(Botanical) growing

Frosty
(Name from a song)
crisp and cool
Frostie

Frula
(German) hardworking

Fuchsia
(Botanical) blossoming
pink
Fuesha

Fructuose
(Latin) bountiful
Fru, Fructuosa, Fruta

Frythe
(English) calm
Frith, Fryth

Fudge
(American) stubborn
Fudgey

Fulvy
(Latin) blonde
Full, Fulvee, Fulvie

Funda
(Turkish)
Fund

Fury
(Latin) raging anger
Furee, Furey, Furie

Fushy
(American) animated;
vivid
Fooshy, Fueshy, Fushee

Gable
(German) farming
woman
*Gabbie, Gabby, Gabe,
Gabell, Gabl*

Gabor
(French) conflicted
Gaber, Gabi

Gabriela
(Italian, Spanish) God is
her strength
*Caby, Gabela, Gabi,
Gabrela, Gabriella*

Gabrielle
(French, Hebrew) strong
by faith in God
*Gabi, Gabraelle,
Gabreelle, Gabreille,
Gabríelle, Gabriele,
Gabriella, Gabrilla,
Gabrille, Gaby, Gaebriell,
Gaebrielle, Garbreal*

Gadar
(Armenian) perfect girl
*Gad, Gadahr, Gaddie,
Gaddy*

Gaegae
(Greek) from Gaea; earthy; happy
Gae, Gaege, Gaegie

Gaia
(Greek) goddess of earth
Gaea, Gaya

Gail
(Hebrew) short for Abigail; energetic
Gaelle, Gale, Gayle

Gaily
(American) fun-loving
Gailai, Galhy

Gaitlynn
(American) hopeful
Gaitlin, Gaitline, Gaitlinn, Gaitlyn, Gaytlyn

Gala
(French, Scandinavian) joyful celebrant
Gaila, Gailah, Galaa, Galuh, Gayla

Galatea
(Greek) sea nymph in mythology
Gal, Gala

Galaxy
(American) universal
Gal, Galaxee, Galaxi

Galen
(American) decisive
Galin, Galine, Galyn, Gaye, Gaylen

Galena
(Latin) metal; tough
Galyna, Galynna

Galiana
(German) vaulted
Galiyana, Galli, Galliana

Galina
(Russian) deserving
Gailina, Gailinna, Galyna, Galynna

Galise
(American) joyful
Galeece, Galeese, Galice, Galyce

Galya
(Hebrew) redeemed; merry
Galia

Garcelle
(French) flowered
Garcel, Garsell, Garselle

Garland
(American) fancy
Garlan, Garlinn, Garlynn

Garlanda
(French) flowered wreath; pretty girl
Gar, Garl, Garlynd, Garlynda

Garlin
(French) variant of Garland; decorative; pretty
Garlyn

Garner
(American) stylesetter
Garnar, Garnir

Garnet
(English) pretty; semi-precious stone

Garnetta
(French) gemstone; precious
Garna, Garnet, Garnie, Garny

Garrett
(Last name as first name) bashful
Garret, Gerrett

Garri
(American) energetic
Garree, Garrey, Garry, Garrye

Garrielle
(American) competent
Gariele, Garielle, Garriella

Garrison
(American) sturdy
Garisen, Garisun, Garrisen, Garrisun

Garrity
(American) smiling
Garety, Garrety, Garity, Garritee, Garritie

Gartha
(American) form of male name Garth; nature-loving

Garyn
(American) svelte
Garen, Garin, Garinne,
Garun, Garynn, Garynne

Gates
(Last name as first
name) careful
Gate

Gauri
(Hindi) golden goddess

Gavin
(American) smart
Gave, Gaven, Gavey,
Gavun

Gavion
(American) daring
Gaveon, Gavionne

Gaviotte
(French) graceful
Gaveott, Gaviot, Gaviott

Gavotte
(French) dancer
Gav, Gavott

Gay
(French) jolly
Gae, Gaye

Gayla
(American) planner
Gaila, Gailah, Gala,
Gaye, Gaylah, Gayluh

Gaylynn
(American) combo of
Gay and Lynn
Gaelen, Gaylene, Gaylyn,
Gay-Lynn

Gaynelle
(American) combo of
Gay and Nelle
Gaye, Gaynel, Gaynell,
Gaynie

Gaynor
(American) precocious
Ganor, Gayner, Gaynorre

Geanna
(American) ostentatious
Geannah, Gianna

Geena
(Italian) form of Gina;
statuesque
Gina, Ginah

Gelacia
(Spanish) treasure
Gela, Gelasha, Gelasia

Gelda
(American) gloomy
Geilda, Geldah, Gelduh

Gem
(American) shining
Gemmy, Gim, Jim

Gemesha
(African-American)
dramatic
Gemeisha, Gemiesha,
Gemme, Gemmy,
Gimesha

Gemini
(Greek) twin
Gem, Gemelle, Gemmy

Gemma
(Latin, Italian, French)
jewel-like
Gem, Gemmie, Gemmy

Gemmy
(Italian) gem
Gemmee, Gemmi,
Gimmy

Gems
(American) shining gem
Gem, Gemmie, Gemmy

Gena
(French) form of Gina;
short for Genevieve
Geena, Gen, Genah,
Geni, Genia

Genell
(American) form of
Janelle
Genill

Genera
(Greek) highborn
Gen, Genere

Generosa
(Spanish) generous
Generosah, Generossa

Genesis
(Latin) fast starter;
beginning
Gen, Gena, Geney,
Genisis, Jenesis

Geneva
(French) city in
Switzerland; flourishing
like juniper
Gena, Janeva, Jeneva

Genevieve
(German, French)
high-minded
*Gen, Gena, Genna,
Genavieve, Genovieve*

Genica
(American) intelligent
*Gen, Genicah, Genicuh,
Genika, Gennica, Jen,
Jenika, Jennika*

Genna
(English) womanly
Gen, Genny, Jenna

Gennelle
(American) combo of
Genn and Elle; graceful
*Genel, Genelle, Ginelle,
Jenele, Jenelle*

Gennese
(American) helpful
*Gen, Geneece, Geniece,
Genny, Ginece, Gineese*

Gennifer
(American) form of
Jennifer
*Genefer, Genephur,
Genifer*

Genoa
(Italian) playful
Geenoa, Genoah, Jenoa

Genoveva
(American) form of
Genevieve; white; light
Genny, Geno

Gentle
(American) kind
*Gen, Gentil, Gentille,
Gentlle*

Gentry
(American) sweet
*Gen, Gentree, Gentrie,
Jentrie, Jentry*

Geoma
(American) outstanding
*Gee, GeeGee, Geo,
Geomah, Geome, Gigi,
Jeoma, Oma, Omah*

Geonna
(American) sparkling
*Gee, Geionna, Geone,
Geonne, Geonnuh*

Georgann
(English) bright-eyed
*Georganne, Jorgann,
Joryann*

Georgene
(English) wandering
*Georgena, Georgene,
Jorgeen, Jorjene*

Georgette
(French) lively and little
Jorgette

Georgia
(Greek, English)
southern; cordial
*Georgi, Georgie,
Georgina, Giorgi, Jorga,
Jorgia, Jorja*

Georgianna
(English) combo of
Georgia and Anna;
bright-eyed
*Georganna,
Georgeanna, Jorjeana,
Jorgianna*

Georgina
(Greek, English) earthy

Geraldine
(German) strong
*Geraldyne, Geri, Gerri,
Gerry*

Geralena
(French) leader
*Gera, Geraleen, Geralen,
Geralene, Gerre,
Gerrilyn, Gerry,
Jerrileena, Lena*

Germaine
(French) of German
origin; important
Germain, Jermaine

Gertrude
(German) beloved
Gerdie, Gerti, Gertie

Gervaise
(French) strong
Gerva, Gervaisa

Gessalin
(American) loving
Gessilin, Gessalyn,
Gessalynn, Jessalin,
Jessalyn

Gessica
(American) form of
Jessica
Gesica, Gesika, Gessika

Gethsemane
(Biblical) peaceful
Geth, Gethse,
Gethsemanee,
Gethsemaney,
Gethsemanie, Gethy

Geynille
(American) womanly
Geynel

Gezelle
(American) lithe
Gezzelle, Gizele, Gizelle

Ghada
(Arabic) graceful
Ghad, Ghadah

Ghadeah
(Arabic) graceful
Gadea, Gadeah

Ghandia
(African) able
Gandia, Ghanda,
Ghandee, Ghandy,
Gondia, Gondiah

Ghea
(American) confident
Ghia, Jeah, Jeeah

Gherlan
(American) forgiving;
joyful
Gerlan, Gherli

Ghita
(Italian) pearl
Gita, Gite

Giacinte
(Italian) hyacinth;
flowering
Gia, Giacin, Giacinta

Gianina
(Itallan) believer
Gia, Giane, Giannina,
Gianyna, Janeena,
Janina, Jeanina

Gianna
(Italian) forgiving
Geonna, Giana, Gianne,
Gianne, Gianni, Giannie,
Gianny, Ginny

Gianne
(Italian) combo of Gi and
Anne; divine
Gia, Gian, Giann, Gigi

Giannelle
(American) hearty
Geanelle, Gianella,
Gianelle, Gianne

Giannesha
(African-American)
friendly
Geannesha, Gianesha,
Giannesh, Gianneshah,
Gianneshuh

Giara
(Italian) sensual
Gee, Geara, Gia, Giarah

Gidget
(American) cute
Gidge, Gidgett, Gidgette,
Gydget

Gift
(American) blessed
Gifte, Gyft

Gigi
(French) small, spunky
Geegee, Giggi

Gilberta
(German) smart
Bertie, Gill

Gilda
(English) gold-encrusted
Gildi, Gildie, Gill

Gilleese
(American) funny
Gill, Gillee, Gilleece,
Gillie, Gilly

Gillen
(American) humorous
Gill, Gilly, Gillyn, Gyllen

Gilli
(American) joyful
Gill, Gillee, Gilly

Gillian
(Latin) youthful
Gila, Gili, Gilian, Giliana, Gilliana, Gilliane, Gillie, Gilly, Jillian

Gillis
(Last name as first name) conservative
Gillice, Gillis, Gilise, Gylis, Gyllis

Gilma
(American) form of Wilma; fortified
Gee, Gilly

Gilmore
(Last name as first name) striking
Gilmoor, Gill, Gillmore, Gylmore

Gina
(Italian) well-born
Geena, Gin, Ginah, Ginny, Jenah

Ginacarol
(American) combo of Gina and Carol
Gina-Carol, Gina-Carrol, Gyna-Carole

Ginamarie
(Italian) combo of Gina and Marie
Gina-Marie, Ginamaria

Ginane
(French) well-born
Gigi, Gina, Gine, Jeanan, Jeanine

Ginger
(Latin) spicy
Gin, Ginny, Jinger

Ginnifer
(American) form of Jennifer
Gini, Ginifer, Giniferr, Ginifir, Ginn

Gioconda
(Italian) pleasing
Gio, Giocona

Giono
(Last name as first name) delight; friendly
Gio, Gionna, Gionno

Giorgio
(Italian) form of George; earthy; vivacious
Giorgi, Giorgie, Jorgio

Giovanna
(Italian) gracious believer; great entertainer
Geo, Geovanna, Gio, Giovahna, Giovana

Giritha
(Sri Lankan) melodic
Giri, Girith

Gisbelle
(American) lovely girl
Gisbel

Giselle
(German) naïve; (French) devoted friend
Gis, Gisel, Gisela, Gisele, Gissel, Gissell, Gissella, Gisselle, Gissie, Jizele

Gita
(Sanskrit) song
Geta, Gete, Git, Gitah

Gitele
(Hebrew) good
Gitel

Gitika
(Sanskrit) little singer
Getika, Gita, Giti, Gitikah

Givonnah
(Italian) loyal; believer
Gevonna, Gevonnuh, Givonn, Givonna, Givonne, Jevonah, Jevonna, Jivonnah, Juvona

Gizela
(Polish) dedicated
Giz, Gizele, Gizzy

Gizmo
(American) tricky
Gis, Gismo, Giz,

Gladiola
(Botanical) blooming; flower
Glad, Gladdee, Gladdy

Gladys
(Welsh) flower; princess
Glad, Gladice, Gladise, Gladdie

Glafira
(Spanish) giving
Glafee, Glafera, Glafi

Gleam
(American) bright girl
Glee, Gleem

Glenda
(Welsh) bright; good
Glinda, Glynda, Glynn, Glynnie

Glenna
(Irish) form of Glenda; fair
Glenn

Glenna
(Irish) valley-living
Glena, Glenah, Glenuh, Glyn, Glynna

Glennesha
(African-American) special
Glenesha, Gleneshuh, Gleniesha, Glenn, Glenneshah, Glenny, Glinnesha

Glennice
(American) topnotch
Glenis, Glennis, Glenys, Glenysse, Glynnece, Glynnice

Gloria
(Latin) glorious
Glorea, Glorey, Glori, Gloriah, Glorrie, Glory

Glorianne
(American) combo of Gloria and Anne
Gloriann, Glori-Ann, Glorianna, Gloryann, Glory-Anne

Glorielle
(American) generous
Gloriel, Gloriele, Glory, Gloree, Glori

Gloris
(American) glorious
Gloeeca, Glores, Gloresa, Glorisa, Glorus, Gloryssa

Glory
(Latin) shining
Gloree, Glori, Glorie

Gloss
(American) showy
Glosse, Glossee, Glossie, Glossy

Glynisha
(African-American) vibrant
Glynesh, Glynn, Glynnecia, Glynnesha, Glynnie, Glynnisha

Glynnis
(Welsh) vivacious; glen
Glenice, Glenis, Glennis, Glinice, Glinnis, Glynn, Glynnie, Glynny

Goala
(American) goal-oriented
Go, GoGo, Gola

Goddess
(American) gorgeous
Godess, Goddesse

Godiva
(English) God's gift; brazen
Godeva, Godivah

Golda
(English) golden
Goldi, Goldie

Golden
(American) shining
Goldene, Goldon, Goldun, Goldy

Goldie
(English) bright and golden girl; form of Yiddish Golda
Goldi, Goldy

Goliad
(Spanish) goal-oriented
Goleade, Goliade

Goneril
(Literature)
Shakespearean name in
King Lear
Gonarell, Gonarille,
Gonereal

Grable
(American) handsome
woman
Gray, Graybell

Grace
(Latin) graceful
Graci, Gracie, Gracy,
Gray, Grayce

Graceann
(American) girl of grace
Gracean, Grace-Ann,
Graceanna, Graceanne,
Gracee, Gracy

Gracie
(Latin) graceful
Graci, Gracy, Graecie,
Gray

Graciela
(Spanish) pleasant; full
of grace
Chita, Gracee, Gracella,
Gracey, Gracie, Graciella,
Gracilla, Grasiela,
Graziela

Graham
(American) sweet
Graehm, Grayhm

Grania
(Irish) love
Grainee, Graini

Gratia
(Scandinavian) beautiful
girl
Gart, Gert, Gertie,
Grasha, Gratea, Gratie

Gratia
(Scandinavian) graceful;
gracious
Grateah

Gray
(Last name as first
name) quiet
Graye, Grey

Grayson
(Last name as first) child
of quiet one
Graison, Grasen,
Greyson

Grazie
(Italian) graceful;
pleasant
Grasie, Grazee, Grazy

Grazyna
(Polish) graceful;
pleasant

Gregory
(American) scholarly
Gregoree, Gregge,
Greggy, Gregoria,
Gregorie

Greshawn
(African-American) lively
Greeshawn, Greshaun,
Greshawna, Greshonn,
Greshun

Gresia
(American) compelling
Grecia, Grasea, Graysea,
Grayshea

Greta
(German) a pearl
Gretah, Grete, Gretie,
Grette, Grytta

Gretchen
(German) a pearl
Gretch, Gretchin,
Gretchun, Grethyn

Gretel
(German) pearl; fanciful
Gretal, Grettel, Gretell,
Gretelle

Greyland
(American) focused
Grey, Greylin, Greylyn,
Greylynne

Griffie
(Welsh) royal
Griff, Griffee, Griffey,
Griffi, Gryffie

Griffin
(Welsh) royal
Griff

Griselda
(German) patient
Grezelda, Grisel, Grissy, Grizel, Grizelda, Grizzie

Grisham
(Last name as first name) ambitious
Grish

Grindelle
(American) livewire
Dell, Delle, Grenn, Grin, Grindee, Grindell, Grindy, Renny

Griselia
(Spanish) gray; patient
Grise, Grisele, Grissy, Seley, Selia

Grizel
(Spanish) longsuffering
Griz, Grizelda, Grizelle, Grizzy

Guadalupe
(Spanish) patron saint; easygoing
Lupe, Lupeta, Lupita

Gubby
(Irish) cuddly
Gub, Gubee, Gubbie

Gudrun
(Scandinavian) close friend; (German) contentious
Gudren, Gudrenne, Gudrin, Gudrinne

Guinevere
(Welsh) queen; white
Guin, Gwen

Gunilla
(Scandinavian) warlike
Gun, Gunn

Gunun
(German) lively
Gunan, Gunen

Gurlene
(American) smart
Gurl, Gurleen, Gurleene, Gurline

Gurshawn
(American) talkative
Gurdie, Gurshauna, Gurshaune, Gurshawna, Gurty

Gussie
(Latin) short for Augusta; industrious
Gus, Gussy, Gustie

Gusta
(German) from Gustava; watchful
Gussy, Gusta, Gustana, Gusty

Guy
(French) guiding; assertive
Guye

Guylaine
(American) combo of Guy and Laine; haughty
Guylane, Gylane

Guylynn
(American) combo of Guy and Lynn; tough-minded
Guylinne, Guylyn, Guylyne

Gwen
(Welsh) short for Gwendolyn; happy
Gwyn, Gweni, Gwenna

Gwendolyn
(Welsh) mystery goddess; bright
Gwenda, Gwendalinne, Gwendalyn, Gwendelynn, Gwendolen, Gwendolin, Gwendoline, Gwendolynn, Gwennie, Gywnne

Gwenless
(Invented) fair
Gwen, Gwenles, Gwenny

Gwenora
(American) combo of Gwen and Nora; playful; fair-skinned
Guinn, Guinna, Guinnora, Guinnoray, Guinore, Gwen, Gwena, Gwenda, Gwendah, Gwenee, Gwenna, Gwennie, Gwennora, Gwenny, Gwenorah, Gwenore, Nora, Nore, Norra

Gwyn
(Welsh) short for
Gwyneth; happy
Gwenn, Gwinn, Gwynne

Gwyneth
(Welsh) blessed
*Gwennie, Gwinith,
Gwynith, Gwynne,
Gwynneth, Win, Winnie*

Gylla
(Spanish) from
Guillermo; determined
Guilla, Gye, Gyla, Jilla

Gynette
(American) form of
Jeannette; believer
*Gyn, Gynett, Gynnee,
Gynnie*

Gypsy
(English) adventurer
Gippie, Gipsie, Gypsie

Gyselle
(German) variant of
Giselle; naïve
Gysel, Gysele

Gythae
(English) feisty
Gith, Gyth, Gythay

Ha
(Vietnamese) happy

Habiba
(Arabic) well-loved
Habibah

Hadassah
(Hebrew) form of Esther;
myrtle; love
*Hadasah, Hadassa,
Haddasah, Haddee,
Haddi, Haddy*

Hadil
(Arabic) cooing

Hadlee
(English) girl in heather
*Hadlea, Hadley, Hadli,
Hadly*

Hady
(Greek) soulful
*Haddie, Hadee, Hadie,
Haidee, Haidie*

Hadyn
(American) smart
Haden

Haelee
(English) form of Hailey

Hagar
(Hebrew) stranger
Haggar, Hager, Hagur

Hagir
(Arabic) wanderer
Hajar

Hailey
(English) natural; hay
meadow
*Hailea, Hailee, Hailie,
Halee, Haley, Hallie*

Halcyone
(Greek) calm
Halceonne, Halcyon

Haletta
(Greek) little country girl
from the meadow
*Hale, Halette, Hallee,
Halletta, Halley, Hallie,
Hally, Letta, Lettie, Letty*

Haleyanne
(American) combo of
Haley and Anne
*Haleyana, Haleyanna,
Haley-Ann*

Halima
(Arabic) gentle

Hall
(Last name as first
name) distinguished
Haul

Hallie
(German) high-spirited
*Halle, Hallee, Haleigh,
Hali, Halie, Hally, Hallye*

Halsey
(American) playful
Halcie, Halsee, Halsie

Halston
(American) stylish
Hall, Halls, Halsten

Halzey
(American) leader
Hals, Halsee, Halsi, Halsy, Halze, Halzee

Hameedah
(Arabic) grateful

Hamilton
(American) wishful
Hamil, Hamilten, Hamiltun, Hamma, Hamme

Hanna
(Polish) grace

Hannah
(Hebrew) merciful; God-blessed; a sweet Biblical name
Hanae, Hanah, Hanan, Hannaa, Hanne, Hanni

Hannette
(American) form of Jannette; graceful
Hann, Hanett, Hannett

Hansa
(Indian) swan-like
Hans, Hansah, Hansey, Hanz

Happy
(English) joyful
Hap, Happee, Happi

Harla
(English) country girl from the fields
Harlah, Harlea, Harlee, Harlen, Harlie, Harlun

Harlan
(English) athletic
Harlen, Harlon, Harlun

Harlequine
(Invented) romantic
Harlequinne, Harley

Harley
(English) wild thing
Harlea, Harlee, Harleey, Harli, Harlie, Harly

Harlinne
(American) vivacious
Harleen, Harleene, Harline, Harly

Harlow
(American) brash
Harlo, Harly

Harmon
(Last name as first name) attuned
Harmen, Harmone, Harmun, Harmyn

Harmony
(Latin) in synchrony
Harmonee, Harmoni, Harmonie

Harper
(English) musician; writer
Harp

Harrell
(American) leader
Harell, Harill, Haryl, Harryl

Harriet
(French) homebody
Harri, Harrie, Harriett, Harriette, Hattie

Hart
(American) romantic
Harte, Hartee, Hartie, Harty, Heart

Hasina
(African) beauty

Hattie
(English) home-loving
Hatti, Hatty, Hettie, Hetty

Haute
(French, American) stylish
Hautie

Hava
(Hebrew) life; lively
Chaba, Chaya, Haya

Havana
(Cuban) loyal
Havanah, Havane, Havanna, Havvanah, Havanuh

Haven
(American) safe place; open
Havin, Havun

Haviland
(American) lively; talented
Havilan, Havilynd

Hawkins
(American) wily
Hawk, Hawkens, Hawkey, Hawkuns

Hawlee
(American) negotiator
Hawlea, Hawleigh, Hawlie, Hawley, Hawly

Haydee
(American) capable
Hady, Hadye, Haydie

Haydon
(American) knowing
Hayden, Hadyn

Hayfa
(Arabic) slim

Hayley
(English) natural; hay meadow
Hailey, Haley, Haylee, Haylie

Hayleyann
(American) combo of Hayley and Ann
Haleyan, Haylee-Ann, Hayley-Ann, Hayli-Ann

Haze
(American) word as a name; spontaneous
Haise, Hay, Hays, Hazee, Hazey, Hazy

Hazel
(English) powerful
Hazell, Hazelle, Hazie, Hazyl, Hazzell

Heart
(American) romantic
Hart, Hearte

Heath
(English) open; healthy
Heathe

Heather
(Scottish) flowering
Heathar, Heathor, Heathur

Heaven
(English) happy and beautiful
Heavyn, Hevin

Heavenly
(American) spiritual
Heaven, Heavenlee, Heavenley, Heavynlie, Hevin

Hedda
(German) capricious; warring
Heda, Heddie, Hedi, Hedy, Hetta

Hedy
(German) mercurial
Hedi

Hedy-Marie
(German) capricious

Heidi
(German) noble; watchful; perky
Heide, Heidee, Heidie, Heidy, Hidi

Heidirae
(American) combo of Heidi and Rae
Heidi-Rae, Heidiray

Heija
(Korean) bright
Hia, Hya

Helaine
(French) ray of light; gorgeous
Helainne, Helle, Helyna, Hellyn

Helanna
(Greek) lovely
Helahna, Helana, Helani, Heley, Hella

Helen
(Greek) beautiful and light
Hela, Hele, Helena, Helyn, Lena, Lenore

Helena
(Greek) beautiful;
ingenious
Helana, Helayna,
Heleana, Helene,
Hellena, Helyena, Lena

Helene
(French) form of Helen;
pretty but contentious
Helaine, Heleen, Heline

Helenore
(American) combo of
Helen and Lenore; light;
darling
Hele, Helen, Helenoor,
Helenor, Helia, Helie,
Hellena, Lena, Lennore,
Lenora, Lenore, Lenory,
Lina, Nora, Norey, Norie

Helga
(Anglo-Saxon) pious
Helg

Helia
(Greek) sun
Heleah, Helya, Helyah

Helie
(Greek) sunny
Heley, Heli

Helina
(Greek) delightful
Helinah, Helinna,
Helinnuh

Helki
(Native American) tender
Helkie, Helky

Heloise
(German) hearty
Hale, Haley, Heley,
Heloese, Heloyse

Hender
(American) embraced
Hendere

Henley
(American) sociable
Hendlee, Hendly, Henli,
Henlie, Hinlie, Hynlie

Henna
(Hindi, Arabic) plant that
releases colorful dye
Hena, Hennah, Hennuh,
Henny

Henrietta
(English, German)
home-ruler
Harriet, Hattie, Henny,
Hetta, Hettie

Hensley
(American) ambitious
Henslee, Henslie, Hensly

Hera
(Greek) wife of Zeus;
radiant

Herendira
(Invented) tender and
dear
Heren

Herise
(Invented) warm
Heree, Hereese, Herice

Herleen
(American) quiet
Herlee, Herlene,
Hurleen, Herley, Herline,
Herly

Hermilla
(Spanish) fighter
Herm, Hermila, Hermille

Hermione
(Greek) sensual
Hermina, Hermine

Hermosa
(Spanish) beautiful
Ermosa

Hersala
(Spanish) lithe and
lovely
Hers, Hersila, Hersilia,
Hersy

Hest
(Greek) star-like; variant
of Hester
Hessie, Hesta, Hetty

Hester
(American) literary
Hestar, Hesther

Hester-Mae
(American) combo of
Hester and Mae; star
Hester May, Hestermae

Hetta
(German)
Hedda, Heta, Hettie, Hetty

Heven
(American) pretty
Hevan, Hevin, Hevon, Hevun, Hevven

Heyzell
(American) form of Hazel; tree; homebody
Hayzale, Heyzel, Heyzelle

Hiah
(Korean) form of Heija; bright
Hia, Hy, Hya, Hye

Hiatt
(English) form of Hyatt; splendid
Hi, Hye

Hicks
(Last name as first name) saucy
Hicksee, Hicksie

Hidee
(American) form of Heidi; wry-humored
Hidey, Hidie, Hidy, Hydee, Hydeey

Hilaria
(Latin, Polish) merrymaker
Hilarea, Hilareeah, Hilariah

Hilary
(Latin) cheerful and outgoing
Hilaire, Hilaree, Hilari, Hilaria, Hillarree, Hillary, Hillerie, Hillery

Hilda
(German) practical; (Scandinavian) fighter
Hildi, Hildie, Hildy

Hildegard
(German, Scandinavian) steadfast protector
Hilda, Hildagarde, Hildegarde, Hildred, Hillie

Hilton
(American) wealthy
Hillie, Hilltawn, Hillton, Hilly

Himalaya
(Place name) upwardly mobile
Hima

Hinton
(American) affluent
Hintan, Hinten, Hintun, Hynton

Hodge
(Last name as first name) confident
Hodj

Holden
(English) willing
Holdan, Holdun

Holder
(English) beautiful voice
Holdar, Holdur

Holiday
(American) jazzy
Holidae, Holidaye, Holladay, Holliday, Holly

Holine
(American) special
Hauline, Holinn, Holli, Holyne

Holland
(Dutch) place name; expressive
Hollan, Hollyn, Holyn

Hollis
(English) smart; girl by the holly
Hollice, Hollyce

Hollisha
(English) ingenious; Christmas-born; holly
Holicha, Hollice, Hollichia, Hollise

Holly
(Anglo-Saxon) Christmas-born; holly tree
Hollee, Holleigh, Holley, Holli, Hollye

Holsey
(American) laidback
Holsee, Holsie

Holton
(American) whimsical
Holt, Holten, Holtun

Holyn
(American) fresh-faced
*Holan, Holen, Holland,
Hollee, Hollen, Holley,
Hollie, Holly, Hollyn,
Hollyn*

Homer
(American) tomboyish
*Homar, Home, Homera,
Homie, Homir, Homma*

Honesty
(American) truthful
*Honeste, Honestee,
Honesti, Honestie,
Honestye*

Honey
(Latin) sweet-hearted
Honie, Hunnie

Honor
(Latin) ethical
Honer, Honora, Honour

Honora
(Latin) honorable
*Honorah, Honoree,
Honoria, Honoura*

Honorata
(Polish) respected
woman

Honoria
(Spanish) of high
integrity; a saint
Honoreah

Honorina
(Spanish) honored
*Honor, Honora,
Honoryna*

Hope
(Anglo-Saxon) optimistic

Hopkins
(American) perky
Hopkin

Hortencia
(Spanish) green thumb
*Hartencia, Hartense,
Hartensia, Hortence,
Hortense, Hortensia*

Hortense
(Latin) caretaking the
garden
*Hortence, Hortensia,
Hortinse*

Houston
(Place name) southern
Houst, Houstie, Huston

Hud
(American) tomboyish
Hudd

Huda
(Arabic) the right way
Hoda

Hudson
(English) explorer;
adventuresome
Hud, Huds

Hueline
(German) smart
*Hue, Huee, Huel, Huela,
Huelene, Huelette,
Huelyne, Huey, Hughee,
Hughie*

Huella
(American) joyous
Huela, Huelle

Hulda
(Scandinavian)
sweetheart

Hun
(American) short for
Hunny
Hon

Hunter
(English) searching;
jubilant
*Hun, Huner, Hunner,
Hunt, Huntar, Huntter*

Hurley
(English) fit
Hurlee, Hurlie, Hurly

Hutton
(English) right
Hutten, Huttun

Huxlee
(American) creative
*Hux, Huxleigh, Huxley,
Huxly*

Hyacinth
  (Greek) flower
  Hy, Hycinth, Hyacinthe
Hyde
  (American) tough-willed
  Hide, Hydie
Hydie
  (American) spirited
  Hidi, Hydee, Hydey, Hydi

Iana
  (Greek) flowering; from
  the flower name Iantha
  Iann
Ida
  (German) kind;
  (English) industrious
  Idah, Iduh
Idahlia
  (Greek) sweet
  Idali, Idalia
Idalia
  (Italian) sweet
Idarah
  (American) social
  Idara, Idare, Idareah
Idelle
  (Celtic) generous
  Idele
Idetta
  (German) serious worker
  Ideta, Idettah, Idette
Idil
  (Latin) pleasant
  Idee, Idey, Idi, Idie, Idyll

Idolina
  (American) idolizes
  Idol, Idolena
Iduvina
  (Spanish) dedicated
  Iduvine, Iduvynna, Vina
Ieesh
  (Arabic) feminine
  *Ieasha, Ieesha, Iesha,
  Yesha*
Ihab
  (Arabic) gift
Ikea
  (Scandinavian) smooth
  Ikee, Ikeah, Ikie
Ikeida
  (Invented) spontaneous
  Ikae, Ikay
Ilamay
  (French) sweet; from an
  island
  *Ila May, Ilamae, Ila-May,
  Ilamaye*
Ilana
  (Hebrew) tree; gorgeous
  *Elana, Ilaina, Ilane, Ilani,
  Illana, Lainie, Lanie*
Ileannah
  (American) soaring
  *Ileanna, Iliana, Ilianna,
  Illeana*
Ilene
  (American) svelte
  Ileen, Ilenia

Ilena
(Greek) regal
Ileena, Ilina

Iliana
(Greek) woman of Troy
Ileanai, Illeana

Ilsa
(Scottish) glowing
*Elyssa, Illisa, Illysa,
Ilsah, Lissie*

Ima
(German) affluent;
(Japanese) current
Imah

Imaine
(Arabic) form of Iman;
exotic; believer
Imain, Iman, Imane

Iman
(Arabic, African)
living in the present
Imen

Imelda
(German) contentious
Imalda

Imogen
(Celtic, Latin) girl who
resembles her mother
Emogen, Imogene

Ina
(Latin) small
Inah

Inca
(Indian) adventurer
Incah

India
(Place name) woman of
India
*Indeah, Indee, Indie,
Indy, Indya*

Indiana
(Place name) salt-of-the-
earth
Inda, India, Indianna

Indiece
(American) capable
Indeece, Indeese

Indigo
(Latin) eyes of deep blue
Indego, Indigoh

Indira
(Hindi) ethereal; god of
heaven and
thunderstorms
Indra

Indra
(Hindi) goddess of
thunder and rain;
powerful
Indee, Indi, Indira, Indre

Indray
(American) outspoken
Indrae, Indee, Indree

Ineesha
(African-American)
sparkling
Inesha, Ineshah, Inisha

Ines
(Spanish) chaste
Inez, Innez, Ynez

Inessa
(Russian) pure
Inesa, Nessa

Inez
(Spanish) lovely
Ines

Infinity
(American) lasting
*Infinitee, Infinitey,
Infiniti, Infinitie*

Inge
(Scandinavian) fertile
Inga

Ingrad
(American) variant of
Ingrid; beauty
Inger, Ingr

Ingrid
(Scandinavian) beautiful
Inga, Inge, Inger, Ingred

Iniguez
(Spanish) good
Ina, Ini, Niqui

Innocence
(American) pure
*Innoce, Innocents,
Inocence, Inocencia,
Inocents*

Integrity
(American) truthful
Integritee, Integritie

Iola
(Greek) dawn
Iole

Iona
(Greek, Scottish)
place name
Ione, Ionia

Ira
(Hebrew) contented;
watchful
Irah

Ireland
(Irish) place name;
vibrant
*Irelan, Irelande, Irelyn,
Irelynn*

Irina
(Greek, Russian)
comforting
*Ireena, Irena, Irenah,
Irene, Irenia, Irenya*

Irene
(Greek) peace-loving;
goddess of peace
Irine

Irina
(Russian) soother
Irena, Iryna, Rina

Iris
(Greek) bright; goddess
of the rainbow

Irma
(Latin) realistic
Irmah

Irodell
(Invented) peaceful
Irodel, Irodelle

Isa
(Spanish) dark-eyed
Isah

Isabel
(Spanish) God-loving
*Isabela, Isabella,
Isabelle, Issie, Iza*

Isabella
(Spanish, Italian)
dedicated to God
Isabela, Izabella

Isadora
(Greek) beautiful; gift of
Isis; fertile
Dora, Dory, Isidora

Isairis
(Spanish) lively
Isa, Isaire

Isela
(American) giving
Iselah

Isis
(Egyptian) goddess
supreme of moon and
fertility

Ismene
(French) from the name
Esme; respected
Isme, Ismyne

Isolde
(Welsh) beautiful
Isolda

Itica
(Spanish) eloquent
Itaca, Iticah

Itzel
(Spanish) from Isabella;
God-loving
Itz

Itzy
(American) lively
Itsee, Itzee, Itzie

Iva
(Slavic) dedicated
Ivah

Ivanna
(Russian) gracious gift
from God
*Iva, Ivana, Ivanka, Ivie,
Ivy*

Ivelisa
(American) combo of Ivy
and Lisa
*Ivalisa, Ivelise, Ivelisee,
Ivelissa, Ivelyse*

Ivette
(French) clever and
athletic
Ivet, Ivett

Ivey
(English, American)
easygoing
Ivee, Ivie, Ivy

Iviannah
(American) adorned
Iviana, Ivianna, Ivie, Ivy

Ivisse
(American) graceful
Ivice, Iviece, Ivis, Ivise

Ivon
(Spanish) light
Ivonie, Ivonne

Ivona
(Slavic) gift
Ivonah, Ivone, Ivonne

Ivonne
(French) athlete
Ivonn

Ivory
(Latin) white
Ivoree, Ivori, Ivorie

Ivy
(English) growing
Iv, Ivee, Ivey, Ivie

Iwona
(Polish) archer; athletic;
gift
Iwonna

Izabella
(American) variant of
Isabella
*Iza, Izabela, Izabelle,
Izabell*

Izanne
(American) calming
*Iza, Izan, Izann, Izanna,
Ize*

Izolde
(Greek) philosophical
Izo, Izolade, Izold

Izzy
(American) zany
Izzee, Izzie

Jacey
(Greek) sparkling
*J.C., Jacee, Jaci, Jacie,
Jacy*

Jacinda
(Greek) attractive girl
Jacey, Jaci

Jacinta
(Spanish) flowering;
sweet

Jacinta
(Spanish) hyacinth
*Jace, Jacee, Jacey,
Jacinda, Jacinna,
Jacintae, Jacinth,
Jacinthia, Jacy, Jacynth*

Jackie
(French) short for
Jacqueline
Jackee, Jacki, Jacky, Jaki

Jackson
(Last name as first
name) swaggering
Jacksen, Jaksin, Jakson

Jaclyn
(French) form of
Jacqueline
*Jacalyn, Jackalene,
Jackalin, Jackalyn,
Jackeline, Jackolynne*

Jacobi
(Hebrew) stand-in
Cobie, Coby

Jacqueline
(French) little Jacquie;
small replacement
*Jacki, Jackie, Jacklin,
Jacklyn, Jaclyn,
Jacqualyn, Jacquel,
Jacquelyn, Jacquelynn,
Jacqui, Jacquie, Jakie,
Jakline, Jaklinn, Jaklynn,
Jaqueline, Jaquie*

Jacquet
(Invented) form of
Jacquelyn
*Jackett, Jackwet,
Jacquee, Jacquie, Jakkett*

Jacqui
(French) short for
Jacquline
*Jacque, Jacquie, Jakki,
Jaki, Jaquay*

Jada
(Spanish) personable;
precious
Jadah

Jade
(Spanish) green
gemstone; courageous;
adoring

Jaden
(African-American)
exotic
*Jadi, Jadie, Jadin, Jadyn,
Jaeden, Jaiden*

Jadwiga
(Polish) religious
Jad, Jadwig, Wiga

Jae
(Latin) small; jaybird
Jay, Jayjay

Jael
(Hebrew) high-climbing
Jaeli

Jaela
(Hebrew) bright
Jael, Jaell, Jayla

Jaelyn
(African-American)
ambitious
*Jaela, Jaelynne, Jala,
Jalyn, Jaylyn*

Jaenesha
(African-American)
spirited
*Jacey, Jae, Jaeneisha,
Jaeniesha, Janesha,
Jaynesha, Nesha*

Jaffa
(Hebrew) lovely

Jagan
(American) form of
Jadan; wholesome
*Jag, Jagann, Jagen,
Jagun*

Jagger
(English) cutter
Jaeger, Jag, Jager

Jaguar
(American) runner
*Jag, Jaggy, Jagwar,
Jagwor*

Jahnny
(American) form of
Johnny
*Jahnae, Jahnay, Jahnie,
Jahnnee, Jahnney,
Jahnnie, Jahny*

Jaidan
(American) golden child
*Jaedan, Jai, Jaide, Jaidee,
Jaidi, Jaidon, Jaidun,
Jaidy, Jaidyn, Jaydan,
Jaydyn*

Jaime
(French) girl who loves;
I love
*Jaeme, Jaemee, Jaimee,
Jaimi, Jaimie, Jaimy,
Jamie, Jaymee*

Jaime-Day
(American) loving

Jakisha
(African-American)
favored
Jakishe

Jaleesa
(African-American)
combo of Ja and Leesa
Gilleesa, Jalesa, Jilleesa

Jalene
(American) combo of
Jane and Lene; pretty
Jaleen, Jaline, Jalinn,
Jalyn, Jalyne, Jalynn,
Jlayna

Jalisa
(American) combo of Jay
and Lisa
Gillisa, Jalise, Jaylisa,
Jelisa

Jalit
(American) sparkling
Jal, Jalitt, Jalitte, Jallit

Jamaica
(Place name) Caribbean
island
Jama, Jamaika, Jamaka,
Jamake, Jamana, Jamea,
Jamiqua

Jamais
(French) ever
Jamay, Jamaye

Jamalita
(Invented) form of
James; little Jama
Jama

Jamar
(African-American)
strong
Jam, Jamara, Jamareah,
Jamaree, Jamarr,
Jamarra, Jammy

Jamashia
(African-American)
soulful
Jamash, Jamashea

Jameah
(African-American) bold
Jamea, Jameea, Jamiah

Jamecka
(African-American)
studious
Jamecca, Jameeka,
Jameka, Jameke,
Jamekka, Jamie, Jamiea,
Jamieka

Jamesetta
(American) form of
James
Jamesette

Jamesha
(African-American)
outgoing
Jamece, Jamecia,
Jameciah, Jameisha,
James, Jamie, Jamisha,
Jay

Jamiann
(American) combo of
Jami and Ann
Jami, Jamia, Jami-Ann,
Jamian, Jamiane

Jamie
(Hebrew) supplants; fun-
loving
Jami, Jamee, James,
Jaymee

Jamielyn
(American) combo of
Jamie and Lyn; pretty
Jameelyn, Jamelinn,
James, Jamie,
Jamie-Lynn, Jamilin,
Jami-Lyn

Jamika
(African-American)
buoyant
Jameeka, Jamey, Jamica,
Jamicka, Jamie

Jamila
(Arabic) beautiful female
Jam, Jameela, Jami,
Jamie, Jamil, Jamilah,
Jamile, Jamilla, Jamille,
Jamilya, Jammell,
Jammie

Jan
(English) short for Janet
or Janice; cute
Jani, Jannie, Janny

Jana
(Slavic, Scandinavian)
gracious
Janna, Janne

Janae
(American) giving
Janea, Jannay, Jennae,
Jannah, Jennay

Janaleigh
(American) combo of
Jana and Leigh; friendly
Jana, Janalea, Janalee,
Janalee, Jana-Lee,
Jana-Leigh, Janlee,
Jannalee, LeeLee, Leigh

Janalyn
(American) giving
Jan, Janalynn, Janelyn,
Janilyn, Jannalyn,
Jannnie, Janny

Janan
(Arabic) soulful
Jananee, Janann, Jannani

Janara
(American) generous
Janarah, Janerah, Janira,
Janirah

Janay
(American) forgiving
Janae, Janah, Janai

Jancy
(American) risk-taker
Jan, Jance, Jancee,
Jancey, Janci, Jancie,
Janny

Jandy
(American) fun
Jandee, Jandey, Jandi

Jane
(Hebrew) believer in a
gracious God
Jaine, Janelle, Janene,
Janeth, Janett, Janetta,
Janey, Janica, Janie,
Jannie, Jayne, Jaynie

Janeana
(American) sweet
Janea, Janean, Janeanah,
Janine

Janene
(American) form of Jane
Janeen, Jenean, Janine,
Jenine

Janella
(American) combo of Jan
and Ella; sporty
Jan, Janela, Janelle,
Janny

Janelle
(French) exuberant
J'Nel, J'nell, Janel, Janell,
Jannel, Jenelle, Nell

Janessa
(American) forgiving
Janessah, Janie, Janyssa

Janet
(English) small; forgiving
Janett, Janetta, Janette,
Jannet, Jannett, Janot,
Jessie, Jinett, Johnette,
Jonetta, Jonette

Janeth
(American) fascinating
Janith

Janice
(Hebrew) knowing God's
grace
Genese, Janece, Janeese

Janie
(English) form of Jane
Janey, Jani, Jany

Janiece
(American) devout;
enthusiastic
Janece, Janecia, Janeese,
Janese, Janesea,
Janesse, Janneece,
Jeneece, Jeneese

Janiecia
(African-American)
sporty
Janesha, Janeisha,
Janeshah, Janisha, Jan,
Jannes, Jannesa

Janika
(Scandinavian) believer
in a gracious God
Janica, Janicah, Janik,
Jannike, Janikka

Janine
(American) kind
Janean, Janeen, Janene, Janey, Janie

Janis
(English) form of Jane
Jenice, Jenis, Janise

Janjan
(Last name as first) sweet; believer
Jan Jan, Jange, Janja, Jan-Jan, Janje, Janni, Jannie, Janny

Janke
(Scandinavian) believer in God
Jankee, Jankey, Jankie

Jan-Marie
(American) combo of Jan and Marie; believer
Jan Marie, Janmarie, Jannemarie

Janna
(Hebrew) short for Johana; forgiving

Jannette
(American) lovely
Jan, Janette, Jannett, Jannie, Janny

Jannie
(English) form of Jane and Jan
Janney, Janny, Jannye

Jansen
(Scandinavian) smooth
Jan, Jannsen, Jans, Jansie, Janson, Jansun, Jansy

Jaqueline
(French) form of Jacquelyn
Jaqlinn, Jaqlyn, Jaqlynn, Jaqua, Jaquaeline, Jaqualine, Jaqualyn, Jaquelina, Jaquelyn, Jaquelynne, Jaquie, Jaqulene

Jaquonna
(African-American) spoiled
Jakwona, Jakwonda, Jakwonna, Jaqui, Jaquie, Jaquon, Jaquona, Jaquonne

Jardana
(American) gardener
Jardana, Jarde, Jardee, Jardy

Jarene
(American) bright
Jare, Jaree, Jareen, Jaren, Jareni, Jarine, Jarry, Jaryne, Jerry

Jarone
(American) optimistic
Jaron, Jaroyne, Jerone, Jurone

Jarren
(American) lovable
Jaren, Jarran, Jarre

Jasalin
(American) devoted
Jasalinne, Jasalyn, Jasalynn, Jaselyn, Jasleen, Jaslene, Jass, Jassalyn, Jassy, Jazz, Jazzy

Jasmine
(Persian, Spanish) fragrant; sweet
Jas'mine, Jasamine, Jasime, Jasimen, Jasimin, Jasimine, Jasmaine, Jasman, Jasme, Jasmie, Jasmina, Jasminah, Jasminen, Jasminne, Jasmon, Jasmond, Jasmone, Jasmyn, Jasmynn, Jasmynne, Jazie, Jazmaine, Jazman, Jazmeen, Jazmein, Jazmen, Jazmin, Jazmine, Jazmon, Jazmond, Jazmyn, Jazmyne, Jazs, Jazsmen, Jazz, Jazza, Jazzamine, Jazzee, Jazzi, Jazzmeen, Jazzmin, Jazz-Mine, Jazzmun, Jazzy

Jasna
(American) talented
Jas, Jazna, Jazz

Ja-Tawn
(African-American)
tawny
J'Tawn, Ja Tawn, Jatawn

Jatsue
(Spanish) lively
Jat, Jatsey

Jaya
(Hindi) winning
Jaia, Jay, Jayah

Jayci
(American) vivacious
Jaycee, Jaycie

Jaydee
(American) combo of Jay
and Dee; perky
*Jadee, Jayde, Jayda,
Jayd, Jaydia, Jaydn, Jayia*

Jayden
(American) enthusiastic
*Jaden, Jay, Jaydeen,
Jaydon, Jaydyn, Jaye*

Jaydie
(American) lively
*Jadie, Jady, Jay-Dee,
Jaydeye, Jaydie*

Jaydra
(Spanish) treasured
jewel; jade
Jadra, Jay, Jaydrah

Jaye
(Latin) small as a jaybird
Jae, Jay

Jayla
(American) smiling
Jaila, Jaylah, Jayle, Jaylee

Jaylo
(American) combo of
Jennifer and Lopez;
charismatic
*J. Lo, Jalo, Jayjay, Jaylla,
Jaylon, J-Lo*

Jayme
(English)
*Jami, Jamie, Jaymee,
Jaymi, Jaymie*

Jayne
(Hindi, American)
winning
*Jane, Janey, Jani, Jaynee,
Jayni, Jaynie*

Jaynell
(American) combo of Jay
and Nell; southern belle
*Janell, Janelle, Jaynel,
Jaynelle, Jeanel, Jeanell,
Jeanelle, Jeanelly*

Jazz
(American) short for
Jasmine; flowering; high-
spirited
*Jas, Jassie, Jaz, Jazzi,
Jazzie, Jazzle, Jazzy*

Jazzell
(American) spontaneous
*Jazel, Jazell, Jazz, Jazzee,
Jazzie*

Jazzlyn
(American) combo of
Jazz and Lyn
*Jaz, Jazilyn, Jazlin,
Jazlinn, Jazlinne, Jazlyn,
Jazlynn, Jazlynne*

Jean
(Scottish) God-loving
and gracious
*Jeana, Jeanie, Jeanne,
Jeannie, Jeanny, Jena,
Jenay, Jenna*

Jeanetta
(American) smallish imp
*Janetta, Jeannet,
Jeannette, Jeanney, Jen,
Jenett, Jennita*

Jeanette
(French) lively
*Janette, Jeannete,
Jeanett*

Jeanie
(Scottish) devout;
outspoken
Jeannie, Jeanny

Jeanine
(Scottish) peace-loving
Jeanene, Jenine

Jeanisha
(African-American)
pretty
*Jean, Jeaneesh, Jeanise,
Jeanna, Jeannie, Jenisha*

Jearlean
(American) vibrant
*Jearlee, Jearlene, Jearley,
Jearli, Jearline, Jearly,
Jerline*

Jecelyn
(Invented) form of
Jocelyn; innovative
Jece, Jecee, Jeselyn, Jess

Jeffrey
(German) peaceful;
sparkling personality
*Jef, Jeff, Jeffa, Jefferi,
Jeffery, Jeffie, Jeffre,
Jeffrie, Jeffy, Jefry*

Jelane
(Russian) light heart
*Jelaina, Jelaine, Jelanne,
Jilane, Julane*

Jelani
(American) pretty sky
*Jelaney, Jelani, Jelanie,
Jelainy, Jelanni*

Jemima
(Hebrew) dove-like
*Jem, Jemi, Jemimah,
Jemm, Jemmi, Jemmy,
Jemora*

Jemine
(American) treasured
Jem, Jemmy, Jemyne

Jemma
(Hebrew, English)
nickname for Jemima;
peaceful
Jem

Jems
(American) form of
Gems; treasured
*Gemas, Jemma, Jemmey,
Jemmi, Jemmy*

Jena
(Arabic); small
*Jenaa, Jenaeh, Jenah,
Jenai, Jenna*

Jencynn
(American) combo of Jen
and Cynn; sweetheart
*Jencin, Jen-Cynn,
Jensynn*

Jenell
(American) combo of
Jenny and Nell
*Janele, Jen, Jenaile,
Jenalle, Jenel, Jenella,
Jennelle, Jenny*

Jenifer
(Welsh) beautiful; fair
*Gennefer, Gennifer,
Ginnifur, Ginnipher, Jay,
Jenefer, Jenifer, Jenjen,
Jenna, Jenni, Jennifer,
Jenny*

Jenilynn
(American) combo of
Jenny and Lynn; precious
*Jennalyn, Jennilin,
Jennilinn, Jennilyn,
Jenny-Lynn, Jennylynn*

Jenna
(Scottish, English)
sweet
Jena, Jynna

Jennifer
(Welsh, English)
fair-haired; beautiful
perfection
*Gennefur, Jen, Jenife,
Jeniferr, Jenn, Jenna,
Jennae, Jennafer,
Jennefer, Jenni,
Jennipher, Jenniphur,
Jenny, Jennyfer,
Jennypher*

Jennings
(Last name as first
name) pretty
Jen, Jenny

Jennis
(American) white;
patient
*J, Jay, Jen, Jenace, Jenice,
Jenis, Jenn, Jennice*

Jennison
(American) variant of
Jennifer; darling
*Gennison, Jenison,
Jennisyn, Jenson*

Jenny
(Scottish, English) short for Jennifer; blessed; sweetheart
Jen, Jenae, Jeni, Jenjen, Jenni, Jennie, Jennye

Jenteale
(American) combo of Jen and Teale; blue-eyed and pretty
Jen, Jenny, Jenteal, Jentelle, Jyn, Jynteale, Teal, Teale

Jenvie
(American) lovely
Jennvey, Jenvee, Jenvy

Jenz
(Scandinavian) form of male name Johannes; believer in God
Jen, Jens

Jeri
(American) hopeful
Geri, Jere, Jerhie, Jerree, Jerri, Jerry, Jerrye

Jeridean
(American) combo of Jeri and Dean; leader; musical
Geridean, Jerdean, Jeri Dean, Jeri-Dean, Jerridean, Jerrydean

Jerikah
(American) sparkling
Jereca, Jerecka, Jeree, Jeri, Jerica, Jerik, Jeriko, Jerrica, Jerry

Jerilyn
(American) combo of Jeri and Lynn
Jeralyn, Jeralynn, Jerrilin, Jerrilyn

Jerin
(American) daring
Jere, Jeren, Jeron, Jerinn, Jerun

Jermaine
(French) form of Germaine
Germaine, Jermane, Jermanee, Jermani, Jermany, Jermayne

Jerrett
(American) spirited
Jerett, Jeriette, Jerre, Jerret, Jerrette, Jerrie, Jerry

Jerrica
(American) free spirit
Jerrika

Jesenia
(Spanish) witty
Jesene, Jess, Jessenia, Jessie, Jessie, Jisenia, Yesenia

Jessa
(American) spontaneous
Jessah

Jessalyn
(American) combo of Jessica and Lynn; exciting
Jesalyn, Jesilyn, Jeslin, Jeslyn, Jessaline, Jessie, Jesslin

Jessamine
(French) form of Jasmine; sassy
Jesamyn, Jess, Jessamin, Jessie, Jessmine

Jesse
(Hebrew) friendly
Jesie, Jessey, Jessi, Jessy

Jessica
(Hebrew) rich
Jesica, Jess, Jessa, Jessie, Jessika, Jessy, Jezika

Jessie
(Scottish) casual
Jesey, Jess, Jessee, Jessi, Jessye

Jessie-Mae
(American) combo of Jessie and Mae; country girl
Jessee-May, Jessemay, Jessie Mae, Jessie May, Jessiemae, Jessmae

Jesusita
    (Spanish) little Jesus
Jett
    (American) high-flying
    Jettie, Jetty
Jette
    (German, Scandinavian)
    lovely gem
    Jet, Jeta, Jetia, Jetta,
    Jette, Jettee, Jettie
Jeudi
    (French) born on
    Thursday
Jeune-Fille
    (French) young girl
Jevae
    (Spanish) desired
    Jevaie, Jevay
Jevonne
    (African-American) kind
    Jev, Jevaughan,
    Jevaughn, Jevie, Jevon,
    Jevona, Jevonn, Jevvy
Jewel
    (French) pretty
    Jeul, Jewelia, Jewelie,
    Jewell, Jewelle, Jewels,
    Jule
Jewellene
    (American) combo of
    Jewel and Lene;
    treasured
    Jewelene, Jeweline,
    Jewels, Julene

Jezebel
    (Hebrew) wanton
    woman
    Jessebelle, Jez, Jeze,
    Jezebell, Jezel, Jezell,
    Jezybel, Jezzie
Jezenya
    (American) flowering
    Jesenya, Jeze, Jezey
Jhamesha
    (African-American)
    lovely; soft
    Jamesha, Jmesha
Jilan
    (American) mover
    Jilyn, Jillan, Jillyn, Jylan,
    Jylann
Jill
    (English) short for Jillian;
    high-energy and
    youthful
    Jil, Jilee, Jilli, Jillie, Jilly
Jilleen
    (American) energetic
    Jil, Jileen, Jilene, Jiline,
    Jill, Jillain, Jilline, Jlynn
Jillian
    (Latin) youthful
    Giliana, Jill, Jillaine,
    Jillana, Jillena, Jilliane,
    Jilliann, Jillie, Jillion,
    Jillione, Jilly, Jilyan
Jimmi
    (American)
    Jim, Jimi, Jimice, Jayjay

Jin
    (Chinese) golden; gem
    Jinn, Jinny
Jinger
    (American) form of
    Ginger; go-getter
    Jin, Jinge
Jinkie
    (American) bouncy
    Jinkee, Jynki, Jinky
Jinny
    (Scottish) form of Jenny
    Jinna, Jinney
Jinx
    (Latin) spell
    Jin, Jinks, Jinxie, Jinxy,
    Jynx
Jinxia
    (Latin) form of Jinx;
    spellbinder
    Jinx, Jynx, Jynxia
Jnae
    (American) darling
    J'Nay, Jenae, Jnay, Jnaye
J'Netta
    (American) form of
    Jeanetta; sweetness
    J'netta, J'Nette, Janetta,
    Janny
J-Nyl
    (American) flirtatious
Jo
    (American) short for
    Josephine; spunky
    Joey, Jojo

Jo-Allene
(American) combo of Jo
and Allene; effervescent
*Jo Allene, Joallene,
Joallie, Joeallene, Joealli,
Jolene*

Joan
(Hebrew) heroine; God-
loving
*Joane, Joane, Joani,
Joanie, Joanni, Joannie,
Jonie*

Joana
(Hebrew) kind
*Joanah, Joanna,
Joannah, Jonah*

Joanie
(Hebrew) kind
*Joanney, Joanni, Joannie,
Joanny, Joany, Joni*

Jo-Ann
(French) believer;
gregarious
*Joahnn, JoAn, JoAnn,
Joann, Joanna, Joanne,
Jo-Anne, Joannie*

Joanna
(English) kind
*Jo, Joeanna, Johannah,
Josie*

Joanne
(English) form of Joan;
excellent friend
*JoAnn, Joann, Jo-Ann,
JoAnne, Joeanne*

Joannie
(Hebrew) forgiving
*Joani, Joany, Joanney,
Joanni*

Jobelle
(American) combo of Jo
and Belle; beautiful
*Jobel, Jobell, Jobi, Jobie,
Joebel*

Jobeth
(American) combo of Jo
and Beth; vivacious
*Beth, Bethie, Jo, Jobee,
Jobie*

Jobi
(Hebrew)
misunderstood;
inventive
Jobee, Jobey, Jobie, Joby

Jo-Carol
(American) combo of Jo
and Carol; lively
Jo Carol, Jocarol, Jocarole

Jocelyn
(Latin) joyful
*Jocelie, Jocelin, Jocelyne,
Jocelynn, Joci, Joclyn,
Joclynn, Jocylan, Jocylen,
Joycelyn*

Joci
(Latin) happy
*Jocee, Jocey, Jocie, Jocy,
Josi*

Jocklyn
(American) combo of
Jock and Lyn; athletic
Jock, Joklyn

Jodase
(American) brilliant
*Jo, Jodace, Jodasse,
Jodie, Jody*

Jo-Dee
(American) combo of Jo
and Dee
Jo Dee, Jodee, Joedee

Jodee-Marie
(American) combo of
Jodee and Marie
Jodeemarie, Jodymarie

Jodelle
(American) combo of Jo
and Delle
Jodel, Jodell, Jodie, Jody

Jodie
(American) happy girl
*Jo, Jodee, Jodey, Jodi,
Jody*

Joedy
(American) jolly
Joedey, Joedi, Joedie

Joe-Leigh
(American) combo of Joe
and Leigh; happy
*Joe Leigh, Joel, Joelea,
Joesey, Jolee, Joleigh,
Jolie, Jollee, Jose, Joze*

Joelle
(Hebrew) willing
Jo, Joel, Joele, Joeleen, Joell, Joella, Joelle, Joelly

Joely
(Hebrew) believer; lively
Jo, Joe, Joey

Joelly
(American) kindhearted
Joelee, Joeli, Joely

Joetta
(American) combo of Jo and Etta; creative
Jo, Joe, Joettah, Joette

Joey
(American) easygoing
Joe, Joeye

Joezee
(American) form of Josey; attractive
Jo, Joe, Joes, Joezey, Joezy

Johanna
(German) believer in a gracious God
Johana, Johanah, Johanna, Jonna

Johnay
(American) steadfast
Johnae, Jonay, Jonaye, Jonnay

Johnica
(American) form of John; believer in a gracious God
Jonica

Johnna
(American) upright
Jahna, John, Johna, Johnae, Jonna, Jonnie

Johnnell
(American) happy
Johnelle, Jonell, Jonnel

Johnnetta
(American) joyful
Johneta, Johnete, Johnetta, Johnette, Jonetta, Jonette, Jonietta

Johnnisha
(African-American) steady
Johnisha, Johnnita, Johnny, Jonnisha

Johnson
(Last name as first name) confident
Johns

Johntell
(African-American) sweet
Johna, Johntal, Johntel, Johntelle, Jontell

Joi
(Latin) joyful
Joicy, Joie, Jojo, Joy

Jo-Kiesha
(African-American) vibrant
Joekiesha

Jolanda
(Latin, Italian) violet; pretty flower
Jolana, Jolande, Jolane

Jolene
(American) jolly
Jo, Joeleane, Joeleen, Joelene, Joelynn, Joleen, Joleene, Jolen, Jolena, Joley, Jolie, Joline, Jolyn, Jolynn

Joletta
(American) happy-go-lucky
Jaletta, Jolette, Joley, Joli, Jolie, Jolitta

Jolie
(French) pretty
Jo, Jolee, Joli, Jollee

Jolienne
(American) pretty
Joliane, Jolianne, Jolien, Jolina, Joline

Jolisa
(American) combo of Jo and Lisa; cheerful
Joelisa, Joli, Jo-Lisa, Jolise, Lisa

Jolyane
(American) sweetheart
Joliane, Jollyane, Jolyan, Jolyann, Jolyanne

Jolynn
(American) combo of Jo and Lynn
Jo, Jolene, Jolynda, Jolyne

Jonelle
(American) combo of Joan and Elle
Jo, Johnel, Jonel, Jonell, Jonnell, Jynel

Jones
(American) saucy

Joni
(American) short for Joan
Joanie, Jonie, Jony

Jonice
(American) casual
Joneece, Joneese, Jonni, Jonise

Jonita
(Hebrew) pretty little one
Janita, Jonite

Jonquill
(American) flower
Jonn, Jonque, Jonquie, Jonquil, Jonquille

Jontelle
(American) musical
Jahntelle, Jontel, Jontlyl

Jorah
(Hebrew) fresh as rain
Jora

Jo-Rain
(American) combo of Jo and Rain; zany
Jo Rain, Jorain, JoRaine

Jordan
(Hebrew) excellent descendant
Johrdon, Jordaine, Jordane, Jorden, Jordenne, Jordeyn, Jordi, Jordie, Jordin, Jordon, Jordyn, Jordynne, Joudane, Jourdan

Jordana
(Hebrew) smart
Giordanna, Jordann, Jordanna, Jordannuh, Jordona, Jordonna, Jourdanna

Jordy
(American) quick
Jordee, Jordey, Jordi, Jordie, Jorey

Jorgina
(Spanish) nurturing
Jorge, Jorgine, Jorgy, Jorgie, Jorgi, Georgina, Georgeena

Jorie
(Hebrew) short for Jordan
Joree, Jorey, Jorhee, Jorhie, Jori, Jorre, Jorrey, Jorri, Jory

Jorja
(American) smart
Georgia, Jorge, Jorgia, Jorgie, Jorgy

Josefat
(Spanish) form of Joseph; gracious
Fata, Fina, Josef, Josefa, Josefana, Josefenna, Josefita, Joseva, Josey, Josie

Josefina
(Hebrew) fertile
Jose, Josephina, Josey, Josie

Joselyn
(German) pretty
Joseline, Josey, Joslyn, Josselen, Josseline, Josselyne, Josslyn, Josslynn, Josylynn

Josephine
(French) blessed
Fena, Jo, Joes, Josefina, Josephene, Josie, Jozaphine

Josette
(French) little Josephine

Josey
(Hebrew, American) saucy
Josee, Josi, Josie, Jozie

Josiann
(American) combo of Josey and Ann; prettiest one
Josann, Josiane, Josianne, Joseyann

Josie-Mae
(American) combo of Josie and Mae
Josee-Mae, Josiemae

Joslyn
(Latin) jocular
Joclyn, Joslene, Joslinn, Josslin, Josslyn, Josslynn

Jostin
(American) adorable
Josten, Jostun, Josty, Jostyn

Jour
(French) day

Jovannah
(Latin) regal
Jouvanna, Jovanee, Jovani, Jovanna, Jovanne, Jovannie

Jovita
(Latin) glad
Joveeta

Jovonne
(American) combo of Jo and Yvonne; queenly
Javonne, Jovaughn, Jovon, Jovonnie

Jovita
(Latin) happy
Joveeda, Jovetta, Jovi, Jovie, Jo-Vita, Jovy

Jowannah
(American) happy
Jowanna, Jowanne, Jowonna

Joy
(Latin) joyful
Joi, Joie, Joya, Joye

Joyce
(Latin) joyous
Joice, Joy, Joyci, Joycie

Joyleen
(American) combo of Joy and Eileen; happy lady
Joyleena, Joylene, Joyline

Joyous
(American) joyful
Joy, Joyus

Joyslyn
(American) form of Jocelyn; cheery
Joycelyn, Joyslin, Joyslinn

Juanisha
(African-American) delightful
Juanesha, Juaneshia, Juannisha

Juanita
(Spanish) believer in a gracious God; forgiving
Juan, Juana, Juaneta, Juanika, Juanna, Juanne, Juannie, Juanny, Wanita

Jubelka
(African-American) jubilant
Jube, Jubi, Jubie

Jubilee
(Hebrew) jubilant
Jubalie

Jubini
(American) grateful; jubilant
Jubi, Jubine

Jucinda
(American) relishing life
Jucin, Jucindah, Jucinde

Judalon
(Hebrew) merry
Judalonn, Juddalone, Judelon

Jude
(French) confident
Judea, Judee, Judde

Judit
(Hebrew) Jewish
Jude, Judi, Juditt

Judith
(Hebrew) woman worthy
of praise
*Jude, Judi, Judie, Juditha,
Judy, Judyth, Judythe*

Judy
(Hebrew) short for Judith
*Judi, Judie, Joodie,
Judye, Jude*

Juel
(American) dependable
*Jewel, Juelle, Juels, Jule,
Juile*

Juirl
(American) careful
Ju, Juirll

Juleen
(American) sensual
Jule, Julene, Jules

Jules
(American) brooding
Jewels, Juels

Julia
(Latin) forever young
Jula, Julina, Julya

Julian
(Latin) effervescent
*Jewelian, Julean, Juliann,
Julien, Juliene, Julienn,
Julyun*

Juliana
(Italian, German,
Spanish) youthful
*Juleanna, Julianna,
Juliannah, Julie-Anna,
Jullyana*

Julianne
(American) combo of
Julie and Anne
Juleann, Jules, Julieann

Julie
(English) young and
vocal
*Juel, Jule, Juli, Juliene,
Julye*

Juliet
(Italian) loving

Juliette
(French) romantic
Julie, Jules, Juliet, Julietta

Julimarie
(American) combo of Juli
and Marie; young;
alluring
*Joolimarie, Julie Marie,
Juliemarie, Julie-Marie*

Julissa
(Latin) universally loved
*Jula, Julessa, Julisa,
Julisha*

Julita
(Spanish) adorable;
young
Juli, Julitte

Juluette
(American) adorable;
young
*Jule, Jules, Julett, Julette,
Julie, Julu, Julue, Juluett,
Julu-Ette, LuLu*

July
(Latin) month; warm

Jumoke
(African) most popular

June
(Latin) born in June
*Juneth, Junie, Junieth,
Juney, Juny*

Junieth
(Latin) from the month
June; heavenly
*Juney, Juni, Junie,
Juniethe*

Juno
(Latin) queenly
Juna, June

Juqwanza
(African-American)
bouncy
*Jukwanza, Juqwann,
Qwanza*

Justice
(Latin) fair-minded
Just, Justise, Justy

Justika
(American) dancing-girl
*Justeeka, Justica, Justie,
Justy*

Justina
 (Latin) honest
 Justeena, Justena
Justine
 (Italian, Latin) fair-minded
 Justa, Juste, Justean, Justeen, Justena, Justene, Justi, Justie, Justina, Justinna, Justyne, Justynn, Justynne, Juzteen
Jutta
 (American) ebullient
 Juta
Juvelia
 (Spanish) young
 Juvee, Juvelle, Juvelya, Juvie, Juvilia, Velia, Velya
Juwanne
 (African-American) lively
 Juwan, Juwann, Juwanna, Juwon, Jwanna, Jwanne

Kacey
 (Irish) daring
 Casey, Casie, K.C., K.Cee, Kace, Kacee, Kaci, Kacy, Kasey, Kasie, Kaycee, Kaycie, Kaysie
Kachina
 (Native American) sacred dancer; doll-like
 Cachina, Kachena, Kachine
Kacondra
 (African-American) bold
 Condra, Connie, Conny, Kacon, Kacond, Kaecondra, Kakondra, Kaycondra
Kaden
 (American) charismatic
 Caden, Kadenn
Kadie
 (American) virtuous
 Kadee
Kady
 (English) sassy
 Cady, K.D., Kadee, Kadie, Kaydie, Kaydy

Kaelin
 (Irish) pure; impetuous
 Kaelan, Kaelen, Kaelinn, Kaelyn, Kaelynn, Kaelynne, Kaylin
Kaelynn
 (American) combo of Kae and Lynn; beloved
 Kaelin, Kailyn, Kay-Lynn
Kai
 (Hawaiian, African) attractive
 Kaia
Kailah
 (Greek) virtuous
 Kail, Kala, Kalae, Kalah
Kailey
 (American) spunky
 Kalee, Kaili, Kailie, Kaylee, Kaylei
Kaitlin
 (Irish) pure-hearted
 Caitlin, Kaitlan, Kaitland, Kaitlinn, Kaitlynn, Kalyn
Kalani
 (Hawaiian) leader
 Kalauni, Kaloni, Kaylanie
Kaleigh
 (Sanskrit) energetic; dark
 Kalea
Kalet
 (French) beautiful energy
 Kalay, Kalaye

Kali
(Greek) beauty
Kalli

Kalidas
(Greek) most beautiful
Kaleedus, Kali

Kalila
(Arabic) sweet; lovable
*Kaililah, Kaleah, Kalela,
Kay, Kaykay, Kaylee, Kyle*

Kalisa
(American) combo of
Kay and Lisa; pretty and
loving
*Caylisa, Kaleesa, Kalisha
Kalyssa, Kaylisa, Kaykay*

Kallan
(American) loving
Kall, Kallen, Kallun

Kallie
(Greek) beautiful
*Callie, Kalley, Kali, Kalie,
Kally*

Kalliope
(Greek) beautiful voice
Calli, Calliope, Kalli

Kallista
(Greek) pretty; bright-
eyed
*Callista, Kalesta, Kalista,
Kalysta*

Kalyn
(Arabic) loved
*Calynn, Calynne, Kaelyn,
Kaelynn, Kalen, Kalin,
Kalinn, Kallyn*

Kami
(Japanese) perfect aura
Cami

Kamilia
(Polish) pure

Kama
(Sanskrit) beloved;
Hindu god of love
Kam, Kamie

Kamala
(American) interesting
*Camala, Kam, Kamali,
Kamilla, Kammy*

Kamea
(Hawaiian) precious
darling
Cammi, Kam, Kammie

Kamela
(Italian) form of Camilla;
wonderful
Kam, Kamila, Kammy

Kameron
(American) spiritual
*Cam, Cameron, Cami,
Cammie, Kamreen,
Kamrin*

Kami
(Italian) spiritual little
one
*Cami, Cammie, Cammy,
Kammie, Kammy*

Kamilah
(North African) perfect

Kamilia
(Polish) perfect
character
*Kam, Kamila, Kammy,
Milla*

Kamyra
(American) light
Kamera

Kandace
(Greek) charming;
glowing
*Candace, Kandace,
Kandi, Kandice, Kandy*

Kandi
(American) short for
Kandace
Candi, Kandie, Kandy

Kandra
(American) light
Candra

Kaneesha
(American) dark-skinned
*Caneesha, Kaneesh,
Kaneice, Kaneisha,
Kanesha, Kaneshia,
Kaney, Kanish, Nesha*

Kanesha
(African-American)
spontaneous
Kaneesha, Kaneeshia,
Kaneisha, Kanisha,
Kannesha

Kansas
(Place name) practical
Kanny

Kaprece
(American) capricious
Caprice, Kapp, Kappy,
Kapreece, Kapri, Kaprise,
Kapryce, Karpreese

Kara
(Danish, Greek) dearest
Cara, Kar, Karah, Kari,
Karie

Karalenae
(American) combo of
Kara and Lenae
Kara-Lenae, Karalenay

Karbie
(American) energetic
Karbi, Karby

Karelle
(French) joyful singer
Carel, Carelle, Karel

Karen
(Greek, Irish) pure-
hearted
Caren, Caryn, Kare,
Kareen, Karenna, Karin,
Karina, Karron, Karyn,
Keren

Karenz
(English) from Kerenza;
sweet girl
Karence, Karens,
Karense

Kari
(Scandinavian) pure
Cari, Karri, Karrie, Karry

Karian
(American) daring
Kerian

Karianne
(American) combo of
Kari and Anne
Kariane, Kariann,
Kari-Ann, Karianna,
Kerianne

Karilynne
(American) combo of
Kari and Lynne
Cariliynn, Kariline,
Karylynn

Karima
(Arabic) giving
Karimah

Karin
(Scandinavian) kind-
hearted
Karen, Karine, Karinne

Karina
(Russian) best of heart;
(Latin) even
Kare, Karinda, Karine,
Karinna, Karrie, Karrina,
Karyna

Karise
(Greek) graceful woman
Karis, Karisse, Karyce

Karissa
(Greek) longsuffering
Carissa, Karessa, Karisa

Karizma
(African) hopeful
Karisma

Karla
(German) bright-eyed;
feminine form of
Carl/Karl
Carla, Karlie

Karla-Faye
(American) combo of
Karla and Faye

Karleen
(American) combo of
Karla and Arleen; witty
Karlene, Karline, Karly

Karly
(Latin, American)
strong-voiced
Carly, Karlee, Karlie,
Karlye

Karma
(Hindi) destined for
good things
Karm, Karmie, Karmy

Karmel
(Hebrew)
Carmel, Karmela,
Karmelle

Karmen
(Hebrew) loving songs
Carmen, Karmin,
Karmine

Karnesha
(American) spicy
Carnesha, Karnisha,
Karny

Karolanne
(American) combo of
Karol and Anne
Karol, Karolan, Karolane,
Karolann, Karolen

Karolina
(Polish) form of Charles
Karo

Karoline
(German) form of Karl
Kare, Karola, Karolah,
Karolina, Lina

Karolyn
(American) friendly
Carolyn, Kara, Karal,
Karalyn, Karilynne,
Karolynn

Karrington
(Last name as first
name) admired
Carrington, Kare, Karring

Karyn
(American) sweet
Caren, Karen

Kasey
(American) spirited
Casey, Kacey, Kasie,
Kaysie

Kashmir
(Sanskrit) place name
Cahmere, Cashmir, Kash,
Kashmere

Kashonda
(African-American)
dramatic
Kashanda, Kashawnda
Koshonda

Kashondra
(African-American)
bright
Kachanne, Kachaundra,
Kachee, Kashandra,
Kashawndra, Kashee,
Kashon, Kashondrah,
Kashondre, Kashun

Kasi
(American) form of
Cassie; seer
Kass, Kassi, Kassie

Kassandra
(Greek) capricious
Cassandra, Kass,
Kasandra, Kassandrah,
Kassie

Kassidy
(Irish) clever
Cassidy, Cassir, Kasadee,
Kass, Kassie, Kassy,
Kassydi

Kassie
(American) clever
Kassee, Kassi, Kassy

Kat
(American) outrageous
Cat

Katarina
(Greek) pure
Katareena, Katarena,
Katarinna, Kataryna,
Katerina, Katryna

Katarzyna
(Origin unknown)
creative
Katarzina

Katchen
(Greek) virtuous
Kat, Katshen

Katchi
(American) sassy
*Catshy, Cotchy, Kat,
Kata, Katchie, Kati,
Katshi, Katshie, Katshy,
Katty, Kotchee, Kotchi,
Kotchie*

Kate
(Greek, Irish) pure-
hearted
Katie, Katy, Kay-Kay

Katelyn
(Irish) pure-hearted
*Caitlin, Kaitlin,
Kaitlynne, Kat, Katelin,
Katelynn, Kate-Lynn,
Katline, Katy*

Katera
(Origin unknown)
celebrant
Katara, Katura

Katharine
(Greek) powerful; pure
*Kat, Katharin, Katherin,
Katherine, Kathy,
Kathyrn, Kaykay*

Kathlaya
(American) fashionable

Kathleen
(Irish) brilliant; unflawed
*Cathleen, Kathlene,
Kathlynn, Kathlyn,
Kathie, Kathy*

Kathryn
(English) powerful and
pure
*Kathreena, Kathren,
Kathrene, Kathrin,
Kathrine, Kathryne*

Kathy
(English) pure;
(Irish) spunky
*Cathy, Kath, Kathe,
Kathee, Kathi, Kathie*

Katia
(French) stylish
Kateeya, Kati, Katya

Katie
(English) lively
*Kat, Katy, Kay, Kaykay,
Kate, Kaytie*

Katina
(American) form of
Katrina; virtuous
Kat, Kateen, Kateena

Katlynn
(Greek) pure
Kat, Katlinn, Katlyn

Katrice
(American) graceful
*Katreese, Katrese,
Katrie, Katrisse, Katry*

Katrina
(German) melodious
Catrina, Katreena, Kay

Katrine
(German, Polish) pure
*Catrene, Kati, Katrene,
Katrinna, Kati*

Katy
(English) lively
*Cady, Katie, Kattee,
Kattie, Kaytee*

Kavinli
(American) form of
Kevin; eager
*Cavin, Kaven, Kavin,
Kavinlee, Kavinley,
Kavinly*

Kavita
(Hindi) poem
Kaveta, Kavitah

Kay
(Greek, Latin) fun-loving
Cay, Caye, Kaye, Kaykay

Kaycie
(American) merrymaker
*CayCee, K.C., Kaycee,
Kayci, Kaysie*

Kayla
(Hebrew, Arabic) sweet
*Cala, Cayla, Kala, Kaela,
Kaila, Kaylah, Keyla*

Kaylee
(American) open
*Cayley, Kaelie, Kaylea,
Kaylie, Kayleigh*

Kayleen
(Hebrew) sweet; combo
of Kay and Eileen
*Kaileen, Kalene, Kay,
Kaylean, Kayleene,
Kaykay*

Kaylin
(American) combo of
Kay and Lynn
Kaylan, Kaylen, Kaylynn

Kaylinda
(American) combo of
Kae and Linda
*Kaelinda, Kaelynda, Kay-
Linda*

Kaylon
(American) form of
Caylin; outgoing
Kay, Kaylen, Kaylun

Kaylon
(Hebrew) crowned
*Kaylan, Kayln, Kaylond,
Kaylon, Kalonn*

Keane
(American) keen
*Kanee, Keanie, Keany,
Keen*

Keanna
(American) curious
Keana, Keannah

Kearney
(Irish) winning
*Kearne, Kearni, KeKe,
Kerney*

Keekee
(American) dancing
*Keakea, KeeKee,
Kee-Kee*

Keeley
(Irish) noisy
Keely, Keylee

Keenan
(Irish) small
Keanan, Keen, Keeny

Kehohtee
(Invented) alternate
spelling for Quixote

Keidra
(American) form of
Kendra; aware
Kedra, Keydra

Keilani
(Hawaiian) graceful
leader
Kei, Lani, Lanie

Keira
(Irish) dark-skinned
Keera, Kera

Keisha
(American) dark-eyed
*Keesha, Keeshah,
Keysha*

Keishla
(American) dark

Kelila
(Hebrew) regal woman
Kelylah

Keller
(Irish) daring
Kellers

Kelley
(Irish) brave
Keli, Kellie, Kelly, Kellye

Kelsey
(Scottish) opinionated
Kelcie, Kelsi, Kelsie

Kember
(American) zany
Kem, Kemmie, Kimber

Kemella
(American) self-assured
*Kemele, Kemellah,
Kemelle*

Kendall
(English) quiet
*Kendahl, Kendelle,
Kendie, Kendylle*

Kendra
(American) ingenious
*Ken, Kendrah, Kennie,
Kindra, Kyndra*

Keneisha
(American) combo of
Ken and Aisha
*Kaneesha, Kenesha,
Kenisha, Kennie, Kaykay*

Kenia
(African) giving (from the
place name Kenya)
Ken, Keneah

Kenna
(English) brilliant
Kennah, Kynna

Kennae
(Irish) form of Ken;
attractive
Kenae, Kenah

Kennedy
(Irish) formidable
Kennedie, Kenny

Kensington
(English) brash
Kensingtyn

Kentucky
(American) place name
Kentuckie

Kenya
(African) place name

Kenyatta
(African)

Kenzie
(Scottish) pretty
Kensey, Kinsey

Keoshawn
(African-American)
clever
Keosh, Keoshaun

Kerdonna
(African-American)
loquacious
*Donna, Kerdy, Kirdonna,
Kyrdonna*

Kerra
(American) bright
Cara, Carrah, Kara, Kerrah

Kerry
(Irish) dark-haired
Carrie, Kari, Keri, Kerrie

Kerthia
(American) giving
*Kerth, Kerthea, Kerthi,
Kerthy*

Kesha
(American) laughing
Kecia, Kesa, Keshah

Keshon
(African-American)
happy
*Keshann, Keshaun,
Keshonn, Keshun,
Keshawn*

Keshondra
(African-American) joy-
filled
*Keshaundra,
Keshondrah, Keshundra,
Keshundrea, Keshundria,
Keshy*

Keshonna
(African-American)
happy
*Keshanna, Keshauna,
Keshaunna, Keshawna,
Keshona, Keshonna*

Keturah
(African) longsuffering

Kevine
(Irish) lively
Kevynne

Keydy
(American) knowing
Keydee, Keydi, Keydie

Keyonna
(African-American)
energetic

Keyshawn
(American) lively
*Keyshan, Keyshann,
Keyshaun, Keyshaunna,
Keyshon, Keyshona,
Keshonna, Keykey, Kiki*

Khadijah
(Arabic)

Khai
(American) unusual
Ki, Kie

Khaki
(American) personality-
plus
*Kakee, Kaki, Kakie,
Khakee, Khakie*

Khali
(Origin unknown) lively
*Khalee, Khalie, Koli,
Kollie*

Khiana
(American) different
*Kheana, Khianah,
Khianna, Ki, Kianah,
Kianna, Kiannah*

Kia
(American) short for
Kiana
Keeah, Kiah

Kiana
(American) graceful
Kianna, Kiannah

Kiara
(Irish) dark-skinned
Chiara, Chiarra, Keearah

Kibibi
(African) small girl

Kidre
(American) loyal
Kidrea, Kidrey, Kidri

Kienalle
(American) light
Kieana, Kienall, Kieny

Kienna
(Origin unknown) brash
Kiennah, Kienne

Kiera
(Irish) dark-skinned
Keara, Keera, Kierra

Kiersten
(Greek) blessed
*Kerston, Kierstin,
Kierstn, Kierstynn, Kirst,
Kirsten, Kirstie, Kirstin,
Kirsty*

Kiki
(Spanish, American)
vivacious
Keiki, Ki, Kiekie, Kikee

Kiko
(Japanese) lively
Kiki, Kikoh

Kiley
(Irish) pretty
*Kilea, Kilee, Kili, Kylee,
Kylie*

Kim
(English, Vietnamese)
*Kimey, Kimmi, Kimmy,
Kym*

Kimberlin
(American) combo of
Kimberly and Lin
*Kimberlinn, Kimberlyn,
Kimberlynn*

Kimberly
(English) leader
*Kim, Kimber-Lea,
Kimberlee, Kimberleigh,
Kimberley, Kimberli,
Kimberlie, Kimmy,
Kymberly, Kimmie*

Kimbrell
(African-American)
smiling
*Kim, Kimbree, Kimbrel,
Kimbrele, Kimby, Kimmy*

Kimeo
(American) form of Kim;
happy
Kim, Kime, Kimi

Kimetha
(American) form of Kim;
happy
Kimeth

Kimi
(Japanese) spiritual

Kimone
(Origin unknown) darling
Kimonne, Kymone

Kineisha
(American) form of
Keneisha
*Keneesha, Keneisha,
Kineasha, Kinesha,
Kineshia, Kiness,
Kinisha, Kinnisha, Kinny*

Kinsey
(English) child
Kensey, Kinsey

Kintra
(American) joyous
Kentra, Kint, Kintrey

Kipling
(Last name as first
name) energetic
Kiplin

Kira
(Russian) sunny; light-
hearted
Kera

Kiran
(Irish) pretty
Kiara, Kiaran, Kira, Kiri

Kirby
(Anglo-Saxon) right
Kirbee, Kirbey, Kirbie

Kirsten
(Scandinavian, Greek)
spiritual
*Karsten, Kirstene,
Kirstin, Kirston, Krystene*

Kirstie
(Scandinavian)
effervescent
Kerstie, Kirstee, Kirsty

Kisha
(Russian) ingenious
Keshah

Kismet
(Hindi) destiny; fate
Kismete, Kismett

Kissa
(African) a baby born
after twins

Kit
(American) strong
Kitt

Kithos
(Greek) worthy

Kitty
(Greek, American) flirty
Kit, Kitti, Kittie

Kiva
(Origin unknown) bright
Keva

Kiwa
(Origin unknown) lively
Kiewah, Kiwah

Kiya
(Australian) from the
name Kylie; always
returning; pretty girl
Kya

Kizzie
(African) energetic
*Kissee, Kissie, Kiz,
Kizzee, Kizzi, Kizzy*

Klarissa
(German) bright-minded
Clarissa, Klarisa, Klarise

Klarybel
(Polish) beauty
Klaribel, Klaribelle

Klea
(American) bold
*Clea, Kleah, Kleea,
Kleeah*

Kleta
(Greek) form of
Cleopatra; noble-born;
temptress
Cleta

Kobi
(American) California girl
Cobi, Kobe

Kogan
(Last name as first) self-
assured
*Kogann, Kogen, Kogey,
Kogi*

Konstance
(Latin) loyal
*Constance, Kon, Konnie,
Konstanze*

Kora
(Greek) practical
Cora, Koko, Korey, Kori

Kori
(Greek) little girl;
popular
*Cori, Corrie, Koree,
Korey, Kory*

Korina
(Greek) strong-willed;
(German) small girl
*Corinna, Koreena,
Korena, Korinna, Koryna*

Kornelia
(Latin) straight-laced
*Cornelia, Korney, Korni,
Kornie*

Kortney
(American, French)
dignified
*Courtney, Kortnee,
Kortni, Kourtney,
Kourtnie*

Koshatta
(Native American) form
of Coushatta; diligent
*Coushatta, Kosha,
Koshat, Koshatte,
Koshee, Koshi, Koshie,
Koushatta*

Krenie
(American) capable
Kren, Kreni, Krenn, Krennie, Kreny

Kris
(American) short for Kristina
Kaykay, Krissie, Krissy

Krishen
(American) talkative
Crishen, Kris, Krish, Krishon

Krissy
(American) friendly
Kris, Krisie, Krissey, Krissi

Krista
(German) short for Christina
Khrista, Krysta

Kristalee
(American) combo of Krista and Lee
Kristalea, Krista-Lee, Kristaleigh

Kristen
(Greek) Christ's follower; (German) bright-eyed
Christen, Cristen, Kristin

Kristian
(Greek) Christian woman
Kristiana, Kristianne, Kristyanna

Kristie
(American) saucy
Christi, Christy, Kristi

Kristin
(Scandinavian) high-energy
Kristen, Kristyne

Kristina
(Greek) anointed; (Scandinavian) Christ's follower
Christina, Krista, Kristie, Krysteena, Tina

Kristine
(Swedish) Christ's follower
Christine, Kristee, Kristene, Kristi, Kristy

Kristy
(American) short for Kristine
Kristi, Kristie

Krysta
(Polish) clear
Chrsta, Krista

Krystal
(American) clear and brilliant
Crystal, Crystalle, Kristel, Krys, Krystelle, Krystie, Krystylle

Krystyna
(Polish) Christian

Kurrsten
(Scandinavian, Greek) form of Kirsten; spiritual
Kurrst, Kurst, Kurstie

Kyla
(Irish) pretty
Kiela, Kila, Ky

Kyle
(Irish) pretty
Kylee, Kylie, Kyll

Kylee
(Australian, Irish) pretty
Kielie, Kiely, Kiley, Kye, Kyky, Kyleigh, Kylie

Kylene
(American) cute
Kyline

Kylynne
(American) fashionable
Kilenne, Kilynn, Kyly

Kym
(American) favorite
Kim, Kymm, Kymmi, Kymmie, Kymy

Kynthia
(Greek) goddess of the moon
Cinthia, Cynthia

Kyra
(Greek) feminine
Kira, Kyrah, Kyrie, Kyry

Kyria
(Greek) form of Kyra;
ladylike
Kyrea, Kyree, Kyrie, Kyry

Labe
(American) slow-moving
Labie

Lace
(American) delicate
*Lacee, Lacey, Laci, Lacie,
Lase*

Lacey
(Greek) cheery
Lacee, Laci, Lacie, Lacy

Lachelle
(African-American)
sweetheart
*Lachel, Lachell, Laschell,
Lashelle*

Lacole
(American) sly
Lucole

Lacreta
(Spanish) form of
Lacretia; efficient
Lacrete, LaLa

Lacretia
(Latin) efficient
*Lacracia, Lacrecia,
Lacrisha, Lacy*

LaDaune
(African-American) the
dawn
Ladaune, LaDawn

Ladda
(American) open
Lada

Ladonna
(American) combo of La
and Donna; beautiful
Ladona, LaDonna

Lady
(American) feminine
Ladee, Ladie

Ladrenda
(African-American) cagy
*Ladee, Ladey, Ladren,
Ladrende, Lady*

Lafonde
(American) combo of La
and Fonde; fond

Laguna
(Place name) Laguna
Beach, California; water-
loving
Lagunah

Laila
(Scandinavian) dark
beauty
Layla, Laylah, Leila

Lainil
(American) soft-hearted
Lainie, Lanel, Lanelle

Lajean
(French) soothing;
steadfast
L'Jean, LaJean, Lajeanne

LaJuana
(American) combo of La
and Juana
Lajuana, Lala, Lawanna

Lake
(Astrology) graceful
dancer

Lakela
(Hawaiian) feminine
Lakla

Lakesha
(African-American)
favored
*Keishia, Lakaisha,
Lakeesha, Lakeisha,
Lakeishah, Lakezia,
Lakisha*

Lalaney
(American) form of
Hawaiian name Leilani;
celestial
Lala, Lalanee, Lalani

Laleema
(Spanish) devoted
Lalema, Lalima

Lalita
(Sanskrit) charmer
*Lai, Lala, Lali, Lalitah,
Lalite, Lalitte*

Lalya
(Latin) eloquent
Lalia, Lall, Lalyah

Lamarian
(American) conflicted
Lamare, Lamarean

Lamia
(Egyptian) calm
Lami

Lamika
(African-American)
variant of Tamika; calm

L'Amour
(French) love
*Amor, Amour, Lamore,
Lamour, Lamoura*

Lana
(Latin) pretty
peacemaker
Lan, Lanna, Lanny

Land
(American) word as
name; confident
Landd

Landa
(American) blonde
beauty
Landah

Landry
(American) leader
Landa, Landree

Landy
(American) confident
*Land, Landee, Landey,
Landi*

Lane
(Last name as first
name) precocious
*Laine, Lainey, Laney,
Lanie, Layne, Laynie*

Lanee
(Asian) graceful

Lanette
(American) healthy
La-Net, LaNett, LaNette

Langley
(American) special
*Langlee, Langli, Langlie,
Langly*

Lani
(Hawaiian) short for
Leilani
Lannie

Lansing
(Place name) hopeful
Lanseng

Laquanna
(African-American)
outspoken
*Kwanna, LaQuanna,
LaQwana, Quanna*

Laquita
(American)
Laqueta, Laquetta

Lara
(Russian) lovely

Laraine
(Latin) pretty
Lareine, Larene, Loraine

Larby
(American) form of
Darby; pretty
*Larbee, Larbey, Larbi,
Larbie*

Larhonda
(African-American)
combo of La and
Rhonda; flashy
LaRhonda, Laronda

Larinda
(American) smart
*Lare, Larin, Larine,
Lorinda*

Larissa
(Latin) giving cheer
Laressa, Larisse, Laryssa

Lark
(American) pretty
Larke

Larkin
(American) pretty
Larken, Larkun

Larrie
(American) tomboyish
Larry

LaRue
(American) combo of La
and Rue
Laroo, Larue

Lasha
(Spanish) forlorn
Lash, Lass

Lashanda
(American) brassy
*Lala, Lasha, LaShanda,
LaShounda*

Lashauna
(American) happy
*Lashona, Leshauna,
Lashawna*

LaShea
(American) sparkling
Lashay, La-Shea, Lashea

Lashoun
(African-American)
content
*Lashaun, Lashawn,
Lashown*

Lassie
(American) lass
Lass

Latanya
(African-American)

Latasha
(American)
*Latacha, LaTasha,
Latayshah*

LaTeasa
(Spanish) tease
*Latea, Lateasa, LaTease,
LaTeese*

Lateefah
(Arabic, African, Hebrew)
kind queen
*Lateefa, Latifa, Latifah,
Lotifah, Tifa, Tifah*

Latesha
(Latin, American)
joyful
*Lateesha, Lateisha,
Lateshah, Laticia,
Latisha*

Latifah
(Muslim) gentle
*Lateefa, Latifa, Latiffe,
Latifuh*

Lathenia
(American) verbose
Lathene, Lathey

Latisehsha
(African-American)
happy; talkative
*Lati, Latise, Latiseh,
Latisha*

Latonia
(African-American) rich
Latone, Latonea

Latosha
(African-American)
happy

Latoya
(American) combo of La
and Toya
LaToya, Lata, Toy, Toya

Latreece
(American) go-getter
*Latreese, Latrice, Letrice,
Lettie, Letty*

Latrelle
(American) laughing
Lettie, Letrel, Letrelle,
Litrelle

Latrice
(Latin) noble
Latreece, Latreese

Latricia
(American) happy
Latrecia, Latreesha,
Latrisha, Latrishah

Latrisha
(African-American)
prissy
Latrishe

Laura
(Latin) laurel-crowned
and joyous
Lara, Lora

Laurann
(American) combo of
Laura and Ann
Lauran, Laurana,
Lauranna, Lauranne

Lauralee
(American) combo of
Laura and Lee
Laura-Lee, Loralea,
Loralee, Lorilee

Laureen
(American) old-
fashioned
Laurie, Laurine, Loreen

Laurel
(American) flourishing
Laurell, Lorel, Lorell

Laurel
(Latin) graceful
Laural, Laurell, Laurella,
Laurelle, Lorel, Lorella,
Lourelle

Lauren
(English, American)
flowing
Laren, Lauryn, Laryn,
Loren

Laurent
(French) graceful
Lorent, Laurente

Lauretta
(American) graceful
Laureta, Laurettah,
Lauritta, Lauritte, Loretta

Laurette
(American) from Laura;
graceful
Etta, Ette, Laure, Laurett,
Lorette

Laurie
(English) careful
Lari, Lauri, Lori

Lauriann
(American) combo of
Laurie and Ann
Laurian, Laurianne

Lavena
(French, Latin)
purest woman
Lavi, Lavie, Lavina

Laverne
(Latin) breath of spring
Lavern, Lavirne, Verna,
Verne

Lavette
(Latin) pure; natural
Laveda, Lavede, Lavete,
Lavett

Lavita
(American) charmer
Laveta, Lavitta, Lavitte

Lavinia
(Greek) ladylike
Lavenia

Lavonne
(American) combo of La
and Yvonne
Lavaughan, Lavaughn,
Lavon, Lavone, Lavonn,
Lavonna, Lavonnah

Lawanda
(American) sassy
LaWanda, Lawonda

Layce
(American) spunky

Layla
(Arabic) dark
Laela, Laila, Lala, Laya,
Laylah, Laylie, Leila

Layne
(French)
Laine, Lainee, Lainey

Lea
(Hawaiian) goddess-like

Leaf
(Botanical) hip

Leah
(Hebrew) tired and
burdened
Lea, Lee, Leeah, Leia, Lia

Leala
(French) steadfast

Leandra
(Greek) commanding as
a lioness
*Leandrea, Leanndra,
Leeandra, Leedie*

Leanna
(English) leaning
Leana, Leelee, Liana

Leanne
(English) sweet
*Lean, Leann, Lee, Leelee,
Lianne*

Leanore
(English, Greek) stately
Lanore

Leatrice
(American) charming
Leatrise

Lecia
(Latin) short for Leticia
*Leecia, Leesha, Lesha,
Lesia*

Leda
(Greek) feminine
Ledah, Lida, Lita

Lee
(English, American,
Chinese) light-footed
Lea, Leelee, Leigh

Leeanne
(English) combo of Lee
and Anne
*Lean, Leann, Lee Ann,
Lee-Ann, Leianne*

Leeannette
(Greek) form of Leandra;
lionine
*Leann, Lee Annette,
Leeanett, Lee-Annette,
Leiandra*

Leelee
(American, Slavic) short
for Leanne, Lena, Lisa,
Leona
Lee-Lee, Lele, Lelee

Leeline
(American) combo of Lee
and Line; pastural; loyal
*Lee, Leela, LeeLee,
Leelene*

Leeo
(American) sunny
Leo

Leeza
(American) gorgeous
Leesa, Leeze, Liza, Lize

Legend
(American) memorable
Legen, Legende, Legund

Legia
(Spanish) bright
Legea

Lei
(Hawaiian) short for
Leilani
Leilei

Léi
(Chinese) open; truthful

Leigh
(English) light-footed
Lee, Leelee

Leila
(Arabic) beauty of the
night
Layla, Leela, Lelah, Leyla

Leilani
(Hawaiian) heavenly girl
Lanie

Lejoi
(French) joy
Joy, Lejoy

Leland
(American) special
Lelan, Lelande

Lelia
(Greek) articulate
Lee, Leelee

Lena
(Latin) siren
Lina

Lenesha
(African-American)
smiling
Leneisha, Lenisha, Lenni,
Lennie, Neshie

Lenice
(American) delightful
Lenisa, Lenise

Lenita
(Latin) gentle spirit
Leneeta, Leneta, Lineta

Lenoa
(Greek) form of Lenore;
light
Len, Lenor, Lenora

Leola
(Latin) fierce; lionine
Lee, Leo, Leole

Leona
(Greek, American)
brave-hearted
Liona

Leondrea
(Greek) strong
Leondreah, Leondria

Leonie
(Latin) lion-like; fierce
Leonee, Leoni, Leoney,
Leony

Leonore
(Greek)
Lenore, Leonor

Leonsio
(Spanish) form of male
name Leon; fierce
Leo, Leonsee, Leonsi

Leopoldina
(Invented) form of
Leopold; brave
Dina, Leo, Leopolde,
Leopoldyna

Leora
(Greek) light-hearted
Liora, Leorah

Lera
(Russian)
Lerae, Lerie, Lira

Leretta
(American) form of
Loretta
Lere, Lerie, Loretta

Lesley
(Scottish) strong-willed
Les, Lesle, Lesli, Leslie,
Leslye, Lezlie

Letha
(Greek) ladylike
Litha

Leticia
(Latin, Spanish)
joyful woman
Letecia, Letisha, Letitia,
Lettie, Letty

Letichel
(American) happy;
important
Chel, Chelle, Leti,
Letichell, Letishell,
Lettichelle, Lettychel

Letsey
(American) form of Letty;
glad
Letsee, Letsy

Lettie
(Latin, Spanish)
happy
Lettee, Letti, Letty, Lettye

Levana
(Hebrew) fair
Lev, Liv, Livana

Levitt
(American) straight-
forward
Levit

Levity
(American) humorous

Levora
(American) home-loving
Levorah, Levore, Livee,
Livie, Livora, Livore

Lexa
(American) effervescent
Lex, Lexah

Lexi
(Greek) helpful;
sparkling
Lex, Lexie, Lexsey,
Lexsie, Lexy

Lexine
(Scottish) helper
Lexus
(American) rich
Lexi, Lexorus, Lexsis,
Lexuss, Lexxus
Lexy
(Scottish) helper
Lezena
(American) smiling
Lezene, Lezina, Lyzena
Li
(Chinese) plum
Lia
(Greek, Russian, Italian)
singular
Li, Liah
Lian
(Latin, Chinese)
graceful
Leane, Leanne, Liane
Liana
(Greek) flowering;
complicated
Leanna, Lee, Liane
Libby
(Hebrew) short for
Elizabeth; bubbly
Lib, Libbi, Libbie
Liber
(American) from the
word liberty; free
Lib, Libby, Lyber

Liberty
(Latin) free and open
Lib, Libbie
Librada
(Spanish) free
Libra, Libradah
Lichelle
(American) combo of Li
and Chelle
Leshel, Leshelle, Licha,
Lili
Licia
(Greek) outdoorsy
Lisha
Lida
(Greek) beloved girl
Leedah, Lyda
Lidia
(Greek) pleasant spirit
Lydia
Liesel
(German) pretty
Leesel, Leezel
Light
(American) light-hearted
Li, Lite
Ligia
(Greek) talented
musician
Ligea, Lygia, Lygy
Likiana
(Invented) likeable
Like, Likia

Lila
(American) short for
Delilah, form of Leila;
(Arabic) playful
Lilah, Lyla, Lylah
Lila-Lynn
(American) combo of Lila
and Lynn; night-loving;
delight
Lilalinn, Lilalyn, Lilalynn,
Lilalynne
Lilac
(American) flowery
Lila
Lilakay
(American) combo of Lila
and Kay
Lilaka, Lilakae, Lila-Kay,
Lilakaye, Lylakay
Lileah
(Latin) lily-like
Lili, Liliah, Lill, Lily, Lilya
Lilette
(Latin) little lily; delicate
Lill, Lillette, Lillith, Lilly,
Lilly
Lilia
(American) flowing
Lileah, Lyleah, Lylia
Liliana
(Italian) pretty
Lilianah, Lylianah

Liliash
(Spanish) lily; innocent
Lil, Lileah, Liliosa, Lilya,
Lyliase, Lylish

Lilith
(Arabic) nocturnal
Lill, Lilli, Lillie, Lilly,
Lilyth, Lilythe

Lillian
(Latin) pretty as a lily
Lileane, Lilian, Liliane,
Lill, Lillie, Lillyan,
Lillyann, Lilyanne, Liyan

Lillibeth
(American) combo of Lilli
and Beth; flower; lovely
girl
Lilibeth, Lillibethe,
Lilybeth

Lily
(Latin, Chinese) elegant
Lil, Lili, Lilie

Lin
(English, Chinese)
beautiful
Linn, Lynn

Lina
(Greek, Latin, Scottish)
light of spirit; lake calm
Lena, Lin, Linah, Lynn

Linda
(Spanish) pretty girl
Lind, Lindy, Lynda

Linden
(American) harmonious
Lindan, Lindun, Lynden,
Lynnden

Lindsay
(English, Scottish)
calming; bright and
shining
Lindsee, Lindsey, Lindsi,
Lindz, Lyndsie, Lyndzee,
Lynz

Lindse
(Spanish) form of
Lindsey; enthusiastic
Linds, Lindz, Lindze,
Lyndzy

Lindy
(American) music-lover
Lind, Lindee, Lindi,
Lindie, Linney, Linnie,
Linse, Linz, Linze

Linette
(French, English,
American) graceful and
airy
Lanette, Linnet, Lynette

Lin-Lin
(Chinese) beauty of a
tinkling bell
Lin, Lin Lin

Ling
(Chinese) delicate

Linnea
(Swedish) statuesque
Lin, Linayah, Linea,
Linnay, Linny, Lynnea

Linsey
(English) bright spirit
Linsie, Linsy, Linzi, Linzie

Linzetta
(American) form of
Linzey; pretty
Linze, Linzette, Linzey

Lisa
(Hebrew, American)
dedicated and spiritual
Lee, Leelee, Leesa,
Leesah, Leeza, Leisa,
Lesa, Lysa

Lisamarie
(American) combo of
Lisa and Marie
Lisamaree, Lisa-Marie,
Lise-Marie, Lis-Maree

Lisarae
(American) combo of
Lisa and Rae
Lisa-Rae, Lisa-Ray,
Lisaray

Lisbeth
(Hebrew) short for
Elizabeth

Lise
(German) form of Lisa;
solemn
Lesa

Lisette
(French) little Elizabeth
Lise, Lisete, Lissette, Liz

Lisha
(Hebrew) short for
Elisha; dark
Lish, Lishie

Lissa
(Greek) sweet
Lyssa

Lisseth
(Hebrew) form of
Elizabeth; devout
*Liseta, Liseth, Lisette,
Lisith, Liss, Lisse, Lissi*

Lissie
(American) short for
Elise; flowery
Lis, Lissi, Lissey, Lissy

Lita
(Latin) short for
Carmelita; life-giving
Leta

Liv
(Latin, Scandinavian)
lively
Leev

Livia
(Hebrew) lively
Levia, Livya

Livona
(Hebrew) vibrant
Levona, Liv, Livvie, Livvy

Liz
(English) short for
Elizabeth; excitable
*Lis, Lissy, Lizy, Lizzi,
Lizzie*

Liza
(American) smiling
*Leeza, Liz, Lizah, Lizzie,
Lizzy, Lyza*

Lizbeth
(American) combo of Liz
and Beth; devout
Liz Beth, Liz-Beth, Lizeth

Lizeth
(Hebrew) ebullient
Liseth, Lizethe

Lizette
(Hebrew) lively
Lizet, Lizett

Lizibeth
(American) combo of Lizi
and Beth
*Lizabeth, Liza-Beth,
Lizzie, Lizziebeth*

Lizzie
(American) devout
*Liz, Liza, Lizae, Lizette,
Lizzee, Lizzey, Lizzi, Lizzy*

Lo
(American) spunky
Loe

Loanna
(American) combo of Lo
and Anna; loving
Lo, Loann, Loanne, LoLo

Logan
(English) climbing
Lo, Logun

Loibeth
(American) combo of Loy
and Beth; popular
*Beth, Loi, Loy Beth, Loy,
Loybeth, Loy-Beth*

Loicy
(American) delightful
*Loice, Loisee, Loisey,
Loisi, Loy, Loyce, Loycy,
Loyse, Loysie*

Lois
(Greek) good
Lo, Loes

Lojean
(American) combo of Lo
and Jean; bravehearted
Lojeanne

Lola
(Spanish) pensive
Lo, Lolah, Lolita

Loleen
(American) jubilant
Lolene

Lolita
(Spanish) sad
Lo, Lola, Loleta, Lita

Lomita
(Spanish) good

Londa
(American) shy
Londah, Londe, Londy

London
(Place name) calming
*Londen, Londun, Londy,
Loney, Lony*

Loni
(American) beauty
*Loney, Lonie, Lonnie,
Loney*

Lonnette
(American) pretty
*Lonett, Lonette, Lonnie,
Lonn*

Lora
(Latin) regal
*Laura, Lorah, Lorea,
Loria*

Loranden
(American) ingenious
*Lorandyn, Lorannden,
Luranden*

Lorelei
(German) siren
Loralee, Lorilie, LoraLee

Lorelle
(American) lovely
*Lore, Loreee, Lorel,
Lorey, Lori, Lorie, Lorille,
Lorel, Lorille*

Loren
(American) form of
Lauren; picture-perfect
*Lorren, Lorri, Lorrie,
Lorron, Lorryn, Lory,
Loryn, Lourie*

Lorena
(English) photogenic
*Loreen, Lorene, Lorrie,
Lorrine*

Loretta
(English) large-eyed
beauty
Lauretta

Lori
(Latin) laurel-crowned
and nature-loving
Laurie, Loree, Lorie, Lory

Lorinda
(American) combo of
Lori and Linda;
gregarious
*Larinda, Lorenda, Lori,
Lorie*

Loris
(Greek, Latin) fun-loving
Lorice, Lauris

Lorna
(Latin) laurel-crowned;
natural
Lorenah

Lorraine
(Latin, French)
sad-eyed
*Laraine, Lauraine,
Lorain, Loraine, Lorrie,
Lors*

Lotis
(Greek) flower
Lottie, Lotty, Lotus

Lotta
(Swedish) sweet

Lottie
(American)
old-fashioned
Lottee, Lotti, Lotty

Lotus
(Greek) flowery
Lolo, Lotie

Lou
(American) short for
Louise
Loulou, Lu

Louisa
(English) patient
*Lou, Loulou, Luisa,
Luizza*

Louise
(German) hardworking
and brave
Lolah, Lou, Loulou, Luise

Lourdes
(French) girl from
Lourdes, France;
hallowed
Lourd, Lordes, Lordez

Lordyn
(American) enchanting
*Lorden, Lordin, Lordine,
Lordun, Lordynn*

Love
(English, American)
loving
Lovey, Lovi, Luv

Loveada
(Spanish) loving
Lova, Lovada

Loveanna
(American) combo of
Love and Anna; loving
*Lovanna, Love-Anna,
Loveanne, Luvana,
Luvanna*

Lovella
(Native American) soft
spirit
Lovela

Lovely
(American) loving
*Lovelee, Loveley, Loveli,
Lovey*

Lovie
(American) warm
Lovee, Lovey, Lovi, Lovy

Lovina
(American) warm
*Lovena, Lovey, Lovinah,
Lovinnah*

Lowell
(American) lovely
Lowel

Loyalty
(American) loyal
Loyaltie

Luann
(Hebrew) combo of Lou
and Ann; happy girl
*Lou, Louann, Louanne,
Loulou, Luan, Luanne*

Luberda
(Spanish) light; dear
Luberdia

Luca
(Spanish) light
Luka

Luceil
(French) light; lucky
Luce, Lucee, Lucy

Lucero
(Italian) light-hearted
Lucee, Lucey, Lucy

Lucia
(Italian, Greek, Spanish)
light; lucky in love
*Chia, Luceah, Lucey,
Lucey, Luci*

Luciana
(Italian) fortunate
*Louciana, Luceana,
Lucianah*

Lucie
(French, American)
lucky girl
Lucy

Lucienne
(French) lucky
*Lucianne, Lucienn,
Lucy-Ann*

Lucille
(English) bright-eyed
Lucie, Lucile, Lucy

Lucina
(American) happy
*Lucena, Lucie, Lucinah,
Lucy, Lucyna*

Lucinda
(Latin) prissy
*Cinda, Cindie, Lu,
Luceenda, Lucynda, Lulu*

Lucja
(Polish) light
Luscia

Luckette
(Invented) lucky
Luckett

Lucretia
(Latin) wealthy woman
*Lu, Lucrecia, Lucreesha,
Lucritia*

Lucy
(Latin, Scottish,
Spanish) light-hearted
*Lu, Luca, Luce, Luci,
Lucie*

Lucyann
(American) combo of
Lucy and Ann
*Luce, Luciana, Luciann,
Lucianne, Lucy, Lucyan,
Lucy-Ann, Lucyanne*

Lucylynn
(American) combo of
Lucy and Lynn;
light-hearted
*Lucilyn, Lucylin, Lucy-
Lynn*

Ludivina
(Slavic) loved
Ludmilla
(Slavic) beloved one
Lu, Ludie, Ludmila,
Ludmylla, Lule, Lulu
Lue-Ella
(English) combo of Lue
and Ella; tough;
assertive
Louel, Luella, Luelle
Luella
(German) conniving
Loella, Louella, Lu, Lula,
Lulah, Lulu
Luenetter
(American) egotistical
Lou, Lu, Luene, Luenette
Luisa
(Spanish) smiling
Louisa
Luisana
(Place name) form of
Louisiana; combative
Luisanna, Luisanne,
Luisiana
Luke
(American) bouncy
Luc, Luka, Lukey, Lukie
Lula
(German)
all-encompassing
Lulu

Lulani
(Polynesian) heavensent
Lula, Lani, Lanie
Lulu
(German, English) kind
Lou, Loulou, Lu, Lulie
Lulubell
(American) combo of
Lulu and Bell; well-
known
Bell, Bella, Belle, Lulu,
Lulubel, Lulu-Bell,
Lulubelle
Luna
(Latin) moonstruck
Loona
Lund
(German) genius
Lun, Lunde, Lundy
Lundyn
(American) different
Lundan, Lunden, Lundon
Lupe
(Spanish) enthusiastic
Loopy, Loopey, Lupeta,
Lupey, Lupie, Lupita
Luquitha
(African-American) fond
Luquetha, Luquith
Lura
(American) loquacious
Loora, Lur, Lurah, Lurie

Lurajane
(American) combo of
Lura and Jane; cuddly
little one
Janie, Loorajane,
Lura-Jane, Luri, Lurijane
Lurissa
(American) beguiling
Luresa, Luressa, Luris,
Lurisa, Lurissah, Lurly
Lurlene
(German) tempting;
(Scandinavian) bold
Lura, Lurleen, Lurlie,
Lurline
Luvelle
(American) light
Luvee, Luvell, Luvey,
Luvy
Luvy
(American) spontaneous
Lovey, Luv
Lux
(Latin) light
Luxe, Luxee, Luxi, Luxy
Luz
(Spanish) light-hearted
Lusa, Luzana, Luzi
Luzille
(Spanish) light
Luz, Luzell
Lyanne
(Greek) melodious
Liann, Lianne, Lyan,
Lyana, Lyaneth, Lyann

Lyawonda
(African-American)
friend
*Lyawunda, Lywanda,
Lywonda*

Lydia
(Greek) musical;
unusual
Lidia, Lidya, Lydie, Lydy

Lyla
(French) island girl
Lila, Lilah, Lile

Lyle
(English) strident
Lile

Lymekia
(Greek) form of Lydia;
royal
Lymekea

Lynda
(Spanish) beautiful
*Linda, Lindi, Lynde,
Lyndie, Lynn*

Lyndsay
(Scottish) bright and
shining
Lindsay, Lindsey

Lynelle
(English) pretty girl;
bright as sunshine
Linelle, Lynel, Lynie, Lynn

Lynette
(French) small and fresh
*Lyn, Lynet, Lynnet,
Lynette, Lynnie*

Lynn
(English) fresh as spring
water
*Lin, Linn, Linnie, Lyn,
Lynne*

Lynsey
(American) form of
Lindsay
*Linzie, Lyndsey, Lynze,
Lynzy*

Lyra
(Greek) musical
Lyre

Lyric
(Greek) musical
Lyrec

Lysa
(Hebrew) God-loving
Leesa, Lisa

Lysandra
(Greek) liberator; she
frees others
Lyse, Lysie

Lysanne
(Greek) helpful
Lysann

Lysett
(American) pretty little
one
Lyse, Lysette

Lyssan
(Greek) form of
Alexandra; supportive
*Liss, Lissan, Lissana,
Lissandra, Lyss*

Lytanisha
(African-American)
scintillating
*Litanisha, Lyta, Lytanis,
Lytanish, Lytanishia,
Nisa, Nisha*

Mab
(Literature)
Shakespearean queen of
fairies
Mabel
(Latin) well-loved
Mabbel, Mable, Maybel,
Maybie
Macallister
(Irish) confident
Macarena
(Spanish) name of a
dance; blessed
Macarene, Macaria,
Macarria, Rena
Macaria
(Spanish) blessed
Maca, Macarea, Macarie,
Maka
Macey
(American) upbeat;
happy
Mace, Macie, Macy

Mackenzie
(Irish) leader
Mac, Mackenzy, Mackie,
Mackinsey, Mckenzie,
McKinsey, McKinzie
Mada
(American) helpful
Madah, Maida
Madalyn
(Greek) high goals
Madelyn
Madchen
(Actress name)
resourceful
Madchan, Madchin,
Maddchen
Maddie
(English) form of
Madeline
Mad, Maddi, Maddy,
Mady
Maddox
(English) giving
Maddax, Maddee,
Maddey, Maddie,
Maddux, Maddy
Madelcarmen
(American) combo of
Madel and Carmen;
old-fashioned
Madel-Carmen,
Madlecarmen
Madeleine
(French) high-minded
Madelon

Madeline
(Greek) strength-giving
Madaleine, Maddie,
Maddy, Madelene, Madi
Madelyn
(Greek) strong woman
Madalyn, Madlynne,
Madolyn
Madge
(Greek, American)
spunky
Madgie, Madg
Madina
(Greek) form of
Madeline; happy
Mada, Maddelina,
Maddi, Maddy, Madele,
Madena, Madlin
Madison
(English) good-hearted
Maddie, Maddison,
Maddy, Madisen,
Madysin
Madonna
(Latin) my lady; spirited
Madrina
(Spanish) godmother
Madra, Madreena,
Madrine
Madrona
(Spanish) mother;
maternal
Madrena

Mae
(English) bright flower
May

Maegan
(Irish) a gem of a woman
Megan

MaElena
(Spanish) light
Elena, Lena

Maeve
(Irish) queen
Mave

Maezelma
(American) combo of
Mae and Zelma;
practical
Mae Zelma, Maez, Mae-
Zelma, Maezie,
Mayzelma

Magan
(Greek) heavy-hearted
Mag, Magen, Maggie

Magda
(Scandinavian) believer
Mag, Maggie

Magdalene
(Greek, Scandinavian)
spiritual
Mag, Magda,
Magdalena, Magdaline,
Magdalyn, Magdelin,
Maggie

Maggie
(Greek, English, Irish)
priceless pearl
Mag, Maggee, Maggi

Magina
(Russian) hard-working
Mageena, Maginah

Magnolia
(Botanical) flower;
(Latin) flowering and
flourishing
Mag, Maggi, Maggie,
Maggy, Magnole, Nolie,

Magryta
(Slavic) desired

Mahal
(Filipino) loving woman
Mah, Maha

Mahala
(Hebrew, Native
American) tender female
Mah, Mahalah, Mahalia,
Mahla, Mahlie

Mahogany
(Spanish) rich as wood
Mahagonie, Mahogony

Mahoney
(American) high energy
Mahhony, Mahonay,
Mahonie, Mahony

Mai
(Scandinavian, Japanese)
treasure; flower; singular
Mae, May

Maia
(Greek) fertile; earth
goddess
Maya, Mya

Maida
(Greek) shy girl
Mady, Maidie, May,
Mayda

Maidie
(Scottish) maiden; virgin
Maidee, Maydee,
Maydie

Maira
(Hebrew) bitter; saved
Mara, Marah

Malred
(Irish) pearl; treasured
Mairead, Mared

Maisie
(Scottish) treasure
Maisee, Maizie, Mazee

Maja
(Scandinavian) fertile

Majidah
(Arabic)

Makala
(Hawaiian) natural
outdoors
Makal, Makie

Makayla
(American) magical
Makaila, Makala,
Michaela, Mikaela,
Mikayla, Mikaylah

Makyll
(American) innovative
Makell

Makynna
(American) friendly
Makenna, Makinna

Malak
(Arabic) angelic

Malay
(Place name) softspoken
Malae

Malaya
(Filipino) free and open
Malea

Malha
(Hebrew) queenlike and
regal

Mali
(Thai) flowering beauty
*Malee, Maley, Mali,
Malley, Mallie*

Malia
(Hawaiian) thoughtful
Maylia

Maliaval
(Hawaiian) peaceful

Malika
(Hungarian)
hardworking and
punctual
Maleeka

Malin
(Native American)
comfort-giver
Malen, Maline, Mallie

Malinda
(Greek, American)
Melinda

Malissa
(American, Greek)
combo of May and
Melissa; sweet
Melissa

Mallika
(Indian) watchful;
tending the garden
Malika

Mallory
(French, German,
American) tough-
minded; spunky
*Mal, Mallari, Mallery,
Mallie, Mallori, Mallorie,
Malorie*

Malu
(Hawaiian) peaceful
Maloo

Malvina
(Scottish) romantic
*Malv, Malva, Malvie,
Melvina*

Mancie
(American) hopeful
Manci, Mansey, Mansie

Manda
(American) short for
Amanda; beloved
*Amand, Mandee, Mandi,
Mandy*

Mandy
(Latin) lovable
*Manda, Mandee, Mandi,
Mandie*

Mandymay
(American) combo of
Mandy and May
*Mandeemae, Mandimae,
Mandimay, Mandymae*

Mane
(American) top
Main, Manie

Manee
(Korean) peace giving
Mani, Manie

Manon
(French) exciting

Mantill
(American) guarded
Mant, Mantell, Mantie

Manzie
(American) musical
Mansie, Manzey, Manzi

Manzie
(Native American) flower
Mansi

Mara
(Greek) thoughtful
believer
Marah, Marra

Marajayne
(American) combo of
Mara and Jayne; lively
*Mara Jayne, Marajane,
Mara-Jayne, Maryjayne*

Maranda
(Latin) wonderful
Marandah, Miranda
Marbella
(Spanish) pretty
Marb, Marbela, Marbelle
Marbury
(American) substantial
Mar, Marbary
Marcella
(Latin) combative
Marce, Marcela, Marci,
Marcie, Marse, Marsella
Marcelline
(French) pretty
Marceline, Marcelyne,
Marcie, Marcy, Marcyline
Marcellita
(Spanish) desired, feisty
Marcel, Marcelita,
Marcelite, Marcelle,
Marcelli, Marcey, Marci
Marcena
(Latin, American)
spirited
Marce, Marceen,
Marcene, Marcie
Marcia
(Latin, American)
combative
Marcie, Marsha
Marcie
(English) chummy
Marci, Marcy, Marsi,
Marsie

Marcilyn
(American) combo of
Marci and Lyn; physical
Marce, Marcie-Lyn,
Marci-Lyn, Marclinne,
Marclyn, Marcy, Mars,
Marse, Marslin, Marslyn
Marcine
(American) bright
Marceen, Marceene
Marcy
(English, American)
opinionated
Marci, Marsie, Marsy
Mardonia
(American) approving
Mardee, Mardi,
Mardone, Mardonne,
Mardy
Mare
(American) living by the
ocean
Maren
(American) ocean-lover
Marin, Marren, Marrin
Marg
(American) tenacious
Mar

Margaret
(Greek, Scottish,
English) treasured pearl;
pure-spirited
Mag, Maggie, Marg,
Margerite, Margie,
Margo, Margret, Meg,
Meggie
Margarita
(Italian, Spanish)
winning
Marg, Margarit,
Margarite, Margie,
Margrita, Marguerita
Margarite
(Greek, German)
pearl
Gretal, Marga, Margit,
Margot
Marge
(English, American)
short for Marjorie;
easygoing
Marg, Margie
Margherita
(Italian, Greek)
treasured pearl
Marg
Margia
(American) form of
Margie; friendly
Marge, Margea, Margy
Margie
(English) friendly
Margey, Margy, Marjie

Margina
(American) centered
Margot
(French) lively
Margaux, Margo
Marguerite
(French) stuffy
Maggie, Marg,
Margerite, Margie,
Margina, Margurite
Maria
(Latin, French, German,
Italian, Polish, Spanish)
desired child
Maja, Malita, Mareea,
Marica, Marike,
Marucha, Mezi, Mitzi
Mariah
(Hebrew) sorrowful
singer
Marayah, Mariahe,
Marriah, Meriah, Moriah
Marializa
(Spanish) combo of
Maria and Liza; desired
Liza, Maria Liza, Maria,
Maria-Liza, Mariliza
Marialourdes
(Spanish) combo of
Maria and Lourdes;
sweet
Maria Lourdes,
Maria-Lourdes

Mariamne
(French) form of Miriam;
sea of sadness
Mariam, Marianne
Marian
(English) thoughtful
Mariane, Marianne,
Maryann, Maryanne
Mariana
(Spanish) quiet girl
Maryanna
Marianella
(French) combo of
Marian and Ella; girl of
the sea
Ella, Marian, Mariane
Mariangela
(American) combo of
Mary and Angela;
angelic
Mary Angela,
Mary-Angela,
Mariangelle
Maria-Teresa
(Spanish) combo of
Maria and Teresa;
desired
Maria Teresa,
Mariateresa,
Maria-Terese,
Maria-Theresa

Maribel
(French, English,
American) combo of
Mary and Belle
EmBee, Marabel,
Maribela, Merrybelle
Maribeth
(American) combo of
Mari and Beth
Mary Beth Mary-Beth,
Marybeth
Marie
(French) form of Mary;
dignified and spiritual
Maree
Mariel
(German) spiritual
Mari, Mariele, Marielle
Marielena
(Spanish) combo of
Marie and Lena; desired
Mari, Mari-Elena, Marie-
Lena, Maryelenna
Mariellen
(American) combo of
Mari and Ellen; dancer
Mare, Marelle, Mariella,
Maryellen, MaryEllen
Mariene
(Spanish) devout
Mari, Marienne
Marietta
(French) combo of Mary
and Etta; spright spirit
Marieta

Marigold
(Botanical) sunny
Maragold, Marigole,
Marrigold

Marihelen
(American) combo of
Mary and Helen;
steadfast friend
Marihelene, MaryHelen

Marika
(Slavic, American)
thoughtful and brooding
Marica, Merica, Merika,
Merk, Merkie

Marikaitlynn
(American) combo of
Mari and Kaitlynn;
desired
Kait, Kaiti, Mari,
Marreekaitlyn, Mary
Kaitlynn, Mary-Kaitlynn

Marilee
(American) combo of
Mary and Lee; dancing
Marylee, Merilee,
Merrilee

Marilou
(American) combo of
Mary and Lou; jubilant
Marilu, Marrilou,
Marylou, Marylu

Marilyn
(Hebrew) fond-spirited
Maralynne, Mare,
Mariline, Marrie,
Marrilyn, Marylyn,
Merilyn, Merrilyn

Marin
(Latin) sea-loving
Mare, Maren

Marina
(Latin) lover of the ocean
Marena, Marina

Marinella
(French) combo of Marin
and Ella; soft
Ella, Marin, Mari-Nella,
Marin-Ella, Nella

Marion
(French) form of Mary;
delicate spirit
Mare, Marrion, Mary,
Maryian

Mariposa
(Spanish) kind
Mari, Mariposah

Mariquita
(Spanish) form of
Margaret; party-loving
Marikita, Marrikita,
Marriquita

Maris
(Latin) sea-loving
Mere, Marice, Meris,
Marys

Marisa
(Latin) sea-loving;
(Spanish) combo of
Maria and Luisa
Marce, Maressa,
Marissa, Marisse, Mariza
Marsie, Marysa, Merisa

Marisela
(Spanish) hearty
Marisella, Marysela

Mariska
(American) endearing
Mareska, Marisca,
Mariskah

Marisol
(Spanish) stunning
Mare, Mari, Marizol,
Marrisol, Marzol, Merizol

Maritza
(Place name) St. Moritz,
Switzerland

Marixbel
(Spanish) pretty
Marix

Marjie
(Scottish) short for
Marjorie
Marji, Marjy

Marjorie
(Greek, English,
Scottish) bittersweet;
pert
Marg, Marge, Margerie,
Margery, Margorie,
Marjie, Marjori

Marky
(American) mischievous
Marki, Markie

Marla
(German) believer;
easygoing
Marlah, Marlla

Marlaina
(American) form of
Marlene; dramatic
Marlaine, Marlane

Marlana
(Hebrew, Greek)
vamp
Marlanna

Marleal
(American) form of
Mary; desired
Marle, Marleel, Marly

Marlee
(Greek) guarded
Marley, Marlie

Marlen
(American) desired
Marl, Marla, Marlin

Marlena
(German) pretty;
bittersweet
*Marla, Marlaina,
Marlina, Marlynne,
Marnie*

Marlene
(Greek) high-minded;
attractive; (English)
adorned
*Marlean, Marlee,
Marleen, Marleene,
Marley, Marline, Marly*

Marley
(English) form of
Marlene
*Mar, Marlee, Marlie,
Marly*

Marlis
(German) combo of
Maria and Elisabeth;
religious
Marl, Marlice

Marlise
(English) considerate
Marlice, Marlis, Marlys

Marlo
(American) vivacious
Marloe, Marloh

Marlycia
(Spanish) desired
Lycia, Marly, Marlysia

Marnie
(Hebrew) storyteller
*Marn, Marnee, Marni,
Marny*

Marnita
(American) worrier
*Marneta, Marni, Marnite,
Marnitta, Marny*

Marolyn
(Invented) form of
Marilyn; desired;
precious
*Maro, Marolin,
Marolinne*

Maromisa
(Japanese) warm; combo
of Maro and Misa
Maromissa

Marquise
(French) noble-spirited
*Markeese, Marquees,
Marquisa, Mars*

Marquisha
(African-American) form
of Marquise
Marquish

Marquita
(Spanish) happy girl
*Marqueda, Marquitta,
Marrie*

Marrie
(American) variant of
Mary; desired
Marry

Marsala
(Italian) of Marseille,
Italy; rambunctious
Marse, Marsela, Marsie

Marsha
(Latin) light-haired;
combative
Marcia, Mars, Marsie

Marshay
(American) exuberant
Marshae, Marshaya

Marta
(Danish) treasure
Mart, Marte, Marty, Merta

Marterrell
(American) changeable
Marte, Marterill, Martrell

Martha
(Aramaic) lady
Marta, Marth, Marti, Marty, Mattie

Marti
(Engllsh) short for Martha; dreamy
Martie, Marty

Martina
(Latin, German) combative
Marteena, Martene, Marti, Martinna, Martyna, Tina

Martivanio
(Italian) form of Martina; feisty; fighter
Mart, Marti, Tivanio

Martonette
(American) form of male name Martin; feisty little girl
Martanette, Martinette, Martonett

Marusya
(Slavic) soft-hearted

Marvella
(French) marvelous woman
Marva, Marvelle, Marvie, Mavela

Mary
(Hebrew) bitter; in the Bible, the mother of Jesus
Maire, Mara, Mare, Maree, Mari, Marie, Mariel, Marlo, Marye, Merree, Merry, Mitzie

Marya
(Arabic) white and bright
Marja

Maryalice
(American) combo of Mary and Alice; friendly
Marialice, Maryalyce

Maryann
(English, American) combo of Mary and Ann; special
Marianne, Maryan

Mary-Catherine
(American) combo of Mary and Catherine; outgoing
Maricatherine, Marycatherine, Mary-Kathryn

Mary-Elizabeth
(American) combo of Mary and Elizabeth; kind
Marielizabeth, Mary Elizabeth, Maryelizabeth

Marykate
(American) combo of May and Kate; splendid
Marikate, Mary-Kate

Marykay
(American) combo of Mary and Kay; adorned
Marikay, Marrikae

Maryke
(Dutch) kind; desired
Mairek, Marika, Maryk, Maryky

Mary-Lou
(American) combo of Mary and Lou; athletic
Mary Lou, Marylou

Mary-Marg
(American) dramatic
Marimarg

Mary-Margaret
(American) combo of Mary and Margaret; dramatic, kind
Marimargaret, Mary Margaret, Marymarg, Marymargret

Marypat
(American) combo of Mary and Pat; easygoing
Mary-Pat, Mary Pat

Marysue
(American) combo of
Mary and Sue; country
girl
*MariSue, Merrysue,
Mersue*

Masha
(Russian) child who was
desired

Mashonda
(African-American)
believer
Masho, Mashonde

Mason
(French) diligent;
reliable

Massey
(German) confident
Massi, Massie

Massiel
(American) giving
*Masie, Masiel, Massey,
Massielle*

Massim
(Latin) great
*Massima, Maxim,
Maxima*

Matia
(Hebrew) a God-given
gift
Matea, Mattea, Mattie

Matilda
(German) powerful
fighter
*Mat, Mathilda, Mattie,
Tilda, Tillie, Tilly*

Mattie
(English) most honored
*Matt, Matte, Matti,
Matty*

Matylda
(Polish) strong fighter
Matyld

Maude
(English) old-fashioned
Maud, Maudie

Maudeen
(American) countrified
*Maudie, Mawdeen,
Mawdine*

Maudisa
(African) sweet
Maudesa, Maudesah

Mauna
(American) attractive
Maune, Mawna, Mon

Maura
(Latin, Irish) dark
Moira, Maurie

Maureen
(Irish, French)
night-loving
*Maura, Maurene,
Maurine, Moreen,
Morene*

Maurelle
(French) petite
*Maure, Maurie,
Maurielle*

Maurise
(French) dark
Morise, Maurice

Mauve
(French) gentle
Mauvey, Mauvie

Mavis
(French) singing bird
Mauvis, Mav, Mave

Maxeeme
(Latin) form of Maxime;
maximum

Maxie
(Latin) fine
Maxee, Maxey, Maxy

Maxime
(Latin) maximum
Maxey, Maxi, Maxim

Maxine
(Latin) greatest of all
*Max, Maxeen, Maxene,
Maxie, Maxy*

May
(Old English) bright
flower
Mae, Maye

Maya
(Latin, Hindi, Mayan) creative; mystical
Maia, Maiya, Mayah, Mya, Myah, Mye

Maybelle
(American) combo of May and Belle; lovely May
Mabelle, Maebelle, Maybell, May-Belle

Maybelline
(Latin)
Mabie, May, Maybeline, Maybie, Maybleene

Mayella
(American) combo of May and Ella; jolly
Ella, Maella, May, Mayela, Mayell, Mella

Mayghaen
(American) fortunate

Mayim
(Origin unknown) special
Mayum

Maykaylee
(American) ingenious
Maykayli, Maykaylie, Maykayly

Mayo
(Irish) place name; vibrant
Mayoh

Mayra
(Spanish) flourishing; creative
Mayrah

Mayrant
(Spanish) industrious
Maya, Mayrynt

Mazel
(American) form of Hazel; shining
Masel, Mazil

Mazel
(Hebrew) lucky girl
Mazal

Mazie
(Scottish) form of Maisie

McCanna
(American) ebullient
Maccanna, McCannah

McCauley
(Irish) feisty
Mac, McCauly, McCawlie

McCay
(Irish) creative
Mackaylee, McCaylee

McCormick
(Irish) last name as first name
MacCormack, Mackey

McGown
(Irish) sensible
Mac, MacGowen, Mackie, McGowen

McKenna
(American) able
Mackenna, Makenna

McKenzie
(Scottish) form of Mackenzie
Mackie, McKinzie, Mickey

McMurtry
(Irish) last name as first name
Mac, McMurt

Mead
(Greek) honey-wine-loving
Meade

Meadow
(English) place name; calm
Meadoh

Meagan
(Irish) joyous; precious
Maegan, Meaghan, Meegan, Meg, Meganne, Meggie, Meggye, Meghan

Meashley
(American) charmer
Meash, Meashlee

Meatah
(American) athletic
Mea, Mia, Miata (car), Miatah

Medalle
(American) pretty
Medahl, Medoll

Medardo
(Spanish) pretty

Medea
(Greek) ruling; cruel
Medeia

Meg
(Greek) able; lovable
Megs

Megan
(Irish) precious, joyful
*Meagan, Meaghen,
Meggi, Meghan,
Meghann*

Meggie
(Greek) best
Meggey, Meggi, Meggy

Mel
(Greek) sporty
Mell

Melana
(Greek) giving; dark

Melancon
(French) dark beauty;
sweet
*Mel, Melance, Melaney,
Melanie, Melanse,
Melanson, Melonce,
Melonceson*

Melania
(Italian) giving;
philanthropic
Mel, Melly

Melanie
(Greek) dark; sweet
Melanee

Melantha
(Greek) dark-skinned;
sweet
Melanthah

Melba
(Australian) talented;
light-hearted
Melbah

Melia
(German) dedicated
Meelia, Melyah

Melina
(Greek) honey; sweet
Melena, Melinah

Melinda
(Latin) honey;
sweetheart
*Linda, Linnie, Linny,
Lynda, Mellie, Melynda,
Milinda, Mylinde*

Melissa
(Greek) a honey
*Melisa, Melyssa,
Melyssuh*

Melody
(Greek) song; musical
*Mel, Mellie, Melodee,
Melodey, Melodie*

Meloney
(American) form of
Melanie; dark and sweet
Mel, Melone, Meloni

Melora
(Latin) good
*Meliora, Melorah,
Melourah*

Melrose
(Place name) sweet girl
Mellrose, Melrosie

Melvia
(American) leader; dark
Mel, Mell, Melvea

Mena
(Egyptian) pretty
Meenah, Menah

Meosha
(African-American)
talented
*Meeosha, Meoshe,
Miosha*

Merary
(American) merry
*Marary, Meraree,
Merarie*

Mercedes
(Spanish) merciful;
rewarded
*Mercedez, Mercides,
Mersadez, Mersaydes*

Mercy
(English) forgiving
*Merce, Mercee, Mercey,
Merci, Mercie*

Meredith
(Welsh) protector
*Mer, Meredithe,
Meredyth, Merridith,
Merry*

Meri
(Irish) by the sea
Merrie

Meridian
(American) perfect
posture
Meredian, Meridiane

Merie
(French) secretive;
blackbird
Mer, Meri, Myrie

Meriel
(Irish) girl who shines
like the sea
*Meri, Merial, Merri,
Merriyl, Merry*

Merilyn
(English, American)
combo of Merry and
Lynn
*Marilyn, Mer, Meralyn,
Merelyn, Meri, Merill,
Merilynn, Merilynne,
Merri, Merrill, Merrylyn*

Merissa
(Latin) ocean-loving
Merisa, Meryssa

Merit
(American) deserving
Merite, Meritte, Mirit

Merribeth
(English) cheerful
Merri-Beth, Merrybeth

Merrilee
(American) combo of
Merri and Lee; happy
*Marilee, Merilee,
Merrylee, Merry-Lee*

Merry
(English) cheerful
Mer, Merie, Merri, Merrie

Merryjane
(English) combo of
Merry and Jane; happy
*Merijane, Merrijane,
Merrijayne, Merryjaine,
Merryjayne*

Mersaydes
(Invented) variant of
Mercedes
Mercy, Mersa, Mersy

Mersey
(Place name)
Merce, Merse

Mersia
(Hebrew) variant of
Mersera; princess
*Mercy, Mers, Mersea,
Mersy*

Meryl
(German) well-known;
(Irish) shining sea
*Mer, Merel, Merri,
Merrill, Merryl, Meryll*

Mesa
(Place name) earthy
Mase, Maysa, Mesah

Mi
(Chinese) obsessive
My, Mye

Mia
(Scandinavian, Italian)
blessed; girl of mine
Me, Mea, Meah, Meya

Miaka
(Japanese) influential

Miana
(American) combo of Mi
and Ana
Mianna

Micah
(Hebrew) religious
Mica, Mika, My, Myca

Michaela
(Hebrew) God-loving
*Meeca, Micaela,
Michael, Michal,
Michala, Michalla,
Mikala*

Michaelannette
(American) combo of
Michael and Annette;
spirited
Annette, Michelannet

Michaele
(Hebrew) loving God

Michele
(Italian, French, American) God-loving
Machele, Machelle, Mechele, Mia, Michell, Michelle, Mish, Mishelle

Michelin
(American) lovable
Michalynn, Mish, Mishelin

Micheline
(French) form of Michele; delightful
Mishelinne

Micki
(American) quirky
Mick, Mickee, Mickey, Micky, Miki, Mycki

Mickley
(American) form of Mickey; fun-loving
Mick, Mickaella, Micklee, Mickley, Mickli, Miklea, Miklee, Mikleigh, Mikley, Myk, Mykkie

Micole
(American) combo of Micha and Nicole; happy-go-lucky girl
Macole, Micolle

Mid
(American) middle child
Middi, Middy

Migon
(American) precious
Mignonne, Migonette, Migonn, Migonne

Mignon
(French) cute
Migonette, Mim, Mimi, Minyon, Minyonne

Miguelinda
(Spanish) combo of Miguel and Linda; strong-willed beauty
Miguel-Linda, Miguelynda

Mika
(Hebrew) wise and pious
Micah, Mikah, Mikie

Mikaela
(Hebrew) God-loving
Mik, Mikayla, Mike, Mikhaila, Miki

Mila
(Russian, Italian) short for Camilla; dearest
Milah, Milla, Millah, Mimi

Milagros
(Spanish) miracle
Mila, Milagro

Milantia
(Panamanian) calm
Mila

Mildred
(English) gentle
Mil, Mildread, Mildrid, Millie, Milly

Milena
(Greek) loving girl
Mela, Mili, Milina

Miliani
(Hawaiian) one who caresses
Mil, Mila

Milissa
(Greek) softspoken
Melissa, Missy

Milla
(Polish) gentle; pure
Mila, Millah

Millay
(Literature) soft

Millicent
(Greek, German) soft-hearted
Melicent, Melly, Millie, Millisent, Milly, Missy

Millie
(English) short for Mildred and Millicent
Mil, Mili, Milly

Mimi
(French) short for Camilla; willful
Meemee, Mim, Mims, Mimsie

Min
(Chinese) sensitive; soft-hearted

Mina
(German, Polish) resolute protector; willful
Mena, Min, Minah

Mindy
(Greek) short for Melinda; breezy
Mindee, Mindi, Mindie, Myndee

Minerva
(Latin, Greek) bright; strong
Menerva, Min, Minnie, Myn

Minette
(French) loyal woman
Min, Minnette, Minnie

Ming
(Chinese) shiny; hope of tomorrow

Minhtu
(Asian) light and clear

Mini
(Scandinavian) mine

Miniver
(English) assertive
Meniver, Minever, Miniverr

Minna
(German) sturdy
Mina, Minnie

Minnie
(German) short for Minerva
Mini, Minni, Minny

Mira
(Latin, Spanish) wonderful girl
Meara, Mirror

Mirabel
(Latin) marvelous; beautiful reflection
Marabelle, Mira, Mirabell, Mirabelle

Mirabella
(Italian) marvelous
Mira, Mirabellah

Miraclair
(Latin) combo of Mira and Clair; wonderful; gentle
Mira-Clair, Miraclaire, Miraclare

Miracle
(American) miracle baby
Merry, Mira, Mirakle, Mirry

Miranda
(Latin) unique and amazing
Maranda, Meranda, Mira, Mirrie, Myranda

Mirella
(Spanish) wonderful
Mira, Mirel, Mirell, Mirelle

Mireya
(Hebrew) form of Miriam; melancholy

Mireyli
(Spanish) wondrous; admirable
Mire, Mirey

Miriam
(Hebrew) living with sadness
Mariam, Maryam, Meriam, Miri, Miriame, Mirriam, Mitzi

Mirka
(Polish) glorious
Mira, Mirk

Mirtha
(Greek) burdened
Meert, Meerta, Mirt, Mirta

Mischanna
(Hebrew) form of Miriam; desired
Misch, Mischana, Mish, Mishanna, Mishke

Mishelene
(French) form of Micheline; pretty; believer
Mish, Misha, Mishlene

Missy
(English) short for Melissa
Miss, Missi, Missie

Misty
(English) dreamy
Miss, Missy, Mistee, Misti, Mistie, Mysti

Mitten
(American) cuddly
Mitt, Mittun, Mitty

Mittie
(American) short for
Matilda and Mitten;
darling
*Mittee, Mittey, Mitti,
Myttie*

Mitzi
(German) dancer
*Mitsee, Mitzee, Mitzie,
Mitzy*

Miya
(Japanese) peaceful as a
temple
Miyah

Mobley
(Last name as first
name) beauty queen
*Moblee, Mobli, Moblie,
Mobly*

Mocha
(Arabic) coffee with
chocolate
Mo, Moka, Mokka

Modesty
(Latin) modest
Modesti, Modestie

Moeshea
(African-American)
talented
*Moesha, Moeshia,
Mosha*

Moira
(English, Irish) pure;
great one
*Maura, Moir, Moirah,
Moire, Moyrah*

Mokysha
(African-American)
dramatic
*Kisha, Kysha, Mokesha,
Mokey*

Moll
(Literature) Moll
Flanders; outgoing
Molly

Molly
(Irish) jovial
*Moli, Moll, Molley,
Mollie*

Momo
(Japanese) peaches

Mona
(Greek) short for
Ramona; shining-
cheeked
Monah, Mone

Moneek
(Invented) form of
Monique; saucy; advisor
Moneeke

Monet
(French) artistic
Mon, Monae, Monay

Monica
(Greek) seeking
company of others
*Mon, Mona, Monicka,
Monika, Monike,
Monique*

Monical
(American) combo of
Monica and L; lively
*Monecal, Moni, Monicle,
Monikal*

Monika
(Polish) advisor

Monique
(French) saucy; advisor
*Mon, Mone, Monee,
Moni*

Monserrat
(Latin) tall
Monserat

Montana
(Place name) mountain
of strength
*Montayna, Montie,
Monty*

Montenia
(Spanish) climber
*Monte, Montenea,
Montynia*

Monya
(American) confident
Mon, Monyeh

Moon
(American) dreamy
*Monnie, Moone,
Moonee, Mooney,
Moonny, Moonnye*

Moon Unit
(Invented) universal
appeal
Moon-Unit

Mor
(Irish) sweet

Mora
(Spanish) sweet as a
blueberry

Morag
(Scottish) goddess
Morrag

Moraima
(Spanish) forgiving
Mora, Morama

More
(American) bonus
Moore, Morie

Morgan
(Welsh) girl on the
seashore
*Mor, Morey, Morgane,
Morgannna, Morgen*

Moriah
(French) dark girl;
(Hebrew) God-taught
*Mareyeh, Mariah,
Moorea, More, Morie,
Morria*

Morine
(American) form of
Maureen; fond of night
Morri

Moritza
(Place name) St. Moritz,
Switzerland; playful

Morla
(American) form of
Marla; easygoing
Morley, Morly

Morven
(American) magical
Morvee, Morvey, Morvi

Morwyn
(Welsh) maiden
*Morwen, Morwenn,
Morwynn, Morwynna*

Moselle
(Hebrew) uplifted
Mose, Mozelle, Mozie

Moya
(Scandinavian) mother
Moy

Mudiva
(Slavic)
Mudeva

Murdina
(Slavic) dark spirit
Murdi, Murdine

Muriel
(Celtic) shining
*Meriel, Mur, Murial,
Muriele, Murielle*

Murphy
(Irish) spirited
*Murphee, Murphey,
Murphi*

Murray
(Last name as first
name) brisk
Muray, Murraye

Musique
(French) musical
Museek, Museke, Musik

Mussie
(American) musical
Muss, Mussi, Mussy

Myeshia
(African-American)
giving
Meyeshia, Mye, Myesha

Mykala
(Scandinavian) giving
Mykaela, Mykela, Mykie

Mykelle
(American) generous
Mykell

Myla
(English) forgiving
Miela, Mylah

Mylene
(Greek) dark-skinned girl
Myleen

Mylie
(German) forgiving
Miley, Mylee, Myli

Mynola
  (Invented) smart
  Minola, Monoa, Mynolla,
  Mynolle
Myra
  (Latin) fragrant
  Myrah
Myrischa
  (African-American)
  fragrant doll
  Myresha, Myri, Myrish,
  Myrisha, Rischa
Myrka,
  (Slavic) great
  Mirk, Mirka, Myrk
Myrka
  (Spanish) rambunctious
  Merka, Mirka, Myrkah
Myrna
  (Irish) loved
  Merna, Mirna, Murna
Myrtle
  (Greek) loving
  Mertle, Mirtle, Myrt,
  Myrtie
Mysha
  (Russian) form of Misha;
  protective
  Mischa, Mish, Misha,
  Mysh
Mysta
  (Invented) mysterious
  Mista, Mystah

Mystique
  (French) intriguing
  woman
  Mistie, Mistik, Mistique,
  Misty, Mystica

Naama
  (Hebrew) sweet
  Naamah, Naamit
Naamah
  (Biblical) sweet
  Nanay, Nayamah,
  Naynay
Naava
  (Hebrew) delightful girl
  Naavah, N'Ava
Nada
  (Arabic) morning dew;
  giving
Nadelie
  (American) form of
  Natalie; Christmas-born
  beauty
  Nadey
Nadeline
  (Invented) born on
  Christmas
  Nad, Nadelyne
Nadia
  (Slavic) hopeful
  Nada, Nadea, Nadi,
  Nadie, Nady, Nadya

Nadine
(Russian, French)
dancer
Nadeen, Nadene, Nadie,
Nadyne, Naidyne

Nadya
(Russian) optimistic;
life's beginnings

Naeemah
(African) breathtaking

Nahtanha
(African) warm

Nai
(Japanese) intelligent
Nayah

Naida
(Greek) nymph-like
Naya

Nailah
(African) successful
Naila

Naimah
(Arabic) happy
Naima

Najet
(African)
Naajet

Nakesha
(African-American)
combo of Na and Kesha
Naka, Nakeisha, Nakie,
Nakisha

Nakia
(Arabic) purest girl
Nakea

Nakita
(Russian) precocious
Nakeeta, Nakeita,
Nakya, Naquita, Nikita

Nala
(African) loved
Nalah, Nalo

Nalani
(Hawaiian) calming
Nalanie, Nalany

Nallely
(Spanish) friend
Nalelee, Naleley, Nallel

Nan
(German, Scottish,
English) bold; graceful
Na, Nana, Nannie,
Nanny

Nanalie
(American) form of
Natalie; graceful;
Christmas-born
Nan, Nana, Nanalee

Nance
(American) giving
Nans

Nancy
(English, Irish) generous
woman
Nan, Nancee, Nanci,
Nancie, Nansee, Nonie

Nanette
(French) giving and
gracious
Nanet

Nani
(Greek) charming beauty
Nan, Nannie

Nanice
(American) open-
hearted
Nan, Naneece, Naneese,
Naniece

Nanna
(Scandinavian) brave
Nana

Nanon
(French) slow to anger
Nan, Nanen

Naomi
(Hebrew) beautiful
woman
Naomie, Naomy, Naynay,
Nene, Noma, Nomah,
Nomi

Nara
(Greek, Japanese)
happy; dreamy
Narah, Nera

Narcissa
(Greek) narcissistic
Narcisse, Nars

Narcissie
(Greek) conceited;
daffodil
Narci, Narcis, Narcissa,
Narcisse, Narcissey,
Narsee, Narsey, Narsis

Nastasia
(Greek, Russian)
gorgeous girl
Nas, Nastasha, Natasie

Natalia
(Russian, Latin) born on
Christmas; beauty
*Nat, Nata, Natala,
Natalea, Natalee,
Natalie, Natalya, Nati,
Nattie, Nattlee, Natty*

Natarsha
(American) splendid
Natarsh, Natarshah

Natasha
(Latin, Russian)
glorious; born on
Christmas
*Natacha, Natashah,
Natashia, Natassia,
Nitasha*

Nathadria
(Hebrew) form of
Nathan; gift of God
*Natania, Nath, Nathe,
Nathed, Nathedrea,
Natty, Thedria*

Nathalie
(French) born on
Christmas
Natalie

Nation
(American) spirited;
patriotic
Nashon, Nayshun

Natosha
(African-American) form
of Natasha; born on
Christmas
*Nat, Natosh, Natoshe,
Natty*

Naveen
(Spanish) snowing

Navita
(Hispanic) original
Nava, Navite

Nayeli
(African) of beginnings

Nazly
(American) idealistic
Nazlee, Nazli, Nazlie

Neal
(Irish) spirited
Neale, Neel, Neil

Neala
(Irish) spirited
*Neal, Neeli, Neelie,
Neely, Neila*

Necie
(Hungarian) intense
Neci

Neda
(Slavic) Sunday baby

Nedda
(English) born to money
Ned, Neddy

Nedra
(English) secretive
Ned, Nedre

Neely
(Irish) sparkling smile
*Nealy, Neelee, Neilie,
Nelie*

Nefris
(Spanish) glamorous
*Nef, Neff, Neffy, Nefras,
Nefres*

Neia
(African) promising

Neith
(Egyptian) feminine
Neithe

Nekeisha
(African-American) bold
spirit
*Nek, Nekeishah,
Nekesha, Nekisha,
Nekkie*

Nelda
(American) friend
*Neldah, Nell, Nellda,
Nellie*

Nelia
(Spanish) short for
Cornelia; yellow-haired
*Neelia, Neely, Nela,
Nelie, Nene*

Nell
(English) sweet charmer
Nelle, Nellie

Nellie
(English) short for
Cornelia and Eleanor
*Nel, Nela, Nell, Nelle,
Nelli, Nelly*

Nelliene
(American) form of
Nellie; charming
Nell, Nelli, Nellienne

Nelvia
(Greek) brash
Nell, Nelvea

Nemoria
(American) crafty
Nemorea

Nereida
(Spanish) sea nymph
*Nere, Nereide, Nereyda,
Neri, Nireida*

Neressa
(Greek) coming from the
sea
*Narissa, Nene, Nerissa,
Nerisse*

Nerys
(Welsh) ladylike
Neris, Neriss, Nerisse

Nessa
(Irish) devout
Nessah

Nessie
(Greek) short for
Vanessa
Nese, Nesi, Ness

Nestora
(Spanish) she is leaving
Nesto, Nestor

Neta
(Hebrew) growing and
flourishing

Netira
(Spanish) flourishing

Netra
(American) maturing
well
*Net, Netrah, Netrya,
Nettie*

Netta
(Scottish) champion
Nett, Nettie

Nettie
(French) gentle
Net, Netti, Netty

Nettiemae
(American) combo of
Nettie and Mae;
small-town girl
*Mae, Netimay,
Nettemae, Nettie,
Nettiemay*

Neva
(Russian, English) the
newest; snow
Neeva, Neve, Niv

Nevada
(Spanish) place name;
girl who loves snow
Nev, Nevadah

Neve
(Irish) promising
princess

Nevina
(Irish) she worships God
Nev, Niv, Nivena, Nivina

Newlin
(Last name as first
name) healing
*Newlinn, Newlinne,
Newlyn, Newlynn*

Neyda
(Spanish) pure
Ney

Nia
(Greek) priceless
Niah

Niamh
(Irish) promising

Niandrea
(Invented) form of
Diandrea; pretty
*Andrea, Nia, Niand,
Niandre*

Nicelda
(American) industrious
Niceld, Nicelde, Nicey

Nichele
(American) combo of
Nicole and Michele;
dark-skinned
Nichel, Nichelle, Nishele

Nichole
(French) light and lively
Nichol

Nichols
(Last name as first name) smart
Nick, Nickee, Nickels, Nickey, Nicki, Nickie, Nicky, Nikels

Nick
(American) short for Nicole
Nik

Nicki
(French) short for Nicole
Nick, Nickey, Nicky, Niki

Nicks
(American) fashionable
Nickee, Nickie, Nicksie, Nicky, Nix

Nico
(Italian) victorious
Nicco, Nicko, Nikko, Niko

Nicola
(Italian) lovely singer
Nekola, Nick, Nikkie, Nikola

Nicolasa
(Spanish) spontaneous; winning
Nico, Nicole

Nicole
(French) winning
Nacole, Nichole, Nick, Nickie, Nikki, Nikol, Nikole

Nicolette
(French) a tiny Nicole; little beauty
Nettie, Nick, Nickie, Nicoline, Nikkolette, Nikolet

Nicolie
(French) sweet
Nichollie, Nikolie

Nidia
(Latin) home-loving
Nidie, Nidya

Niesha
(African-American) virginal
Neisha, Nesha, Nesia, Nessie

Nieves
(Spanish) snows
Neaves, Ni, Nievez, Nievis

Nike
(Greek) goddess of victory; fleet of foot; a winner

Niki
(American) short for Nicole and Nikita
Nick, Nicki, Nicky, Nik, Nikki, Nikky

Niki-Lynn
(American) combo of Niki and Lynn
Nicki-Lynn, Nicky-Lynn, Nikilinn, Nikilyn

Nikita
(Russian) daring
Nakeeta, Niki, Nikki, Niquitta

Nikithia
(African-American) winning; frank
Kithi, Kithia, Nikethia, Niki

Nikole
(Greek) winning
Nik, Niki

Nima
(Arabic) blessed
Nimah

Nina
(Russian, Hebrew, Spanish) bold girl
Neena, Nena, Ninah

Nina-Lina
(Spanish) combo of Nina and Lina; lovely
Nina Lina, Ninalena, Ninalina

Nirvana
(Hindi) completion; oneness with God
Nirvahna, Nirvanah

Nissa
(Hebrew) symbolic
Niss, Nissah, Nissie

Nissie
(Scandinavian) pretty; elf
Nisse, Nissee

Nita
(Hebrew) short for
Juanita
Neeta, Nite, Nittie

Niu
(Chinese) girlish;
confident

Nixi
(German) mystical
Nixee, Nixie

Niy
(American) lively
Nye

Noa
(Hebrew) chosen
Noah

Noel
(Latin) born on
Christmas
*Noela, Noelle, Noellie,
Noli*

Nohelia
(Hispanic) kind
Nohelya

Nola
(Latin) sensual
Nolah, Nole, Nolie

Nomble
(African) beautiful
Nombi

Nona
(Latin) ninth; knowing
*Nonah, Nonie, Nonn,
Nonna*

Nora
(Greek, Scandinavian,
Scottish) light; bright;
from the north
Norah, Noreh

Noranna
(Irish) combo of Nora
and Anna; honorable
*Anna, Nora, Norana,
Norannah, Noranne,
Noreena*

Noreen
(Latin) acknowledging
others
*Noire, Norin, Norine,
Norinne, Nureen*

Norika
(Japanese) athletic
Nori, Norike

Norma
(Latin) gold standard
*Noey, Nomah, Norm,
Normah, Normie*

Norris
(English) serious
Nore, Norrus

Nota
(American) negative
Na, Nada, Not

Nova
(Latin) energetic; new
*Noova, Novah, Novella,
Novie*

Novak
(Last name as first
name) emphatic
Novac

Novia
(Spanish) sweetheart
Nov, Novie, Nuvia

Nu
(Vietnamese) confident
Niu

Nueva
(Spanish) new; fresh
Nue, Nuey

Numa
(Spanish) delightful
Num

Numa-Noe
(Spanish) combo of
Numa and Noe; delight
Numanoe

Nunibelle
(American) combo of
Nuni and Belle; pretty
Nunibell, Nunnibelle

Nunu
(Vietnamese) friendly

Nura
(Aramaic) light-footed
Noora, Noura, Nurrie

Nuria
(Arabic) light
Noor, Noura, Nur

Nurlene
(American) boisterous
Nerlene, Nurleen

Nuvia
(American) new
Nuvea
Nydia
(Latin) nest-loving;
home and hearth
woman
Ny, Nydie, Nydya
Nylene
(American) shy
*Nyle, Nylean, Nyleen,
Nyles, Nyline*
Nysa
(Greek) life-starting
*Nisa, Nissa, Nissie,
Nysa, Nyssa*
Nyx
(Greek) lively
Nix

Obede
(English) obedient
Obead
Obedience
(American) obedient
Obey
Obey
(American) obedient
Oceana
(Greek) ocean-loving;
name given to those
with astrological signs
that have to do with
water
*Oceonne, Oceane, Ocie,
Oh*
Octavia
(Latin) eighth child; born
on eighth day of the
month; musical
Octivia, Octtavia
Odalis
(Spanish) humorous
*Odales, Odallis,
Odalous, Odalus*

Odele
(Hebrew, Greek)
melodious
Odela, Odelle, Odie
Odelia
(Hebrew, Greek) singer
of spiritual songs
*Odele, Odelle, Odie,
Odila*
Odelita
(Spanish) vocalist
Odelite
Odessa
(Place name) traveler on
an odyssey
Odessah, Odie, Odissa
Odette
(French) good girl
Oddette, Odetta
Odile
(French) sensuous
Odyll
Odilia
(Spanish) wealthy
*Eudalia, Odalia, Odella,
Odylia, Othilia*
Ohara
(Japanese) meditative
Oh
Oksana
(Russian) praise to God
Oksanah, Oksie
Ola
(Scandinavian) bold
Olah

Olaide
(American) lovely;
thoughtful
Olai, Olay, Olayde

Olga
(Russian) holy woman
Ola, Olgah, Ollie

Olidie
(Spanish) light
Oli, Olidee, Olydie

Olino
(Spanish) scented
Olina, Oline

Olive
(Latin) subtle
Olyve

Olivia
(English) flourishing
*Olive, Olivea, Oliveah,
Ollie*

Olwen
(Welsh) magical; white
Olwynn

Olya
(Latin) perfect
Olyah

Olympia
(Greek) heavenly woman
Olimpia, Ollie

Olynda
(Invented) form of
Lynda; fragrant; pretty
*Lyn, Lynda, Olin, Olinda,
Olynde*

Oma
(German) grandmother;
(Hebrew) pious
Omah

Omanie
(Origin unknown)
exuberant
Omanee

Omayra
(Latin) fragrant
(Spanish) beloved
Oma, Omyra

Omesha
(African-American)
splendid
Omesh, Omie, Omisha

Omie
(Italian) homebody
Omee

Omorose
(African) lovely

Ondina
(Latin) water spirit
Ondi, Ondine, Onyda

Oneida
(Native American)
anticipated
*Ona, Oneeda, Onida,
Onie, Onyda*

Oni
(African) desired child

Onie
(Latin) flamboyant
Oh, Oona, Oonie, Una

Opal
(Hindi) the opal;
precious
Opale, Opalle, Opie

Ophelia
(Greek) helpful woman;
character from
Shakespeare's Hamlet
Ofelia, Ophela, Phelie

Oprah
(Hebrew) one who
soars; excellent
*Ophie, Ophrie, Opra,
Oprie, Orpah*

Ora
(Greek) glowing
Orah, Orie

Oraleyda
(Spanish) light of dawn
Ora, Oraleydea, Oralida

Oralie
(Hebrew) light of dawn
Oralee, Orla

Orbelina
(American) excited,
dawn
*Lina, Orbe, Orbee,
Orbeline, Orbey, Orbi,
Orby*

Orene
(French) nurturing
Orane, Orynne

Orfelinda
(Spanish) pretty dawn
Orfelinde, Orfelynda

Orianna
(Latin) sunny; dawn
Oriana, Oriannah, Orie

Orin
(Irish) dark-haired
Oren, Orinn

Oriole
(Latin) golden light
Oreole, Oriel, Oriol

Orlanda
(German) famed

Orly
(French) busy
Orlee

Ormanda
(Latin) noble
Ormie

Orna
(Irish) dark-haired
Ornah

Ottolee
(English) combo of Otto
and Lee; appealing
Ottalie, Ottilie

Otylia
(Polish) rich
Oteelya

Ovalia
(Spanish) helpful
Ova, Ove, Ovelia

Owena
(Welsh) feisty
Oweina, Owina, Owinne

Ozara
(Hebrew) treasured
Ozarah

Pabiola
(Spanish) small girl
Pabby, Pabi, Pabiole

Pace
(Last name as first
name) charismatic
Pase

Pacifica
(Spanish) peaceful
Pacifika

Padgett
(French) growing and
learning; lovely-haired
Padge, Padget, Paget

Page
(French) sharp; eager
*Pagie, Paige, Paje,
Payge*

Pageant
(American) theatrical
*Padg, Padge, Padgeant,
Padgent, Pagent*

Paisley
(Scottish) patterned
Paislee, Pazley

Pal
(American) friend; buddy

Palemon
(Spanish) kind
Palem, Palemond

Paley
(Last name as first name) wise
Palee, Palie

Pallas
(Greek) wise woman
Palace, Palas

Palma
(Latin) successful
Palmah, Palmeda, Palmedah

Paloma
(Spanish) dove
Peloma

Pam
(Greek) sweet as honey
Pama, Pamela, Pammie, Pammy

Pamela
(Greek) sweet as honey
Pam, Pamala, Pamalla, Pamee, Pamelinn, Pamelyn, Pammee, Pammi, Pammie, Pammy, Pamyla, Pamylla

Pandora
(Greek) a gift; curious
Pan, Pand, Pandie, Pandorah

Pang
(Chinese) innovative

Pansy
(Greek) fragrant
Pan, Pansey, Pansie, Panze, Panzee, Panzie

Panther
(Greek) wild; all gods
Panthar, Panthea, Panthur, Panth

Paola
(Italian) firebrand

Paolabella
(Italian) lovely firebrand

Paris
(French) capital of France; graceful woman
Pareece, Parie, Parice, Parris

Parker
(English) noticed; in the park
Park, Parke, Parkie

Parminder
(Hindi) attractive

Parnelle
(French) small stone
Parn, Parnel, Parnell, Parney

Parslee
(Botanical) complementary
Pars, Parse, Parsley, Parsli

Parthenia
(Greek) from the Parthenon; virtuous
Parthe, Parthee, Parthene, Parthine, Thenia

Pascale
(French) born on a religious holiday
Pascal, Paschale, Paskel, Paskil

Paschel
(African) spiritual
Paschell

Pash
(French) clever
Pasch

Pasha
(Greek) lady by the sea
Passha

Passion
(American) sensual
Pashun, Pasyun, Pass, Passyun

Pat
(Latin) short for Patricia; tough
Patt, Patty

Patia
(Latin) short for Patricia; hard-minded

Patience
(English) woman of patience
Pacience, Pat, Pattie

Patrice
(French) form of Patricia; svelte
Pat, Patreas, Patreece, Pattie, Pattrice, Trece, Treecc

Patricia
(Latin) woman of nobility; unbending
Pat, Patrisha, Patsie, Patsy, Patti, Pattie, Patty

Patrina
(American) noble; patrician
Patryna, Patrynna, Tryna, Trynnie

Patsy
(Latin) short for Patricia; brassy
Pat, Patsey, Patsi, Patsie, Patti, Patty

Patty
(English) short for Patricia and Patrice
Pat, Pati, Patti, Pattie

Paula
(Latin) small and feminine
Paulah, Paulie, Pauly, Pawlah

Paulette
(French) form of Paula; little Paula
Paula, Paulett, Paulie, Paullette

Paulina
(Latin) small;
(Italian) lovely
Paula, Paulena, Paulie

Pauline
(Latin) short for Paula; precocious
Pauleen, Paulene

Pax
(Latin) peace goddess

Paxton
(Latin) place name; peaceful
Pax, Paxten, Paxtun

Payton
(Last name as first name) aggressive
Pay, Paye, Payten, Paytun, Peyton

Paz
(Spanish, Hebrew) sparkling; peaceful
Pazia

Paza
(Hebrew) golden child
Paz

Pazzy
(Latin) peaceful
Paz, Pazet

Peace
(English) peaceful woman
Pea, Peece

Peaches
(American) outrageously sweet
Peach, Peachy

Pearl
(Latin) jewel from the sea
Pearlie, Pearly, Perl, Perla

Pecola
(American) brash
Pekola

Peggy
(Greek) pearl; priceless
Peg, Peggi, Peggie

Pei
(Chinese) place name; from Tang Pei

Peigi
(Scottish) pearl; priceless

Pele
(Hawaiian) volcano; conflicted

Pelham
(English) thoughtful
Pelhim, Pellam, Pellham, Pellie

Pelia
(Hebrew) marvelous
Peliah, Pelya, Pelyia

Pendant
(French) necklace; adorned
Pendan, Pendanyt

Penelope
(Greek) patient; weaver
of dreams
*Pen, Penalope, Penni,
Pennie, Penny*

Peninah
(Hebrew) pearl; lovely
Peni, Penny

Penny
(Greek) short for
Penelope; spunky
*Pen, Penee, Penni,
Pennie*

Peony
(Greek) flowering; giving
praise
Pea, Peoni, Peonie

Pepita
(Spanish) high-energy
Peppita

Pepper
(Latin) spicy
Pep, Peppie, Peppyr

Peppy
(American) cheerful
*Pep, Peppey, Peppi,
Peps*

Perfecta
(Spanish) perfection
Perfekta

Perla
(Latin) substantial
Perlah

Peridot
(Arabic) green gem;
treasured
Peri

Perlace
(Spanish) small pearl
*Perl, Perlahse, Perlase,
Perly*

Perlette
(French) pearl; treasured
*Pearl, Pearline, Peraline,
Perl, Perle, Perlett*

Perlie
(Latin) form of Pearl
Perli, Purlie, Perly

Perlina
(American) small pearl
*Pearl, Perl, Perlinna,
Perlyna*

Perouze
(Armenian) turquoise
gemstone
*Perou, Perous, Perouz,
Perry*

Perri
(Greek, Latin) outdoorsy
Peri, Perr, Perrie, Perry

Persephone
(Greek) breath of spring
*Pers, Perse, Persefone,
Persey*

Pesha
(Hebrew) flourishing
Peshah, Peshia

Pershella
(American) philanthropic
*Pershe, Pershel,
Pershelle, Pershey,
Persie, Persy*

Persia
(Place name) colorful
Persha, Perzha

Persis
(Latin) from Persian
Pers, Persus, Perz

Peta
(English) saucy
Pet, Petty

Petra
(Slavic) glamorous;
capable
*Pet, Peti, Petrah, Pett,
Petti, Pietra*

Petronilla
(Greek) form of Peter;
rock; dependable
*Petria, Petrina, Petrine,
Petro, Petrone,
Petronela, Petronella,
Pett*

Petula
(Latin) petulant song
Pet, Petulah, Petulia

Petunia
(American) flower; perky
Pet, Petune

Phaedra
(Greek) bright
Faydra, Faydrah, Padra,
Phae, Phedra

Phashestha
(American) decorative
Phashey, Shesta

Phernita
(American) articulate
Ferney, Phern

Phila
(Greek) loving
Phil, Philly

Philadelphia
(Greek) place name;
loving one's fellow man
Fill, Phil, Philly

Philana
(Greek) loving
Filana, Filly, Philly

Philippa
(Greek) horse lover
Feefee, Felipa, Phil,
Philippe, Phillie,
Phillippah

Philise
(Greek) loving
Felece, Felice, Philese

Philly
(Place name) wild spirit
Filly, Philee, Phillie

Philomena
(Greek) beloved
Filomena, Filomina,
Mena, Phil,
Phillomenah, Philomen

Phoebe
(Greek) bringing light
Febe, Fee, Feebe, Feebs,
Phebee, Phoeb,
Phoebey, Phoebie,
Phoebs

Phoenix
(Place name) U.S. city;
(Greek) rebirth
Fee, Fenix, Fenny,
Phenix, Phoe

Phylicia
(Greek) fortunate girl
Felicia, Phillie, Phyl,
Phylecia

Phyllida
(Greek) lovely; leafy
bough
Filida, Phyll, Phyllyda

Phyllis
(Greek) beautiful; leafy
bough; articulate;
smitten
Fillice, Fillis, Phil, Philis,
Phillisse, Phyl, Phylis,
Phyllys

Pia
(Latin) devout
Peah, Piah

Picabo
(American) place name
Peekaboo

Pier
(Greek) form of Peter;
rock; reliable
Peer

Pierette
(Greek) reliable
Perett, Perette, Piere

Pierina
(Greek) dependable
Peir, Per, Perina, Perine,
Pieryna

Pilar
(Spanish) worthwhile;
pillar of strength

Pilvi
(Italian) cheerful
Pilvee

Pink
(American) blushing
Pinkee, Pinkie, Pinky,
Pinkye, Pynk

Piper
(English) player of a
pipe; musical

Pippa
(English) ebullient;
horse-lover
Pip, Pipa

Pippi
(English) blushing;
(French) loving horses
Pip, Pippie, Pippy

Pirouette
(French) ballet term
Piro, Pirouet, Pirouetta

Pita
(English) comforting
Peta, Petah

Pitarra
(American) interesting
Pitarr

Pity
(American) sad
Pitee, Pitey, Pitie

Pixie
(American) small; perky
Pixee, Pixey, Pixi

Platinum
(Metal) refined
Plati, Platnum

Pleshette
(American) plush
Plesh

Po
(Italian) effervescent
Poe

Pocahontas
(Native American) joyful
Poca, Poka

Poe
(Animal and river)
peacock; Po River
Po, PoPo

Poetry
(Word as name)
romantic
Poe, Poesy, Poet,

Polina
(Russian) small
Po, Pola, Polya

Polly
(Irish) devout; joyous
Paulie, Pol, Polli, Pollie

Pollyanna
(American, English)
combo of Polly and
Anna; happy-go-lucky
*Polianna, Polliana,
Pollie-anna, Polly*

Pomona
(Latin) apple of my eye
Pomonah

Pompa
(Last name as first
name) pompous
Pompy

Pompey
(Place name) lavish
*Pomp, Pompee, Pompei,
Pompy*

Pony
(American) wild-west girl
Poney, Ponie

Poodle
(American) dog; froufrou
girl
Poo, Pood, Poodly

Poppy
(Latin) flower; bouncy
girl
Pop, Poppi, Poppie

Porsche
(Latin) giving; high-
minded
*Porsh, Porsha, Porshe,
Porshie, Portia*

Portia
(Latin) a giving woman
Porsh, Porsha, Porshuh

Posh
(American) fancy girl
Posha

Posy
(American) sweet
Posee, Posey, Posie

Poupée
(French) French word for
doll
Pou

Powder
(American) gentle; light
*Pow, Powd, Powdy,
Powdyr, PowPow*

Precia
(Latin) important
*Preciah, Presha,
Presheah, Preshuh*

Precious
(English) beloved
*Preshie, Preshuce,
Preshus*

Prema
(Hindi) love

Prescilian
(Hispanic) fashionable
Pres, Priss

Presley
(English) talented
Preslee, Preslie, Presly, Prezlee, Prezley, Prezly

Price
(Welsh) loving
Pri, Prise, Pry, Pryce, Pryse

Prima
(Latin) first; fresh
Primia, Primie, Primma

Primalia
(Spanish) prime; first

Primavera
(Italian) spring child

Primola
(Botanical) flower; from primrose; first
Prim, Prym, Prymola

Primrose
(English) rosy; fragrant
Prim, Primie, Rosie, Rosy

Princess
(English) precious
Prin, Prince, Princie, Prinsess

Prinscella
(American) combo of Princess and Priscilla; princess
Princella, Prins, Prinsce, Prinscilla, Prinsee, Prinsey

Prisciliana
(Spanish) prissy; wise; old
Cissy, Priscili, Priss, Prissy

Priscilla
(Latin) wisdom of the ages
Cilla, Pris, Priscella, Prisilla, Priss, Prissie, Prissy

Prisisima
(Spanish) wise and feminine
Priss, Prissy, Sima

Prissy
(Latin) short for Priscilla; wise; feminine
Prisi, Priss, Prissie

Priti
(Hindi) lovely

Priya
(Hindi) sweetheart
Preeya, Preya, Priyah

Promise
(American) sincere
Promis

Prova
(French) place name; Provence
Pro, Proa, Provah

Pru
(Latin) short for Prudence
Prudie, Prue

Prudence
(Latin) wise; careful
Perd, Pru, Prudie, Prudince, Pruds

Prunella
(Latin) shy
Pru, Prue, Prune, Prunie

Pryor
(Last name as first name) wealthy
Prieyer, Pryar, Prye, Pryer

Psyche
(Greek) soulful
Sye, Sykie

Puma
(Animal) cougar; wild spirit
Poom, Pooma, Poomah, Pumah, Pume

Purity
(English) virginal
Puretee, Puritie

Pyera
(Italian) sturdy; formidable; rock
Pyer, Pyerah

Pyllyon
(English) enthusiastic
Pillion, Pillyon, Pillyun

Pyria
(Origin unknown) cherished
Pyra, Pyrea

Q-Malee
(American) form of
Cumale; open-hearted
Cue, Q, Quemalee,
Quemali, Quemalie

Quan
(Chinese) goddess of
compassion

Quanda
(English) queenly
Kwanda, Kwandah,
Quandah, Qwanda

Quanella
(African-American)
sparkling
Kwannie, Quanela

Quanesha
(African-American)
singing
Kwaeesha, Kwannie,
Quaneisha, Quanisha

Quantina
(American) brave queen
Kwantina, Kwantynna,
Quantinna, Quantyna,
Tina

QueAnna
(American) combo of
Que and Anna; genuine
Keana, KeAnna,
KeeAnna, Queana

Queen
(English) regal; special

Queenie
(English) queen-like;
royal and dignified
Kweenie, Quee, Queen,
Queeny

Queenverlyn
(Invented) combo of
Queen and Verlyn; lady
Queenee, Queenie

Quenby
(Swedish) feminine
Quenbee, Quenbey,
Quenbi, Quenbie,
Quinbee

Quenna
(English) feminine
Kwenna

Questa
(French) looking for love
Kesta

Queta
(Spanish) head of the
house
Keta

Quilla
(English) writer
Kwila, Kwilla, Quila,
Quillah

Quinby
(Scandinavian) living
like royalty
Quenby, Quin, Quinbie,
Quinnie

Quinceanos
(Spanish) fifteenth child
Quin, Quince, Quincy

Quincy
(French) fifth
Quince, Quincie

Quincylla
(American) popular; fifth
child
Cylla, Quince, Quincy

Quinella
(Latin) betting term; a
girl who is as pretty as
two
Quinn

Quinn
(English, Irish) smart
Quin, Quinnie

Quinta
(Latin) fifth day of the
month

Quintana
(Latin) fifth; lovely girl
Quentana, Quinn

Quintessa
(Latin) effervescent
Quinn

Quintilla
(Latin) fifth girl
Quintina

Quintona
(Latin) fifth
Quintwana
(American) fifth girl in
the family
Quintuana
Quinyette
(American) likeable; fifth
child
Kwenyette, Quiny
Quisha
(African-American)
beautiful mind
Keisha, Kesha, Key
Quita
(Latin) peaceful
Keeta, Keetah

Rabbit
(American) lively;
energetic
Rabit
Rachael
(Hebrew) peaceful as a
lamb
*Rach, Rachaele, Rachal,
Rachel, Rachie, Raechal,
Rasch, Raye*
Racheline
(American) combo of
Rachel and Line
Rachelene
Rachelle
(French) calm
*Rach, Rachell, Rashell,
Rashelle, Rochelle*
Racquel
(French) friendly
Racquelle, Raquel
Rada
(Polish) glad
Radmilla
(Slavic) glad;
hardworking

Rae
(English) raving beauty
Raedie, Raena, Ray, Raye
Raegan
(French) delicate
Reagan, Regan, Regun
Rafaela
(Hebrew) spiritual
Rafayela
Rafferty
(Irish) prospering
*Raferty, Raff, Raffarty,
Rafty*
Rain
(German) actor; tearful
Rainie, Reign
Raina
(German) dramatic
Raine, Rainna, Rayna
Rainbow
(American) hope
*Rain, Rainbeau, Rainbo,
Rainie*
Raine
(Latin) helpful friend
Raina, Rainie, Rane
Rainey
(Last name as first
name) giving
Rainee, Rainie, Raney

Rainey-Anne
(American) combo of
Rainey and Anne;
languid
Rainee, Raineeann,
Rainee-Anne, Rainey,
Raneyann, Raneyanne

Raisa
(Russian) embraced
Rasa

Raka
(Hindi) royal

Ramona
(Teutonic) beautiful
protector
Rae, Ramonah,
Ramonna, Raymona

Rana
(Hindi) beauty

Randa
(Latin) admired
Ran, Randah

Randall
(English) protective of
her own
Rand, Randal, Randi,
Randy

Randelle
(American) wary
Randee, Randele

Randi
(English) audacious
Randee, Randy

Rane
(Scandinavian) queen-
like
Rain, Raine, Ranie

Rani
(Hebrew) joyous; (Hindi)
queen
Rainie, Ranie

Rania
(Sanskrit) regal
Ranea, Raneah, Raney,
Ranie

Raphaela
(Hebrew) helping to heal
Rafaela, Rafe

Raquel
(Spanish) sensual
Racuell, Raquelle,
Raqwel

Rasheeda
(Indian) pious
Rashee, Rashida,
Rashie, Rashy

Rashel
(Spanish)
Rashell, Rashelle

Rashidah
(Arabic) on the right
path
Rashida

Rashinique
(African-American) rash
Rash, Rashy

Raven
(English) blackbird
Ravan, Rave, Ravin

Rawnie
(Slavic) ladylike
Rawani, Rawn, Rawnee

Rayleen
(American) popular
Raylene, Raylie, Rayly

Raynelle
(American) giving hope;
combo of Ray and Nelle
Nellie, Rae, Raenel,
Raenelle

Raynette
(American) ray of hope;
dancer
Raenette, Raynet

Razia
(Hebrew) secretive
Razeah, Raziah

Rea
(Polish) flowing
Raya

Reagan
(Last name as first
name) strong
Regan, Reganne, Reggie

Reannah
(English) combo of Rae
and Annah; divine
Reana, Reanna, Rennie

Reanne
(American) happy
Reann, Rennie, Rere,
Rianne

Reba
(Hebrew) fourth-born
Rebah, Ree, Reeba

Rebecca
(Hebrew) loyal
Becca, Becki, Beckie,
Becky, Rebeca, Rebeka,
Rebekah

Rebi
(Hebrew) friend who is
steadfast
Reby, Ree, Ribi

Rebop
(American) zany
Reebop

Reenie
(Greek) peace-loving
Reena, Reeni, Reeny,
Ren, Rena

Reese
(American) style-setting
Ree, Reece, Rees, Rere

Reeve
(Last name as first
name)

Regan
(Irish) queenly
Reagan

Regeana
(American) form of
Regina; queen
Rege, Regeanah,
Regeane

Regina
(English, Latin)
thoughtful
Gina, Rege, Regena,
Reggie, Regine

Regine
(Latin) royal
Regene, Rejean

Rehema
(African) well-grounded
Rehemah, Rehemma,
Rehima

Rela
(German) everything
Reila, Rella

Reina
(Spanish) a thinker
Rein, Reinie, Rina

Reith
(American) shy
Ree, Reeth

Remah
(Hebrew) pale beauty
Rema, Remme, Remmie,
Rima, Ryma

Remember
(American) memorable
Remi, Remmi, Remmie,
Remmy

Remi
(French) woman of
Rheims; jaded
Remee, Remie, Remy

Rena
(Hebrew) joyful singer
Reena, Rinah, Rinne

Renae
(French) form of Renee
Renay, Rennie, Rere

Renard
(French) fox; sly
Ren, Renarde, Rynard,
Rynn

Renata
(French) reaching out
Renie, Renita, Rennie,
Rinata

Rene
(Greek) hopeful
Reen, Reenie, Reney

Renea
(French) form of Renee;
renewal
Renny

Renee
(French) born again
Rene, Rennie, Rere

Renetta
(French) reborn
Ranetta, Renette

Renita
(Latin) poised
Ren, Renetta, Rennie

Renite
(Latin) stubborn
Reneta, Renita

Renzia
(Greek) form of Renee;
peaceful
Renze

Resa
(Greek) productive;
laughing
Reesa, Reese, Risa

Reseda
(Spanish) helpful;
(Latin) fragrant flower
Res, Reseta

Reshauna
(African-American)
combo of Re and
Shauna
*Reshana, Reshawna,
Reshie*

Reva
(Hebrew) rainmaker
Ree, Reeva, Rere

Reveca
(Spanish) form of
Rebecca; charming
Reba, Rebeca, Reva

Rexanne
(English) combo of Rex
and Anne; gracious
Rexan, Rexann, Rexanna

Rexella
(English) combo of Rex
and Ella; lighthearted
*Rexalla, Rexel, Rexela,
Rexell, Rexey, Rexi, Rexy*

Rexie
(American) confident
Rex, Rexi, Rexy

Reyna
(English) elegant;
(Greek) peaceful woman
Raina, Rayna, Rey

Reynalda
(German) wise
Raynalda, Rey, Reyrey

Reynolds
(Scottish) wispy
*Rey, Reye, Reynells,
Reynold*

Rhea
(Greek) earthy; mother
of gods; strong
Ria

Rhianna
(Welsh) pure
Rheanna

Rhiannon
(Welsh) goddess;
intuitive
*Rhian, Rhiane, Rhianen,
Rhiann, Rhianon, Rhyan,
Rhye, Riannon*

Rhoda
(Greek) rosy
*Rhodie, Roda, Rodi,
Rodie, Rody, Roe*

Rhona
(Scottish) power-
wielding
Rona, Ronne

Rhonda
(Welsh) vocal;
quintessential
*Rhon, Ron, Ronda,
Ronnie*

Rhondie
(American) perfect
Rond, Rondie, Rondy

Rhonwen
(Welsh) lovely
*Rhonwenne, Rhonwin,
Ronwen*

Ria
(Spanish) water-loving;
river
Reah, Riah

Riana
(Irish) frisky
*Reana, Rere, Rianna,
Rinnie*

Riane
(American) attractive
Reann, Reanne

Rica
(Spanish) celestial
*Ric, Ricca, Rickie, Rieka,
Rika, Ryka*

Richelle
(French) strong and artistic
Chelle, Chellie, Rich, Richel, Richele, Richie

Richesse
(French) wealthy
Richess

Ricki
(American) sporty
Rici, Rick, Rickie, Ricky, Rik, Riki, Rikki

Rico
(Italian) sexy
Reko, Ricco

Rida
(Arabic) satisfied
Ridah

Riley
(Irish) courageous; lively
Reilly, Rylee, Ryleigh, Ryley, Rylie

Rima
(Arabic) graceful; antelope
Rema, Remmee, Remmy, Rimmy, Ryma

Rinda
(Scandinavian) loyal
Rindah

Ring
(American) magical
Ringe, Ryng

Riona
(Irish) regal
Rina, Rine, Rionn, Rionna, Rionne

Ripley
(American) unique
Riplee, Ripli, Riplie

Rissa
(Latin) laughing
Resa, Risa, Riss, Rissah, Rissie

Rita
(Greek) precious pearl
Reda, Reita, Rida

Ritalinda
(Spanish) combo of Rita and Linda; treasured
Linda, Retalinda, Retalynde, Rita, Ritalynd, Ritalynda

Ritz
(American) rich
Rits

Riva
(Hebrew) joining; sparkling
Reva, Revi, Revvy

Rivalee
(Hebrew) combo of Riva and Lee; joined
Rivalea, Riva-Lee

River
(Latin) woman by the stream
Riv

Rivers
(American) trendy

Riza
(Greek) dignified
Reza, Rize

Roberta
(English) brilliant mind
Robbie, Robby, Robertah, Robi

Robin
(English) taken by the wind; bird
Robbie, Robby, Robinn, Robinne, Robyn

Robina
(Scottish) birdlike; robin
Robena

Robinetta
(American) combo of Robin and Etta; graceful dancer
Robbie, Robineta, Robinette

Rochelle
(French) small and strong-willed; (Hebrew) dream-like beauty
Roch, Roche, Rochel, Rochi, Rochie, Rochy, Roshelle

Rockella
(Invented) rocker
Rockell, Rockelle

Rocky
(American) tomboy
Rock, Rockee, Rockey,
Rockie

Roddy
(German) well-known
Rod, Roddee, Roddey,
Roddi, Roddie

Roderica
(German) princess
Rica, Roda, Roddie,
Rodericka, Rodrika

Rogertha
(American) form of
Roger; substantial
Rodge

Roksana
(Polish) dawn
Roksanna, Roksona

Rolanda
(German) rich woman
Rolane, Rollande, Rollie

Rolandan
(German) form of
Roland; from a famous
land
Roland, Rolanden,
Rollie, Rolly

Roma
(Italian) girl from Rome;
adventurous
Romy

Romaine
(French) daredevil
Romain, Romane,
Romayne, Romi

Roman
(Italian) adventurous
Romi, Romie, Rommie,
Rommye, Romyn

Romilda
(Latin) striking
Romelda, Romey, Romie,
Romy

Romilla
(Latin) from Rome; she
who wanders
Romella, Romi, Romie,
Romila

Romilly
(Latin) wanderer
Romillee, Romillie,
Romily

Romona
(Spanish) form of
Ramona
Mona, Rome, Romie,
Romy

Romy
(French) short for
Romaine; roaming
Roe. Romi, Romie

Rona
(Scandinavian, Scottish)
powerful
Rhona, Ronne, Ronni

Ronda
(Welsh) form of Rhonda;
a standout
Ronni

Ronelle
(English) winner
Ronnie

Roney
(Scandinavian) form of
Rona; lively
Roneye, Roni

Ronneta
(English) go-getter
Roneda, Ronnete,
Ronnette, Ronnie

Ronni
(American) energetic
Ron, Ronee, Roni,
Ronnie, Ronny

Rori
(Irish) spirited; brilliant
Rory

Rosa
(Italian) rose;
(German) blushing
beauty
Rose, Rossah, Roza

Rosabella
(Italian) combo of Rosa
and Bella; beautiful rose

Rosabelle
(French) combo of Rosa
and Belle; beautiful rose
Belle, Rosa, Rosabel,
Rosa-Belle

girls

Rosalba
(Latin) glorious as a rose
Rosalbah, Rosey, Rosi,
Rosie, Rosy

Rosalia
(Italian) hanging roses
Rosa, Rosalea,
Rosaleah, Rosaliah,
Roselia, Rosey, Rosi,
Rosie, Rossalia, Rosy

Rosalie
(English) striking dark
beauty
Leelee, Rosa, Rosalee,
RosaLee, Rosa-Lee,
Rosie, Rossalie, Roz,
Rozalee, Rozalie

Rosalind
(Spanish) lovely rose
Lind, Ros, Rosa,
Rosalyn, Rosalynde,
Rosie, Roslyn, Roslynn

Rosalinda
(Spanish) lovely rose
Rosa-Linda, Rosalynda

Rosalvo
(Spanish) rosy-faced
Rosa, Rosey

Rosamaria
(Italian) combo of Rosa
and Maria; rose; devout
Rosa-Maria

Rosamond
(English) beauty
Rosa, Rosamun,
Rosamund, Rose,
Rosemond, Rosie

Rosanna
(English) lovely
Rosannah

Rosaoralia
(Spanish) combo of
Rosa and Oralia; rosy
Rosa Oralia, Rosa-Oralia,
RoseyO

Rose
(Latin) rose; blushing
beauty
Rosa, Rosey, Rosi, Rosie,
Rosy, Roze, Rozee

Roseanna
(English) combo of Rose
and Anna
Rosana, Rosannah,
Rose, Roseana, Rosie

Roseanne
(English) combo of Rose
and Anne
Rosann, Rosanne, Rose
Ann, Rosie

Rosellen
(English) pretty
Roselinn, Roselyn

Rosemarie
(Latin, Scandinavian)
combo of Rose and
Marie
Rose-Marie, Rosemary

Rosemary
(English) combo of Rose
and Mary; sweetheart
Ro, Rose Mary, Rose,
Rosie

Rosenda
(Spanish) rosy
Rose, Rosend, Rosende,
Rosey, Rosie, Senda

Rosetta
(Italian) longlasting
beauty
Rose, Rosy, Rozetta

Rosette
(Latin) flowering; rosy
Rosett, Rosetta

Roshall
(African-American) form
of Rochelle; dreamy
Rochalle, Roshalle

Roshawna
(African-American)
combo of Rose and
Shawna
Rosh, Roshanna, Roshie,
Roshona, Shawn

Roshell
(French) form of
Rochelle; small and
strong-willed
Rochelle, Roshelle

Roshumba
(African-American)
gorgeous
Rosh, Roshumbah

Roshunda
(African-American)
flamboyant
*Rosey, Roshun,
Roshund, Rosie, Roz*

Rosie
(English) bright-cheeked
Rose, Rosi, Rosy

Rosita
(Spanish) pretty
*Roseta, Rosey, Rosie,
Rositta*

Rotella
(American) smart
Rotel, Rotela

Roth
(American) studious
Rothe

Rotnei
(American) bright
Rotnay

Rowena
(Scottish) blissful;
beloved friend
Roe, Roenna, Rowina

Roxanna
(Persian) bright
Roxana, Roxie

Roxanne
(Persian) lovely as the
sun
*Roxane, Roxann, Roxie,
Roxy*

Roxy
(American) sunny
Rox, Roxi, Roxie

Royetta
(American) combo of
Roy and Etta; cowgirl
*Etta, Roy, Roye, Royett,
Royette*

Roynale
(American) motivated
Roy, Royna, Roynal

Roz
(French) short for
Rosalind
Ros, Rozz, Rozzie

Rozena
(American) form of
Rosena; pretty
Roze, Rozenna

Rozonda
(American) pretty
*Rosonde, Rozon,
Rozond*

Rubena
(Hebrew) sassy
Rubyn, Rubyna, Rueben

Rubianney
(American) combo of
Rubi and Anney; shining
*Rubi, Rubianey,
Rubianne, Rubi-Anney,
Rubyann*

Rubilee
(American) combo of
Ruby and Lee; shining
Ruby Lee, Rubylee

Rubina
(Pakistani) gem
Rubi

Rubra
(French) from Ruby;
jewel
Rube, Rue

Ruby
(French) precious jewel
Rubi, Rubie, Rue

Ruby-Jewel
(American) combo of
Ruby and Jewel; sassy
*Rubijewel, Rubyjewel,
Ruby-Jule*

Ruchi
(German) brash

Rudy
(German) sly
Rudee, Rudell, Rudie

Rue
(English, German)
looking back
Ru

Ruelynn
(American) combo of
Rue and Lynn; smart and
famous
*Rue Lynn, Ruelin,
Ruelinn, Rue-Lynn,
Rulynn*

Rufaro
(African) happy

Rula
(American) wild-spirited
Rue, Rulah, Rewela

Rumer
(English) unique
Ru, Rumor

Ruri
(Japanese) emerald
Rure, Rurrie, RuRu

Rusbel
(Spanish) beautiful girl
with reddish hair
Rusbell, Rusbella

Russo
(American) happy
Russoh

Rusty
(English) red-haired girl
Rustee, Rusti

Ruta
(Lithuanian) practical
Rue, Rudah, Rutah

Ruth
(Hebrew) loyal friend
Rue, Ruthie, Ruthy

Ruthanne
(American) combo of
Ruth and Anne
Ruthann

Ruthemma
(American) combo of
Ruth and Emma
Routhemma, Ruthema

Ruthie
(Hebrew) friendly and
young
*Ruth, Ruthey, Ruthi,
Ruthy*

Ryan
(Irish) royal; assertive
*Ryann, Ryen, Ryunn,
Rian*

Ryanna
(Irish) leader
*Rianna, Rianne, Ryana,
Ryanne, Rynn*

Ryba
(Hebrew) traditional
Reba, Ree, Riba, Ribah

Rylee
(Irish) brave
*Rilee, Rili, Ryelee, Ryley,
Ryli, Ryly*

Ryn
(American) form of Wren
Ren, Rynn

Ryne
(Irish) form of Ryan;
divine; special
Rynea, Ryni, Rynie

Rynie
(American) woods-loving
Rinnie, Ryn

Rynn
(American) outdoorsy
woman
*Rin, Rynna, Rynnie,
Wren*

Rynnea
(American) sun-lover
Rynnee, Rynni, Rynnia

Saba
(Arabic) morning star
Sabah

Sabella
(English) spiritual
Bella, Belle, Sabela, Sabell, Sabelle, Sebelle

Sabina
(Latin) desirable
Sabeena, Sabine, Sabinna, Say

Sable
(English) chic
Sabelle, Sabie

Sablette
(American) luxurious
Sable, Sablet

Sabra
(Hebrew) substantial
Sabe, Sabera, Sabrah

Sabrina
(Latin) place name; passionate
Breena, Brina, Brinna, Sabe, Sabreena, Sabrinna

Sacha
(Greek) helpful girl
Sachie, Sachy

Sachi
(Japanese) girl
Sachie, Sashi, Shashie

Sadie
(Hebrew) charmer; princess
Sade, Sadee, Sady, Sadye, Shaday

Saffron
(Indian) spice
Saffrone, Safron

Saga
(Scandinavian) sensual
Sagah

Sagal
(American) action-oriented
Sagall, Segalle

Sage
(Latin) wise
Saige

Sahare
(American) loner

Sahri
(Arabic) giving

Saida
(Hebrew) happy girl
Sada, Sadie

Sailor
(American) outdoorsy
Sail, Saile, Sailer, Saylor

Sajah
(Hindi) meritorious
Sajie, Sayah

Salama
(African) safe

Salena
(Latin) needed; basic
Salene, Sally

Salima
(Arabic) healthy
Salma

Salina
(French) quiet and deep
Sale, Salena

Sally
(Hebrew) princess
Sal, Salli, Sallie

Salma
(Hebrew) peaceful; (Spanish) ingenious
Sal, Sally, Salmah

Salma
(Hindi) safe
Sal, Salwah

Salome
(Hebrew) sensual; peaceful
Sal, Salohme, Salomey, Salomi

Salowmee
(Invented) form of
Salome; peaceful
Sal, Salomee, Salomie,
Salomy, Slowmee

Salvadora
(Spanish) saved
Sal, Salvadorah

Samantha
(Hebrew) good listener
Sam, Samath, Sammi,
Sammie

Samara
(Hebrew) God-led;
watchful
Sam, Samora

Sami
(Hebrew) insightful
Sam, Sammie, Sammy

Samia
(Hindi) joyful
Sameah, Samee,
Sameea, Samina,
Sammy

Samuela
(Hebrew) selected
Samm, Sammi, Sammy,
Samula

Samyrah
(African-American)
music-loving
Samirah, Samyra

Sandi
(Greek) defends others
Sand, Sanda, Sandee,
Sandie, Sandy

Sandra
(Greek) helpful;
protective
Sandrah, Sandy

Sandrea
(Greek) selfless
Sandreea, Sandie,
Sanndria

Sandreen
(American) great
Sandrene, Sandrin,
Sandrine

Sanila
(Indian) full of praise
Sanilla

Sanjuana
(Spanish) from San Juan;
God-loving
Sanwanna

Sanjuanita
(Spanish) from San Juan;
combo of San Juan and
Juanita; believer
Juanita, Sanjuan

Sanna
(Scandinavian) truthful
Sana

Santana
(Spanish) saintly
San, Santanne, Santie,
Santina

Santeene
(Spanish) passionate
Santeena, Santene,
Santie, Santina, Santine,
Satana

Santia
(African) lovable
Santea

Santonina
(Spanish) ardent

Sapphire
(Greek) precious gem
Safire, Saphire, Sapphie,
Sapphyre

Sara
(Hebrew) God's princess
Sae, Sarah, Saree, Sarrie

Sarah-Jessica
(American) charismatic
Sarah Jessica, Sara-Jess,
Sarajessee, Sarajessica

Sarai
(Hebrew) contentious
Sari

Sarajane
(American) combo of
Sara and Jane
Sarahjane

Saralee
(American) combo of
Sara and Lee

Saramay
(American) combo of
Sara and May
Sarah-May, Saramae

Saree
(Hebrew) woman of value
Sarie, Sary

Sarilla
(Spanish) princess
Sarella, Sarill, Sarille

Sarina
(Hebrew) strong
Sareena, Sarena, Sarrie

Sarita
(Spanish) regal
Sareeta, Sarie, Saritah

Sasha
(Russian) beautiful courtesan; helpful
Sacha, Sachie, Sascha, Sasheen, Sashy

Saskia
(Dutch) dramatic
Saskiah

Sassy
(Irish) Saxon girl; flirtatious
Sass, Sassi, Sassie

Satchel
(American) unusual
Satchal

Satin
(French) shiny
Saten

Saturine
(American) form of Saturn
Saturenne, Saturinne, Saturn, Saturyne

Saundra
(Greek) defender
Sandi, Sandra, Sandrah

Savannah
(Spanish) place name; open heart
Sava, Savana, Savanah, Savanna, Seven

Sawyer
(Last name as first name) industrious
Sawya, Sawyar, Sawyhr, Sawyie, Sawyur

Sayde
(American) form of Sadie; charming
Saydey, Saydie

Scally
(Last name as first) introspective
Scalley, Scalli

Scarlett
(English) seductive; unpredictable
Scarlet, Scarletta, Scarlette

Schemika
(African-American) form of Shameka
Schemi, Schemike

Scherry
(American) form of Sherry
Scherri, Scherrie

Schmoopie
(American) baby; sweetie
Schmoopee, Schmoopey, Schmoopy, Shmoopi

Schulyer
(Dutch) form of Skyler; protective
Schulyar, Sky, Skye

Scooter
(American) wild-spirit
Scooder, Scoot

Scotty
(Scottish) girl from Scotland
Scota, Scotti, Scottie

Scout
(French) precocious
Scouts

Scyllaea
(Greek) mythological monster; menace
Cilla, Scylla, Silla

Sea
(American) sea-loving; flowing
Cee, See

Sealy
(Last name as first name) fun-loving
Celie, Seal, Sealie

Seana
(Irish) giving
Seane, Seanna, Suannea

Seandra
(American) form of Deandra; intuitive
Seandre, Seandreah, Seanne

Season
(Latin) special; change
Seas, Seasee, Seasen, Seasie, Seasun, Seazun, Seezun

Sebastiane
(Latin) respected female
Sebastian, Sebbie

Seema
(Hebrew) treasured; softhearted
Seem

Seine
(French) river; flowing
Sane

Sela
(Hebrew) short for Cecilia; substantial
Cela, Celia, Selah, Selia

Selda
(German) sure-footed
Seda, Seldah, Selde, Seldee, Seldey, Seldi, Seldie

Selena
(Greek) like the moon; shapely
Celina, Sela, Seleene, Selene, Selina, Sylena

Selima
(Hebrew) peacemaker
Selema, Selemmah

Selin
(Turkish) calm

Selma
(German) fair-minded female
Selle, Sellma, Selmah, Zele, Zelma

Selona
(Greek) form of Selena; goddess
Celona, Sela, Seli, Selo, Selone

Selsa
(Hispanic) enthusiastic
Sel, Sels

Sema
(Greek) earthy
Semah, Semale, Semele

Semilla
(Spanish) earth mother
Samilla, Sem, Semila, Semillah, Semmie, Semmy, Sumilla

Semone
(American) sentimental
Semonne

Sendy
(American) form of Cindy
Sendee, Sendie

Seneca
(Italian, Native American) leader
Seneka

September
(Latin) serious; month
Seppie, Sept

Septima
(Latin) seventh child
Septimma, Septyma

Sequoia
(Cherokee) giant redwood; formidable
Sekwoya

Serafina
(Hebrew) ardent
Serifina, Seraphina, Seraphine

Seren
(Latin) serene
Ceren, Seran

Serena
(Latin) calm
Sarina, Sereena,
Serenah, Serina

Serendipity
(Invented) mercurial;
lucky
Sere, Seren,
Serendipitee, Serin

Serenity
(American) serene
Sera, Serenitee,
Serenitie

Sesame
(American) inventive
Sesamee, Sezamee

Seth
(Hebrew) set;
appointed; gentle
Sethe

Seymoura
(Invented) form of male
name Seymour; calm
Seymora

Shade
(English) cool
Shadee, Shadi, Shady

Shadow
(English) mysterious
Shado, Shadoh

Shae
(Hebrew) shy
Shay

Shaela
(Irish) pretty
Shae, Shaelie, Shala

Shaelin
(Irish) pretty
Shae, Shaelyn,
Shaelynn, Shalyn

Shaeterral
(African-American)
well-shaped
Shatey, Shatrell,
Shayterral

Shail
(American) pretty
Shale

Shaine
(Hebrew) pretty girl
Shanie, Shay, Shayne

Shainel
(African-American)
animated
Shainell, Shainelle,
Shaynel

Shakira
(Arabic, Spanish) pretty
movement
Shak, Shakeera,
Shakeerah, Shakeira,
Shakie, Skakarah

Shakonda
(African-American) lovely

Shalanda
(African-American) vivid
Shalande, Shally,
Shalunda

Shaleah
(Hebrew) combo of Sha
and Leah; funny
Shalea, Shalee,
Shaleeah

Shaleina
(Turkish) humorist
Shalina, Shalyna,
Shalyne

Shalonda
(African-American)
enthusiastic
Shalie, Shalondah,
Shalonna, Shelonda

Shamara
(Arabic) assertive
Shamarah, Shemera

Shameena
(Arabic) beautiful
Shamee, Shameenah,
Shamina, Shaminna

Shamika
(African-American)
loving
Shameika, Shameka,
Shamekah, Shamika,
Shemeca

Shamsa
(Pakistani) adorable

Shana
(Hebrew) pretty girl
Shaina, Shan, Shanah,
Shane, Shannah,
Shanni, Shannie,
Shanny, Shayna, Shayne

Shanae
   (Irish) generous
   Shan, Shanea, Shanee
Shandee
   (English) hopeful
   Shandi, Shandie,
   Shandy
Shandilyn
   (American) not forsaken
   Shandi, Shandy
Shandra
   (American) fun-loving
   Chandra, Shan, Shandrie
Shane
   (Irish) softspoken
   Shanee, Shanie
Shaneka
   (African-American)
   perky; pretty
   Chaneka, Shan,
   Shanekah, Shanie,
   Shanika
Shanelle
   (African-American)
   variant of Chanel; stylish
   Shanel, Shannel,
   Shannell, Shanny
Shania
   (African) ambitious;
   bright-eyed
   Shane, Shaniah, Shanie,
   Shaniya, Shanya

Shanice
   (African-American)
   bright-eyed
   Chaniece, Shaneese,
   Shani, Shaniece
Shanika
   (African-American)
   pretty; optimistic
   Shan, Shane, Shanee,
   Shaneeka, Shaneika,
   Shaneikah, Shanequa,
   Shaney, Shaneyka
Shaniqua
   (African-American)
   outgoing
   Shane, Shanequa,
   Shanie, Shanikwa,
   Shaniquah, Shanneequa
Shanique
   (African-American)
   outgoing
Shanisha
   (African-American)
   bright
   Chaneisha, Chanisha,
   Shan, Shanecia,
   Shaneisha, Shanie
Shanna
   (Irish) lovely
   Shanah, Shanea,
   Shannah

Shannon
   (Irish) smart
   Shann, Shanna,
   Shannen, Shannyn,
   Shanon
Shanny
   (Irish) bubbly
   Shannee, Shanni,
   Shannie
Shanta
   (French) singing
   Shantah, Shante,
   Shantie
Shantara
   (French) bright-eyed
   Shantay, Shantera,
   Shantie
Shantell
   (American) bright singer
   Chantel, Shantal,
   Shantel
Shanti
   (Hindi) calm
Shaquan
   (American) fine
   Shak, Shaq, Shaquanda,
   Shaquanna, Shaquie,
   Shaquonda
Shaquita
   (African-American)
   delight
   Shaq, Shaqueita,
   Shaqueta, Shaquie

Shara
(Hebrew) form of
Sharon; open
Sharah, Sharra, Sherah

Shardae
(Arabic) wanderer
Chardae, Sade, Shaday,
Sharday, SharDay

Sharee
(American) dear
Sharie

Shari
(French) beloved girl
Shar, Sharree, Sher,
Sherri

Sharice
(French) graceful
Cherise, Shar, Shareese,
Shares

Sharif
(Russian) mysterious
Shar, Shareef, Sharey,
Shari, Sharrey, Shary

Sharita
(French) charitable
Shar, Shareetah, Shareta

Sharla
(American) friendly
Sharlah

Sharlene
(German) form of
Charlene
Charleen, Charlene,
Shar, Sharl, Sharleen,
Sharline, Sharlyne

Sharmeal
(African-American)
exhilarating
Sharm, Sharma, Sharme,
Sharmele

Sharna
(Hebrew) broad-minded
Sharn, Sharnah

Sharnea
(American) quiet
Sharnay, Sharnee,
Sharney

Sharnelle
(African-American)
spiritual
Sharnel, Sharnle, Sharny

Sharnette
(American) fighter
Chanet, Charnette,
Shanet, Sharn, Sharnett,
Sharney

Sharon
(Hebrew) open heart;
desert plain
Shar, Sharen, Shari,
Sharin, Sharren,
Sharron, Sharry, Sharyn,
Sheron, Sherron

Sharonda
(African-American) open
Sharondah, Sheronda

Sharrona
(Hebrew) open
Sharona, Sharonne,
Sherona, Shironah

Sharterica
(African-American)
beloved
Sharter, Sharterika,
Shartrica, Sharty

Shasta
(American)
majestic mind
Shastah

Shatoya
(African-American)
spirited
Shatoye, Shay,
Shaytoya, Toya

Shauna
(Hebrewm, Irish)
giving heart
Shauhna, Shaunie,
Shaunna, Shawna

Shaune
(American) wide smile
Shaun, Shaunie, Shawn

Shauntee
(Irish) dancing eyes
Shaun, Shawntey,
Shawntie, Shawnty

Shavon
(Irish) devout; energetic
Chavon, Chavonne,
Shavaun, Shavon,
Shavonne

Shawana
(African-American)
dramatic
Shavaun, Shawahna,
Shawanna, Shawnie

Shawandreka
(African-American) gutsy
Shawan, Shawand,
Shawandrika, Shawann,
Shawuan

Shawn
(American) smiling
Shawne, Shawnee,
Shawnie, Shawny

Shawnda
(Irish) helpful friend
Shaunda, Shaundah,
Shona

Shawneequa
(African-American)
loquacious
Shauneequa,
Shawneekwa

Shawnel
(African-American)
audacious
Shaune, Shaunel,
Shaunelle, Shawn,
Shawnee, Shawnelle,
Shawney, Shawni

Shawnie
(American) playful
Shaunie, Shawni

Shayjuana
(African-American)
combo of Shay and
Juana; cheerful
Shajuana, Shajuanna,
Shay

Shaylie
(Latin) playful
Shaleigh, Shaylea,
Shaylee, Shealee

Shayne
(Hebrew) form of Shane;
pretty
Shaine, Shane, Shay,
Sheyne

Shayonda
(African-American) regal
Shay, Shaya, Shayon,
Shayonde, Sheyonda,
Yona, Yonda

Shea
(Irish) soft beauty
Shae, Shay

Sheba
(Hebrew) short for
Bathsheba; queenly
Chebah, Sheeba,
Sheebah

Sheddreka
(African-American)
dynamo
Shedd, Sheddrik,
Shedreke

Sheela
(Hindi) gentle spirit
Sheelah, Sheeli, Sheila

Sheelyah
(Irish) form of Shelia;
woman
Sheel, Sheil

Sheena
(Hebrew) shining
Sheen, Sheenah, Shena

Sheeneva
(American) combo of
Sheena and Eva; shiny
Shee, Sheen, Sheena,
Sheeny

Sheila
(Irish) vivacious; divine
woman
Shaylah, Sheela, Sheilia,
Sheilya, Shel

Shelby
(English) dignified
Chelby, Shel, Shelbee,
Shelbi, Shelbie

Shelia
(Irish) woman; gorgeous
Shelya, Shelyah, Shillya

Shelita
(Spanish) little girl
Chelita, Shelite, Shelitta

Shelley
(English) outdoorsy;
meadow
Shelee, Shelli, Shelly

Shena
(Irish) shining
Shenae, Shenea, Shenna

Sheneeka
(African-American) easygoing
Shaneeka, Shaneka, Sheneecah, Sheneka

Shepard
(English) vigilant
Shep, Sheperd, Shepherd, Sheppie

Shera
(Hebrew) light-hearted
Sheera, Sheerah, Sherah

Sheray
(French) saucy
Cheray, Sherayah

Sherael
(American) form of Sherry; distinctive
Sheraelle, Sherelle, Sherryelle

Sheree
(French) dearest girl
Sheeree, Sher, Shere

Sherele
(French) bouncy
Sher, Sherell, Sherrie

Sheresa
(American) dancer
Sher, Sherisa, Sherissa, Sherri

Sheretta
(American) sparkling
Shere, Sherette

Sheri
(French) sparkling eyes
Sher, Sherri, Sherrie

Sherice
(French) artistic
Cherise, Sher, Shereece, Sherisse

Sheridan
(Irish) free spirit; outstanding
Cheridan, Cheridyn, Sheridyn, Sherridan

Sherilyn
(American) combo of Sheri and Lyn
Sharilyn, Sheralyn, Sheri-Lyn, Sheri-Lynn, Sherry-Lynn

Sherita
(French) stylish
Cherita, Sheretta

Sherleen
(American) easygoing
Sherl, Sherlene, Sherline, Sherlyn, Shirline

Sherlitha
(Spanish) feminine
Sherl, Sherli

Sherolynna
(American) lovely
Cherolina, Sher, Sheralina, Sherrilina

Sherrill
(English) bright
Cheril, Cherrill, Sherelle, Sheril, Sherrell, Sheryl

Sherrunda
(African-American) free spirit
Sharun, Sharunda, Sherr, Sherrunde, Sherunda

Sherry
(French) outgoing
Sher, Sheri, Sherreye, Sherri, Sherrie, Sherye

Sherrylynn
(American) combo of Sherry and Lynn
Sharolyn, Sher, Sherilyn, Sherry, Sherylynn

Sheryl
(French) beloved woman
Cheryl, Sharal, Sher, Sheral, Sheril, Sherill

Shevonne
(Gaelic) ambitious
Shavon, Shevaune, Shevon

Sheyenne
(Native American) form
of Cheyenne; audacious
*Shey, Shianne, Shyann,
Shyanne, Shyenne*

Sheyn
(Hebrew) beauty

Shifra
(Hebrew) beautiful
woman
Sheefra, Shifrah

Shikendra
(African-American)
spirited
Shiki, Shikie, Skikend

Shiloh
(Hebrew) gifted by God
Shilo, Shy

Shine
(American) shining
example
Shena, Shina

Shiney
(American) glowing
Shine, Shiny

Shinikee
(African-American)
glorious
*Shinakee, Shinikey,
Shynikee*

Shira
(Hebrew) song; singer
Shirah, Shiree

Shireen
(English) charmer
*Shareen, Shiree,
Shireene, Shirene, Shiri,
Shiry, Shoreen, Shureen,
Shurene*

Shirleen
(American) nature-loving
Shirlene, Shirline

Shirley
(English) bright
meadow; cheerful girl
*Sherlee, Sherley, Sherly,
Shir, Shirl, Shirly*

Shlonda
(African-American)
bright
Londa, Schlonda, Shodie

Shola
(Hebrew) spirited
Sholah

Shona
(Irish) open-hearted
Shonah, Shonie

Shonda
(Irish) runner
*Shondah, Shonday,
Shondie, Shounda,
Shoundah*

Shonta
(Irish) fearless
*Shauntah, Shawnta,
Shon, Shontie*

Shony
(Irish) shining
*Shona, Shonee, Shoni,
Shonie*

Shoshana
(Hebrew) beautiful; lily
*Shoshanna,
Shoshannah, Shoshauna*

Shulondia
(African-American)
dynamic
*Shulee, Shuley, Shuli,
Shulonde, Shulondea,
Shulondiah*

Shuntay
(African-American)
Shuntae

Shura
(Greek) protective

Shyanne
(Native American) form
of Cheyenne
Shy

Shyla
(English) creative
Shila, Shy, Shylah

Shyne
(American) standout
Shine

Sia
(Welsh) calm; believer
Cia, Seea

Sian
(Welsh) believer

Siana
(Welsh) ebullient
Sian, Siane

Sibley
(Anglo-Saxon) related
Siblee, Sibly

Sibyl
(Greek) intuitive
Cibyl, Cyb, Cybil, Cybill, Cybyl, Sib, Sibbi, Sibbie, Sibby, Sibella, Sibylla, Sybela, Sybil, Sybyl

Sidonia
(French) spiritual
Sid, Sidoneah, Sydonya

Sidonie
(French) appealing
Sidonee, Sidony, Sydoni

Sidra
(Latin) star
Cidra, Siddey, Siddie, Siddy, Sidi, Sidrie, Sydra

Sienna
(Place name) delicate; reddish-brown
Siena, Siene

Sierra
(Place name) peaks; outdoorsy
Cierra, Searah, Searrah, Siera, Sierrah, Sierre

Sigfrid
(German) peacemaker
Sig, Sigfred, Sigfreid, Siggy

Signe
(Latin) symbol
Sig, Signie, Signy

Sigourney
(English) leader who conquers
Sig, Siggie, Signe, Signy, Sygourny

Sigrid
(Scandinavian) lovely
Segred, Sig, Siggy, Sigrede

Sigrun
(Scandinavian) winning
Cigrun, Segrun

Sikita
(American) active
Sikite

Silvanna
(Spanish) nature-lover
Sil, Silva, Silvana, Silvane, Silvanne, Silver

Silver
(Anglo-Saxon) light-haired
Silva, Silvar, Sylver

Silvia
(Latin) deep; woods-loving
Sill, Silvy, Siviah, Sylvia

Simi
(Lebanese)
Sim

Simica
(American)
Sim, Simika, Simmy

Simona
(American) form of Simon; wise
Sim, Simon, Sims

Simona
(Hebrew) svelte
Simonah, Symmie, Symona, Syms

Simone
(French) wise and thoughtful
Sim, Simonie, Symone

Sinai
(Place name)
Mt. Sinai

Sinclair
(French) person from St. Clair; admired; (Last name as first name) dynamic
Cinclair, Sinclare, Synclair, Synclare

Sinead
(Irish) singer; believer in a gracious God
Shanade

Siobhan
(Irish) believer; lovely
Chevon, Chevonne, Chivon, Shavonne, Shevon

Siphronia
(Greek) sensible
*Ciphronia, Sifronea,
Sifronia, Syfronia*

Siren
(Greek) enchantress
Syren

Sirena
(Greek) enchantress
*Sireena, Sirenah, Sirine,
Sisi, Sissy, Syrena*

Sissy
(Latin) short for Cecilia
or little sister; immature;
ingenue
*Cissee, Cissey, Cissy, Sis,
Sissi, Sissie*

Sistene
(Italian) spiritual
Sisteen, Sisteene

Skye
(Scottish) place name;
high-minded; head in
the clouds

Skyler
(Dutch) protective;
sheltering
*Schuyler, Skieler, Skilar,
Skiler, Skye, Skyla,
Skylar, Skylie, Skylor*

Slane
(Irish) form of Sloane;
striking
Slaine

Sloane
(Irish) strong
Sloan, Slone

Smiley
(American) radiant
*Smile, Smilee, Smiles,
Smili, Smily*

Snooks
(American) sweetie
Snookee, Snookie

Snow
(American) quiet
Sno, Snowdrop, Snowy

Socorro
(Spanish) helpful
Socoro

Sofya
(Russian) wise
Sofi, Sofie, Sofiya

Solana
(Spanish) sunny
Solanah, Soley, Solie

Solange
(French) sophisticated
Solie

Soledad
(Spanish) solitary
woman
*Saleda, Solada, Solay,
Sole, Solee, Solie, Solita*

Soleil
(French) sun

Soline
(French) solemn
Solen, Solenne, Souline

Sommer
(English) warm
*Sommie, Summer,
Summi*

Sonay
(Asian) bright-eyed
Sonnae

Song
(Chinese) independent

Sonia
(Slavic) effervescent
*Soni, Sonnie, Sonny,
Sonya*

Sonja
(Scandinavian) bright
woman

Sonnet
(American) poetic
Sonnett, Sonni, Sonny

Sonoma
(Place name) wine-
loving
Sonomah

Sonora
(Place name) easygoing
Sonorah

Sonseria
(American) giving
Seria, Sonsere, Sonsey

Sonya
(Greek) wise
Sonia, Sonje

Soo
(Korean) gentle spirit

Soon-Yi
(Chinese) delightful;
assertive
Soozi
(American) form of Suzy;
friendly
*Soos, Sooz, Souz,
Souze, Souzi*
Sophia
(Greek) wise one
*Sofeea, Sofi, Sofia,
Sofie, Sophea, Sophie,
Sophy*
Sorangel
(Spanish) heavenly
Sorange
Soraya
(Persian) royal
Sorcha
(Irish) bright
Shorshi, Sorsha, Sorshie
Sorrel
(English) delicate
*Sorel, Sorell, Sorie,
Sorree, Sorrell, Sorri,
Sorrie*
Sozos
(Hindi) clingy
Sosos
Spencer
(English) sophisticate
Spence, Spenser

Spirit
(American) lively;
spirited
Spirite, Spyrit
Sprague
(American) respected
Sprage
Spring
(English) springtime;
fresh
Spryng
Stacey
(Greek) hopeful and
spiritual
*Stace, Staci, Stacie,
Stacy, Staycee*
Stacia
(English) short for
Anastasia; devout
*Stace, Stacie, Stasia,
Stayshah*
Stanise
(American) darling
*Stanee, Staneese, Stani,
Stanice, Staniece*
Starla
(American) shining
Starlah, Starlie
Starlite
(American) extraordinary
Starlight, Starr
Starr
(English) shining star
Star

Stasia
(Greek, Russian)
Stacie, Stasie, Stasya
Stefanie
(Greek) regal; (German)
crowned
*Stafanie, Stefannye,
Stefany, Steff, Steffany,
Steffie, Stephanie*
Steffi
(Greek) short for
Stephanie; crowned;
athletic
Steffie, Steffy, Stefi
Stefnee
(American) form of
Stephanie/Stefanie;
regal
Stef, Steffy
Stella
(Latin) bright star
Stele, Stelie
Stephanie
(Greek) regal
*Stefanie, Steff, Steffie,
Stephenie, Stephney*
Stephene
(French, Greek) dignified
Steph, Stephie, Stephine
Stephney
(Greek) crowned
*Stef, Steph, Stephie,
Stephnie*

Sterla
(American) quality
Sterl, Sterlie, Stirla
Stevie
(Greek, American) jovial
Steve, Stevee, Stevey, Stevi
Stockard
(English) stockyard; sturdy
Stockerd, Stockyrd
Storelle
(Invented) legend
Storee, Storell, Storey, Stori
Stormy
(American) impulsive
Storm, Stormi, Stormie
Story
(American) creative
Stori, Storie, Storee, Storey
Sue
(Hebrew) flower-like; lily
Susy, Suze, Suzy
Suellen
(American) combo of Sue and Ellen
SueEllen, Sue-Ellen
Sugar
(American) sweet
Shug

Sugy
(Spanish) short for the name Sugar; sweet
Sug, Sugey, Sugie
Suki
(Japanese) beloved
Suke, Sukie, Suky
Sula
(Greek) sea-going
Soola, Sue, Suze
Sullivan
(Last name as first name) brave-hearted
Sulli, Sullie, Sullivin, Sully
Summer
(English) summery; fresh
Somer, Sommer, Sum, Summie
Sun
(Korean) obedient girl
Suna, Suni, Sunnie
Sundancer
(American) easygoing
Sunndance
Sunday
(Latin) day of the week; sunny
Sun, Sundae, Sundaye, Sundee, Sunney, Sunni, Sunnie, Sunny, Sunnye
Sunna
(American) sunny
Sun, Suna

Sunny
(English) bright attitude
Sonny, Sun, Sunni, Sunnye
Sunshine
(American) sunny
Suprina
(American) supreme
Suprinna
Surrender
(Word as name) dramatic
Surren
Susan
(Hebrew) lily; pretty flower
Soozan, Sue, Susahn, Susanne, Susehn, Susie, Suzan
Susannah
(Hebrew) gentle
Sue, Susah, Susanna, Susie, Suzannah
Susie
(American) short for Susan
Susey, Susi, Susy, Suze, Suzi, Suzie, Suzy
Suz
(American) short for Susan; lily; pretty flower
Suze

Suzanne
(English) fragrant
Susanne, Suzan,
Suzane, Suzann, Suze

Suzette
(French) pretty little one
Sue, Susette, Suze

Svea
(Swedish) patriotic
Svay

Svetlana
(Russian) star bright
Sveta, Svete

Swanhildda
(Teutonic) swan-like;
graceful
Swan, Swanhild, Swann,
Swanney, Swanni,
Swannie, Swanny

Sweeney
(Irish) young and
rambunctious
Sweenee, Sweeny

Sweetpea
(American) sweet
Sweet-Pea, Sweetie

Swell
(Invented) good
Swelle

Swift
(Last name as first
name) bold
Swiftie, Swifty

Swoosie
(American) unique
Swoose, Swoozie

Sybil
(Greek) future-gazing
Sibel, Sibyl, Syb, Sybill,
Sybille, Sybyl

Sydlyn
(American) quiet
Sidlyn, Sydlin, Sydlinne

Sydney
(French) enthusiastic
Sidney, Syd, Sydnee,
Sydnie

Syl
(Latin) woods-loving
Sill

Sylvana
(Latin) forest; natural
woman
Silvanna, Syl, Sylvie

Sylvia
(Latin) sylvan; girl of the
forest
Syl, Sylvea

Sylvie
(Latin) sylvan;
peacefulness
Sil, Silvie, Silvy, Syl,
Sylvey, Sylvi, Sylvy

Sylwia
(Polish) serene; in the
woods
Silwia

Symira
(American) enthusiastic
Sym, Symra, Syms,
Symyra

Symone
(Hebrew) good listener
Sym

Symphony
(American) musical
Simphony, Symfonie,
Symfony, Symphonee,
Symphonie

Synora
(American) languid
Cinora, Sinora, Synee,
Syni, Synor, Synore

Synpha
(American) capable
Sinfa, Sinpha, Synfa

Syreta
(American)
Sireta

Tabia
(African) talented girl
Tabitha
(Greek) graceful; gazelle
Tabatha, Tabbatha, Tabbi, Tabytha
Tacha
(American) form of Tasha (from Natalie); born on Christmas
Tach
Tacho
(American) form of Tasha (from Natalie); born on Christmas
Tacie
(American) healthy
Tace, Taci, Tacy
Taesha
(American) sterling character
Tahisha, Taisha, Taisha, Tisha

Taffeta
(American) shiny material
Tafeta, Taffetah, Taffi, Taffy
Taffy
(Welsh) sweet and beloved
Taffee, Taffey, Taffi
Tai
(American) fond
Tie, Tye
Tajudeen
(Spanish) clingy
Taj, Tajjy, Taju
Takara
(Japanese) beloved gem
Taka, Taki
Takeya
(African-American) knowing
Takeyah
Takia
(Arabic) spiritual
Taki, Tikia, Tykia
Takira
(American) combo of Ta and Kira; prayerful
Kira, Takera, Tikiri
Takisha
(African-American) combo of Ta and Kisha; joyful
Takeisha, Takish, Tekisha, Tykisha

Talent
(American) self-assured
Talynt
Talesha
(African-American) friendly
Tal, Taleesh, Taleisha, Talisha, Tallie, Telesha
Tali
(Hebrew) confident
Talia
(Greek) golden; dew from heaven
Tahlia, Tali, Tallie, Tally, Talya, Talyah
Talibah
(African) intellectual
Tali, Talib, Taliba
Talitha
(African-American) inventive
Taleta, Taletha, Talith, Tally
Tallulah
(Native American) leaping water; sparkling girl
Talie, Talley, Tallula, Talula, Talulah
Talluse
(American) bold
Talloose, Tallu, Taluce

Talou
(American) saucy
Talli, Tallou, Tally

Tam
(Japanese) decorative

Tamaka
(Japanese) bracelet;
adorned female

Tamala
(American) kind
*Tam, Tama, Tamela,
Tammie, Tammy*

Tamar
(Hebrew) palm; breezy
Tama, Tamarr

Tamara
(Hebrew) royal female
*Tamera, Tammy, Tamora,
Tamra*

Tamay
(American) form of
Tammy; soft
Tamae, Tamaye

Tambara
(American) high-energy
*Tam, Tamb, Tambra,
Tamby, Tammy*

Tamber
(American) combo of T
and Amber; energetic
*Amber, Tam, Tambey,
Tambur*

Tambusi
(African) frank
Tam, Tambussey, Tammy

Tame
(American) calm

Tamefa
(African-American) form
of Tameka
Tamefah, Tamifa

Tamesha
(African-American) open
face
*Tamesh, Tamisha,
Tammie, Tammy*

Tamesis
(Spanish) name for the
Thames River
Tam, Tamey

Tamika
(African-American) lively
*Tameca, Tameeka,
Tameka, Tamieka,
Tamikah, Tammi,
Tammie, Tammy, Temeka*

Tamiko
(Japanese) the people's
child
Tami, Tamico, Tamika

Tamirisa
(Indian) night; dark
*Risa, Tami, Tamirysa,
Tamrisa, Tamyrisa*

Tammi
(American) sweetheart
*Tam, Tammie, Tammy,
Tammye*

Tamra
(Hebrew) sweet girl
Tammie, Tamora, Tamrah

Tamsin
(English) benevolent
*Tam, Tami, Tammee,
Tammey, Tammy,
Tammye, Tamsa,
Tamsan, Tamsen*

Tamyrah
(African-American)
vocalist
Tamirah

Tana
(Slavic) petite princess
Taina, Tan, Tanah, Tanie

Tandy
(English) team player
Tanda, Tandi, Tandie

Tane
(Polynesian) fertile

Tanesha
(African) strong
*Tanish, Tanisha,
Tannesha, Tannie*

Tangela
(American) combo of Tan
and Angela
T'Angela

Tangelia
(Greek) angel
Gelia, Tange, Tangey

Tangenika
(American) form of
former country
Tanganyika
Tange, Tangi, Tangy

Tangi
(American)
Tangee

Tango
(Spanish) dance
Tangoh

Tangyla
(Invented) form of
Tangela; special
Tange, Tangy

Tani
(Slavic) glorious
Tahnie, Tanee, Tanie

Tania
(Russian, Slavic)
queenly
Tannie, Tanny, Tanya

Tanina
(American) bold
*Tan, Tana, Tanena,
Taninah, Tanney, Tanni,
Tannie, Tanny, Tanye,
Tanyna*

Tanise
(American) unique
Tanes, Tanis

Tanish
(Greek) eternal
Tan, Tanesh, Tanny

Tanisha
(African-American)
talkative
*Taniesha, Tannie,
Tenisha, Tinishah*

Tansy
(Latin) pretty
Tan, Tancy, Tansee, Tanzi

Tanuneka
(African-American)
gracious
Nuneka, Tanueka, Tanun

Tanya
(Russian) queenly
bearing
*Tahnya, Tan, Tanyie,
Tawnyah, Tonya*

Tanyanika
(African-American)
combo of Tayna and
Nika; wild spirit
*Nike, Tanya, Tanyani,
Yanika*

Tanyav
(Slavic) regal
Tanyev

Tanyette
(Italian) talkative
Tanye, Tanyee, Tanyett

Tanze
(Greek) form of Tansy;
eternal
*Tans, Tansee, Tanz,
Tanzee, Tanzey, Tanzi*

Tapa
(Spanish) little snack
Tapas

Tapice
(Spanish) covered
*Tapeece, Tapeese,
Tapese, Tapiece, Tapp,
Tappy*

Taquanna
(African-American) noisy
*Takki, Takwana,
Taquana, Taque, Taquie*

Taquesha
(African-American) joyful
Takie, Takwesha

Taquilla
(Spanish) form of
tequila, the liquor; lively
*Takela, Takelah, Taque,
Taquella, Taqui, Taquile,
Taquille*

Tara
(Gaelic) towering
Tarah, Tari, Tarra

Taro
(Card name) farsighted
Taroh

Tarsha
(American) combo of
Tasha and Tara
Tarsh, Tay

Taryn
(American) combo of
Tara and Karyn;
exuberant; (Irish) bright;
combo of Tara and Erin
*Taran, Taren, Tarran,
Tarrin, Tarron*

Tasha
(Russian) Christmas-
born baby
*Tacha, Tahshah, Tash,
Tashie, Tasia, Tasie, Tasy,
Tasya*

Tashanah
(African-American)
spunky
Tash, Tashana

Tashanee
(African-American) lively
Tashaunie

Tashawndra
(African-American)
bright smiling
*Tasha, Tashaundra,
Tashie*

Tashel
(African-American)
studious
*Tasha, Tashelle, Tashelle,
Tochelle*

Tashza
(African-American) form
of Tasha; bright
Tashi, Tashy, Tashzah

Tassi
(Slavic) bold
Tassee, Tassey, Tassy

Tate
(English) short

Tateeahna
(Invented) form of
Tatiana; snow queen

Tatiana
(Russian) snow queen
*Tanya, Tatania, Tatia,
Tatianna, Tatiannia,
Tatie, Tattianna, Tatyana,
Tatyanna*

Tatum
(English) cheery; high-
spirited
Tata, Tate, Tatie, Tayte

Tavia
(Latin) short for Octavia;
light
Tava, Taveah, Tavi

Tawannah
(African-American)
talkative
*Tawana, Tawanda,
Tawanna, Tawona*

Tawanner
(American) loquacious
Tawanne, Twanner

Tawanta
(African-American) smart
Tawan, Tawante

Tawny
(American) tan-skinned
*Tawn, Tawnee, Tawni,
Tawnie*

Tawnya
(American) form of
Tonya; tan
*Tawnie, Tawnyah, Tonya,
Tonyah*

Tawyn
(American) reliable; tan
*Tawenne, Tawin,
Tawynne*

Tayla
(American) doll-like
Taila, Taylah

Taylor
(English) tailor by trade;
style-setter
*Tailor, Talor, Tay, Taye,
Taylar, Tayler*

Teagan
(Irish) worldly; creative
Teague, Teegan, Tegan

Teague
(Irish) creative
Tee, Teegue, Tegue

Teah
(Greek) goddess
Tea

Teale
(English) blue-green;
bird
Teal, Teala

Teamikka
(African-American) form
of Tamika; lively
Teamika

Teana
(American) form of Tina;
high-energy
Teanah, Teane

Tecoa
(American) precocious
Tekoa

Teddi
(Greek) cuddly
Ted, Teddie, Teddy

Tedra
(Greek) outgoing
Teddra, Tedrah

Tejuana
(Mexican) place name
T'Juana, Tijuana

Tekira
(American) legendary
Tekera, Teki

Tekla
(Greek) legend; divine
glory
*Tekk, Teklah, Thekla,
Tikla, Tiklah*

Telina
(American) storyteller
*Teline, Telyna, Telyne,
Tilina*

Telsa
(American) form of
Tessa; successful
Telly

Temetris
(African-American)
respected
*Teme, Temi, Temitris,
Temmy*

Tempest
(French) tempestuous;
stormy
*Tempeste, Tempie,
Tempyst*

Templa
(Latin) spiritual;
moderate
Temp, Templah

Tenesha
(African-American)
clever
*Tenesia, Tenicha,
Tenisha, Tennie*

Tennille
(American) innovative
*Tanielle, Tanile, Ten,
Teneal, Tenile, Tenneal,
Tennelle, Tennie*

Teo
(Spanish) from Spanish
male name Teodoro;
God's gift
Teeo, Teoh

Teodora
(Scandinavian) God's gift
Teo, Teodore

Tequila
(Spanish) alcoholic
beverage
*Tequela, Tequilla, Tiki,
Tiquilia*

Teresa
(Greek) gardener
*Taresa, Terese, Terhesa,
Teri, Terre, Tess, Tessie,
Treece, Tressa, Tressae*

Terese
(Greek) nurturing
Tarese, Therese, Treece

Tereso
(Spanish) reaper
Tere, Terese

Teri
(Greek) reaper
Terre, Terri, Terrie

Terilyn
(American) combo of Teri
and Lynn
*Terelyn, Terrelynn,
Terrilynn, Terri-Lynn*

Terolyn
(American) combo of
Tere and Carolyn;
harvesting; flirtatious
*Tarolyn, Tero, Terolinn,
Terolinne*

Terra
(Latin) earthy; name for
someone born under an
astrological earth sign
Tera, Terrie
Terrell
(Greek) hardy
*Ter, Teral, Terell, Terrelle,
Terrie, Teryl*
Terrena
(Latin) smooth-talking
Terina, Terrina, Terry
Terry
(Greek) short for
Theresa
*Teri, Terre, Terrey, Terri,
Tery*
Tertia
(Latin) third
*Ters, Tersh, Tersha,
Tersia*
Tess
(Greek) harvesting life
Tesse
Tessa
(Greek) reaping a
harvest
Tesa, Tessie, Teza
Tessica
(American) form of
Jessica; friendly
*Tesica, Tess, Tessa,
Tessie, Tessika*

Tessie
(Greek) form of Theresa;
wonderful
Tessey, Tessi, Tezi
Thada
(Greek) appreciative
Thadda, Thaddeah
Thadyne
(Hebrew) worthy of
praise
Thadee, Thadine, Thady
Thalassa
(Greek) sensitive
*Talassa, Thalassah,
Thalasse*
Thalia
(Greek) joyful; fun
Thalya
Tharamel
(Invented) form of the
word caramel; dedicated
Thara
Thea
(Greek) goddess
*Teah, Teeah, Theah,
Theeah, Theo, Tiah*
Theda
(American) confident
Thada, Thedah
Thelma
(Greek) giver
Thel

Theodora
(Greek) sweetheart;
God's gift
*Dora, Teddi, Teddie,
Teddy, Tedi, Tedra,
Tedrah, Theda, Theo,
Theodorah, Theodrah*
Theola
(Greek) excellent
Theo, Theolah, Thie
Theone
(Greek) serene
Theonne
Theresa
(Greek) reaping a
harvest
*Reza, Teresa, Terri,
Terrie, Terry*
Therese
(Greek) reaping a
harvest
*Tereece, Terese, Terise,
Terry*
Theta
(Greek) letter in Greek
alphabet; substantial
Thayta, Thetah
Thim
(Thai) ice cream; sweet
Thirzah
(Hebrew) pleasant
Thirza, Thursa, Thurza

Thomasina
(Hebrew) twin
*Tom, Toma, Tomasa,
Tomasina, Tomina,
Tommie, Toto*

Thora
(Scandinavian) thunder-
like
Thorah

Thyra
(Scandinavian) loud
Thira

Tia
(Greek) princess;
(Spanish) aunt
Teah, Tee, Teia, Tiah

Tian
(Greek) lovely
*Ti, Tiane, Tiann, Tianne,
Tyan, Tyann, Tyanne, Tye*

Tiana
(Greek) highest beauty
*Tana, Teeana, Tiane,
Tiona*

Tianth
(American) pretty and
impetuous
*Teanth, Tia, Tian,
Tianeth*

Tiara
(Latin) crowned goddess
*Teara, Tearra, Tee,
Teearah, Tierah, Tira*

Tibby
(American) frisky
Tib, Tibb, Tybbee

Tibisay
(American) uniter
Tibi, Tibisae

Tichanda
(African-American)
stylish
Tichaunda, Tishanda

Tiena
(Spanish) earthy
Teena

Tierah
(Latin) jeweled;
ornament
Tia, Tiarra, Tiera

Tierney
(Irish) wealthy
*Teern, Teerney, Teerny,
Tiern*

Tifaya
(Greek) form of Tiffany
*Tifaya, Tifayane, Tiff,
Tiffy*

Tiffany
(Greek) lasting love
*Tifanie, Tiff, Tiffanie,
Tiffenie, Tiffi, Tiffie, Tiffy,
Tiphanie, Tyfannie*

Tigerlily
(English) flower

Tigress
(Latin) wild
Tigris, Tye, Tygris

Tiki
(Place name) kinetic
energy
Tekee

Tilda
(German) short for
Matilda; powerful
Telda, Tildie, Till, Tylda

Tilla
(German) industrious
Tila

Tilly
(German) cute; strong
Till, Tillee, Tillie

Timmie
(Greek) short for
Timothie; honorable
Tim, Timi, Timmy

Timothie
(Greek) honorable
*Tim, Timmie, Timothea,
Timothy*

Tina
(Latin, Spanish) little
and lively
Teena, Teenie, Tena, Tiny

Tionne
(American) hopeful
Tionn

Tipper
(Irish) pourer of water;
nurturing
Tip, Tippy, Typper

Tippett
(American) giving

Tippie
(American) generous
Tippi, Tippy

Tirrza
(Hebrew) sweet;
precious
*Thirza, Thirzah, Tirza,
Tirzah*

Tisa
(African) ninth child
Tesa, Tesah, Tisah

Tish
(Latin) happy
Tysh

Tisha
(Latin) joyful
*Tesha, Ticia, Tishah,
Tishie*

Tishunette
(African-American)
happy girl
Tish, Tisunette

Tobago
(Place name) West
Indies island; islander
Bago, ToTo

Tobi
(Hebrew) good
Tobie, Toby

Toffey
(American) spirited
*Toff, Toffee, Toffi, Toffie,
Toffy*

Toinette
(Latin) wonderful
*Toin, Toinett, Toney,
Tony, Toynet*

Tollie
(Hebrew) confident
*Toll, Tollee, Tolli, Tolly,
Tollye*

Toma
(Latin) short for
Tomasina
*Tomas, Tomgirl, Tommi,
Tommie, Tommy*

Tomeka
(African-American) form
of Tamlka
Tomeke

Tomiko
(Japanese) wealthy
Miko, Tamiko, Tomi

Tomitria
(African-American) form
of Tommy
Tomi

Tommie
(Hebrew) sassy
Tom, Tomi, Tommy

Tonaya
(American) valuable
Tona, Tone

Tonia
(Latin) a wonder
*Toneah, Tonya, Tonyah,
Toyiah*

Tonietta
(American) combo of
Toni and Etta; valuable
Toni, Toniett, Toniette

Tonisha
(African-American) lively
*Nisha, Tona, Toneisha,
Tonesha, Tonie, Tonish*

Toni
(Latin) meritorious
Tone, Tonee, Tonie, Tony

Tonia
(Latin) daring
*Tonni, Tonnie, Tony,
Tonya*

Topaz
(Latin) gemstone;
sparkling
Tophaz

Topekia
(American) form of
Topeka
*Topeka, Topeke,
Topekea*

Topsy
(English) topnotch
Toppie, Topsi, Topsie

Tora
(Scandinavian) thunder

Tori
(Scottish) rich and
winning
*Toree, Torri, Torrie, Torry,
Tory*

Torill
(Scandinavian) loud
Toril, Torille

Torrance
(Place name) confident
Torr, Torri

Tosha
(American) form of Tasha
Tosh

Tosha
(Slavic) priceless
Tosh, Toshia

Tova
(Hebrew) good woman
Tovah

Toy
(American) playful
Toia, Toya, Toye

Tracey
(Gaelic) aggressive
*Trace, Tracee, Traci,
Tracie, Tracy*

Tracilyn
(American) combo of
Tracy and Lynn;
combative
*Trace, Tracelynn,
Tracilynne, Tracy-Lynn*

Tranell
(American) confident
*Tranel, Tranelle, Traney,
Trani*

Traniqua
(African-American)
hopeful
*Tranaqua, Tranekwa,
Tranequa, Trani,
Tranikwa, Tranney,
Tranniqua, Tranny*

Trazanna
(African-American)
talented
Traz, Trazannah, Traze

Tree
(American) sturdy

Treece
(American) short for
Terese
Treese, Trice

Treena
(American) form of Trina
Treen

Tremira
(African-American)
anxious
Tremera, Tremmi

Treneth
(American) smiling
Trenith, Trenny

Trenica
(African-American)
smiling
Trenika, Trinika

Trenise
(African-American)
songbird
*Tranese, Tranise,
Trannise, Treenie,
Treneese, Treni,
Trenniece, Trenny*

Trenyce
(American) smiling
Trienyse, Trinyce

Tressa
(Greek) reaping life's
harvest
*Tresa, Tresah, Tress,
Trisa*

Tressie
(American) successful
*Tress, Tressa, Tressee,
Tressey, Tressi, Tressy*

Tricia
(Latin) humorous
*Tresha, Trich, Tricha,
Trish, Trisha*

Trina
(Greek) perfect;
scintillating
Tina, Treena, Trine, Trinie

Trinidad
(Place name) spiritual
person
Trini, Trinny

Trinlee
(American) genuine
Trinley, Trinli, Trinly

Trinity
(Latin) triad
Trin, Trini, Trinie,
Trinitee, Triniti

Trish
(American) short for
Patricia; funny
Trysh

Trisha
(American) short for
Patricia: funny
Tricia

Trishelle
(African-American)
humorous girl
Trichelle, Trichillem,
Trish, Trishel, Trishie

Trissy
(American) tall
Triss, Trissi, Trissie

Trista
(Latin) pensive;
sparkling love
Tresta, Trist, Tristie,
Trysta

Tristen
(Latin) bold
Tristan, Tristie, Tristin,
Trysten

Tristica
(Spanish) form of Trista;
pretty
Trist, Tristi, Tristika

Trixie
(Latin) personable
Trix, Trixi, Trixy

Trixiebelle
(American) combo of
Trixie and Belle; sweet
personality
Belle, Trix, Trixeebel,
Trixiebell, Trixybell

Trudy
(German) hopeful
Trude, Trudi, Trudie

True
(American) truthful
Truee, Truie, Truth

Truette
(American) truthful
Tru, True, Truett

Truffle
(Food name)
Truff, Truffy

Trulencia
(Spanish) honest
Lencia, Tru, Trulence,
Trulens, Trulense

Truly
(American) honest
True, Trulee, Truley

Trusteen
(American) trusting
Trustean, Trustee,
Trustine, Trusty, Trusyne

Truth
(American) honest
Truthe

Try
(American) earnest
Tri, Trie

Tryna
(Greek) form of Trina
Trine, Tryne, Trynna

Tsonka
(American) capricious
Sonky, Tesonka,
Tisonka, Tsonk

Tuenchit
(Thai)

Tuesday
(English) weekday

Tulia
(Spanish) glorious
Tuli, Tuliana, Tulie,
Tuliea, Tuly

Tully
(Irish) powerful; dark
spirit
Tull, Tulle, Tulli, Tullie

Turin
(American) creative
Turan, Turen, Turrin,
Turun

Turquoise
(French) blue-green
Turkoise, Turquie,
Turrkoise

Tursha
(Slavic) warm
Tersha

Tweetie
(American) vivacious
Tweetee, Tweetey, Tweeti

Twiggy
(English) slim
Twiggie, Twiggee, Twiggey

Twyla
(English) creative
Twila, Twilia

Twynceola
(African-American) bold
Twin, Twyn, Twynce

Tye
(American) talented

Tyeoka
(African-American) rhythmic
Tioka, Tyeo, Tyeoke

Tyesha
(African-American) duplicitous
Tesha, Tisha, Tyeisha, Tyiesha, Tyisha

Tyisha
(African-American) sweet
Isha, Tisha, Ty, Tyeisha, Tyish

Tyler
(American) stylish; tailor
Tielyr, Tye

Tymitha
(African-American) kind
Timitha, Tymi, Tymie, Tymith, Tymy, Tymytha

Tyne
(American) dramatic; (Old English) sylvan
Tie, Tine, Tye

Tyneil
(African-American) combo of Ty and Neil; helpful
Tyne, Tyneal, Tyniel

Tynisha
(African-American) fertile
Tinisha, Tynesha, Tynie

Tyra
(Scandinavian) assertive woman
Tye, Tyrah, Tyre, Tyrie

Tyrea
(African-American) form of Thora; thunder
Tyree, Tyria

Tyrina
(American) ball-of-fire
Tierinna, Tye, Tyreena, Tyrinah

Tyronna
(African-American) combo of Tyronne and Anna; special
Tierona, Tye, Tyrona, Tyronnah

Tyson
(French) son of Ty
Ty, Tysen

Tyzna
(American) ingenious, assertive
Tyze, Tyzie

Udavine
(American) thriving
Uda

Udele
(English) prospering
woman
Uda, Udell

Ula
(Celtic) jewel-like beauty
Ule

Ulanda
(American) confident
Uland, Ulandah, Ulande

Ulani
(Hawaiian) happy;
(Polynesian) happy
Ulanee

Ulrika
(Teutonic) leader
*Ulree, Ulric, Ulrica, Ulrie,
Ulry, Urik*

Ulyssia
(Invented) from Ulysses;
wanderer
*Lyss, Lyssia, Uls, Ulsy,
Ulsyia*

Uma
(Hebrew) nation;
worldview
Umah

Una
(Latin) unique
Unah

Undine
(Latin) from the ocean
Undene, Undyne

Undra
(American) one; long-
suffering

Unique
(Latin) singular
Uneek

Unity
(English) unity of spirit
Unitee

Unn
(Scandinavian) loving
Un

Ural
(Place name) Ural
Mountains
Ura, Uralle, Urine, Uris

Urania
(Greek) universal beauty
Uraine, Uraneah

Urith
(Hebrew) bright
Urit

Ursa
(Greek, Latin) star; bear-
like
Urs, Ursah, Ursie

Ursula
(Latin) little female bear
Ursa, Urse, Ursela, Ursila

Usha
(Indian) dawn;
awakening

Usher
(Word as name) helpful
Ush, Ushar, Ushur

Utopia
(American) idealistic
Uta, Utopiah

Uzbek
(Place name) for
Uzbekistan
Usbek

Uzetta
(American) serious
Uzette

Uzma
(Spanish) capable
Usma, Uz, Uzmah

Vada
(German) form of Valda;
winner
Vaida, Vay

Val
(Latin) short for Valerie;
strong

Valarie
(Latin) strong
Val, Valerie

Valda
(German) high spirits
Val, Valdah

Vale
(English) valley; natural
Vail, Vaylie

Valeda
(Latin) strong woman
Val, Valayda, Valedah

Valencia
(Spanish) place name;
strong-willed
Val, Valensha, Valincia

Valentina
(Latin) romantic
*Val, Vala, Valentin,
Valentine*

Valeny
(American) hard
Val, Valenie

Valeria
(Spanish) having valor
Valeri, Valerie, Valery

Valerie
(Latin) robust
Val, Valarie, Valery, Vallie

Valerta
(Invented) form of
Valerie; courageous
Valer, Valert

Valeska
(Polish) joyous leader
Valeske

Valetta
(Italian) feminine
Valettah, Valita, Valitta

Valkie
(Scandinavian) from
Valkyrie; fantastic
*Val, Valkee, Valki, Valkry,
Valky*

Vallie
(Latin) natural
Val, Valli, Vally

Vallie-Mae
(Latin) from Valentina
and Mae; romantic
*Valliemae, Vallimae,
Vallimay*

Valora
(Latin) intimidating
Val, Valorah, Valorie

Valore
(Latin) courageous
Val, Valour

Valoria
(Spanish) brave
Vallee, Valora, Valore

Value
(Word as name) valued
Valu, Valyou

Valyn
(American) perky
Valind, Valinn, Valynn

Vamia
(Hispanic) energetic
Vamee, Vamie

Vanda
(German) smiling beauty
Vandah, Vandi

Vanessa
(Greek) flighty
*Nessa, Van, Vanesah,
Vanessah, Vanna,
Vannie, Venesa*

Vania
(Hebrew) gifted
Vaneah, Vanya

Vanille
(American) from vanilla;
simplistic
*Vana, Vani, Vanila,
Vanile, Vanna*

Vanity
(English) vain girl
Vaniti

Vanna
(Greek) golden girl
Van, Vana, Vannah

Vanya
(American) form of
Vanna; self-assured
*Vani, Vanja, Vanni,
Vanyuh*

Vara
(Greek) strange
Varah, Vare

Varda
(Hebrew) rosy
Vardah

Varaina
(Invented) form of
Loraine

Vasteen
(American) capable
*Vas, Vastene, Vastine,
Vasty*

Vaughan
(Last name as first
name) smooth talker
Vaughn, Vawn, Vawne

Veata
(Cambodian) smart;
organized
Veatah

Veda
(Sanskrit) wise woman
Vedah, Veida, Vida

Vedette
(French) watchful
Veda, Vedett

Vega
(Scandinavian) star
*Vay, Vayga, Vegah,
Veguh*

Veleda
(German) intelligent
Vel, Veladah, Velayda

Velinda
(American) form of
Melinda; practical
*Vel, Velin, Velind, Vell,
Velly, Velynda*

Vell
(American) short for
Velma; practical
Vel, Velly, Vels

Velma
(German) hardworking
Vel, Velmah

Velvet
(French) luxurious
Vel, Vell, Velvete, Velvett

Veneradah
(Spanish) honored;
venerable
Ven, Venera, Venerada

Venice
(Place name) coming of
age
*Vanice, Vaniece,
Veneece, Veneese*

Venitia
(Italian) forgiving
*Esha, Venesha, Venn,
Venney, Venni, Vennie,
Venny*

Vennita
(Italian) from Venice,
Italy; having arrived
*Nita, Vanecia, Ven,
Venesha, Venetia,
Venita, Vennie, Vinetia*

Venus
(Latin) loving; goddess
of love
Venise, Vennie

Vera
(Russian) faithful friend
Verah, Verie

Verda
(Latin) breath of spring
Ver, Vera, Verdah, Verde

Verdad
(Spanish) verdant;
honest
*Verda, Verdade, Verdie,
Verdine, Verdite*

Verdie
(Latin) fresh as
springtime
*Verd, Verda, Verdee,
Verdi, Verdy*

Verena
(English) honest
*Veren, Verenah, Verene,
Virena*

Verenase
(Swiss) flourishing;
truthful
Ver, Verenese,
Verennase, Vy, Vyrenase,
Vyrennace

Verity
(French) truthful
Verety, Veritee, Veriti,
Veritie

Verlene
(Latin) vivacious
Verleen, Verlie, Verlynne

Vermekia
(African-American)
natural
Meki, Mekia, Verme,
Vermekea, Vermy,
Vermye

Verna
(Latin) springlike
Vernah, Verne

Vernice
(American) natural
Verna, Vernie, Verniece

Vernicia
(Spanish) form of
Vernice; springtime
Vern, Verni, Vernisia

Veronica
(Latin) real
Nica, Ronica, Varonica,
Veron, Veronika,
Veronnica, Von

Veronique
(French) realistic
woman; form of Veronica
Veroneek, Veroneese,
Veroniece

Versperah
(Latin) evening star
Vesp, Vespa, Vespera

Vertrelle
(African-American)
organized
Vertey, Verti, Vertrel,
Vetrell

Vesela
(Origin unknown) open
Vess

Vesta
(Latin) home-loving;
goddess of the home
Vess, Vessie, Vestah

Vevay
(Latin) form of Vivian;
lively
Vevah, Vi, Viv, Vivay, Vivi,
Vivie

Vi
(Latin) short for Viola;
kind
Vy

Vianey
(Spanish) form of Vivian;
alive
Via, Viana, Viane, Viani,
Vianne, Vianney, Viany

Vianne
(French) striking
Vi, Viane, Viann

Vicky
(Latin) short for Victoria
Vic, Vick, Vickee, Vicki,
Vickie, Vikki

Victoria
(Latin) winner
Vic, Vicki, Victoriah,
Vikki, Viktoria

Victory
(Latin) a winning woman
Vic, Viktorie

Vida
(Hebrew) short for
Davida
Veeda

Vidella
(Spanish) life
Veda, Vida, Videline,
Vydell

Vidette
(Hebrew) loved
Viddey, Viddi, Viddie,
Vidett, Videy

Vienna
(Latin) place name
Viena, Viennah, Vienne

Viennese
(Place name) from
Vienna
Vee, Viena, Vienne

Viet
(Place name) form of
Viet Nam
Vee, Viette

Vilma
(Spanish) form of Velma;
industrious
Vi, Vil

Vina
(Hindi) musical
instrument
Vin, Vinah, Vinnie, Vinny

Vinah
(American)
up-and-coming
Vi, Vyna

Vincentia
(Latin) winner
Vin, Vinnie

Vincia
(Spanish) forthright;
winning
Vincenta, Vincey, Vinci

Viola
(Latin) violet; lovely lady
Vi, Violah

Violanth
(Latin) from the purple
flower violet
*Vi, Viol, Viola, Violanta,
Violante*

Violet
(English, French) purple
flower
*Vi, Viole, Violette,
Vylolet*

Violyne
(Latin) from the purple
flower violet
*Vi, Vio, Viola, Violene,
Violine*

Virgilee
(American) combo of
Virgi and Lee; pure girl
*Virge, Virgee, Virgi,
Virgilea, Virgileigh,
Virgy, Virgylee*

Virginia
(Latin) pure female
*Giniah, Verginia, Virgie,
Virginya, Virgy*

Viridiana
(Spanish) combo of Viri
and Diana; ostentatious
*Di, Diana, Diane, Viri,
Viridi, Viridiane*

Virtue
(Latin) strong; pure

Vita
(Latin) animated; lively;
life
Veda, Veeta, Veta, Vete

Viv
(Latin) short for Vivian;
vital

Viva
(Latin) alive; lively
Veeva

Vivecca
(Scandinavian) lively;
energetic
*Viv, Viveca, Viveka,
Vivica, Vivie*

Vivi
(Hindi) vital
Viv

Vivian
(Latin) bubbling with life
*Viv, Vive, Vivi, Viviana,
Vivien, Vivienne, Vivyan*

Vivianna
(American) inventive
Viviannah, Vivianne

Vivilyn
(American) vital
Viv, Vivi

Vix
(American) short for
Vixen
Vixa, Vixie, Vyx

Vixen
(American) flirt
Vix, Vixee, Vixie

Voila
(French) attention; seen
Vwala

Voletta
(French) mysterious
Volette, Volettie

Vonda
(Czech) loving
Vondah, Vondi

Vondrah
(Czech) loving
Vond, Vondie, Vondra

Vonese
(American) form of
Vanessa; pretty
*Vonesa, Vonise, Vonne,
Vonnesa, Vonny*

Voni
(Slavic) affectionate
Vonee, Vonie

Vonna
(French) graceful
*Vona, Vonah, Vonne,
Vonni, Vonnie*

Vonnala
(American) sweet
*Von, Vonala, Vonnalah,
Vonnie*

Vonshae
(American) combo of
Von and Shae; confident
Von, Vonshay

Voyage
(Word as name) trip;
wanderer
Voy

Wade
(American) campy

Wafa
(Arabic) loyal

Wakeen
(American) spunky
*Wakeene, Wakey,
Wakine*

Wakeishah
(African-American)
happy
*Wake, Wakeisha,
Wakesha*

Walda
(German) powerful
woman
Waldah, Wally

Waleria
(Polish) sweet

Waleska
(Last name as first
name) effervescent
Wal, Walesk, Wally

Walker
(English) active; mover

Wallis
(English) from Wales;
openminded
*Walis, Wallace, Wallie,
Wally*

Wanda
(Polish) wild; wandering
*Wandah, Wandie,
Wonda*

Warma
(American) warmth-filled
Warm

Warner
(German) outgoing;
fighter
Warna, Warnar, Warnir

Wenda
(German) adventurer
Wend, Wendah, Wendy

Wendy
(English) friendly;
childlike
*Wenda, Wende, Wendee,
Wendi, Wendie, Wendye*

Weslie
(English) woman in the
meadow
Wes, Weslee, Wesli

Wheeler
(English) inventive
Wheelah, Wheelar

Whitley
(English) outdoorsy
Whitlee, Whitly, Witlee

Whitman
(English) white-haired
man
Whit, Wittman

Whitney
(English) white; fresh
Whit, Whitne, Whitnee,
Whitnie, Whytnie

Whitson
(Last name as first)
white
Whits, Whitty, Witte,
Witty

Whittier
(Literature)
distinguished
Whitt

Whoopi
(English) excitable
Whoopee, Whoopie,
Whoopy

Whynesha
(African-American) kind-
hearted
Whynesa, Wynes,
Wynesa, Wynesha

Wiktoria
(Polish) victor
Wikta

Wilda
(English) wild-haired girl
Willie, Wyle

Wile
(American) coy; wily
Wiles, Wyle

Wilhelmina
(German) able protector
Willa, Willhelmena,
Willie, Wilma

Willa
(English) desirable
Will, Willah

Willette
(American) open
Wilet, Wilett, Will, Willett

Willine
(American) form of Will;
willowy
Will, Willene, Willy,
Willyne

Willis
(American) sparkling
Wilice, Will, Willice

Willow
(American) free spirit;
willow tree
Willo

Wilona
(English) desirable
Wilo, Wiloh, Wilonah,
Wylona

Wilma
(German) sturdy
Wilmah, Wylm

Win
(German) flirty
Winnie, Wyn, Wynne

Wind
(American) breezy
Winde, Windee, Windey,
Windi, Windy, Wynd

Winetta
(American) peaceful;
country girl
Winette, Winietta, Wyna,
Wynette

Winifred
(German) peaceful
woman
Win, Windy, Winefred,
Winnie, Winniefred,
Winnifreed

Winkie
(American) vital
Winkee, Winky

Winner
(American) outstanding

Winnie
(English) winning
Wini, Winny, Wynnie

Winnielle
(African) victorious
female
Winielle, Winniele,
Wynnielle

Winona
(Native American)
firstborn girl
Winonah, Wye, Wynona,
Wynonah, Wynonna

Winter
(English) child born in winter
Wynter

Wonder
(American) filled with wonder
Wander, Wonda, Wondee, Wondy, Wunder

Wonila
(African-American) swaying
Waunila, Wonilla, Wonny

Wood
(American) smooth talker
Woode, Woodee, Woodie, Woody, Woodye

Wova
(American) brassy
Whova, Wovah

Wren
(English) flighty girl; bird
Renn, Wrin, Wryn, Wrynne

Wyanda
(American) form of Wanda; gregarious
Wyan

Wyetta
(French) feisty

Wylie
(American) wily
Wylee, Wyley, Wyli

Wymette
(American) vocalist
Wimet, Wimette, Wymet, Wynette

Wynne
(Welsh) fair-haired
Win, Winwin, Wynee, Wynn, Wynnie

Wyomie
(Native American) horse-rider on the plains
Why, Wyome, Wyomee, Wyomeh

Wyss
(Welsh) spontaneous; fair
Whyse

Xanadu
(Place name) *Kubla Khan*'s Xanadu is an idyllic, exotic place
Zanadu

Xandra
(Greek) protective
Xandrae, Zan, Zandie, Zandra

Xanthe
(Greek) beautiful blonde; yellow
X, Xanth, X-Anth, Xantha, Xanthie, Xes, Zane, Zanthie

Xaviera
(French) smart
Zavey, Zavie, Zaviera, Zavierah, Zavy

Xena
(Greek) girl from afar
Zen, Zena, Zennie

Xeniah
(Greek) gracious entertainer
Xen, Xenia, Zenia, Zeniah

Xiomara
(Spanish) congenial
Xylene
(Greek) outdoorsy
Leen, Lene, Xyleen,
Xyline, Zylee, Zyleen,
Zylie
Xylia
(Greek) woods-loving
Zylea, Zylia

Yadira
(Hindi) dearest
Yaffa
(Hebrew) beautiful girl
Yafa, Yafah
Yahaira
(Hebrew) precious
Yajaira
Yahnnie
(Greek) giving
Yahn, Yanni, Yannie,
Yannis
Yaki
(Japanese) tenacious
Yakee
Yamileth
(Spanish) girl of grace
Yami
Yana
(Slavic) lovely
Yanah, Yanni, Yannie,
Yanny
Yannette
(American) combo of
J and Annette; melodic
Yanett, Yannett, Yanny

Yaquelin
(Spanish) form of
Jaqueline
Yackie, Yacque,
Yacquelyn, Yaki, Yakie,
Yaque, Yaquelinn,
Yaquelinne
Yara
(Spanish) expansive;
princess
Yarah, Yare, Yarey
Yarine
(Russian) peaceful
Yari, Yarina
Yarita
(Hispanic) flashy
Yasmine
(Arabic) pretty
Yasmeen, Yasmen,
Yasmin
Yaura
(American) desirous
Yara, Yaur, YaYa
Yazmin
(Persian) pretty flower
Yazmen
Yebenette
(American) little
Yebe, Yebey, Yebi
Yelena
(Russian) friendly
Yemaya
(African) smart; quirky
Yemye

Yenny
(American) combo of Y and Jenny; happy
Yen, Yeni, Yenney, Yenni

Yessenia
(Spanish) devout
Jesenia, Yesenia

Yeva
(Russian) lively; loving
Yevka

Yina
(Spanish) winning
Yena

Yodelle
(American) old-fashioned
Yode, Yodell, Yodelly, Yodette, Yodey

Yoko
(Japanese) good; striving
Yokoh

Yola
(Spanish) form of Yolanda; violet
Yolanda, Yoli

Yolanda
(Greek) pretty as a violet flower
Yola, Yolana, Yolandah, Yolie, Yoyly

Yolie
(Greek) violet; flower
Yolee, Yoli

Yonaide
(American)
Yonade, Yonaid

York
(English) forthright
Yorkie, Yorkke

Young
(Korean) forever

Ysanne
(English) graceful
Esan, Esanne, Essan, Ysan, Ysann

Yu
(Asian) jade; a gem

Yue
(Asian) happy

Yuette
(American) capable
Yue, Yuete, Yuetta

Yuliana
(Invented) combo of Y and Juliana
Ana, Yuli, Yuliann, Yulianne

Yuna
(African) gorgeous
Yunah

Yurianna
(Invented) combo of Yuri and Anna; royal
Yuri, Yuriann, Yurianne

Yuta
(American) dramatic
Uta

Yvette
(French) lively archer
Yavet, 'Yevette, Yvete

Yvonne
(French) athletic
Vonne, Vonnie, Yavonne, Yvone, Yvonna

Zachah
(Hebrew) Lord remembered; brave-hearted
Zach, Zacha, Zachie, Zachrie

Zahavah
(Hebrew) golden girl
Zahava, Zeheva, Zev

Zahra
(African) blossoming
Zara, Zarah

Zaida
(Spanish) peacemaker
Zada, Zai

Zainab
(Arabic) brave

Zaira
(Arabic) flower
Zara

Zaire
(Place name)
Zai, Zay, Zayaire

Zambee
(Place name) from Zambia
Zambi, Zambie, Zamby, Zamby

Zan
(Greek) supportive; (Chinese) praiseworthy
Zander, Zann

Zana
(Greek) defender; energetic
Zanah

Zandra
(Greek) shy; helpful
Zan, Zondra

Zane
(Scandinavian) bold girl
Zain

Zanita
(American) gifted
Zaneta, Zanetta, Zanette, Zanitt, Zeneta

Zanth
(Greek) leader
Zanthe, Zanthi, Zanthie, Zanthy

Zara
(Hebrew) dawn; glorious
Zahra, Zarah, Zaree

Zarmina
(Origin unknown) bright
Zar, Zarmynna

Zaylee
(English) heavenly
Zay, Zayle, Zayley, Zayli, Zaylie

Zayna
(Arabic) wonderful
Zayne

Zazalesha
(African-American) zany
Lesha, Zaza, Zazalese, Zazalesh

Zazula
(Polish) outstanding

Zeb
(Hebrew) Jehovah's gift

Zef
(Polish) moves with the wind
Zeff

Zela
(Greek) blessed; smiling

Zelda
(German) practical
Zell, Zellie

Zelia
(Latin) sensual
Zeleah

Zenae
(Greek) helpful
Zen, Zenah, Zennie

Zenia
(Greek) open
Zeniah, Zenney, Zenni, Zennie, Zenny, Zenya

Zephyr
(Greek) the west wind; wandering girl
Zefir, Zeph, Zephie, Zephir

Zesta
(American) zestful
Zestah, Zestie, Zesty

Zeta
(English) rose; Greek letter
Zetah

Zett
(Hebrew) olive; flourishing
Zeta, Zetta

Zhenia
(Latin) bright
Zennia, Zhen, Zhenie

Zhi
(Chinese) of high character; ethical

Zhong
(Chinese) honorable

Zhuo
(Chinese) smart; wonderful
Zuo

Zi
(Chinese) flourishing; giving

Zia
(Latin) textured
Zea, Ziah

Zila
(Hebrew) shadowy
Zilah, Zilla

Zimbab
(Place name) from Zimbabwe
Zimbob

Zina
(Greek) hospitable woman
Zinah, Zine, Zinnie

Zinnia
(Botanical) flower
Zenia, Zinia, Zinny, Zinya

Zipporah
(Hebrew) bird in flight
Ziporah, Zippi, Zippie, Zippy

Zita
(Spanish) rose; (Arabic) mistress
Zeeta, Zitah

Zoann
(American) combo of Zo and Ann; alive
Zoan, Zoanne, Zoayn

Zoe
(Greek) lively; vibrant
Zoee, Zoey, Zoie, Zooey

Zofia
(Polish) skilled

Zola
(French) earthy
Zolah

Zolema
(American) confessor
Zolem

Zona
(Latin) funny; brash
Zonah, Zonia, Zonna

Zoom
(American) energetic
Zoomi, Zoomy, Zoom-Zoom

Zora
(Slavic) beauty of dawn
Zorah, Zorrah, Zorre, Zorrie

Zoralle
(Slavic) ethereal
Zoral, Zoralye, Zorre, Zorrie

Zorianna
(American) combo of Zori and Ann; practical
Zoree, Zori, Zoriannah, Zory

Zorka
(Slavic) dawn
Zorke, Zorky

ZsaZsa
(Hungarian) wild-spirited
Zsa, Zsaey

Zulah
(African) country-loving
Zoola, Zoolah, Zula

Zuleyka
(Arabic) sparkling
Zelekha, Zue, Zuleika,
Zuley
Zulma
(Arabic) vibrant
Zul, Zule, Zulmah
Zuni
(Native American)
creative
Zu
Zuwena
(African) good
Zuzanna
(Polish) misunderstood
Zu, Zue, Zuzan

Bibliography

'America's 40 Richest Under 40.' *Fortune* Online. 16 Sept. 2002
    <http://www.fortune.com>.

'The American States.' Collin, P.H., ed. *Webster's Concise Desk Dictionary*. New York:
    Barnes & Noble Books, 2001.

'The Animal Kingdom.' Collin, P.H., ed. *Webster's Concise Desk Dictionary*. New York:
    Barnes & Noble Books, 2001.

Baby Center Baby Name Finder Page. 1 Dec. 2002
    <http://www.babycenter.com/babyname>.

Baby Chatter Page. 1 Dec. 2002 <http://www.babychatter.com>.

Baby Names/Birth Announcements Page. 1 Oct. 2002
    <http://www.princessprints.com>.

Baby Names Page. 1 Dec. 2002 <http://www.yourbabysname.com>.

Baby Names Page. 1 Nov. 2002 <http://www.babynames.com>.

Baby Names Page. 1 Oct. 2002 <http://www.babyshere.com>.

Baby Names World Page. 15 Jan. 2003 <http://www.babynameworld.com>.

Baby Zone Page. 'Around-the-World Names.' 15 Jan. 2003
    <http://www.babyzone.com/babynames>.

'Biographical Names.' Collin, P.H. ed. *Webster's Concise Desk Dictionary*. New York:
    Barnes & Noble Books, 2001.

'Biographical Names.' *The Merriam-Webster Dictionary*. Springfield, Mass: Merriam
    Webster, Inc., 1998.

'Books of the Bible.' Collin, P.H., ed. *Webster's Concise Desk Dictionary*. New York:
    Barnes & Noble Books, 2001.

Celebrity Names Page. 1 Nov. 2002 <http://www.celebnames.8m.com>.

'Common English Given Names.' *The Merriam-Webster Dictionary*. Springfield, Mass: Merriam Webster, Inc., 1998.

Death Penalty Info Page. 1 Feb. 2003 'Current Female Death Row Inmates.' <http://www.deathpenaltyinfo.org/womencases.html>.

Dunkling, Leslie. *The Guinness Book of Names*. Enfield, UK: Guinness Publishing, 1993.

eBusinessRevolution Page. 1 Nov. 2002 <http://www.ebusinessrevolution.com/babynames/a.html>.

ePregnancy Page. 1 Dec. 2002 <http://www.Epregnancy.com/directory/Baby_Names>.

'Fifty Important Stars.' Gove, Philip Babcock, ed. *Webster's Third New International Dictionary of the English Language Unabridged*. Springfield, Mass: Merriam-Webster, Inc., 1981.

'Gambino Capos Held in 1989 Mob Hit.' Jerry Capeci. This Week in Gangland, The Online Column Page. 1 Aug. 2002 <http://www.ganglandnews.com/column289.htm>.

Hanks, Patrick, and Flavia Hodges. *A Dictionary of First Names*. Oxford: Oxford University Press, 1992.

Harrison, G.B. ed. *Major British Writers*. New York: Harcourt, Brace &World, Inc., 1959.

HypoBirthing Page. 'Baby Names.' 1 Oct. 2002 <http://www.hypobirthing.com>.

Indian Baby Names Page. 1 Nov. 2002 <http:// www.indiaexpress.com/specials/babynames>.

Irish Names Page. 15 Jan. 2003 <http://www.hylit.com/info>.

Jewish Baby Names Page. 15 Jan. 2003 <http://www.jewishbabynames.net>.

Kaplan, Justin, and Anne Bernays. *The Language of Names: What We Call Ourselves and Why It Matters.* New York: Simon & Schuster, 1997.

'Months of the Principal Calendars.' Gove, Philip Babcock, ed. *Webster's Third New International Dictionary of the English Language Unabridged.* Springfield, Mass: Merriam-Webster Inc., 1981.

'Most Popular Names of the 1990s.' Social Security Administration Online. 1 Nov. 2002 <http://www.ssa.gov/OACT/babynames>.

'Most Popular Names of the 1980s.' Social Security Administration Online. 1 Nov. 2002 <http://www.ssa.gov/OACT/babynames>.

'Most Popular Names of the 1970s.' Social Security Administration Online. 1 Nov. 2002 <http://www.ssa.gov/OACT/babynames>.

'Most Popular Names of the 1960s.' Social Security Administration Online. 1 Nov. 2002 <http://www.ssa.gov/OACT/babynames>.

'Most Popular Names of the 1950s.' Social Security Administration Online. 1 Nov. 2002 <http://www.ssa.gov/OACT/babynames>.

'Most Popular Names of 2001.' Social Security Administration Online. 1 Nov. 2002 <http://www.ssa.gov/OACT/babynames>.

'Most Powerful Women in Business.' *Fortune* Online. 14 Oct. 2002 <http://www.fortune.com>.

'Movie-Star Names.' Internet Movie Database online. 1 Nov. 2002 <http://www.imdb.com>.

Origins/Meanings of Baby Names from Around the World Page. 1 Nov. 2002 <http:// www.BabyNamesOrigins.com>.

Oxygen Page. 'Baby Names.' 1 Nov. 2002 <http://www.oxygen.com/babynamer>.

Parenthood Page. 1 Nov. 2002
<http:// www.parenthood.com/parent_cfmfiles/babynames.cfm>.

'The Plant Kingdom.' Collin, P.H., ed. *Webster's Concise Desk Dictionary*. New York: Barnes & Noble Books, 2001.

Popular Baby Names Page. 1 Nov. 2002 <http://www.popularbabynames.com>.

'Presidents of the United States.' Collin, P.H., ed. *Webster's Concise Desk Dictionary*. New York: Barnes & Noble Books, 2001.

'Prime Ministers of the U.K.' Collin, P.H., ed. *Webster's Concise Desk Dictionary*. New York: Barnes & Noble Books, 2001.

Racketeering and Fraud Investigations Page. 4 Feb. 2003
<http://www.oig.dol.gov/public/media/oi/mainz01.htm>.

Rick Porelli's AmericanMafia.com Page. 21 June 2002
<http://www.americanmafia.com/news/6-21-02_Feds_Bust.html>.

Rosenkrantz, Linda, and Pamela Redmond Satran. *Baby Names Now*. New York: St. Martin's Press, 2002.

Rosenkrantz, Linda, and Pamela Redmond Satran. *Beyond Charles and Diana: An Anglophile's Guide to Baby Naming*. New York: St. Martin's Press, 1992.

Rosenkrantz, Linda, and Pamela Redmond Satran. *Beyond Jennifer and Jason*. New York: St. Martin's Press, 1994.

Schwegel, Janet. *The Baby Name Countdown*. New York: Marlowe & Company (Avalon), 2001.

'Signs of the Zodiac.' Gove, Philip Babcock, ed. *Webster's Third New International Dictionary of the English Language Unabridged*. Springfield, Mass: Merriam-Webster Inc. Publishers, 1981.

Television-show credits. 1 Oct. 2002–25 Feb. 2003.

Texas Department of Criminal Justice Page. 'Offenders on Death Row.' 1 Feb. 2003 <http://www.tdcj.state.tx.us/stat/offendersondrow.htm>.

Trantino, Charlee. *Beautiful Baby Names from Your Favorite Soap Operas*. New York: Pinnacle Books, 1996.

20,000+ Names Page. '20,000+ Names from Around the World.' 1 Nov. 2002 <http:// www.20000-names.com>.

United Kingdom Baby Name Page. 15 Jan. 2003 <http://www.baby-names.co.uk>.

Wallace, Carol McD. *The Greatest Baby Name Book Ever*, New York: Avon, 1998.

About the Author

With daughter Jennifer Shoquist, M.D., Diane Stafford co-authored *Potty Training for Dummies, No More Panic Attacks, Migraines for Dummies,* and *The Encyclopedia of Sexually Transmitted Diseases.*

Stafford has been Editor-in-Chief of *Health & Fitness Magazine, Texas Woman Magazine, Houston Home & Garden Magazine, Dallas-Fort Worth Home & Garden Magazine, Philanthropy in Texas,* and *Latin Music Magazine.* Stafford also co-owned *Health & Fitness* and *Texas Woman,* and helped with startups of *Health & Fitness* in New Orleans, Philadelphia, and Miami. Today, she writes and edits books and does volunteer work for Houston's Emergency Aid Coalition Clothing Center. She has written hundreds of magazine articles.

Order further Vermilion titles from your local bookshop,
or have them delivered direct to your door by Bookpost

☐	The New Contented Little Baby Book	0091882338	£9.99
☐	Finger Food for Babies and Toddlers	0091889510	£9.99
☐	Secrets of a Baby Whisperer	0091857023	£9.99
☐	What to Expect When You're Breast-feeding	0091856744	£7.99

FREE POSTAGE AND PACKING

Overseas customers allow £2.00 per paperback

ORDER:

By phone: 01624 677237

**By post: Random House Books
c/o Bookpost, PO Box 29, Douglas
Isle of Man, IM99 1BQ**

By fax: 01624 670923

By email: bookshop@enterprise.net

**Cheques (payable to Bookpost)
and credit cards accepted**

Prices and availability subject to change without notice.
Allow 28 days for delivery.
When placing your order, please mention if you do not wish
to receive any additional information.

www.randomhouse.co.uk